CAMBRIDGE LATIN AMERICAN STUDIES

Editors

Malcolm Deas   Clifford T. Smith   John Street

23

The African Experience in Spanish America
1502 to the Present Day

THE SERIES

The African Experience in Spanish America

1502 TO THE PRESENT DAY

LESLIE B. ROUT, Jr.

Associate Professor, Department of History
Michigan State University

CAMBRIDGE UNIVERSITY PRESS

CAMBRIDGE

LONDON · NEW YORK · MELBOURNE

Published by the Syndics of the Cambridge University Press
The Pitt Building, Trumpington Street, Cambridge CB2 1RP
Bentley House, 200 Euston Road, London NW1 2DB
32 East 57th Street, New York, NY 10022, USA
296 Beaconsfield Parade, Middle Park, Melbourne 3206, Australia

First published 1976

Typeset by Computer Productions Inc., New York, New York
Printed in the United States of America
by R. R. Donnelley & Sons Company, Crawfordsville, Indiana

Library of Congress Cataloging in Publication Data

Rout, Leslie B.   1936—
The African experience in Spanish America, 1502 to the present day.

(Cambridge Latin American studies ; 23)
Bibliography: p.
Includes index.
1. Blacks — Latin America — History.
2. Slavery in Latin America. I. Title. II. Series.
F1419. B55R68   980'.004'96   75-9280
ISBN 0 521 20805 X hardcovers
ISBN 0 521 29010 4 paperback

CONTENTS

Part II: Since Independence

I would like to express my appreciation to the following for their assistance: David Bailey, John Bratzel, Emily Cumberland-Whitaker, Martha Phaneuf, Judith Spratling, and Robert Greene. In particular, I want to dedicate these humble efforts to:

> "Big Charlie" – who thought it up;
> "Rapid Robert" – who had faith and bread;
> "Gino G." – who had a better idea; and
> "Smoochie" – who will pick up the profits.

PREFACE

Walk into a bookstore or meet with a textbook salesperson, and you'll have no trouble finding a dozen books that purport to tell the story of the people of African origin in America. Almost without exception, "America" in these books extends only as far southward as the Río Grande or the Gulf of Mexico. During the 1950s and the early 1960s the Afro-American was "hot copy" and virtually any work dealing with Negro slavery or the oppression of black people was likely to rack up excellent sales. These were the years of civil rights marches, "we shall overcome," and the general belief that Negroid peoples were oppressed only in the United States and the Union of South Africa.

The peculiar aspect of this situation is that the majority of the African peoples removed from their continent and brought to this hemisphere between roughly 1443 and 1870 became residents of the Spanish or Portuguese-speaking regions in the two continents. Much has already been written about the African presence in Brazil, but where is the story of these people in Spanish America? It does not yet exist in complete form, although there is little question that a multivolume study of the subject will one day be written. This book is a comprehensive primer that provides basic historical information about the blacks and mulattoes in the eighteen American states where Spanish is the official spoken language. It is the first holistic study on this topic in any language and is intended for use not only by scholars and students of Spanish America but also by those interested in Afro-American history and general studies in Western civilization.

The origin of this work lies in my first trip to Latin America as a jazz musician in 1962. What became grossly evident was that racial problems were by no means absent from Latin America, even though they were often swept under the rug. Returning to Latin America as both musician and researcher in 1965, 1968, and 1970, I conducted interviews and sought the opinions of leading Latin intellectuals on racial questions. Some readers may see little connection between playing jazz and doing academic research, but, in fact, this proved an ideal way to obtain candid answers to sensitive questions: People seemed much less suspicious of a saxophone player than of a history professor.

There should be no doubt that the point of view manifested on the following pages is that of a black North American. This perspective is not the only one from which the topic may be approached, but it does provide one type of insight. On 1 December 1973 for example, Bob Foster, an Afro-American and the light-heavyweight champion of the world, defeated Pierre Fourie, a white South African, before 42,000 people in Johannesburg. This was the first time a black had fought a white professionally in South Africa. In the Detroit Free Press (3 December 1973), Foster announced himself "unimpressed" with the historical aspects of the match; he felt a bizarre attraction, however, to the idea that he and the blacks in his party had been given the status of "honorary whites" during their stay. When I read the story, the first thing that came to mind was that in Spanish America the status of "honorary white man" had been legally sanctioned almost two centuries ago! Not much has changed; many whites still seem to believe that the best thing they can do for black people is to "improve" their color.

January 1976   Leslie B. Rout, Jr.

GLOSSARY

SPANISH TERMINOLOGY

Almojarifazgo: A duty charged on imports and exports. In the slave trade the duty was 7.5 percent of the cost of each slave sold until 1543; in 1566 it was raised by 10 percent. The tax was cut in half if prepaid in Seville to the Casa de Contratación. During the eighteenth century the amount of this tax varied widely among the viceroyalties.

Asiento (de negros): A formal contract between the crown and an individual or company for the privilege of providing colonial Spanish America with African slaves.

Casa de Contratación: The House of Contracts and Trade established in 1503 to organize and regulate all forms of oceanic trade between Spain and its American colonies.

Cabildo: Town Council. In colonial Spanish America members of this local ruling body were appointed by the governor, usually upon the recommendation of outgoing councillors. Occasionally, some council members were elected by the local populace, but most of them were royal, viceregal, or *audiencia* selections.

Cédula: A decree promulgated by the Spanish king.

Consejo de las Indias: The Council of the Indies created in 1524 to advise the king on American affairs. It played a major political role, determining policy, drafting *cédulas* for the king to sign, and acting as a final court of judicial appeal.

Consulado: A guild of merchants conducting trade between Spain and Spanish America. In some port cities such as Buenos Aires these organizations became extremely powerful, and during the early nineteenth century they were often sources of revolutionary activity.

Fuero militar: A military privilege granted to royal army and militia personnel in colonial Spanish America that exempted them from trial by civilian jury.

Gracias al sacar: (literally, "thanks for the exclusion") A royal concession from exemption from some existing restriction. In this text, the term refers specifically to the issuance or purchase of a royal dispensation that freed a person from the status of *casta*.

Hacienda: A large, agrarian estate.

Licencia: A royal authorization allowing an individual to take slaves to a particular region of the Indies. Obtaining this privilege usually required payment of a large sum, but the recipient of the grant paid no *almojarifazgo*. The terms of the *licencia* prohibited resale but did not oblige the recipient to make full use of the authorization granted.

Palenque: The general name given to a settlement of Negroid fugitives. In Venezuela these sites were called *cumbes*, and in Cuba, *mambises*.

Pieza de Indias: (literally, "piece of the Indies") A term referring to the theoretical mean used to define the ideal slave: an African male between the ages of eighteen and thirty, with no physical defects, and at least five feet tall.

Patronato real: Special power grudgingly granted to the King of Spain in 1508 by Pope Julius II. Under terms of this agreement the royal government was allowed to select all bishops for the New World, collect all ecclesiastical tithes, and examine and sanction all communications between the papacy and the New World clerics.

Recopilación de las leyes de los reinos de las Indias: ("Compilation of the laws of the kingdoms of the Indies") A codification of the multitude of royal decrees and ordinances issued by the Spanish kings and their councils. The *Recopilación* was published in 1680 and in its final form contained 6,377 laws under 218 headings in a nine-volume set.

Visitador: ("visitor") A royal official empowered to supervise the examination of the regime of a departing viceroy. On occasion specially appointed officials, also called *visitadores* were sent by the royal government to oversee the execution of special projects.

POLITICAL TERMINOLOGY

Throughout this work the current name of a particular state is generally used. For purposes of accurate historical explanation, however, the name of a territory as it was known by the Spanish between 1493 and 1810 is used in specific cases.

Viceroyalties

Viceroyalties, or New World Kingdoms, were the general political subdivisions of Spain's American possessions. Each of these was ruled by a viceroy appointed by the Crown. The following viceroyalties were established:

> *New Spain* (1535): The area that included all of Mexico, Central America, and present-day California, New Mexico, Arizona, and Texas. The viceregal seat was Mexico City.

> *Peru* (1542): Originally the region that encompassed all of Spanish South America. It was later reduced to Peru, Chile, Bolivia, and Ecuador. After 1778 it included only Peru and Chile. The viceregal seat was Lima.

> *New Granada* (1717-1726, 1739-1810): The political subdivision that covered Venezuela, Colombia, Panama, and after 1739, Ecuador. The viceregal seat was Bogotá.

> *La Plata* (1776): The area that consisted of Argentina, Uruguay, Bolivia, and Paraguay. The viceregal seat was Buenos Aires.

Captaincy Generals

Captaincy Generals were territories under the rule of special governors called captain generals. Although in theory they were responsible to the viceroy, they were in fact directly responsible to the Crown and the Council of the Indies. Usually captain generals were also sent to military frontiers and strategic territories. The following captaincy generals were established:

> *Central America* (1542): The division that included Costa Rica, Nicaragua, Guatemala, and San Salvador. The seat of government was Guatemala City.

> *Havana* (1764): The administrative unit originally established in 1607 and restructured in 1764 to include Cuba, the Louisiana Territory (ceded by France in 1763), and after 1783 present-day Florida. Governmental headquarters were established at Havana.

> *Caracas* (1777): The region that included all of contemporary Venezuela. The government seat was Caracas.

Chile (1778): The area that covered all of present-day Chile. The seat of government was Santiago.

Audiencia

Audiencia was the judicial and administrative council that acted as the highest court in the area and, although often under the control of a viceroy or captain general, it nevertheless exercised partial executive powers. It consisted of eight to twelve judges (*oidores*, or "hearers"). Normally the viceroy or captain general acted as president of the *audiencia* located in the administrative capital. *Audiencias* that exercised some degree of independence include those in Quito (1563), which governed most of what is now Ecuador, and Charcas (1563), whose jurisdiction included contemporary Bolivia.

SOCIO-RACIAL TERMINOLOGY

Caucasian

Peninsular: A Spaniard born on the Iberian Peninsula who settled in Spanish America. In Mexico, he was termed *gachupin* ("spur") and in Peru, *Chapeton* ("greenhorn"). Virtually all viceroys, bishops, and *audiencia* members were *peninsulares*.

Criollo: A person of Spanish descent born in America.

Zonite: A United States citizen who lives and works in the Panama Canal Zone. Many were born there and feel that their jobs are semi-hereditary. Virtually all of those considered *zonites* are Caucasians.

Negroid and Mixed Blood

Black: In this text, a person of full-blooded African origin, equivalent to the Spanish *negro*.

Bozal: A slave brought directly to the New World from Africa and, therefore, neither Christianized nor Spanish speaking.

Casta: ("caste") A derogatory term for all persons of mixed blood including freed blacks.

Chumbo: An insulting name given to a West Indian born or English-speaking Negroid who has settled in the Republic of Panama.

Cimarrón: ("wild black") An escaped African slave who often established independent settlements in inaccessible places and refused to recognize Spanish royal authority.

Criollo moreno: A black born in the New World. The term was most often applied during colonial times to children born of *bozal* parentage.

Emancipado: An African captured by British antislavery patrol vessels and released in Cuba. This supposedly freed black was usually treated as a slave by the Cubans.

Ladino: As originally used, a Christianized African slave who spoke Spanish or had some knowledge of Spanish culture. Subsequently the term came to include any descendant of African slaves born in the New World and eventually any Hispanicized Negroid.

Liberto: (literally "freed one") A descendant of slaves given his legal freedom under the terms of free-womb laws passed during the nineteenth century in Argentina, Uruguay, Peru, and Paraguay. In theory, he was legally bound to his mother's master only until he reached the age of fifteen to twenty-five. In practice, the laws were easily evaded and a *liberto* remained a slave in everything but name.

Manumiso: The term for *liberto* in Venezuela, Colombia, and Ecuador.

Mestizo: A person of Spanish and Indian heritage.

Moreno: A darkskinned person. The term generally denoted any person of authentic African ancestry.

Mulato: ("mulatto") A derivation of the word *mulo*, which denominated the hybrid offspring of a horse and a mule. Probably intended in a negative sense, *mulato* became the term used to designate a human of mixed blood, in this case, a person of Caucasian and African descent.

Mulecón: A male slave between the ages of seven and twelve. The female counterpart was referred to as a *mulecona*.

Muleque: A male slave between the ages of twelve and sixteen. A female in this age group was dubbed a *muleca*.

Negro: (literally "black") A full-blooded African.

Negroid: In this text, a person possessing any degree of African blood.

Pardo: An indefinite term usually referring to a mulatto or a person possessing some African blood. On occasion, very darkskinned persons who held commissioned officers' status in the colonial militia were called *pardos* as a form of courtesy.

Retinto: (literally "redyed") A derogatory term employed in Peru to identify a very darkskinned person.

Zambo: ("sambo") In Spain, a knock-kneed or cross-eyed person. In Spanish America, a person of Afro-Indian origin.

PART ONE

The Colonial Period

1
The Iberian Connection

THE PORTUGUESE BACKGROUND

Prince Henry and Portuguese control of
the African slave trade to Europe

The initial arrival of sub-Saharan Africans in the Iberian Peninsula is an event lost in antiquity. Quite likely a few accompanied Gebel-el-Tarik (Tariq ibn-Ziyad) when he and his Moorish
legions crossed over from North Africa and, after six years of
campaigning (A.D. 711 to 716), consolidated Islamic rule in
Iberia. Some of the defeated Christians retreated into the vastness of the Pyrenees, but during the eighth century they commenced the *Reconquista*, an intermittent series of wars with the
Muslims aimed at reconquering the previously held territories.[1]
By the thirteenth century European Christians had come to
view the struggle in Iberia as a Western crusade. The papacy
granted plenary indulgences to all those who fought the Moors,
and this factor undoubtedly encouraged some Frankish knights
to enter the fray. By 1250 Moorish rule was permanently terminated in the Portuguese kingdom.

In the wake of victory, the newly liberated kingdom of Portugal found itself the victim of an acute shortage of manual
laborers as a result of the flight of numerous Moors. The end of
major warfare meant a reduction in the number of slaves, for
Christians and Muslims captured in battle had been subject to
ransom or condemned to a life of servitude. Even during the
conflict, the increasing likelihood of Muslim defeat forced many
believers in Allah to flee the country and take up residence in

3

Granada, the only area of Iberia still held by their coreligionists. In addition, several hundred years of recurrent fighting had seriously diminished the native population of the area.

During the centuries of bitter struggle, the black African had become known to the Christians essentially as a soldier fighting for the Moors or as a slave laborer.[2] The Portuguese, therefore, looked upon blacks as the logical answer to their problem of a cheap source of labor after 1250, and as early as 1258 Moorish traders appeared at fairs at Guimarães (northern Portugal) offering sub-Saharan Africans for sale.[3] A few Portuguese traders traveled to the Barbary Coast, where they bought blacks, but the cost was high because control of the trans-Sahara trade routes rested with desert tribesmen who delivered the captives to Barbary Coast middlemen for sale. Aside from an occasional raid on Moorish vessels by Portuguese pirates, purchases from these Muslim dealers represented the only way Christians could obtain black slaves. The result was that black slavery did exist in thirteenth and fourteenth-century Portugal but was too expensive to be common.

The combination of technological advancement in ship navigation and construction, a favorable geographical position astride the Atlantic Ocean and Africa, and the belief that the *Reconquista* could be successfully pursued in Morocco were among the factors which fueled a fifteenth-century Portuguese policy of discovery and expansion. In August 1415 an expeditionary force seized Ceuta (Morocco), a major terminal on the trans-Sahara trade route. In keeping with their past history, the Portuguese claimed they were fighting a holy war since, until the seventh century A.D., all of North Africa had been Christian.[4] They were supported in their pretensions by the papacy, which urged general European backing for Lisbon and authorized a new round of plenary indulgences for the combatants.

Nevertheless, an impecunious Portugal could not immediately follow up its initial success with another campaign. Moreover, one important personality viewed the frontal attack in Morocco as only a part of a gigantic effort that would be needed to smash the Islamic states on the Barbary Coast. This was Prince Henry (later termed "the Navigator"), Duke of Viscu, who became the commander at Ceuta in 1418. He intended to sponsor exploratory voyages down the western coast of Africa, hoping to discover some way by which the hated Muslims could be taken in the flank. In 1420 he became director of the Military Order of Christ, a post that provided him with the financial means to support his ambitions. Curiously enough, his first efforts were not directed against the followers of the Prophet, but against the neighboring state of Castile. Fearing that the latter kingdom might attempt to occupy the recently discovered Madeira Islands, he dispatched João Gonçalves Zarco and Tristão Vaz to seize them. The settlement and annexation of these territories in 1419 and 1420 represented the true beginning of Portuguese colonization in Africa.

One great question confronting Henry and all Europeans at this time was, What lay beyond the Madeiras? Old and semimythological accounts suggested that a great deal did, although there were no specific details. Gomes Eanes de Zurara, whose chronicles are the most knowledgeable records of Portuguese explorations up to 1450, provides a mixed assortment of motives for Henry's sponsorship of voyages beyond that point:

1. The zeal for knowledge
2. The acquisition of gold and other forms of wealth
3. The solicitation of converts to Christianity
4. The vanquishment of the followers of Islam in North Africa and elsewhere
5. The establishment of contact with Prester John, the legendary black Christian king[5]

While some of these aims may seem pompous and hypocritical, they must be considered in the context of their times. For several centuries Europeans had been purchasing not only blacks but also quantities of spices, ivory, and gold dust from Barbary Coast dealers. Given their monopoly over the supply of these products, the Moors could charge Europeans whatever the market would bear. This disadvantageous situation was further aggravated by the decline of gold and silver production throughout Europe during the fourteenth century. In fact, the value of some undebased gold coins in Portugal reached astronomical proportions, rising as much as 1,000 percent by the fifteenth century.[6] There was some hope that this pressing metal shortage might eventually be alleviated. The Portuguese believed that somewhere south of the Barbary Coast lay the Rio de Ouro ("River of Gold"), which, with its adjacent mines, supplied the entirety of Islam. If this treasure trove could be located and seized, Christendom (and Portugal in particular) would alleviate its shortage of precious metals, while Islam would slump into devastating poverty.

The role of Prester John – in reality, the emperor of Ethiopia – in Henry's scheme was tied to the mistaken assumption that Ethiopia was in western Africa. In addition to exchanging ambassadors, Henry probably hoped to form a black–white alliance aimed at catching Muslim North Africa in a vise. Obviously, it was not certain that Prester John would believe it was Henry's Christian duty to attack the Muslims; but if the black ruler could be persuaded to cooperate, so much the better.

A problem for twentieth-century humanitarians, perhaps, is how Henry could simultaneously be so zealous about spreading Catholicism and so hostile toward the followers of Islam. It should be borne in mind that the prince was a creature of an intolerant age, and his conscience had been forged in the embers of the *Reconquista*. A possibly more inexplicable problem is why, between 1419 and 1441, Henry persisted in financing exploratory voyages that rendered virtually no profit. Only the aforementioned Eanes de Zurara provides an answer to this question, stating that

> his ascendant [Henry's star] was Aries, which is in the house of Mars . . . and is lord in the eleventh house, in the company of the sun, and because said Mars was in Aquarius, which is in the house of Saturn, and in the mansion of hope, it signified that the lord [Henry] should toil at high and mighty conquests.[7]

There is no proof that the motion of the heavenly bodies dictated the prince's actions, or even that he was a fervent believer in astrological forecasts. What cannot be denied is that Henry definitely acted as if he believed that fate was on his side.

By 1434 Portuguese mariners in the pay of the prince had reached Cape Bojador (about 26° north latitude),[8] which, with its high winds, treacherous currents, and October-to-April fogs, seemed to mark the much feared edge of the earth. In that year, after allegedly having failed on fourteen separate occasions, Gil Eanes rounded Cape Bojador and sailed a few leagues beyond it. In two succeeding voyages (1435 to 1436) he and Gonçales Baldais (Prince Henry's cupbearer) pushed farther southward, eventually reaching a point Baldais called "Rio de Ouro" (approximately 22°3′ north latitude). Unfortunately, none of that precious metal was discovered there, and the few barrels of seal oil obtained did little to justify the continued expense of Henry's limited resources on the outfitting of expeditions.

In 1441 the fortunes of the prince took a turn for the better, although black people would certainly come to rue the events that transpired. In that year, Nuno Tristão reached Cape Branco (now Cape Blanc, about 21° north latitude). Subsequently, he turned northward, encountering Antão Gonçalves, Prince Henry's chamberlain, who had also been dispatched on a voyage of investigation. The two decided that it was incumbent upon them to return to Portugal with some cargo of value. Landing at a point north of Cape Blanc (roughly 21°52′ north latitude),[9] they seized a group of eleven *azenagues*[10] and one black woman, with whom Gonçalves returned to Portugal. For his "feat" Henry made Gonçalves his private secretary.

One of the captured *azenagues* was named Adahu, and since he spoke Arabic as well as his local dialect, he was able to suggest to an interpreter that if he and two other captives were returned to Africa, Prince Henry would receive ten black slaves. Gonçalves agreed to carry out this exchange, and even though Adahu, when released, reneged on his promise, the other two captives were traded for ten blacks, some ostrich eggs, and the first gold dust that any of the expeditions had managed to obtain.[11]

With the success of this voyage, Henry's exploration policies were deemed vindicated and he was hailed both at home and abroad as "the New Alexander." Additional rewards subsequently came his way: (1) in 1443 Nuno Tristão reached the island of Arguim (located about 20°5' north latitude) and returned with twenty-nine *azenague* prisoners; (2) Prince Henry of England awarded him the Order of the Garter; (3) King Affonso of Portugal granted him a monopoly on all trade south of Cape Bojador. Others were also convinced that ample profit could be derived from the western coast of Africa. In 1444 Lançarote de Freitas, a customs officer in league with a group of local merchants, formed the Lagos Company and applied for a license to trade in the newly discovered areas. The prince readily agreed to this request in exchange for 20 percent of the profits, and that same year a six-ship flotilla commanded by Freitas set sail. He found no gold or ivory and made no significant discoveries but returned with 235 *azenague* and "black-moor"[12] prisoners. The royal share of this booty came to forty-six souls, whom Henry distributed among his followers. The company sold the others in Lagos or Lisbon, and it is essentially from this period that the market for blackmoors began to mushroom.

The growth and development of the African slave trade

The voyages down the African coast continued. The indefatigable Nuno Tristão reached the Senegal River in 1444, and Dinis Dias discovered Cape Verde in 1445. In effect, "Guinée," or the land of the black people, had finally been reached.[13] It should be recalled that, in raids like those conducted by Antão Gonçalves in 1441 and Lançarote de Freitas in 1444, the Portuguese had initially attempted to enslave all the *azenagues* and blackmoors they could catch. Dinis Dias had picked up four blacks at Cape Verde, but in 1445 and 1446 kidnapping expeditions in the Senegal River region yielded meager results. Indeed, on one of these raids, Nuno Tristão suffered an ignominious end. The Portuguese, therefore, decided to change their tactics. Raiding parties shouting "São Jorge" or "Portugal" became passé. Instead, Portuguese commercial interests established trading stations on the island of Arguim, at Cape Verde, on the Gambia and Geba Rivers, and, from 1455 to 1460, in Sierra Leone. It was these business ventures that achieved the regularization of trade with the local inhabitants, exchanging wheat, cloth, weapons, and especially horses for gold dust, spices, ivory, and black captives.[14] As early as 1445, Lagos Company representatives operating from the island of Arguim were trading with *azenagues* for blacks; by 1448 almost 1,000 captives had been shipped to Portugal.[15] But bases established in the Rivers of Guinea[16] and in the Gulf of Guinea supplied the bulk of the captives obtained after 1460. During the period from 1450 to 1500, the importation of black slaves averaged perhaps 700 to 900 per year, and estimates of the total imported into Portugal and its Madeira Islands possessions range from 40,000 to 100,000.[17] The principal consideration, however, is that by the beginning of the sixteenth century the value of the black traffic had equaled or surpassed that of either the gold or spice trades.[18]

Prince Henry had primarily been interested in crushing the Muslim, converting the heathen, and finding Prester John. In 1446, however, he had found it necessary to prohibit the enslavement of the *azenagues*, for they had become regular suppliers of desired goods. And when the Navigator died in 1460, although none of the ideals that Eanes de Zurara had enunciated was officially discarded, the course of Portuguese expansion in Africa took an unabashedly materialistic turn. Traffic with black chiefs and tribal leaders south of the Senegal River was producing larger numbers of slaves, and the prospect of sales to other European nations further whetted the acquisitive appetites of both Portuguese and foreign capitalists. In 1468 the Portuguese crown sold to Fernão Gomes a five-year *assento* ("monopoly") over slave, spice, and other traffics in the region south of the Senegal River. The price was 1,000 ducats a year and a promise to finance the exploration of the African coast at least 250 miles beyond Sierra Leone.[19] The cost of this exclusive privilege skyrocketed during the next forty years, but Venetian and Genoese merchants hastened to pay it, accurately foreshadowing developments that were yet to come.[20]

Perhaps the only objections to this burgeoning slave traffic were raised by metropolitan agricultural interests, which complained that, although most of the blacks obtained were landed at Lisbon or Lagos, they were immediately reshipped to other countries where prices were higher. In 1472 and 1473 members of the Portuguese Cortes – the legislative branch of the government – complained vigorously to the king because Portuguese home interests could not obtain black slaves either as cheaply as they wanted or in the quantity that they desired. Affonso V, however, had no intention of allowing the Cortes to take any action that might make the sale of slaves less lucrative. He made no recommendations to the *assento* holders and continued pocketing the duties that had to be paid on sub-Saharan properties before they could be reshipped elsewhere.[21] Still, a few steps had to be taken to provide some semblance of control over the growing trade. It was the most energetic of the Portuguese kings of that age, João II (1481–1505), who established a customs and counting agency for slaves (*casa da escravos*) in 1486. Fifteen years later he promulgated a code intended to govern the commercial operations of slave importers. Taken together, these steps suggest both that the slave trade was highly profitable and that Portuguese kings intended to continue profiting from it for a long time.

The Portuguese view of the black man

Prior to 1441 the Portuguese had displayed no unusual preference for black slaves. Any non-Christian they could capture was fair game, and even Christian slaves could be found in that country as late as the sixteenth century. After the disastrous defeat at Algiers in 1437, Portuguese expansion in Morocco simply ground to a halt, and, although occasional raids and subsequent campaign revivals might net some territory and a few prisoners, a steady supply of Muslims never developed. The fact was that only blacks could be obtained with relative ease. In an avowedly Christian country, however, the continued enslavement of these peoples could not be explained simply as another profit-making enterprise; an assembly of moral defenses became a necessity. The nature of the arguments offer both an unusual insight into the nature of the society that produced them and a sobering comprehension as to why a basically inhumane institution resisted all efforts to destroy it for hundreds of years.

For the Portuguese, a moral argument justifying the enslavement of the Moors had not been necessary. A war against Islam was an unalloyed battle against evil and, therefore, was innately righteous. Even the slavery of white Christians was a long-time tradition in Iberia and, although the Catholic church gradually adopted an intransigently hostile position toward it,[22] the practice continued. It was adjudged a phenomenon involving unfortunate individuals rather than races, and if an individual succeeded in emancipating himself, he could become a full-fledged member of society.

Justification for the enslavement of sub-Saharan Africans lay in papal bulls issued by Nicholas V (1454) and Calixtus III (1456). These documents established Lisbon's drive down the western coast of Africa as a crusade and intimated that the enslavement of pagans was beneficial since they could then be Christianized.[23] The papal pronouncements in this last regard did not represent a marked departure from generally held beliefs. As early as 1444, for example, in accepting his share of captives from Lançarote de Freitas's raid, Prince Henry had suggested that slavery was not an outrageous price for the African to pay for his Christianization.[24]

Other justifications were found in the writings of Aristotle, who argued that soldiers or fighting men taken in just wars are licitly subjugated. He also believed it was clear that while "some men are by nature free, so others are by nature slaves."[25] It is the first argument that was most commonly espoused, at least in the beginning. Thus, in 1489 Pedro Dias, a Lisbon resident, sold a black woman and her daughter to a lady in Barcelona, signing a letter to the effect that the two were "captives taken in just war."[26] Conceivably, the mother could have been a combatant in some sort of African conflict, but it is exceedingly unlikely that the child was. Obviously, the separation of the two could have resulted in terrible suffering on the part of the offspring, but this fact was hardly a moral justification for selling the girl as a slave.

The shallowness of the "just war" explanation as applied to African slaves apparently troubled some persons; thus, other Portuguese thinkers seized upon Aristotle's natural slave argument and trotted it out, decked in religious garb. The noted chronicler Gomes Eanes de Zurara, who himself had been a participant in a pre-1448 slave raid, was perhaps the first to blaze this trail. He wrote that, after the Flood mentioned in the Old Testament,[27] Noah had blessed two of his sons but cursed the third, Ham, and condemned the latter's offspring, Canaan, to be "a servant of servants . . . unto his brethren." Referring to the ten Muslim blacks brought to Portugal in 1442 by Antão Gonçalves, Eanes de Zurara states that they were slaves

> in accordance with ancient custom, which I believe to have been because of the curse which after the Deluge, Noah laid on his son Cain [Canaan] cursing him in this way: that his race would be subject to all the other races of the world.[28]

Notice that in this context, Canaan's descendants had suddenly become a race! Still, for a person seeking proof to sanction an action, this type of "evidence" was conclusive. Concerning the hapless blacks among Lançarote's 1444 prisoners, Eanes de Zurara further observed that "they had no understanding of good but only knew how to live in bestial sloth."[29] Such people were innately servile; therefore, the morally superior Europeans needed to entertain no scruples about enslaving them. Moreover, by Christianizing the abominable blacks, the Europeans were bestowing upon them the greatest favor possible: spiritual salvation.

This urge to demonstrate the utter depravity of the sub-Saharan peoples is also etched deeply in the work of Duarte Pacheco Pereira. He dismissed the natives of Sierra Leone as "idolators," condemned those he labeled *mandingos* as having "all the badness of bad men," and even questioned the descendency of black Africans from the universal father, Adam.[30] One may be permitted to disregard some of the judgment of this observer, however, for he also reported that there existed 5,000-foot snakes in the Senegal River![31] Furthermore, his final conclusion mimics that of Eanes de Zurara: The black man is so depraved that, by enslaving him and bringing him in contact with a superior culture, the Portuguese are really helping him advance to higher goals.

There is ample evidence that the complex of ideas promoted by Pacheco Pereira and Eanes de Zurara gained an audience. Following the arrival of numbers of black slaves in Portugal during the fifteenth and early sixteenth centuries, the general condition of all the captives in the country seems to have deteriorated.[32] The crown, in particular, displayed a conspicuous enmity toward servile blacks, for in 1515 it ordered that they could not be buried with other Christians. Instead, their corpses were to be thrown into a special trench containing only the remains of deceased Negroids.[33] Proscriptions like this suggest that the belief in black inferiority had apparently come to be shared by some relatively important segments of Portuguese society.

THE SPANISH BACKGROUND

The black slave in a multiracial system of bondage

Spain's history between the eighth and thirteenth centuries is, in many respects, analogous to that of Portugal. The Moors held sway over much of what is presently Spain, but there is also ample evidence of the presence of sub-Saharan Africans. Virtually all the blacks reaching al-Andalus (as Muslim Spain was called) were bondmen brought across Tunisia, but as the Omayyad rulers generally incorporated foreign mercenary and slave elements into their armies, the prospects for emancipation by this route were not unfavorable. One Omayyad emir, al-Hakam I (796–822), feared palace plots against his life and virtually surrounded himself with "Mamelukes and Negroes."[34] He also used black troops as palace guards and garrison forces, freeing many and allowing a few to reach the position of *mawla*, a military–religious prayer leader in the Muslim faith.[35]

In general, the position of the black as slave–soldier seems to have both waxed and waned. Arabic documents of the tenth century are laconic in that they speak of the sub-Saharan peoples in al-Andalus either as *'abid* ("slaves") or as blacks from *bilad-al-Sudan* ("country of the Sudan"),[36] suggesting that they were respected but viewed essentially as strangers.[37] Certainly under Abd-al-Rahman III (912–961), the status of some, if not all, blacks suffered. Sometime before having himself declared caliph (929), this crafty suzerain demanded as tribute from a minor princeling at Ceuta thousands of Berber and black slaves for military service. Unlike al-Hakam I, however, Abd-al-Rahman III denied them rank and promotion and limited their placement to labor-batallion service.[38]

The pendulum swung in the other direction under al-Hakam II (961–975). This ruler drafted and mobilized large numbers of slaves of all races for military service and even established a black honor guard, which solemnly paraded on official occasions.[39] Al-Mansur (978–1002), royal chamberlain but de facto ruler of the caliphate, added a new wrinkle to the traditional practice of importing black slaves for military service by also utilizing them as couriers, carrying messages both to and from his armies in the field.[40] Relevant also were the policies of Yusef ibn-Tashufin, founder of Almoravid dynastic rule in Muslim Iberia, who was known to have exchanged black slaves for "(white) Christian boys."[41] Affected with a touch of malevolence, Yusef believed that nothing would demoralize his Christian enemies more than the sight of blue-eyed Europeans fanatically wielding their swords in the name of Allah. Throughout his military campaigns, however, he also made good use of the black bondmen he managed to acquire.

Curiously enough, it seems that more black female slaves were imported than males, and these served essentially as domestic workers and concubines.[42] As a result, a number of mulattoes were to be found in al-Andalus, and several of them allegedly enjoyed positions of importance in the national aristocracy and bourgeoisie. Overall, then, the sub-Saharan peoples in al-Andalus did not possess great power and influence. Neither were they only servitors nor was their status as slaves necessarily permanent.

Yusef ibn-Tashufin's brief reign marked the sunset of Iberian Islam's political glory. A century of internal strife and intrigue weakened the caliphate and provided the Christian states of the north with ample opportunities to exploit the situation. After the battle of Las Navas de Tolosa in 1212, the caliphate was doomed, and by 1249 all but the mountainous territory around Granada had passed under the control of Aragon and Leon-Castile.

Meanwhile, Christian merchants had lifted a page from the Muslim book and decided that they too ought to have a few black slaves. By the eleventh century merchants from Barcelona had begun purchasing small numbers of darkskinned servitors at Tunis and other Cyrenaican ports. This traffic between Barbary Coast Muslims and Barcelona Christians continued at least until the mid-fifteenth century.[43] At least from the time of Henry III of Castile (1390–1406), blacks were purchased in North Africa and sold in Cádiz, although no records of the degree of this traffic are presently available.[44] As in the Portuguese case, shortages of precious metals and the rise in the value of undebased coins made the prices of *sarracenos negros* (literally, "black Muslims") prohibitive.[45] Beginning about 1462, however, Portuguese dealers began regularly supplying the Spanish market with cheap black captives. These merchants ensconced themselves in the port towns of Valencia, Barcelona, Seville, and Cádiz, and despite the bitter resentment of some Spanish commercial interests,[46] they consistently succeeded in underselling their competitors.

As part of the Treaty of Alcaçovas signed in 1479, Spain limited its penetration into Africa to the Canary Islands and thereby assured Portugal uncontested control over the rest of that continent. Not spelled out but definitely implied in this agreement was Spanish acceptance of Portuguese domination of the black trade in both countries. Ferdinand and Isabella, the "Catholic Monarchs," may not have realized that the concession was permanent, but subsequent rulers would certainly come to rue this diplomatic arrangement.[47]

Just how many sub-Saharan Africans the Portuguese delivered to Spain as bondmen cannot be determined. Between 1479 and 1516 roughly 5,200 were disembarked at Valencia,[48] and a 1616 census in Cádiz established that black captives outnumbered Moorish slaves by more than 20 percent.[49] Seville represented probably the largest concentration of Negroids and, according to 1565 figures, there were 14,760 slaves in the greater archdiocese. Unfortunately, it cannot be determined whether these were all Negroid; indeed, in one district where an intensive study has been conducted, blacks and mulattoes, free or enslaved, represented only one in every thirty inhabitants.[50] In any event, the demand for blacks, especially as mine laborers, continued in metropolitan Spain until 1785.[51]

The mass of the sub-Saharan slaves sold in Spain after 1462 by the Portuguese were designated *negros de jalof* (*gelofes*), meaning that their alleged places of embarkation were stations somewhere between the Senegal River and Sierra Leone. Toward the end of the fifteenth century, blacks called *mandingos* (from the same general region) were marketed, but the first so-called *bantu* slaves did not arrive from Congo River stations until 1513.[52] Prices for these captives varied a great deal; in Valencia, for example, during the period from 1479 to 1516, prices ranged from approximately $53 to $170 per black. White slaves, in comparison, generally sold for higher prices, the maximum reaching as high as $253.[53] One of the reasons blacks sold for a generally lower price was that they were usually offered in large lots, and, after the prime properties had been sold, the Portuguese dealers disposed of the sick and the undesirables for whatever price they could get. Another reason was that the black slave had to be taught the Spanish language and Christian customs, and, while he underwent this orientation process, he could not often be effectively utilized as a worker.

The kind of labor performed by sub-Saharan captives tended to vary according to sex. Female captives were almost totally committed to domestic service, but males performed a variety of tasks. Wealthy Spaniards purchased some males and converted them into footmen, coachmen, and butlers, while others functioned as stevedores, factory workers, farm laborers, miners, and assistants to their owners in crafts. Male and female domestics working in wealthy homes lived in relative comfort, and those who learned a marketable skill were sometimes able to purchase their freedom. A common practice in Seville – but apparently not elsewhere – was to allow slaves to live separately from their owners, providing them instead with a weekly sum that they might earn from a potpourri of endeavors. At the other end of the spectrum were those unenviable souls owned by the Spanish crown. They served essentially as construction workers or galley slaves, their only prospect of release being royal dispensation or death; in most cases, the latter event was the more likely to occur.[54] By the last quarter of the fifteenth century, at least six types of bondmen were to be found in Spain: (1) Jewish; (2) Moorish; (3) "Turkish" (actually Egyptians, Syrians, Lebanese); (4) white Christian (Sardinians, Greeks, Russians, even Spaniards); (5) *guanches* (Canary Islanders);[55] and (6) sub-Saharan Africans.

During the reign of Ferdinand and Isabella, general regulations governing slavery in the entirety of their Iberian domains began to be promulgated. A 1498 decree issued by these two sovereigns prohibited slaves in Aragon and Castile from selling gold, pearls, or products that included these items in their makeup.[56] Laws like these made no distinctions among bondmen, and in that sense they were color-blind.

The primary regulations governing slave conduct, according to some Spanish historians of slavery, were local customs and practices, and these were subject to enormous variation.[57] One of the traditional privileges that a slave in Spain ostensibly enjoyed was the liberty to purchase his freedom if he could pay a price that he and his owner had agreed upon. The degree to which this and other historic rights were actually exercised is uncertain; in Valencia, for example, a slave could not sue his master in court, and in parts of Aragon law enforcement officers were known for their utter disregard of slave rights.[58]

At the same time, local customs, statutes, and practices also bestowed special advantages upon bondmen, but these were often dependent upon an assortment of racial and religious considerations. White Christian slaves who fled their masters and managed to reach Toulouse (France) were rarely repatriated by French authorities, but this exemption was not extended to

Moors, *guanches*, or blacks.[59] Jewish and occasionally Moorish slaves who converted to Christianity were often freed, but for blacks and *guanches*, Christian baptism was no ticket to emancipation. A white Christian slave could flee into white Spain and, with some luck, pass himself off as a serf or urban worker. Jewish captives might drop out of sight in their ghettos, and until 1492 Moorish fugitives reaching Granada could evade repatriation. Even the *guanches* could seek the intercession of those Canary Island chieftains who had influence in the Spanish court.[60] For the black African, however, there was nothing.

Equality under national law was a reality in Spain, but a host of customary practices and unfavorable conditions usually nullified any advantage that sub-Saharan captives might have derived from this situation.

The free man of color

As is natural in the circumstances of slavery, males of the owner class had easy access to females in bondage, and in Spain (as everywhere the sub-Saharan African was transported) a race of mixed blood eventually appeared. Most of the free Negroids who attained any importance in Spanish society were mulattoes. Outstanding among these were Cristóbal de Meneses, a Dominican priest; Juan de Pareja and Sebastián Gómez, both painters; and Leonardo Ortiz, a lawyer who expressed a preference for his female parent "because I owe much to my mother, who gave me so honorable a father, and very little to my father who gave me so humble a mother."[61] Meneses and Ortiz were illegitimate, but their fathers were highborn Spaniards, a consideration that partially explains their social ascension. Blacks did not fare as well, but two notable exceptions were Juan de Valladolid and Juan Latino. The former held only a service position[62] in the city of Seville, but in 1475 Ferdinand and Isabella declared him "Chief and Judge" over the free and enslaved *negros* and *loros*[63] in both the town and the archdiocese. The commission was certainly not ceremonial in character, for it established that Juan de Valladolid was "of noble lineage among Negroes." At the same time, however, the command limited Valladolid's authority to Negroid peoples and made no provision by which he could pass the title on to his descendants.[64]

Possibly more distinguished but unlike either the mulattoes mentioned or Juan de Valladolid was the sixteenth-century figure known only as Juan Latino. He began life as a slave and claimed to have been brought to Spain from Ethiopia.[65] Juan must have demonstrated an unusual intellectual precocity, because he was allowed to accompany his master, the young duke of Sesa, to class when the latter began attending the preparatory school attached to the cathedral of the city of Granada. Eventually his prodigious scholastic erudition plus the duke's protection and financial assistance enabled Juan to attain the status of regular student. Subsequently, this black scholar matriculated at the University of Granada, where he received both his bachelor's degree (1546) and licentiate (1556).[66] But even in the halls of academe, Juan discovered that genius did not necessarily neutralize racial barriers. When he graduated in 1546, his name was placed last on the list of fellow graduates. More significantly, even though he taught at the University of Granada and his skills in the utilization of the language of Horace and Vergil gained him wide renown, he apparently never received an official faculty appointment at that institution.[67] There is little question, however, that in the eyes of Spanish dramatists Juan Latino was the most preeminent Negroid figure in the national history. His memory has been cultivated by the master playwright, Lope de Vega,[68] and a fictionalized version of his life was written for staging by Diego Jiménez de Enciso.[69]

While the relative success of this handful of liberated blacks and mulattoes is indeed impressive, it should in no way suggest that opportunities for socioeconomic advancement were normally made available to all emancipated Negroids. In general, they found employment in the same occupations they had as slaves, namely, stevedores, domestics, day laborers, and agricultural hands. They suffered harassment from law enforcement officers, and during the sixteenth century the legislature of Castile (Cortes de Castilla) even considered the passage of a law preventing freedmen from moving to new regions and from fraternizing with slaves.[70] Economic ascent had become virtually impossible when, during the last quarter of the fifteenth century, the various craft guilds passed regulations prohibiting persons with African blood from entering their ranks.[71] Neither the royal government nor the Church condemned such prejudicial practices, a situation that strongly suggests that most freed Negroids enjoyed no more de facto options in life style than they had as slaves.

In the face of this adversity, the associative spirit of the black African did not fail him. With the permission of the Church, religious brotherhoods (*cofradías*) were formed in Barcelona (1454 or 1455), Valencia (1472), and Seville (1475). One important service provided by these organizations was the procurement of burial grounds for blacks and mulattoes, for in Spain as well as in Portugal they were denied plots and tombs in other cemeteries.[72] Prominent too were the recreational and social activities of these groups, which provided the freedman with a sense of community. As a rule, gala festivals were held on the feast day of the patron saint of each brotherhood. Entertainment on the grand scale cost money, however, and in order to obtain sufficient funds for the annual celebration held on Corpus Christi,[73] the *Cofradía de los Negritos* ("Brotherhood of the Little Negroes") in Barcelona would sometimes sell a consenting brother into slavery. Later, the group would assess its membership a specific sum in order to manumit the enslaved member.[74] Practices such as this one emphasize the general poverty of most freedmen in Spain; they also accentuate the good faith that the members had in their fraternal bonds.

The overall status of Negroids in Spain

Like Eanes de Zurara and Pacheco Pereira, many Spaniards came to believe that the black African was a racially inferior creature. The "natural slave" theory of Aristotle and the contention that blacks were the descendants of Ham or Canaan both had their adherents in the realm of Ferdinand and Isabella. However, the official justification that the Spanish gave for buying slaves provided by the Portuguese was that the blacks were prisoners taken *en buena guerra*.[75] If the slaves had really been obtained through illicit means, it was a problem for the Portuguese and the African salesmen, not for the Spaniards who made their purchases in good faith.[76]

It is not from these theoretical arguments, however, that one gains a sense of the more common attitudes toward Negroid people in Spain, but from the theatrical works of the sixteenth and seventeenth centuries, particularly those of the celebrated Lope de Vega. In his fascinating *Los peligros de ausencia*, for example, mulatto slaves, partly as a result of their mixed biological heritage, are singled out and condemned as unscrupulous persons, prone to betray their masters.[77] Blacks invariably are also the performers of menial tasks and the victims of heartless mockery. Both unforgettable and illuminating is the situation in *El mayor imposible* in which a black slave-servitor scrubbed himself thoroughly, only to discover that his pigmentation had not come off; or as Lope would have it, "The Negro . . . finds it necessary to return [i.e., after his bath] to being a Negro."[78] The particular incident is humorous, but the question pertinent to our discussion is, What kind of society makes black Africans feel obsessed with the desire to rid themselves of their coloration? An appropriate reply would be that in sixteenth and seventeenth-century Spain the adjective *negro* was often a synonym for evil.[79] Conceivably, white Spaniards who used the word in this fashion did not think twice about the matter, but we can be certain that the Negro did!

In addition to these considerations, a comprehensive assessment of the status of Negroids in Spain must also examine other sociopolitical and dynastic conditions. After 2 January 1492 the last vestiges of Moorish political rule in Iberia were eliminated, but in the conglomeration of states ruled by Ferdinand and Isabella there still existed large concentrations of Moors and Jews who were Spanish by birth. Considering that the different segments of the Spanish population were dissimilar in appearance, culturally diverse, and attached to their regional customs, the only possible unifying principle was the one chosen – religion. In 1492 and 1502, therefore, Isabella issued two edicts that forced Moors and Jews in Castile to convert to Roman Catholicism or face exile. Those who defied these decrees, or who publicly converted but clandestinely persisted (or were thought to persist) in practicing non-Catholic rites, became fair game for the ubiquitous engine of persecution, the Inquisition.

Ultimately, to the white Christians of Spain, the captive from

Negrería[80] and/or his *ladino* descendant were believed to be
loyal, superstitious, lighthearted, of low mentality, and distinctly in need of white supervision.[81] In the words of the Spanish
author Hipólito Sancho de Sopranis, the blacks were possessed
of an "ungovernable character," and while indulgently tolerated
by authorities, they were always considered a "weak and desti-
tute" element in the population.[82] At the same time, they were
nominally Christian, and in late fifteenth-century Spain this
made them politically reliable. The emancipated black or mulatto in Spain played the role of a jackal, tolerated because of
circumstance, but condemned to be content with the crumbs
that society chose to throw his way.

THE FATEFUL DECISION: BLACK SLAVES
FOR THE NEW WORLD

Curiously enough, the first slaves to make the long trip across
the Atlantic Ocean were Indians shipped to Spain by Christo-
pher Columbus in 1495.[83] The Admiral of the Ocean Sea appears to have had few scruples about subjugating the indigenous
population, but Queen Isabella proved a great deal more consci-
entious in this case. In her 1501 instructions to Nicolás Ovando,
the first royal governor of Hispaniola, she ordered that the Indian leaders on the island be informed that they were under her
special protection and that the natives could be compelled to
work only as tributaries of the crown of Castile.[84]

No such solicitousness governed the royal attitude toward
blacks. Another 1501 order barred the entry into the New
World of all Jews, Moors, and "New Christians," a provision
that should have included all *ladinos* in the Iberian Peninsula.
Nevertheless, special exception was made for those "born in the
power of Christians,"[85] and, as a result, an unknown number of
black and mulatto servitors were in Ovando's entourage when it
landed at Hispaniola in April 1502.

Within a year of this landing, however, Ovando had requested
that Isabella prevent the further dispatch of *ladinos* to the New
World. He reported that those already on the island had been a

source of scandal to the Indians, and some had fled their owners and established independent settlements in the mountains. Concerned that the Indians might be led from the path of Christian righteousness, Isabella immediately barred the shipment of *ladinos*.

No sooner had this issue been settled than new developments necessitated its reappraisal. Ovando admitted to having an increasingly difficult time making the Indians work the gold diggings or adapt themselves to plantation agriculture, and King Ferdinand (Isabella died in 1504), therefore, chose to take a hand in the proceedings. In 1505 he shipped seventeen blacks to the island, informing Ovando that they were to be used as agrarian laborers. In November of that same year, he promised that 100 more would be dispatched, and in 1510 another 250 were landed and pressed into service in the mines at Buenaventura and Concepción.[86] Ferdinand's decision to ship more *ladino* slaves was undoubtedly influenced by his awareness that the Indians were still not adjusting to the Spanish labor demands; in addition, the ravages of overwork, influenza, and smallpox were annually depleting the indigenous population. Thus, in 1511 he wrote that the Indians appeared to be "very frail," and that "one black could do the work of four Indians."[87] In this fashion another myth was born, the total effects of which are still apparent.

Grounds for assuming that King Ferdinand was coming to view the Africans as necessary for the successful exploitation of the New World can be seen in his 1513 decree, which created a head tax of 2 ducats on any black slave landed in the Indies. By 1514 the number of *ladinos* in Hispaniola had apparently surpassed that of whites, a potent result of the king's policy.[88] But with Ferdinand's death in 1516, Cardinal Jiménez Cisneros became regent and, citing the rebelliousness of *ladinos*, renewed Isabella's ban on New World black cargoes.

This prohibition did nothing to reduce the demand, and, somewhat unexpectedly, the cry for black laborers in Hispaniola took on a moral tone. Friar Bartolomé de Las Casas, who had received the title of "Protector of the Indians," declared in

1517 that unless the indigenous people received some relief, they would soon disappear from Hispaniola. In order to remedy the situation, he proposed that each white resident receive a *licencia* allowing the importation of up to twelve blacks. Already during that year a special commission composed of several Heronymite priests and Alonso Zuazo, a judiciary official, had journeyed to Hispaniola and, upon its return, reported that black slave labor was a necessity if the colony was to survive. Meanwhile, Cardinal Jiménez Cisneros had died during the summer of 1517, and in November of that year Charles I ascended the throne. Taking what in retrospect was a momentous step, in August 1518 Charles voided the deceased cardinal's prohibition and awarded to a member of the royal household a monopoly on the slave trade. It is more than likely that this decision would have been made even if Charles's friend, Las Casas, never suggested the importation of blacks into Hispaniola. In addition, the direct shipment of blacks from Africa to the New World was sanctioned.

The definitive elucidation of Spanish policy in regard to black slavery in the Indies was still some nine years away. A 1522 rebellion of bondmen in Santo Domingo touched off a review of royal policy, and the conclusion was that a combination of Muslim-influenced *gelofes* and disgruntled *ladinos* had been responsible for this frightening challenge to white authority. The further shipment of either *ladinos* or *gelofes* to America was therefore declared an illegal action. This prohibition was followed by decrees on 25 February 1530 and 13 September 1532 that specifically proscribed the dispatch of any white, Moorish, Jewish, or *ladino* slave to the Indies.[89] Only African *bozales* who were not *gelofes* were to be disembarked because they were considered "peaceful and obedient."[90] Noteworthy also was the royal government's insistence upon these points in *cédulas* issued in 1543 and 1550 and in the monopoly slave-trade contracts of 1595, 1601, 1605, and 1609. In fact, so cautious did the crown become once it had reached a decision on this issue that in the 1595 agreement it specifically limited the importation to *bozales* who were *negros atezados* (literally, "blackened blacks")![91]

The casually committed atrocity

The crown initially attempted to create a New World society in which the indigenous people and the whites were separated into a "Republic of Spaniards" and a "Republic of Indians."[92] Naturally the premier political and clerical offices were to be held by Spaniards, but the Indians were to live in separate settlements under the rule of their own chiefs. Most important, since the crown would ultimately govern both republics and recognize the Indians' personal rights as royal vassals, Spanish settlers would theoretically have to respect them. Separation was thus conceived of as a means of protecting the Indians rather than of subjugating them.

What in fact caused the breakdown of this hypothetical societal contract almost as soon as it was conceived was the increasing inability of the Indians to perform the aggregate of manual labor tasks that the Spaniards demanded. More toters of barges and lifters of bales had to be found, but powerful considerations militated against the establishment of the multiethnic slavery system long prevalent in Spain. Most of the Moors and Jews left in Spain had, by 1505, undergone at least a formal conversion to Catholicism. They were of questionable orthodoxy, however, and no one was more aware of this than the crown. If religion was to be the unifying principle in the New World, Muslim or Hebraic religious influence could not be tolerated. This situation immediately focused the spotlight on the *ladinos*, but these Hispanicized blacks often fled rather than function as field hands or miners. Furthermore, as Spaniards soon discovered (witness the 1522 Santo Domingo affair), the *ladinos* were highly adept at rousing *bozales* to rebellion.[93]

By process of elimination, the only other conceivable laborer, barring the capture and enslavement of some peoples as yet unknown, was the *bozal*. Several additional considerations also prompted this choice:

> 1. As a captive in the New World, the *bozal* could be baptized and molded into the kind of "model" Christian the Spaniards wanted him to be.

2. The *bozal* would be clearly recognized as a slave. Some Spanish *ladinos* were mulattoes and not much darker than white Iberians. In the triracial society to which the Spaniards were committed after 1518, the *bozal*'s black skin made his status immediately discernible. Likewise in Spanish America there would be almost no possibility that the white or the red man would be confused about the status of the Africans they encountered.

3. The Spaniards believed that the *bozal* could be psychologically intimidated into performing the excruciating manual labor needed.

4. The *bozal* could be bought at a relatively cheap price and in the numbers that would soon be needed.

The Old Testament has been used to justify almost everything, and this situation is no exception. In Leviticus, it is stated that

> of the stranger that sojourn among you, or that were born of them in your land, these you shall have for servants: and by right of inheritance, shall leave them to your posterity and shall possess them forever. But oppress not your brethren, the children of Israel by might.[94]

The decrees issued after 1492 made the unconverted Moor or Jew the "stranger," the person whom all Christians could openly loathe and the malefactor for whom bondage and detention were natural conditions. Under these conditions in Spain, the African became a kind of "little brother"; but in the New World all persons were to become Catholics. The question of who would play the role of "nigger" in the Indies would necessarily be decided on different grounds, a consideration that, along with the reasons already cited, made the black man a prime candidate for this infamous position.

2
The Slave Trade
to Spanish America

THE ORIGINS OF THE SLAVES

A distinctly Herculean task for modern investigators has been the determination of the exact geographical origins of the many slaves landed in Spanish America. One reason for the difficulty of this investigation is Spain's failure to obtain stations in western Africa, which meant that captives came from a host of regions rather than from one predominant area. Also, slave dealers and middlemen, for the purpose of stimulating sales, occasionally circulated all manner of false information regarding the humanity they were attempting to sell. As if these problems were not enough, the disagreements and vagaries of scholars who have researched this field must be tackled. Professor Peter Boyd-Bowman for example, defines the *bram* or *bran* peoples as captives who came from the Senegambia region of western Africa.[1] In contrast, Aquiles Escalante and Gonzalo Aguirre Beltrán argue that these same blacks lived near the Gold Coast (contemporary Ghana) and were shipped as slaves from São Jorge da Mina.[2] Miguel Acosta Saignes accepts the latter geographical position but insists that the *bran* people are today called the *brong*.[3]

These scholarly disagreements aside, the underlying difficulty would seem to be that the Spanish government, while concerned with the religious status of the captives unloaded in the Indies, was generally indifferent to their origins. It should hardly be surprising, therefore, that the information derived from Spanish records is not always helpful. A captive from the Hausa nation, for example, might be considered an *adra*[4] if he was loaded on a slave ship at Grand Popo in the Gulf of Guinea, but if the same black was embarked at a port on the Niger River delta, he might be offered for sale as a *calabari*.[5] A *yoruba* tribesman might be known in most of Spanish America as a *nago*, but in Mexico, Cuba, and Colombia this same prisoner was dubbed a *lucumi*.[6] Considering this confusion of names and origins plus the previous difficulties mentioned, the wonder is that any accurate data is available.

To obtain a clearer picture of slave origins, let us first delineate the major areas from which Europeans tended to obtain slaves:

> 1. Upper Guinea, now occupied by the contemporary states of Senegal, Guinea, the Republic of Guinea-Bissau, Sierra Leone, western Mali, and Liberia.
> 2. Lower Guinea, the leeward coast of the Gulf of Guinea including the Bights of Benin and Biafra. The territory encompassed includes the republics of Ghana, Togo, Dahomey, Nigeria, and northern Cameroon.
> 3. Congo River delta and Angola, the region around the mouth of the Congo River belonging presently to the republics of Gabon and Congo (Brazzaville) as well as the former Portuguese colony of Angola.
> 4. Mozambique, the former Portuguese possession in eastern Africa.

The first major shippers of blacks, the Portuguese, followed a standard policy of naming slaves on the basis of the region from which they were obtained or the port from which they were shipped. Thus, *castas de rios de Guinea*[7] ("nations of the Rivers of Guinea") were blacks from Upper Guinea who were often subcategorized as *gelofes*, *biafras*, and *mandingos*. Until 1570 the Portuguese had the lucrative slave trade entirely to themselves, and since Upper Guinea was closer to Spanish America than any of the other slave centers, it initially provided the mass of the blacks needed. Thereafter, Dutch and English raiders and other competitors forced a discreet withdrawal southward. The isle of San Tomé, located in the Bight of Biafra, subsequently

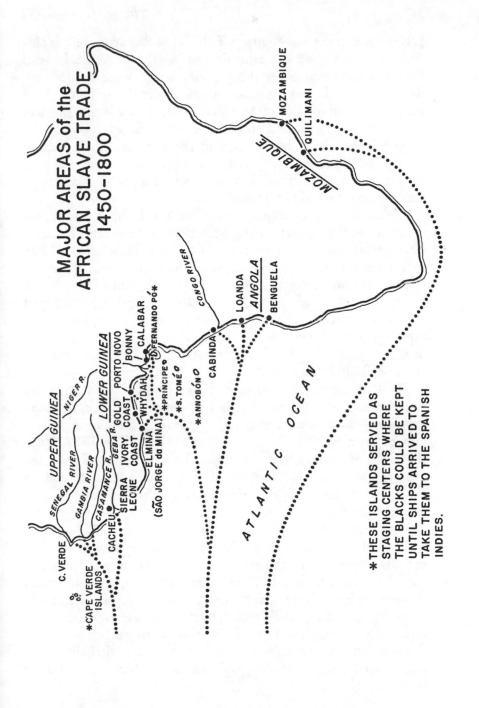

MAJOR AREAS of the AFRICAN SLAVE TRADE 1450-1800

UPPER GUINEA

LOWER GUINEA

C. VERDE

*CAPE VERDE ISLANDS

SENEGAL RIVER

GAMBIA RIVER

CASAMANCE R.

NIGER R.

GEBA R.

CACHEU

SIERRA LEONE

IVORY COAST

GOLD COAST

ELMINA (SÃO JORGE da MINA)

PORTO NOVO

BONNY

CALABAR

WHYDAH

FERNANDO PÓ

PRINCIPE

S. TOMÉ

ANNOBÓN

CABINDA

CONGO RIVER

LOANDA

ANGOLA

BENGUELA

ATLANTIC OCEAN

MOZAMBIQUE

MOZAMBIQUE

QUILIMANI

*THESE ISLANDS SERVED AS STAGING CENTERS WHERE THE BLACKS COULD BE KEPT UNTIL SHIPS ARRIVED TO TAKE THEM TO THE SPANISH INDIES.

became the major slave entrepôt. Africans dispatched from this port became known as *castas de San Tomé*. These blacks who were called, among other things, *terra novas*, were chiefly captives taken in Lower Guinea and the Niger River delta. Juan Rodríguez Cutiño, the second major Portuguese *asentista*, was governor of Angola, and thus there was little question of the origin of the blacks he shipped to the New World. Especially after 1600 these *castas de Angola*, subcategorized as *loandas*, *benguelas*, *congos*, and *manicongos*, were shipped in quantity to almost every area of the Spanish Indies.[8]

The two most important aberrations in this southward movement of the Portuguese slaving operations were the unsuccessful attempts of the Royal Company of Guinea from 1696 to 1701 to rejuvenate the Upper Guinea traffic, and the intermittent trade between eastern Africa and Spanish America's Pacific coast. A small number of *castas de Mozambique* were shipped across the Pacific Ocean to Acapulco (Mexico), where they were mysteriously dubbed *chinos* ("Chinese"). This traffic eventually died out, probably because the great distances involved made it an unprofitable operation.[9]

The Dutch became significant exporters of slaves to Spanish America after the Dutch West India Company began seizing the Portuguese slave depots in the Gulf of Guinea; the most important of these was São Jorge da Mina, which fell in 1637. Since the Gulf of Guinea was the region in which virtually all the captured stations were located, it is reasonable to assume that the mass of the slaves reaching Spanish America under Dutch auspices came from this zone.[10]

The French held the *asiento* from 1701 to 1713, during which time they unsuccessfully attempted, to exploit the Upper Guinea region as the source of slaves for most of Spanish America. Simultaneously, however, they dispatched several thousand blacks from Congo River stations to the Río de la Plata region, Chile, and Peru. Great Britain came to dominate this traffic during the rest of the eighteenth century and sent slaves to Spanish America from a host of bases, virtually all of which were north of the equator (i.e., Upper and Lower Guinea).[11]

In the Americas the best evidence concerning the origins of the slaves landed is provided in those national histories and special studies that deal with African slavery. In this regard the Mexican slave trade has been the most thoroughly researched. One study, based on records from 1549, which concentrates specifically on the captives held by Hernán Cortés, demonstrates that 15 out of some 20 blacks working a sugar mill were from Upper Guinea, while 39 out of 79 others employed in the Cuernavaca region were Upper Guineans.[12] Investigations conducted by Peter Boyd-Bowman based on records in Cuba and Mexico up to 1578 reveal that of about 169 black slaves reported, 70 percent were from Upper Guinea and only 12 percent were from the Congo and Angola.[13] Another student of these questions, Aguirre Beltrán, surmises that only after the seventeenth century did slaves from the Congo and Angola begin to appear in large numbers, and the mass of those from Lower Guinea did not reach Mexico until 1650.[14] These findings coincide closely with the argument that prior to 1570 the mass of blacks transported to the Spanish Indies by the Portuguese were *castas de rios de Guinea.*

Carlos Larrazábal Blanco argues that the *zapes* of Upper Guinea were quite numerous in Santo Domingo,[15] while Carlos Meléndez reports that until 1713 in Costa Rica Congolese elements outnumbered their nearest numerical competitors, Angolan bondmen, by two to one. Thereafter, slaves brought from Lower Guinea by the South Sea Company, tended to predominate.[16] In Cuba the ubiquitous English traders helped to make the *lucumí* (from Lower Guinea) the most common black servitor,[17] and in Venezuela no one group predominated, although Congolese and Lower Guineans were apparently more numerous than the others.[18]

The proximity of Angola and Mozambique to the southerly regions of the Spanish Indies proved to be the decisive consideration in regard to profitability and slave concentration there. Also, because as early as 1601 Juan Rodríguez Cutiño had found that shipping slaves from Luanda and Benguela (Angola) north to Cartagena (Colombia) or Veracruz (Mexico) resulted in a prohibitive number of deaths,[19] the focal point of disembarkation for slaves from the subequatorial regions of Africa became Buenos Aires and, eventually, Montevideo. A good many of those landed were taken overland to Chile, Paraguay, and Peru, where they seem to have become the predominant group of servitors.[20]

Dealers and slaveholders in each Spanish American region came to express a distinct preference for certain types of blacks. In Peru *congos* and *angolas* were considered jovial and docile and for these reasons were more highly valued.[21] In Cuba and Colombia *lucumis* were the choice since they were viewed as industrious workmen,[22] while in sixteenth-century Mexico *terra novas* were deemed the pick of the lot.[23] Even after the Portuguese had lost the *asiento*, slaves peddled as *cabos verdes* drew generally higher prices because of their reputation for physical stamina.[24]

A few tentative hypotheses may be drawn from the available information concerning the African slaves sent to the Spanish Indies:

1. Blacks from virtually every area of western Africa and Mozambique were brought to the Spanish Indies.
2. Blacks from Upper and Lower Guinea eventually became the most prevalent in the Caribbean, Central America, and northern South America.
3. In the Río de la Plata region, Chile, and Peru, Angolan and Congolese elements were probably more numerous.

Little substantial information is available concerning the percentage of blacks who died making the transatlantic passage. Obviously, those traveling from Upper Guinea to Cuba were better off than the hapless souls who had to travel from Angola or the Congo to the same island. Luck also played a prominent role in determining who survived; witness the case of a 1629 slave ship that foundered in Cartagena harbor, killing 870 of the 900 blacks said to have been on board.[25] The 1595 *asiento* contract of Gómez Reynal provides a reasonable idea of the losses the Spaniards expected. This *asentista* agreed to deliver 4,250 blacks a year, but he had to land at least 3,500 of them alive or pay a penalty; in effect, the mortality allowance was

17.6 percent.[26] This mathematical reckoning does not take into consideration the many blacks who died in the foul, vermin-ridden slave warehouses in ports like Veracruz or Cartagena once they had disembarked. Probably the real miracle is that so many of them survived at all.

THE MORAL QUESTION

The Spanish government's justification of the shipment of *bozales* to America was a carbon copy of the argument that sanctioned the same traffic to Spain: The blacks obtained from the Portuguese were prisoners taken *en buena guerra*. Even prior to the mid-sixteenth century, however, some Spanish ethical thinkers began to regard this argument as a conscience salve that no longer did the job. As early as the 1520s, Bartolomé de Las Casas renounced his previous advocacy of black enslavement, explaining that he now realized that the *bozales* delivered were not captives taken in just wars.[27] But, since the only replacement for the black seemed to be the much harassed Indian, Las Casas failed to propose any solution for the future.

Other priest–authors, including Tomás de Mercado, Luis de Molina, and Alonso de Sandoval,[28] questioned or rejected the *buena guerra* contention in their writings.[29] In particular, Sandoval wrote in 1610 to a Portuguese Jesuit, Luis Brandão, in Luanda (Angola) inquiring whether the slaves dispatched to the Indies were obtained by moral means. Brandão admitted that some blacks were illicitly obtained but insisted that the vast majority were not. He also argued that the Mesa de Consciencia[30] in Lisbon had never prohibited the traffic and that most slaves who said they had been kidnapped were probably lying.[31]

Despite Brandão's bland assurances, the admission that injustice was being committed, even on a small scale, highlighted the dubious moral nature of the *buena guerra* rationalization. Particularly after 1640 the major suppliers of slaves to the Spanish Indies were the Dutch, the French, and the English. These powerful states did not even bother to employ the "prisoners of a just war" charade, and it eventually lost its serviceability.

More morally comforting than the *buena guerra* explanation

was the argument that slavery was the impost the black was expected to pay in exchange for his conversion to Christianity. This position was championed by Tomás de Solórzano Pereira, possibly "the most distinguished of Spanish colonial jurists."[32] On the other hand, some found this rationalization as spurious as the other. Alonso Montúfar, archbishop of Mexico City, wrote to King Philip II in 1560, and this cleric's misgivings underline the basic flaw in the argument:

> We do not know of any cause why the Negroes should be captives any more than Indians, since we are told that they receive the Gospel in good will and do not make war on Christians.[33]

The court at Madrid ignored the archbishop's inquiry, but his was not the only protest to be heard. Bartolomé Frías de Albornoz, former law professor at the University of Mexico City, raised similar questions and provided devastating answers. In his *Arte de contratos* (*Art of Contracts*, 1573) Frías de Albornoz denied that Aristotle's "natural slave" theories were in any way applicable to the black African. Most significantly, he insisted that the Christianization of blacks was no excuse for their enslavement; assuming that conversion was a primary policy goal, he reasoned that Spain should instead send missionaries to Africa. Frías de Albornoz virtually denied the contention that Spain had any moral basis for subjugating the black man. Predictably, some administrators in Madrid came to view his book as a dangerous assault on the credibility of royal policy. The Holy Office of the Inquisition intervened, and *Arte de contratos* wound up on the *Index of Forbidden Books*.[34]

Conditional condemnations of the African slave trade had been forthcoming from Pius II (1462) and Paul V (1537), and in 1639 Urban VII barred all Catholic Christians from participating in the black traffic. These prohibitions do not seem to have had any discernible effect on Spanish colonial policy. A major crisis did develop, however, when in 1685 the Dutch Jew Balthasar Coymans sought to obtain control of the slave-trade monopoly to the Indies. The Holy Office vociferously opposed this concession, insisting that the Protestant Dutch might obtain blacks through all manner of immoral means. Moreover, since the slaves to be shipped often spent long periods under Dutch control on islands like Curaçao or Aruba, they might become "infected" with the germs of heretical doctrine; naturally, heretics could not be allowed in the Indies. The ludicrous aspect of the situation was that for almost two decades the alleged possessors of the slave-trade monopoly had trafficked regularly with Dutch suppliers at Curaçao, and with the much maligned Mynheer Coymans in particular. The Spanish royal government was in an extremely uncomfortable position because it could not publicly admit what had been going on without acknowledging that many "Protestant" *bozales* had already been allowed to enter the Indies. Coymans neatly outflanked the grand inquisitors by promising to allow Capuchin monks to make journeys to Spanish America on his slave vessels.[35] Nevertheless, the issue had been prominently raised, and Charles II deemed it wise to initiate a full-scale review of royal slave-trade policy. The task was assigned to the Royal Council of the Indies.

In its final report, the council allowed a modicum of candor to surface in that sea of sophistry upon which royal policy had so long floated. Was it moral to purchase *bozales* from heretics? Would the heretics supply only prisoners taken *en buena guerra*? Ignoring Urban VII's 1639 declaration, the council assured Charles II that sufficient moral reasons sanctioned the Coymans contract, but the report really sidestepped this question and emphasized mundane considerations:

> There cannot be any doubt as to the necessity of these slaves for the support of the kingdoms of the Indies, and . . . to the importance of the public welfare of continuing and maintaining the procedure without any change.[36]

On at least one occasion during the eighteenth century, the Spanish government was again confronted with the difficult problem of countenancing certain iniquitous aspects of this profitable trade to its American possessions. In August 1735 Governor Antonio de Salas informed Madrid that the

South Sea Company, which then held the monopoly contract, was introducing "black Christians of the Congo" as slaves into the port of Cartagena (Colombia). In a *cédula* issued on 23 October 1736, Philip V provided a highly revealing reply to Salas's report. The king initially insisted that "it is not licit to enslave anyone borne free, nor is it licit that any Christian enslave another."[37] But having expressed his adherence to these enlightened moral concepts, Philip shifted gears and ordered Governor Salas to accept the Congolese blacks as slaves, the same as any other captive disembarked at Cartagena.

In providing the rationale for his position, Philip declared that since the Congolese were Catholic, they were infinitely better off as captives in Spanish lands than as bondmen in territories ruled by the Protestant English.[38] But assuming that the king was sincere in his belief that no Christian should enslave another Christian, why did he not order the blacks in question restored to freedom? Moreover, should he not have forced the South Sea Company to stop the shipment of these Africans to Spanish America? None of these questions is dealt with in the 1735 *cédula*, but it is clearly implied that Philip's commitment to the liberation of Christian bondmen did not include initiating a conflict with the South Sea Company that might result in the disruption of the slave traffic.[39] As in the previously cited cases, political and economic considerations continued to prevail over moral and theological concerns.

Although the 1685 Council of the Indies report and the 1735 *cédula* differ in their relative importance in the history of the slave traffic, both were essentially cut from the same cloth. For those whose sensibilities required assurance that royal policy was always guided by the highest moral standards, verbal confirmation was to be found in the opening paragraphs of each document. But the unvarnished reality was that if the colonial empire was to flourish and the flow of profit to the royal coffers to continue unabated, somebody had to sustain the endless drudgery. The black bondman was a proven workman with many capabilities; until some cheap and practical replacement for him could be discovered, the African slave trade would remain "legal," "moral," and most of all, necessary.

1518–1580: YEARS OF EXPERIMENTATION
AND INDECISION

In a special message sent to the Casa de Contratación on 18 August 1518, seventeen-year-old Charles I declared that he had given permission to Lorenzo de Garrevod, duke of Bresa, to ship 4,000 *bozales* "to the Indies, the islands and the mainland of the Ocean Sea." No customs duties were to be charged on these slaves, and all other dealers in captive blacks were prohibited from making similar shipments for four years without the express permission of the crown.[40] With this contract Spain initiated a policy of controlled provision of blacks who could be shipped directly from Africa to the Indies.

The reason for the award of this monopoly, referred to as the *asiento de negros*, was probably that Garrevod was majordomo of the royal household and had the young king's ear. But having neither slave ships nor African depots, the slave-traffic monopolist quickly sold the entry permits for the 4,000 blacks to a group of Genoese merchants for 25,000 ducats.[41] The merchants were not supposed to resell the permits obtained, but of course they did. Portuguese sea captains and other slave dealers were the chief purchasers. For their pains, the Genoese garnered a profit of at least 300,000 ducats.[42] Thus, from the beginning, the sordid business of contracting to supply blacks for the Indies labor force proved both an immensely lucrative venture and a constant source of corruption and duplicity.

Still exploiting his intimacy with the young king, Garrevod sought and received an extension of his monopoly in 1521 for another eight years, but in 1523 the exclusivity of his privilege was abruptly canceled.[43] Perhaps the duke had committed some error that accelerated his fall from grace; what is certain is that the 4,000 slaves who originally were slated for delivery had not arrived. Possibly more important, Charles had become aware of the benefits that the sale of the *asiento* might produce for the royal exchequer. Subsequently, a second monopoly, this time for a four-year contract, was sold in 1528 for 20,000 ducats to Heinrich Ehinger and Hieronymus Seiler, surrogates for the German banking house of Welsher. As in the previous case, they

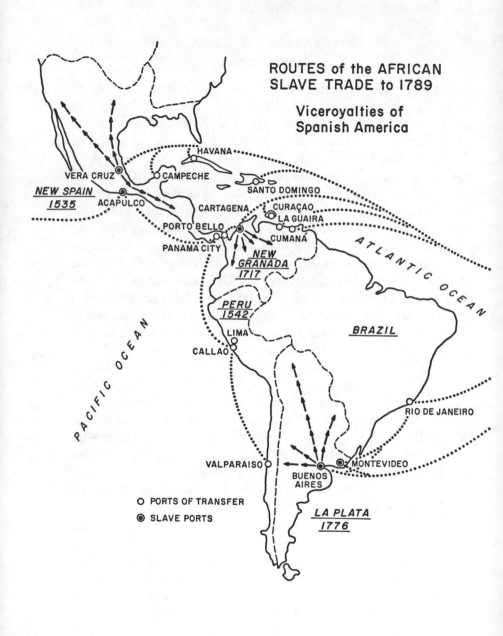

ROUTES of the AFRICAN
SLAVE TRADE to 1789

Viceroyalties of
Spanish America

HAVANA

VERA CRUZ   CAMPECHE
NEW SPAIN   SANTO DOMINGO
1535   ACAPULCO
                    CARTAGENA   CURAÇAO
                                LA GUAIRA
            PORTO BELLO   CUMANA
        PANAMA CITY   NEW
                        GRANADA
                        1717

                    PERU
                    1542
                    LIMA
        CALLAO

ATLANTIC OCEAN

BRAZIL

PACIFIC OCEAN

                            RIO DE JANEIRO

VALPARAISO   MONTEVIDEO
        BUENOS
        AIRES

O PORTS OF TRANSFER
◎ SLAVE PORTS   LA PLATA
                        1776

intended to act only as middleman, selling the 4,000 permits to the highest bidders. They seem not to have paid much attention to a contract clause that fixed the maximum price for a *bozal* at 40 ducats. The result was that agricultural interests in Santo Domingo complained vehemently to the King, declaring that good slaves were not available at 40 ducats and that those who were offered at that price were old, emaciated, or decrepit. As in the case of the Garrevod *asiento*, the 4,000 slaves were never legally delivered. With the expiration of the agreement in 1532, neither Charles nor the Germans indicated any desire for renewal.[44]

No new *asiento* was granted until 1537, at which time two Sevillians, Cristóbal Francisquime and Domingo Martínez, received permission to transport 1,500 *bozales* to the Indies free of customs duties in exchange for a 9,750 ducat payment to the royal exchequer. Since neither merchant had any means of completing the contract, the inevitable sale of the permits to Portuguese dealers and shippers soon followed. Charles seems to have concluded, however, that the resale system either allowed the Portuguese too great a profit or more access to the Indies than it was deemed proper for them to have. In any case, neither he nor his successor, Philip II, would grant another *asiento* for almost fifty years.

The policy in vogue from 1540 until 1586 was the awarding of *licencias* to an assortment of individuals and groups.[45] In reality, this policy had been prevalent for some time, for Charles I had granted special permission to court favorites for the importation of slaves even while the Garrevod and Welsher monopolies had been in effect. The holder of a *licencia* might arrange for the delivery of a specific number of *bozales* from Africa, or he might even choose not to make use of this permit. He could not, however, resell it or give it to any other person. In essence, the official switch to a *licencia* system was the crown's response to the problem of smuggling, to colonial complaints about the high prices charged, and to the inability of some *asentistas* to fulfill their contracts.

Unfortunately for Spain, the actual operation of this system proved less than satisfactory. It seems to have been designed chiefly to facilitate situations such as the one that occurred in 1539, when merchants of the city of Panama obtained a license to import 50 *bozales*. These merchants actually were only some of the many persons with contacts in the royal court who snapped up thousands of permits through purchase or intrigue. María de Toledo, wife of the viceroy of New Spain, became the great go-between for *licencia* procurement during the 1540s, and in 1553 and 1554 Fernando Ochoa de Ochandiana attempted to corner the market, proposing to pay 184,000 ducats for 23,000 permits.[46] Both in Spain and in the Indies it was believed that this noble favorite planned to obtain all the *licencias* available and then dictate the prices that purchasers would have to pay for slaves. In response to protests, the crown ordered the establishment of a maximum price on slaves in each of the regions of the Indies in 1556. Had this ceiling been effective, the cost of *bozales* disembarked would have been reduced as much as 60 percent, but its most startling effect was a rapid shrinkage in the occasionally abundant supply.[47] Realizing its mistake, the royal government acted with surprising dispatch and revoked the decree in 1561.

The demand for blacks in Spanish America continued to grow rapidly, so the impoverished Spanish kings constantly raised the price for which *licencias* were sold. The rate of increase between 1513 and 1578 was some 300 percent.[48] This cost factor, the inability of many persons to obtain either licenses or cheap slaves, and the fact that all the blacks still had to come from Portuguese sources all contributed to a dramatic rise in contraband traffic. The royal government probably realized that Portuguese interests were responsible for this illicit trade, but to deal realistically with the problem, Spain would have had to acquire its own depots in western Africa or allow the Portuguese a chunk of the Indies trade. Powerful commercial interests in the Casa de Contratación violently opposed the second course of action, and in the Treaty of Tordesillas (1494),[49] Spain had unwisely renounced its right to seek African holdings. What saved the crown from having to admit the unsound nature of its *licencia* program was a European dynastic development that the government could only have considered fortuitous.

1580–1640: THE PORTUGUESE PREDOMINANCE

Following the death of King Sebastián in 1578, Philip II of Spain, through a show of force and a series of minor intrigues, gained the Portuguese crown in 1580. As a result, he became sovereign ruler of both the Portuguese and Spanish empires, although administrative direction of the colonial possessions remained rigidly separated. Because of the union at the top, however, Portuguese dealers could now directly and legitimately tap the Indies market, and Spanish America could get all the slaves it wanted. Indeed, offering powerful Portuguese commercial interests an opportunity to fatten their purses was probably seen by Philip as a means of ensuring their loyalty. Six years after ascending the throne in Lisbon, he resurrected the policy of negotiating *asientos*, awarding one to the Portuguese merchant Gaspar Peralta. The terms of this agreement stipulated that the signatory was to transport 2,800 blacks to the Indies and pay Philip 84,000 ducats for the privilege. In return, however, Peralta was relieved of the necessity of paying the regular customs duties on one-third of his blacks, no small factor in the apparent success of this arrangement.[50]

The Peralta contract paved the way for the celebration of what historians have generally considered to be the first major slave-trade monopoly.[51] Its purchaser was Pedro Gómez Reynal, who agreed in May 1595 to pay 100,000 ducats annually for nine years and deliver 4,250 blacks (38,250 overall). This agreement was terminated with his death in 1600. Thereafter, the *asiento* was held by Juan and Gonzalo Rodríguez Cutiño (1601–1609), Antonio Rodríguez Delvas (1615–1622), Antonio Lomego (1623–1631), and the combine of Melchor Gómez Ángel and Cristóbal Méndez de Sossa (1631–1639). The general terms of these contracts differed only slightly, except that Pedro Gómez Reynal and Juan Rodríguez Cutiño could utilize the port of Buenos Aires, a privilege denied to subsequent *asentistas*. Moreover, no matter whose names appeared on the contract, a small circle of Portuguese slave importers and Genoese bankers actually controlled the operation. Perhaps the best evidence of this continuity is the fact that although five separate contracts were signed between 1595 and 1640, the *asentista* agents in the Spanish American ports rarely changed.[52]

The actual operation of the *asiento* was by no means an uneventful business, nor even necessarily a profitable one. Gómez Reynal suffered grievous setbacks as a result of Dutch attacks on his ships and their capture of the great slave station on the island of San Tomé in 1600. Throughout the period from 1595 to 1640, Portuguese interests encountered stiff opposition from the Casa de Contratación, which resented "foreign" participation in the trade of the Indies and accused the Portuguese of promoting contraband slave sales. Also, the crown did not prove greatly interested in keeping the *asentistas* happy. After Gómez Reynal negotiated his contract, Philip II restrained his appetite for selling or granting special *licencias*, but neither Philip III nor Philip IV felt similarly constrained.[53] As a result, contraband sales continued, for the Portuguese *asentistas* considered them an effective means of protecting themselves against royal caprice.

Another unresolved source of friction was the status of the port of Buenos Aires, which after 1605 was generally closed to the traffic. Slaves bound for Bolivia, Paraguay, Chile, or Argentina could easily have been disembarked at Buenos Aires, but Casa de Contratación opposition made this initiative impossible. Merchants from Seville dominated the Casa, and, in conjunction with their counterparts in Lima (Peru), determined the basic routes by which all goods legally entered the Indies.[54] Not merely slaves, but all imports destined for the territories mentioned above had to be landed at Cartagena or Porto Bello, shipped from Panama City to Callao (the port nearest to Lima) by sea, and then rerouted. The added travel costs naturally increased the price of slaves and reduced the market available to the Portuguese *asentistas*. Their solution to the problem was to land as many contraband blacks as possible at Buenos Aires and sell them to overland traders, a practice surreptitiously supported by local merchants who resented the dominance exerted by the Seville–Lima clique. So conspicuous did this traffic become that the bishop of Santiago, Francisco de Salcedo, loudly protested to Philip III concerning the notorious indifference of royal officials in Chile in this regard. In 1622 Madrid took significant action; an interior customs house (*aduanilla seca*) was established near the city of Córdoba (Argentina) in an effort to intercept traders with illicit slaves. Its existence initially caused consternation, but soon the contraband traffic regained its previous levels as routes around the official post were developed.[55]

The end of Portuguese control of the Indies slave traffic came unexpectedly in 1640, although for several years the colonies of Portugal had been targets of opportunity for both France and the Netherlands. In 1638 France had seized the isle of Arguim, while the year before Dutch West India Company forces had captured the slave base at São Jorge da Mina. The Hollanders would follow up their initial triumph in 1641 with conquests of San Tomé Island and the colony of Angola. Despite these crippling losses, Portuguese dealers could still have acquired blacks from Mozambique or Guinea-Bissau, but from the Spanish point of view, an even more dramatic event had occurred. In 1640 a revolt in Portugal culminated in the end of Hapsburg rule and the reassertion of national independence. An angry and vindictive Philip IV, egged on by Casa de Contratación elements, took the only revenge immediately available to him; he canceled the *asiento* and prohibited his American subjects from buying slaves from Portuguese sources.

1640–1712: THE *ASIENTO* BECOMES
AN INTERNATIONAL PRIZE

When Spain dismissed Portugal as its chief provisioner of slaves, it was confronted with the same difficult choices that had plagued it since 1518. It either had to obtain slave depots on the western coast of Africa, or it had to ensure regular Indies slave shipments by some country which did. In 1640, however, Madrid was deeply involved in European conflicts and was unable to embark upon any African territorial adventure. Considering the alternative solution, if Philip IV refused to do business with the Portuguese, that left the Dutch, English, or French. The first two were Protestant states, and the crown could not bring itself to trade openly with heretics. There remained only France, but that nation was at war with Spain until the 1659 Peace of the Pyrenees and would remain the sworn enemy of all Hapsburgs until 1700.

Obviously, a major policy reappraisal should have been undertaken; instead, Philip IV sanctioned a return to the *licencia* program, and the Casa de Contratación eventually issued slightly over 100,000 permits in twenty-two years.[56] But what was theoretically practical in the sixteenth century was unfeasible one hundred years later, for fundamental changes had occurred in the European balance of power. Not only was Spain on its way to becoming a military nonentity but also the Dutch had seized Curaçao (1634), the French had taken the islands of Guadaloupe and Martinique (1635), while the English would annex Jamaica in 1655. Poised in their island strongholds, these European states began to mount contraband campaigns in slaves and goods, the volume of which would "eventually threaten the very foundations of Spanish commercial policy."[57]

Adjustment to a changed political situation is always difficult, but the hypocrisy of Spain's official position did absolutely nothing to enhance the process. It refused to negotiate a slave contract with England, France, or the Netherlands, even though the king and the Council of the Indies knew that the *licencia* holders had to obtain the needed blacks from these same powers. Vessels from both Spain and the Indies were soon sailing to Dutch, French, and English Caribbean ports, and returning with more slaves than the *licencias* granted had allowed. Furthermore, ships flying foreign flags regularly visited ports, selling slaves to eager buyers and dispensing bribes to corruptible officials. The ultimate result was that royal control over the traffic diminished rather than increased.

Over two decades passed before Philip IV finally acknowledged that the *licencia* program was an abject failure and that the contraband trade had exceeded the level of acceptability. In 1662 he agreed to a reinstatement of the *asiento* system. Domingo Grillo and Ambrosio Lomelín were the contractors until 1673, Sebastián de Silíceo and Antonio García acted as *asentistas* from 1674 to 1676, and Juan Barroso and Nicolás Porcio were the nominal controllers from 1682 to 1685. With the exception of Grillo and Lomelín, none of the others delivered more than half the slaves they had contracted for. Excluding that same pair, all the other *asentistas* were wholly dependent upon the Dutch West India Company depots at Curaçao for slaves and the bank of Balthasar Coymans for financing.[58]

Madrid was prepared to ignore the fact that the desired blacks were being supplied by heretics, but not the fact that Curaçao was the traffic center. Operating from this island, the Dutch West India Company was brazenly utilizing the slave traffic in order to further all manner of contraband trade with the Spanish Indies. With this knowledge in mind, the Spanish government in 1676 awarded the *asiento* for five years to the Consulado of Seville with the understanding that no trading whatsoever would take place at Curaçao. This group of merchants rapidly encountered serious difficulties in trying to obtain slaves from either Dutch or English sources, and they soon found it virtually impossible to obtain any slaves at all. In 1679 the Consulado returned the privilege to the crown, but not before it made a shamefaced effort to fulfill its commitments by trading for blacks at the forbidden island.[59]

In the light of these events, Balthasar Coymans's application for the *asiento* in 1685 should be regarded as essentially the move of a king-maker out of the shadows. The terrible anguish caused by the Coymans contract was that its very existence was blatant testimony of the desperate need of slaves in the Indies and of the naked impotence of a Spain that could neither supply them nor control the traffic that did. Coymans became an *asentista* in 1685 with the right to complete the Barroso–Porcío contract to 1687 plus a two-year extension, but he was granted this only after making a large cash payment to the Spanish treasury and promising to construct three warships. The Dutch dealer died unexpectedly in November 1686, and successive efforts on the part of his brother John and the Dutch West India Company to obtain a refund or Spanish cooperation in the execution of the 1685 contract proved fruitless. In 1689 the crown returned the *asiento* to Nicolás Porcío, who claimed that he had been unjustly treated as a result of intrigues by Balthasar

Coymans. The award of the Coymans contract to this Hispanicized Italian changed little, for, although blacks were obtained at Jamaica and Barbados, the major portion continued to come from Curaçao until 1694.[60]

The end of Dutch hegemony (except for smuggled blacks) can be dated from 1692, when Charles II solicited a new *asentista,* and an American-born Spaniard, Bernardo Marín de Guzmán, grabbed the prize. It was no secret that Marín de Guzmán's backers were the Portuguese Companhia de Cabo Verde e Cacheu de negocios dos Prêtos ("Cape Verde and Cacheu Company for the Sales of Blacks"). In granting the monopoly, however, the crown believed that it was finally escaping its dependency upon the Dutch, while simultaneously assuring that the necessary *bozales* would be forthcoming from a less troublesome supplier. It is possible that this arrangement might have functioned effectively, but ensuing developments did not provide sufficient time for results to take place. The very year the *asiento* was to have gone into effect, Marín de Guzmán was murdered, presumably by Dutch interests in Curaçao.[61] Representatives of the Companhia de Cacheu promptly petitioned Madrid, arguing that since their organization had been Marín de Guzmán's silent partner, the operation of the *asiento* should revert to them. Madrid absolutely rejected this position, insisting instead that arrangements made between Marín de Guzmán and the Companhia de Cacheu were in no way binding upon the Spanish government.

Aside from masses of legal briefs, controversies of this nature produced only contraband *bozales* for the mines and plantations of the Indies. A new *asiento* had to be offered but, since Spain would no longer tolerate the Dutch, was frightened of the English,[62] and was at war with the French,[63] the only potential supplier left was Portugal. Not surprisingly, therefore, on 12 July 1696 a contract was signed between Madrid and the Portuguese Company of Guinea (actually the Companhia de Cacheu reorganized).[64] The Lisbon-based enterprise immediately advanced Madrid a desperately needed 200,000-peso loan, but because of the aforementioned reluctance to allow potential shippers to compete for the prize, no further important concessions could be extracted from the wily Portuguese.

The history of the *asiento* prior to 1696 can be interpreted as a validation of the cynic's dictum that "anything that can go wrong, will"; the next episode, even more than some of the previous ones, was almost totally in character. Hardly had the Portuguese Royal Company become the concessionaire when French forces attacked and devastated slave depots in Portuguese Guinea. Virtually shorn of their intended source of supply, the new *asentistas* were forced to sign subcontracts with the British for the procurement of slaves.[65] Not until January 1698 did the first company slave ship make a legitimate delivery in the Spanish Indies. Shortly thereafter, new problems erupting at Cartagena, the company's major distribution center, threatened to effect a cancellation of the contract. In 1697 French corsairs had sacked and burned Cartagena. Fearful that the French might return, and lacking a sufficient number of vessels to beat off a future attack, Governor Diego del Ríos proceeded to commandeer several British slave ships sailing from Jamaica under orders from the Portuguese company. These acts generated a threat of British intervention, and the Portuguese had to make restitution to the irate Jamaican slave dealers. The final blow, however, fell shortly after Juan Díaz Pimienta replaced Diego del Ríos as governor of Cartagena in June 1699. In six months Díaz Pimienta closed the company's operation in the port and arrested Gaspar de Andrade, its chief representative, for dealing in contraband goods and conspiring to defraud Spain of the duties to be paid on incoming slaves.[66] Infuriated by these actions, the company charged Díaz Pimienta with theft and extortion, sought his dismissal, and presented a demand to Madrid for 752,000 pesos in compensation for damages.[67]

In retrospect, Díaz Pimienta's charges essentially seem to have been justified. At least 2,500 slaves had been smuggled into the small port of Río del Hacha (Colombia),[68] and an unknown number clearly was disembarked at Cartagena without any duties paid, the Portuguese falsely claiming that the blacks in question were sick or dying.[69] As a result of these and other contraband activities in the harbor of Cartagena alone, Díaz Pimienta claimed that the Portuguese Royal Company of Guinea owed the Spanish crown over 500,000 pesos.[70] This figure is probably a gross exaggeration; nevertheless, it is certain that a large sum was involved. It is also clear that the company failed to pay all the duties on the 9,853 slaves it legally disembarked at Cartagena between 1698 and 1702.[71] Defrauding the Spanish was apparently a prime motive of the company from the beginning, and only the determined opposition of Juan Díaz Pimienta, among others, prevented the Portuguese from gaining even greater profits.

Meanwhile, the company's damage claims received short shrift in Madrid until momentous events transpiring upon the European scene eventually forced Spain to reassess its diplomatic position. Before his death in 1700, Charles II named Philip of Anjou, grandson of Louis XIV, as his successor. The procurement of the Spanish throne by the House of Bourbon was indeed a *coup de maître*, but other European powers were certain to oppose what they viewed as an ominous extension of Louis XIV's influence. If continental war broke out, Philip would need French assistance, and granting the *asiento* to his former motherland was unquestionably a propitious manner of demonstrating both his gratitude and recognition of his dependency. As early as 19 June 1701, the basic details of a new contract had been negotiated,[72] but technically the 1696 pact guaranteed that the Portuguese would remain the legal *asentistas* until 1703. Moreover, Pedro II, the Lusitanian king, was the largest individual stockholder in the Portuguese Company of Guinea, and unless conciliatory moves were made, he might join the general alliance of European states that was already forming against Spain and France.[73]

It is against this backdrop of events that the agreement of 2 August 1701, by which Portuguese interests ceded the slave-trade monopoly back to Spain, necessarily must be analyzed. In return for its withdrawal, the Portuguese Royal Company of Guinea was to receive roughly 1 million pesos, allegedly for property damages.[74] Moreover, from a diplomatic perspective, Pedro II effected an important change in Article 12, for it was in his role as king (not as stockholder) that he declared Spain's payment full and final restitution to the Portuguese company.[75] It is not evident whether the Spanish realized it at the time, but this article decisively undermined Madrid's contention that the *asiento* was merely an arrangement between the crown and a group of private entrepreneurs. The road was now clear for the French to become the official *asentistas*, and, despite the veiled bribe that the 1701 treaty really was, the Portuguese formally allied themselves in May 1703 with the nations warring against France and Spain. Philip V retaliated by canceling all payments to the Portuguese.[76] It has been said that there is no honor among thieves; there does not seem to have been much among slave traders either.

On 27 August 1701 the French Royal Company of Guinea was ushered onto the stage as the new *asentista*. The contractual terms offered to this organization were easily the most favorable proffered to any supplier yet. Specifically, the French concessionaire was to provide 48,000 *piezas de Indias* over a ten-year period and disembark these at any Spanish Indies port not specifically prohibited. It advanced 200,000 pesos to the Spanish government for this privilege and, in return, paid a duty that was 4.5 percent lower than the one that the Portuguese had been granted. Furthermore, a rebate of 17 percent of the duties was to be paid in any year in which 4,800 *piezas* were delivered.[77]

The most revealing aspect of these arrangements was the agreement made between the company, Louis XIV, and Philip V. One-fourth of the stock in this enterprise was awarded to Philip, another fourth was allotted to Louis and the remainder was sold to French investors. But the Guinea company also agreed to advance Philip a loan to cover all the stock he was to have paid for.[78] The fact is that Philip V became a major partner in the French Royal Company solely on credit.

Although the new Spanish king believed that both he and Spain would profit from this change in *asentistas*, the Casa de Contratación and especially the Council of the Indies were of quite another opinion. They bitterly opposed what they perceived as growing French interference in Spanish internal affairs. Recognizing this opposition, Philip refused to provide any details concerning the pact concluded with the French Royal Company until 29 August, two days after the contract had been formally signed. In addition, he denied the Casa de Contratación an opportunity to review the document and begrudgingly allotted the Council of the Indies exactly seventy-two hours to present its objections and recommendations. Nevertheless, the council (which had been known to dawdle over some reports for years) managed to make the deadline. In its reply it argued that the new *asentistas* would utilize the contract not only for selling slaves but also as a "cover" for the marketing of all manner of French goods. It further concluded that Spanish mercantile interests would suffer as a result of the agreement and declared itself "morally unable to make the reasonable judgment as to the convenience and inconvenience of the *asiento* for Spanish national interests."[79]

If this report accomplished anything, it was to convince Philip that some sop had to be thrown the aggrieved commercial and bureaucratic contingents in his government. Subsequent negotiations with the French company resulted in the barring of company vessels from Pacific Ocean ports in the Indies and a 10 percent reduction in the number of slaves to be landed at Buenos Aires.[80] These steps only temporarily mollified the opposition, for once the actual shipment of slaves commenced in 1703, Spanish colonial officials moved to harass the French at every turn. *La Gaillarde*, for example, docked at Cartagena on 26 November 1703, after a difficult transatlantic passage. The company inspector and the port surgeon reported that of the 103 males on board, 36 were suffering from various maladies, and half of the afflicted were either dying or had become permanently disabled. Nevertheless, Spanish officials, led by the redoubtable Juan Díaz Pimienta, refused to allow any discounts; instead, they taxed each of the debilitated blacks as one full *pieza*. So incensed were company officials by these and other incidents that in October 1704 Madrid was informed that unless Díaz Pimienta was removed or chastized, Cartagena would be abandoned as a port for slave disembarkation.[81]

An even more blatant example of obstructionism can be seen

in the June 1702 order of the Council of the Indies prohibiting the sale of *Mina* or *Cabo Verde* slaves in Indies ports. The French company protested this prohibition, and merchant groups in the Indies also demanded its rescission, but the council refused to retreat from its position. On 19 August 1704 it announced that "according to information supplied by the Casa de Contratación and the Consulado [of Seville]," Mina and Cabo Verde slaves were "exceedingly barbarous," difficult to convert to Catholicism, and known to "eat human flesh with voracity."[82] That both the Portuguese and Dutch had supplied these slaves to Spanish America prior to the award of the *asiento* to the French appears to have been a consideration the council conveniently overlooked. Finally, in 1706 a royal order sanctioned the shipment of these suspected "cannibals" to Indies slave ports.

Unfortunately for the French company, the relief provided by this order and another allowing it to recoup the duties on slaves who died within fifteen days after landing proved insufficient. First, many of the slaves shipped to Spanish America were supposedly to have come from French slave stations in Upper Guinea. This region, however, had been mercilessly combed for almost two hundred years and no longer could provide all the slaves needed. Second, because of the War of Spanish Succession, it became almost impossible for French slavers to obtain blacks from Portuguese, Dutch, or British stations on the Lower Guinea coast. Indeed, the company reported that of some twenty vessels sent to obtain slaves on the African coast between 1703 and 1706, at least two had been lost and few of the others had been able to embark a full load of captives.[83]

The total collapse of the slave-supply system was averted chiefly because the enemies of France and Spain had no compunction about selling slaves to the French Royal Company from their depots at Jamaica and Curaçao. A 1706 *cédula* permitted the French to supply the Spanish Indies through British and Dutch subcontractors. So completely did these erstwhile enemies soon come to dominate the slave traffic that, after 1708, all but three of the slave ships reaching Cartagena came from Jamaica.[84] The frustrating problem for the French was that once they allowed the British and Dutch to commence deliveries, more and more Anglo-Dutch vessels began appearing in Spanish American harbors, and the total of contraband slaves landed began rising rapidly. The company moved to restrict the number of ports to which the Anglo-Dutch suppliers could deliver the legally contracted slaves, but since it lacked control over both the sea lanes and the sources of slave supply, these security measures proved largely unsuccessful.[85]

Incongruously enough, while the French were fighting a losing battle against English and Dutch smugglers in the Caribbean, they were funneling all manner of illicit merchandise into Spanish America through the port of Buenos Aires.[86] One may recall that the Council of the Indies had predicted that the French company would seek to defraud the Spanish crown, and this in effect was happening. The most ignominious aspect of this situation, however, was that Philip V remained a nominal director of an organization that was violating the laws of his government and abetting the corruption of his colonial bureaucracy. Not even the admittedly inept Hapsburg rulers of Spain's past had managed to maneuver themselves into such an absurd position!

Ultimately, any advantages that Philip V may have hoped Spain would derive from this *asiento* proved illusory. Having contracted to deliver a maximum of 48,000 *piezas*, the French Royal Company of Guinea legally delivered no more than 12,798 between 1702 and 1713.[87] Even more disgruntled were the company's French stockholders, for the staggering effects of the War of Spanish Succession, and heavy losses caused by financial mismanagement brought this enterprise to the brink of ruin in 1710.[88] An angry Louis XIV, in conjunction with the other stockholders, openly accused Spanish officials of seeking to break the contract and surreptitiously pass it on to the English. Then, in 1712 the French Royal Company of Guinea presented to Spain a memorandum calling for the payment of over 5 million pesos in debts, interest, and damages. Sixty years would pass before these claims were finally dropped.[89]

After 1640 the Dutch, Portuguese, and French all held the *asiento* contract, and each attempted to smuggle into the Spanish American colonies as many slaves and commercial goods as possible. In their eyes, Spain had accumulated the gold and silver of the Indies by forcing subject peoples to render it up; despoiling the despoilers was hardly a crime. Conversely, by 1713 the Spanish probably viewed themselves as having been sorely abused by their European neighbors. The problem for Madrid, unfortunately, was that the worst was yet to come.

1713–1805: THE *ASIENTO* AND
ENGLISH DOMINANCE

When in January 1712 the negotiations that finally settled the War of Spanish Succession commenced, the most powerful member of the coalition facing Spain and France was Great Britain. The badly desired peace could not be achieved unless London received its price, and what the English clearly wanted was the *asiento*.[90] This demand was tenaciously resisted, but since neither Spain nor its French ally was in any position to continue the struggle, the eventual outcome could easily be foreseen. It was, therefore, no accident that the preliminary peace treaty between Spain and England was not signed until the accords consigning the *asiento* to the British government had been duly ratified (26 March 1713).

The essentials of the new contract generally resembled those granted the French Royal Company. Great Britain was to provide 144,000 *piezas* over a thirty-year period and pay a duty of 33 1/3 pesos per *pieza*. A 200,000-peso advance was paid to the Spanish government, and all the ports to which the French company had been given access in 1701 were to be open to the slave ships flying the Union Jack. The one new concession granted the English was that annually they would be able to send a "permission ship"[91] to sell British-made commercial products in Buenos Aires, Porto Bello, or Cartagena.[92]

Also like the French, the British government did not propose to operate the *asiento* directly. The contract was sold for £7.5 million to the South Sea Company, a combination formed in 1711. At this point, the arrangements between the company and the crowned heads of both Spain and England necessitate

more careful scrutiny. Philip V and Queen Anne held 28 and
22½ percent of the company stock, respectively, but to pay for
his shares, the Spanish monarch borrowed 1 million pesos from
his South Sea Company associates. Despite their massive share-
holdings, neither head of state could control South Sea policy.
Philip could not demand an audit of the company's books, for
"the English had taken care to specify that they [the king's
representatives to the board] could 'only interpose' and could
not decide."[93]

Article 42 of the 1713 *asiento* contract forbade the operator
of the concession to participate in unlawful trade. In contrast,
as early as August 1713 Lord Bolingbroke, Queen Anne's chief
minister, publicly declared that he considered the primary value
of the contract to be its ability to act as a "shield for illicit
trade."[94] The South Sea Company always denied that it was
involved in any illicit traffic, but, from the start, a small coterie
of directors and insiders encouraged and maintained a wide variety of contraband trade activity.[95] The legal sale of slaves, no
matter how lucrative, was only a secondary concern compared
to the incredible income they accurately assumed could be derived from the sale of English goods in Spanish America.[96] But
neither the Spanish nor the vast majority of the stockholders
was privy to the thoughts and plans of the company directors
and their small circle of associates. The victims of the fraud that
would be perpetrated were, therefore, Englishmen as well as
Spaniards.

The arrival of the first permission ship at Buenos Aires demonstrated precisely how accurate Lord Bolingbroke's forecast of
South Sea intentions was. This vessel (the *Kingston*) was loaded
with merchandise that was sold without the payment of duties,
a lapse of law enforcement for which the Spanish governor
received roughly 25 percent of the profits earned. The first such
ship (the *Bedford*) to enter Cartagena disposed of its cargo under similar circumstances, an activity to which Governor Gerónimo Badillo assented, in exchange for a "gift" of 75,000
pesos. Don Guillermo Eon, the representative of the Spanish
king on the company's board of directors, received £1,000 plus
an £800 yearly pension in return for remaining oblivious to

these and other commercial irregularities.[97] So brazen did the South Sea Company's inner clique become that they actually maintained an informer "very close . . . to the Council of the Indies," and, through this agent, they "succeeded in learning the secret instructions of the Council of the Indies."[98]

As previously noted, Madrid had ceded the *asiento* to Great Britain only under pressure, and following the outbreak of war with the latter in 1718 Madrid acted to remove the South Sea "viper" from its bosom. In October of that year, Philip V ordered the confiscation of all company property in the Americas. With the cessation of hostilities in 1721, the Consulados of Seville, Mexico City, and Lima all complained of the English contraband activities and demanded the termination of the South Sea Company's contract. A puny Spain, however, was dealing with too strong a foe and could not easily extract itself from the shackles it had begrudgingly accepted in 1713. In the Treaty of Madrid, signed in June 1721, the *asiento* was renewed with the company without any changes.

The legal traffic was resumed during the following year, but the determined opposition of the Council of the Indies made effective operation of the concession increasingly difficult. Unaffected, in contrast, was the contraband traffic, for permission ships that were to have docked only at Buenos Aires, Cartagena, and Porto Bello entered harbors such as Veracruz and sold their cargoes without harassment.[99] But in 1726 the threat of general European conflict again brought Spain and Britain close to war. For a second time, Philip V strove to rid himself of his *bête noire*, and in March 1727 all South Sea Company property was again confiscated.

The threatened conflict was averted, but, in a 1729 treaty, Britain once again forced the Spanish to return the *asiento* to the South Sea Company. Madrid's reluctance proved wholly justifiable because during the period from 1730 to 1739 the volume of the contraband traffic rose to a level in which it threatened the very stability of the Spanish commercial system. In 1733 the king ordered that merchants leaving the viceroyalty of Peru would not be able to bring gold and silver to ports where British permission ships might be loading.[100] Then, in

1737 the Casa de Contratación reported to Philip V that it had become impossible for Spanish dealers to ship clothing to the Spanish Indies because the colonial market was utterly saturated with contraband.[101] At the same time, however, Spain was beginning to fight the contrabandists more effectively. The signed confessions of two ex-South Sea Company officials, Matthew Plowes and John Burnett, provided Madrid with all the moral ammunition it needed, and in 1730 a special fleet of coastal security vessels was created. It was the commander of one of these vessels who in 1731 cut off the ear of a Robert Jenkins, an English shipmaster suspected of smuggling. This event would eventually serve England as the *cause célèbre* for the war that broke out eight years later, although in fact the conflict could have been touched off by a whole raft of seizures that transpired between 1730 and 1739.

The last act of this drama began when, at British insistence, both London and Madrid signed a convention on 14 January 1739 calling for an end to all search and seizure operations in order "to prevent an open rupture between the two crowns."[102] The South Sea Company, however, then rejected a Spanish demand for an audit of its books and, in rebuttal, demanded that Spain pay £400,000 for impounded cargoes and property damages. On 28 November 1739, after citing South Sea Company smuggling as the *casus belli*, Philip V declared war on Great Britain.[103] Decrying, among other things, Mr. Jenkins's severed ear, Britain replied in kind, and this conflict eventually merged with the War of Austrian Succession (1740–1748).

The initiation of a general conflict in Europe in no manner reduced Spanish America's need for slaves, and Madrid was soon faced with the necessity of obtaining the needed blacks by any means possible. *Licencias* were issued allowing individual shippers to try their luck on the African coast, but the ubiquitous British navy made such endeavors exceedingly hazardous. Much more effective was a *cédula* issued on 1 September 1746, granting José Ruiz de Noriega permission to bring 5,000 *piezas* to Cartagena and Porto Bello. Reminiscent of the era of Grillo and Porcio, Madrid sanctioned this agreement without specifying or limiting the source from which Ruiz de Noriega was to obtain the slaves. One suspects that Madrid had more than a passing idea of what his plans were, for upon receipt of the royal permission, he traveled to Jamaica. There he quickly reached an accord on slave purchases with George Frier, the last South Sea Company representative stationed in Cartagena.[104] Whether or not the British government approved of these purchases is unknown, but the fact that they occurred tends to underscore a preeminent rule governing the slave trade: European wars might come and go, but, as long as Spanish America needed slaves and could pay the price, there was always some interest group that would supply them.

The Treaty of Aix-la-Chapelle ended the War of Spanish Succession in 1748, but, for the third time, Britain used its power to coerce Spain into allowing the South Sea Company to resume its operations in Spanish America until 1752. Nevertheless, by this time, not even the company directors felt optimistic about trade prospects, and, when Spain offered a quit-claim payment of £100,000 in 1750, the acceptance was swift.[105] Exactly how many African slaves the South Sea Company legally introduced cannot be now known, but available statistics suggest that at least 28,300 *piezas* were landed at five major ports between 1715 and 1738.[106] Obviously, the company did not produce anywhere near the 144,000 *piezas* contracted for, but Madrid's unyielding determination to cancel the 1713 treaty and thwart the company's contraband operations meant that the delivery question had become a moot issue.

The lessons drawn from the South Sea Company's term as *asentista* were that the slave-supply contract had to be kept out of the international diplomatic arena, and under no circumstances was a comprehensive monopoly to be granted to a nation stronger than Spain. Unfortunately, the need for slaves remained acute and some system of supply would have to be developed unless Madrid intended to grant smugglers *carte blanche*. The solution that was gradually implemented was a mixed system of *licencias* and limited *asientos*. In Central America, the Caribbean, and northern South America, the return to *licencia* policy was tied chiefly to the appearance and growth of the Spanish-owned joint stock company. As early as 1730, a series of arrangements was made with the Guipúzcoa (Caracas) Company allowing that organization to import thousands of slaves over a forty-eight-year period.[107] A similar package was fashioned with the Royal Havana Company, which introduced from 4,000 to 11,000 blacks into Cuba between 1740 and 1760.[108] Unfortunately, evidence that its directors were engaged in smuggling slaves and bribing customs officials ruined the Royal Havana Company's reputation and led to its rapid decline.[109]

Another *asiento* for the Caribbean and Central American regions was not granted until 1765, when Don Miguel de Uriarte received a ten-year contract. By terms of the agreement, Uriarte could sell slaves at no more than 300 pesos per *pieza*, and Puerto Rico became his center for slave distribution. No payment for possession of the *asiento* was designated, but there was a charge of 40 pesos per *pieza* to cover customs and port fees.[110] From the beginning, the successful implementation of this contract was a questionable affair. American-based slave importers, especially at Cartagena, had come into their own after the commencement of the War of Austrian Succession had terminated South Sea Company supply operations. They had obtained slaves in Jamaica even though Spain and England had been enemies, and this traffic had continued, with Madrid's begrudging permission, even after termination of the war in 1748.[111] The Uriarte *asiento* was bitterly resented by these Indies-based interests, for in essence it imposed a needless middleman who would have to obtain slaves from the same source that they used. Resistance to the *asentista* was strong, and it was further abetted by the indifference to contraband activities displayed by colonial customs officials, underpaid civil servants whose venality was notorious.

Uriarte was only the titular head of a Cádiz-based corporation which called itself La Compañía Gaditana de Negros. Subsequently, Francisco Aguirre, Lorenzo de Aristegui, José Enrile, and José Octavio Ramírez emerged as the actual controllers, and the latter pair either withdrew or was forced out of the combination. The Aguirre–Aristegui duo seemed determined to hang on, but in August 1772 they declared themselves bankrupt and returned the *asiento* to the crown. Fixed prices on the blacks sold, colonial commercial opposition, and indifference to smuggling by colonial officials had resulted in a reported loss of 1 million pesos.[112] Madrid accepted these explanations for bankruptcy, and, since no other national group exhibited an interest in the monopoly, it chose to be conciliatory. Under a new contract sanctioned on 1 May 1773, the 40-peso import tax was dropped until 1776, and the necessity of maintaining a slave distribution center at Puerto Rico was also set aside. Finally, the Compañía General de Negros (as the Aguirre–Aristegui combine now called itself) was granted a four-year extension on its original ten-year contract. Unfortunately, royal favor did little to improve real conditions for the *asentistas*, and when another Anglo–Spanish conflict broke out in 1779 closing Jamaica as a legal port of entry, the Compañía General de Negros simply retired from the business. Still another slave-trade experiment had ended unsuccessfully.

Spanish policy in the Caribbean during the next decade was, if nothing else, pragmatic. A royal decree in 1780 authorized colonial officials in that region to allow any Spaniard to go to the French Caribbean colonies of Guadaloupe, Saint Domingue, or Martinique to obtain slaves. When in 1783 the Peace of Paris again made Great Britain and Spain noncombatants, a limited *asiento* was granted to the firm of Peter Baker and John Dawson, Ltd., of Liverpool. The two-year contract signed in 1784 allowed these dealers to bring 4,000 blacks to Venezuela and Trinidad, while another accord reached in 1786 called for the delivery of 5,000 to 6,000 slaves to Venezuela and Cuba.[113] The last known contracts were granted to an Irishman, Edward Barry, who transported about 4,000 slaves to Venezuela sometime between 1795 and 1805.[114]

After 1740 in the lands of the Río de la Plata region, Chile, and Peru, privileged individuals were sold or granted *licencias* that allowed them to obtain as many blacks as they could from any nation not then at war with Spain. A royal concession issued on 12 November 1750, for example, empowered Don Ramón Palacio to import "2,000 or more Negros" and sell them in the abovementioned areas free of customs duties.[115] When in

1779 war with Britain threatened to drive Spanish commerce from the Atlantic, Charles III granted numerous *licencias*, his intention being to encourage the procurement of slaves from any source that was not British. Between 1780 and 1783 at least seventeen licenses were granted sanctioning the introduction of 3,400 blacks through Buenos Aires or Montevideo, and, during the next nine years, another ten *licencias* permitted the disembarkation of 4,600 more.[116]

During the period from 1787 to 1788, however, no *licencias* were granted for the southern part of South America because Charles III granted an *asiento* covering the Río de la Plata region, Chile, and Peru to the Royal Company of the Philippines. This organization, established in 1733 and reorganized in 1785, acted essentially as a proxy for the crown. The Philippines company was exempted from the payment of all customs and sales taxes, and it established agents to direct the slave traffic in London, Bristol, and Liverpool. The trouble was that the company could not exercise real control over the varied activities of the British dealers with whom it contracted, and, since its own profits proved meager, the will to persevere was soon dissipated. Late in 1788 the company gave up its monopoly.[117]

The Spanish rendezvous with reality was finally accomplished when Charles IV authorized the beginning of the "free" slave trade on 28 February 1789.[118] From then on, any Spanish or colonial Spanish citizen could go in his own vessel to any port and obtain as many blacks as he desired, provided the source was not a country then at war with Spain. Foreigners in Spain or its colonies were also allowed to introduce slaves, but their representatives in the Indies had to be Spaniards. No duty was to be charged on the incoming slaves, and in some areas the crown paid a subsidy of 4 pesos per head to individuals who went out and brought back the needed slaves.

The new policy was first instituted for Cuba, Santo Domingo, Puerto Rico, and Venezuela, because the first three regions were places where Spain hoped to institute an intensive sugar culture. Similar privileges were granted to the Viceroyalty of New Granada in 1791 and to those of the Río de la Plata and Peru in 1795. How "free" this new policy actually was can be debated, for, following the Saint Domingue uprisings of 1790, slaves from the French islands were prohibited from entering the Spanish colonies. Eventually, all slaves except *bozales* who were newly shipped from Africa were denied entry, but a law prohibiting foreign slave ships from remaining longer than twenty-four hours in Spanish colonial ports was eased. Also Spanish citizens were permitted to import agricultural equipment from foreign suppliers if they could not find available slaves. Most of the time between 1796 and 1810, however, Great Britain and Spain were in conflict, so that men-of-war flying the Union Jack again made the sea lanes hazardous for Spanish vessels. Nevertheless, the contraband traffic continued, and, at least in the Río de la Plata, the Portuguese moved to fill the void created by the withdrawal of Great Britain from the trade in 1807.

Spain's quixotic efforts to halt contraband activities had only facilitated the passage of the wealth of the Indies into the pockets of the Dutch, Portuguese, French and English. It had been a painful process, but in 1789 Spain bowed to the inevitable. Thereafter, if the colonists wanted slaves, they could negotiate the business by themselves.

THE SLAVE TRAFFIC: AN ASSESSMENT

How many slaves were shipped from Spain and Africa to Spanish America between 1518 and the beginning of the Latin American wars of independence in 1810? To this date, all figures provided in published studies have been highly conjectural and distinctly unconvincing because of deficiencies in the several areas.

First of all, between 1518 and 1808 both the kings of Spain and an assortment of royal agencies handed out thousands of *licencias* allowing groups and individuals to import blacks. The number of *licencias* distributed is unknown, and no one has ever been able to determine how many of these permits were actually used.

Also, beginning with Domingo Grillo and Ambrosio Lomelín (1662–1673), several of the *asiento* contracts established the *pieza de Indias* as the standard by which each *bozal* was to be evaluated.[119] Thus, while the French Royal Company of Guinea reported that it had sold 16,791 slaves during its term as *asentista*, these slaves were considered as only 12,798 *piezas*, thereby establishing a ratio of 1 *pieza* to 1.31 persons.[120] During the period of South Sea Company predominance, however, 1 *pieza* was sometimes deemed to equal 1.74 persons, and, under unusual conditions, as many as 11 persons.[121]

Another reason for the difficulty in computing the number of imported slaves was the *tonelada* ("ton") measure. A few pacts like the 1676 *asiento* that was granted to the Consulado of Seville called for the importation of *toneladas* of slaves.[122] When speaking of ship cartage, the Spanish *tonelada* was defined as a "measure of capacity equal to the volume of 100 English cubic feet."[123] Bearing this criterion in mind, the crucial question becomes, How many slaves could be transported in a space perhaps 2 cubic feet high, 9 cubic feet long, and 5½ cubic feet wide? The standard figure given is 3, but as many as 7 *bozales* have sometimes been calculated to weigh or represent 1 ton of slaves.[124]

Probably the most difficult calculation scheme of all was that embodied in the 1696 *asiento* signed by the Portuguese Royal Company of Guinea. This arrangement stipulated that 3 *piezas* rather than persons equaled 1 *tonelada* of slaves. Thus, 3 males or females in good health could be counted as 3 *piezas*, or 1 taxable *tonelada* of slaves. A common practice, however, was to consider 2 *muleques* (or *mulecas*) as 1 *pieza*, or even 3 of these young Africans as 2 *piezas*.[125] Thus, 4½ or even 6 *muleques*, depending on their condition, might be taxed as 1 *tonelada* of slaves.

There was little that was ordinary about any scheme of computing the value of a *bozal*, and a method as complicated as the tonnage system lent itself to all manner of inexplicable variations. Witness the case of *El Defensor*, a slaver that docked at Cartagena in November 1700. A group of 12 *mulecones* and *muleconas*, 5 *muleques*, 48 *macarrones*,[126] 9 infants, and 4 blacks reported to be dying was adjudged to represent slightly more than 18 tons of slaves (4.33 persons to 1 ton).[127] By what standard the *macarrones*, the infants, and the dying were evaluated as *piezas* cannot be determined.

This entire process of computation aptly demonstrates that *bozales* were considered to be something less than human by the persons who arranged for or dealt in the traffic. It also strongly suggests that despite the appearance of some standardized rules of measurement, subjective factors and questions of supply and demand were probably of the utmost importance in determining how many slaves equaled a *pieza* or a ton. Using the assorted means employed in colonial Spanish America for evaluating slaves, one may never be able to make more than highly speculative assessments concerning the number of *bozales* landed prior to 1810.

Unquestionably, the worst problem facing anyone attempting a serious assessment of the transatlantic traffic to the Indies is determining the extent of the contraband black trade. Faced with high duties, docking fees, and occasional special charges, it was in the interest of the *asentista* to sell as many of his properties as he could on a market where no taxes would be charged and where the potential buyer might purchase more blacks because he could obtain them more cheaply.

As early as 1527, the royal government issued a decree prohibiting the sales of contraband blacks in America, but fifteen years later, at least in the Caribbean, "for every 100 [slaves] entering openly, 200 were introduced secretly."[128] The Venezuelan scholar Federico Brito Figueroa has argued that at least 20 percent of the blacks landed in Venezuela during the eighteenth century were illegal entrants, while Gonzalo Vial Correa believes that half of those reaching Chile were smuggled.[129] Elena Fanny Scheüss de Studer concluded that perhaps 50 percent of the blacks landed between 1680 and 1806 in the Río de la Plata area were contraband arrivals; indeed, during the period from 1606 to 1655, only 288 of some 12,788 slaves were legally disembarked.[130]

Finally, a point rarely discussed but not to be ignored is the unknown number of captives reshipped from Rio de Janeiro to Montevideo in contravention of both Spanish and Portuguese royal dicta.[131] It would seem, then, that no census of the Spanish American slave traffic can be considered authoritative unless a reasonably convincing effort is made to determine the approximate extent of the illegal traffic.

Table 1. *Slaves delivered to the Spanish Indies*

Author	Total	Time
Edward G. Bourne	700,000	1550–1750
Federico Brito Figueroa	1,037,900	1500–1810
Philip Curtin	925,100	1521–1807
Arthur Corwin	2,000,000	colonial period
Arthur Helps	5,000,000–6,000,000	1517–1807
Rolando Mellafe	3,000,000	1500–1810 (approx.)
Magnus Mörner	3,000,000	1500–1810 (approx.)

Sources: Edward G. Bourne, *Spain in America: 1450–1580* (New York, 1904), pp. 275–76; Federico Brito Figueroa, *Estructura económica de Venezuela colonial* (Caracas, 1963), p. 110; Arthur Corwin, *Spain and the Abolition of Slavery in Cuba: 1817–1886* (Austin, 1967), p. 8; Philip Curtin, *The Atlantic Slave Trade: A Census* (Madison, 1969), p. 46; Arthur Helps, *Spanish Conquest in America and Its Relation to Slavery*, 4 vols. (London, 1861), 1: 371; Rolando Mellafe, *La esclavitud en Hispano-América* (Buenos Aires, 1964), pp. 59–60; Magnus Mörner, *Race Mixture in the History of Latin America* (Boston, 1967), p. 17.

Bearing these considerations in mind, let us examine the opinions vouchsafed by the authors listed in table 1 regarding the delivery of slaves to the Spanish Indies.

Brito Figueroa's study of slave arrivals probably represents the first attempt at a comprehensive reckoning of the *licencia* traffic over a three-century time span. He states quite candidly that his figures cover only the legal trade to the Spanish Indies and that the illegal counterpart was "intense."[132] There are, unfortunately, two serious flaws in his methodology. For some unexplained reason, he computes one *pieza de Indias* as the equivalent of one slave, an assumption that is totally unacceptable in view of the previously cited examples. Second, he calculates that between 1773 and 1810 roughly 123,000 blacks were imported into the "Hispanic American colonies."[133] In contrast, credible statistics produced by Baron Alexander von Humboldt reveal that during the period from 1764 to 1810 over 140,000 Africans were disembarked in Cuba alone.[134] Even if one accepts only Humboldt's 1791 to 1810 customs-house figure of 107,512 slave imports and assumes it to be distinctly inflated,

Brito Figueroa's 1773–1810 totals become highly questionable. The suspicion is strong that the Venezuelan author included only continental Spanish American possessions in his survey.

Philip Curtin's importation census is a laudable effort, but one with definite weaknesses. This scholar divides the slave trade into two major periods, 1521 to 1773 and 1773 to 1807. Unlike Brito Figueroa, he makes no particularly serious effort to study the *licencia* trade. As to the contraband slave traffic up to 1773, Curtin recognizes its existence, but his conclusion that this trade was "extremely difficult to estimate"[135] does nothing to further our knowledge concerning the issue. Ambiguous also are the bases upon which Professor Curtin chose to accept some statistics while rejecting others. In tabulating his totals for 1773 to 1807, he accepts the figures given by Elena Fanny Scheüss de Studer and Brito Figueroa for the illegal traffic to Venezuela and the Río de la Plata region. For some unexplained reason, however, Curtin completely ignores Humboldt's measurement of the contraband Cuban traffic.[136] Omissions of this sort do little to strengthen the credibility of Curtin's computations.

The totals produced by Magnus Morner, Arthur Helps, Raymond Corwin, and Edward Bourne are presumably little more than knowledgeable guesses, since none of these writers provides detailed rationales explaining how they arrived at the figures presented. Rolando Mellafe, in contrast, presents some interesting, though controversial, data and opinions. He reached the conclusion that at least 1.5 million slaves were brought from African sources to the Spanish Indies prior to the beginning of the wars of independence. But this is only the visible part, as it were, of the tabulational iceberg. Mellafe further ponders the high number of "small *licencias* and . . . that which is most important of all . . . contraband" and decides that 3 million imported slaves are a more likely total. This investigator should perhaps be lauded for attempting to compute the incomputible (i.e., the illicit trade), but in his estimates, no attempt was made to compensate for the fact that many of the *asientos* were never legally fulfilled.[137] Thus, while the illegal and *licencia* traffic could have equaled the *asiento* and all other forms of lawful traffic, a sizable reduction in the original computation may well be in order.

Until there emerges some Goliath equipped with new weapons in the struggle to dissipate the fog that shrouds many aspects of man's past, all efforts at making an acceptable census of the Spanish American slave traffic will be innately flawed. A likely "guesstimate" would be that Brito Figueroa's figure of roughly 1 million, plus an addition of 500,000 to 600,000 for *licencia* traffic and smuggled slaves, is a realistic numerical assessment of the traffic to 1810. *Chacun à son goût.*

SPANISH SLAVE-TRADE POLICY:

A REFLECTION

In establishing its American colonies, Spain acted in harmony with the prevailing mercantilist beliefs of the age. These held that a nation's wealth lay in its stock of precious metals, that the maintenance of a favorable balance of trade with other nations was an absolute necessity, and that colonies existed primarily for the furtherance of the interests of the mother country. The dispatch of black Africans to the Spanish Indies was merely a means to enhance the production and shipment of goods that Spain desired.

The problem, unfortunately, was that the slave-procurement policies Spain employed and the traffic-control practices it attempted to implement were virtually always doomed to failure. The event that best exemplifies the crown's stubborn refusal to read the handwriting on the wall was the annexation of Fernando Po and Annobón, islands off the Cameroonian coast in western Africa. In 1776 Spain had pressured Portugal, possibly the only European nation upon which it could still enforce its will, to surrender these islands.

Charles III and the Council of the Indies told themselves that they had at last acquired slave depots. Spain still had no base on the African mainland, however, and without one, these islands could not serve the purpose envisioned. The royal government also seemed to be unaware that the Portuguese did not consider these islands to be useful staging centers, and that England's control of the sea lanes made them vulnerable to blockade and difficult to defend. One need not have been a soothsayer to predict that occupying these isles would do nothing to increase the flow of slaves to the Indies. The 1789 "free" slave-trade *cédula* is proof that even Spain finally drew this conclusion.

Judged on the bases of the previously mentioned situations and their contingencies, Spanish slave-trade policy would seem to have been the work of deranged men hopelessly addicted to hallucinogenic drugs. Fortunately, a more favorable picture emerges if these problems are viewed against another kind of background. Consider, for example, the 1542 rebellion which broke out in Peru following the promulgation of the New Laws there.[138] Charles I would have preferred to dispatch an army to the New World in order to crush these malcontents, but he was then busy battling Protestants in Germany, Barbary Coast corsairs, and Francis I, who would soon attack him in the fourth in the series of Valois–Hapsburg wars. An overextended Charles simply had to be discreet. He never officially rescinded the New Laws; instead, he allowed royal colonial officials in Peru to enforce only those provisions that they deemed enforceable.[139] In leaving his representatives to make the compromises, Charles saved face and avoided a dangerous confrontation that could have resulted in a political conflagration.

Governing the far-flung Spanish empire was always a prodigious task, and expediency was often the only policy. Plagued with a chronic shortage of funds, the crown sold *licencias* to obtain immediate cash, even though the *asentistas* might retaliate by smuggling. It kept raising the customs duties for the same reasons, even though the short-sightedness of this strategy had to be self-evident. Charles I could not have imagined selling the *asiento* to Protestant England or the Netherlands, but Charles II, who needed all the money he could get, swallowed his pride and took the funds proffered by Balthasar Coymans.

The Spanish kings would have preferred to create a comprehensive and functional slave trade system. Unfortunately, international embroilments, a paucity of African holdings, chronic financial problems, and long distances simply nullified this possibility. Therefore, unless contrabandists became too brazen, or the question of slave supply forced some change in the existing administrative arrangements, the Spanish kings applied to this problem the same solution Charles I had adopted in sixteenth-century Peru: try to find out what's going on, but if you cannot dominate the situation, stick your head in the sand.

3

The African Slave
in Spanish America

THE BUSINESS OF BUYING AND
SELLING SLAVES

Picture the arrival of a legally operated African slaver at Cartagena or some other designated port. After anchoring in the
roadsteads, the vessel would soon be subjected to a number of
inspection processes. Initially, the *protomédico*, or royal health
inspector, would attempt to determine whether the human
cargo imprisoned below decks was infected with a contagious
disease such as yellow fever, smallpox, or elephantiasis (called
mal de San Lázaro).[1] If the *protomédico* concluded that all the
blacks were infected and would cause the outbreak of an
epidemic, the vessel might be quarantined and refused permission to disembark its living freight. But in the sixteenth, seventeenth, and eighteenth centuries, disease detection and prevention methods were rudimentary at best, and the demand for
slaves often outweighed other considerations.[2] The normal
practice in Cartagena, therefore, was to quarantine those slaves
believed to be carriers of dangerous disorders in accomodations
outside the city walls. Those blacks deemed "safe" would be
disembarked in the customs area as soon as royal officials had
checked the cargo inventory and the ship's log (*visita de recono-
cimiento e inventario*). The ship would then be searched for
contraband (*visita de fondeo*) and the captain questioned
regarding his crew, the status of any other passengers aboard,
and the vessel's itinerary (*visita de entrada*).[3] If these inquiries
were satisfactorily answered, the disembarked blacks were re-

leased either to the *asentista*'s representative or, if no company then held the slave-trade monopoly, to the ship's captain. They were then moved from the immediate harbor area and were marched or driven, depending on their condition, to *barraconas* ("barracks") within the city limits.[4] The bestial conditions prevalent in these compounds were notorious, and ironically enough, many slaves who had survived the rigors of the Atlantic passage contracted some illness in these hovels and succumbed to it before they could be sold.[5]

The procedures for ship inspection and slave disembarkation noted in Cartagena seem to have been followed in varying degrees in all Spanish Indies slave ports, although important differences existed. In Buenos Aires, for example, slaves considered to be infected with some virulent disease were often left on board ship, and the *visita de fondeo* and *visita de entrada* practices were usually merged.[6] In addition, from the time of the French *asiento* in 1702, all *chacras* ("cabins") for incoming slaves were located outside the city limits,[7] and the two week interim before customs inspection, a routine delay in Cartagena, was apparently dispensed with in the Río de la Plata port.[8]

Despite these differences, the *palmeo*, or customs clearance inspection, was probably the most meticulous procedure involving incoming bondmen. Those *bozales* judged to be salable were marched from their quarters to a central location where they were grouped according to size, physical condition, and sex. Each one was then rigorously examined to determine disabilities, injuries, or previously undetected illnesses. Depending upon his or her condition and often after a good deal of haggling, the slave was classified for tax purposes as one *pieza de Indias* or some fraction of that denomination.[9] Once all the slaves in a group had been graded, the total customs tax was tabulated and paid to the port governor by either the *asentista*'s agent, the ship captain, or some individual merchant who had already contracted to buy the slaves processed. The culmination of the *palmeo* procedure was the branding of the slave with a small silver iron called a *carimba*, an act designed to furnish permanent proof that the slave had been legally introduced.[10] Sometimes he was branded a second time with the *asentista*'s

emblem to prevent his theft before being sold.[11] One undoubtedly bemused Englishman, speaking about the *carimba* ceremony, assured his readers that "the application (of the iron) is
instantaneous, and the pain momentary."[12] One wonders how
objective and dispassionate the observer would have been had a
red-hot iron been placed against his arm, breast, or back.

These formalities completed, the blacks were ready for the
auction bloc. There, *caveat emptor* became the rule for the
hundreds of small merchants who came from the interior to buy
slaves to take back to Mexico City, Potosí, or a host of other
inland centers. One such merchant was Sebastián Duarte, who
around 1628 journeyed from Peru to Cartagena to make purchases. He eventually bought almost 250 blacks from various
dealers in that port's markets. Five of these died, but their
demise was apparently foreseen because the Peruvian received
an undetermined number of *muleques* and *mulecones* as a kind
of bonus, probably because he bought in quantity and could
demand extras. Duarte's expenses came to 44,916 pesos, an
amount that included: (1) royal taxes; (2) medicine; (3) food;
(4) payment to a *ladino* who understood African tongues and
could act as a translator; (5) payment to guards to prevent the
escape of the slaves; (6) cost of transporting the slaves by ship
from Cartagena to Porto Bello, overland across the Isthmus of
Panama, and again by sea from Panama City to Callao (the port
of Lima). Apparently no more slaves died, and Duarte disposed
of all his properties to other dealers and individuals in Peru at
an average of 250 pesos a head. His gross income was 61,250
pesos, leaving him a profit of approximately 16,334 pesos.
Some of these slaves were probably sold on credit, and payment
in some instances was in goods rather than specie. Still, a profit
of roughly 36 percent was a substantial reward indeed.[13]

A continuing supply of *bozales* was an absolute requirement
because, in general, the slaves brought to the Spanish Indies
failed to reproduce themselves[14] and were worn out rapidly in
the mines and on the agricultural plantations. Moreover, since
the *bozal* was sought primarily to perform the hard labor that
no one else would perform, males (*varones*) were preferred to
females (*hembras*). An indication of this preference can be seen

in some of the *asentista* contracts, where the general ratio of importation was fixed at roughly two to one.[15] It is then understandable that *hembras* often sold for 10 to 25 percent less than equivalent males.[16] There were, however, certain discrepancies to this general rule. In Cuba slaves from Angola were considered poor workers, while *lucumís* of either sex were seen as superior slaves. Therefore, an *hembra* designated a *lucumí* might easily sell for more than a *varón* shipped from Angola.[17] Local prejudice and supply and demand considerations all exercised critical roles in determining the actual selling price.

Overall, prices for *bozales* were lower in the Antilles and the Caribbean coast and higher in Bolivia, Peru, and Chile. The collusion between Sevillian merchants and Lima-based commercial groups, aimed at keeping Buenos Aires closed (1605-1702) as a slave entrepôt, was the major reason for this economic distortion.[13] Slaves landed at Cartagena and subsequently transported (recall the experience of Sebastián Duarte) to Porto Bello, Panama City, Callao (Peru), or Valparaiso (Chile) simply had to be more expensive. As a result, in 1630 a prime male *bozal* cost about 370 pesos in Mexico City, 500 in Lima, 600 in Santiago (Chile), 800 in Potosí (Bolivia), but only 250 to 275 in Cartagena.[19] Almost a century and a half later, quality *piezas de Indias* in Lima were still selling at 500 pesos, roughly 60 percent higher than the cost of prime *bozales* on the coast of Venezuela. In addition to geography, methods of payment also had a weighty effect upon prices. Eighteenth-century English suppliers, for example, were often paid in Venezuela with cacao and indigo rather than money.[20] What price these products brought on the London market is difficult to determine, but the fact that goods were accepted as payment suggests that the sale of the products when the demand was high must have brought a reasonable profit to the English slave dealers.

In addition to the legal trade in *bozales*, there was also the internal slave trade, which concerned only persons of African origin already resident in the Spanish Indies. One difference between the two was that, while a buyer like Sebastián Duarte took a chance when buying *bozales*, local laws and customs regulated the workings of the internal market more closely.

When selling acculturated blacks (billed as *ladinos* or *criollos morenos*, the latter term indicating birth in the New World), a dealer had to provide a list of physical or psychic defects (*tachos*) for the prospective purchaser. To meet this require-ment, slaves were frequently offered for sale with advertise-ments that were fastidiously written but that did not always state what the buyer would really want to know. This situation provides a revealing insight into the deceitful nature of the business itself. On 1 August 1564 in Santiago (Chile), for example, Guillermo de Niza sold to General Juan Jofre a slave who was described as a "drunkard, thief (and) debaucher," and, in addition, physically depreciated — "skin and bones." Strange-ly enough, this apparently useless individual was sold for 300 pesos "of good gold." Six weeks later, in the same town, a black woman of "more than thirty years old," castigated as a "drunk-ard, thief (and) runaway" was auctioned off for a sum of 270 gold pesos.[21] It is possible that the relative shortage of black slaves, common in Chile to about 1700,[22] induced the payment of what otherwise appears to have been exhorbitant prices. It is also possible that the sellers simply stated every possible defect, fault, or flaw in order to cover themselves if subsequently the buyer became disenchanted with his purchase and initiated a legal suit.

Some purchasers, of course, did become aggrieved and later sued to recover their purchase price. Witness the case of José Miguel Múñoz Naranjo, city clerk (*escribano*) in the town of Remedios (Colombia), who in February 1760 charged that Don Salvador Lara had sold him a slave named Germán, who was a thief and a drunkard. The judicial official hearing the case, Don Manuel Calderón, decided in Múñoz Naranjo's favor and or-dered Lara to return the 200 gold pesos that the plaintiff had paid. The angry defendant denounced Calderón as a "shyster" and appealed the ruling.[23] By some unexplained maneuver, the judge selected for the retrial was Don Fermín García, who, like Salvador Lara, was a city magistrate (*alcalde ordinario*). In March of the same year, Calderón's decision was completely reversed, a development that suggests that in colonial Spanish America, as elsewhere, rank enjoyed its share of privileges.[24]

Often the highest prices charged were not for *bozales* but for skilled slaves obtained on the internal market. Not surprisingly, in Chile (1631) "a *ladino* called Jacinto," who was billed as having the capacity to be a "manager of an estate," was offered for sale at a minimum acceptable bid of 600 pesos. At the same time, a black bricklayer named Sebastián was offered for 700 pesos. On the internal market, female seamstresses, dressmakers, and cooks of heralded abilities often sold for 600 to 700 pesos.[25] Another example also shows the universality of the situation in both time and place: A prime *bozal* sold for an average of 250 pesos in 1805 in Cartagena while *criollos morenos* who were carpenters and brick masons, when they could be purchased, sold for a minimum of 500 to 600 pesos.[26]

As has been noted, the slave dealer, acting as middleman between shipper and purchaser, took many risks. The undetected infectious disease carried by one *bozal* could result in the death or incapacitation of an entire group, and the vicissitudes of wind and weather could easily cause financial disaster. They also had to contend with local taxes and the problems that invariably arose from credit sales. But the peddlers of Negroid flesh persevered for the most obvious of reasons. As early as 1536, colonists in Santo Domingo complained to the crown that the middlemen in the slave trade were making profits of 100 percent.[27] Two wealthy dealers in Cartagena made profits of "various millions of pesos"[28] from 1748 to 1752. Prominent in the same community was José de Anchederreta, a trader of bondmen, who in 1759 gifted the viceroy of New Granada with 25,000 gold pesos for the express purpose of building new defense works for Cartagena harbor.[29] Also, at least one operative in the black traffic would be favorably cited in the national histories of his country. This man was Francisco García de Huidobro, the builder of the Casa de Moneda and possibly the premier slave vender in eighteenth-century Chile.[30]

Many of the slave middlemen of the Indies were probably involved in the contraband black traffic as well, but all the money obtained that way could be plowed into legal enterprises or used to purchase legitimate titles and advantages. Today we look upon the sale of one person of any race to another as a crime against humanity; in colonial Spanish America, however, this "crime" paid propitious rewards, often allowing the slave trafficker to stifle his conscience while he counted his pesos.

THE BLACK SLAVE AS COMPATRIOT
IN THE CONQUEST

The English landed at Jamestown in 1607, but the first blacks did not arrive until 1619. Although the Puritans established themselves at Plymouth in 1620, African slaves did not make an appearance there until perhaps two decades later. In Spanish America the situation evolved quite differently. *Ladinos* entered Cuba about 1511, no more than two years after Castilians had made their first settlement there. At least one black slave, Nuflo de Olano, was in the company of Vasco Núñez de Balboa when the latter claimed the South Sea for Spain in 1513. When Pedrarias de Ávila became royal governor of the colony on the Isthmus of Panama in 1514, he brought a group of *ladino* servants in his entourage. Hernán Cortés's expedition to the Aztec empire also included at least two blacks, Juan Garrido and Juan Cortés. And in 1520, when Pánfilo de Narváez was sent to subdue the future conqueror of Mexico, one of the Negroid servitors in his assemblage soon made his presence felt. Already suffering from smallpox, this unfortunate slave introduced the plague, which subsequently eliminated thousands of hapless Indians.[31]

Spaniards who followed in the footsteps of Cortés, Balboa, and other explorers generally brought three things with them: horses, guns, and African bondmen. Pedro de Alvarado included slaves in his expeditionary force into Guatemala in 1523, while the presence of blacks was recorded at Santa Marta (Colombia) before 1529. Francisco de Montejo carried at least a dozen slaves to the Yucatán peninsula for his first campaign there in 1532, and a considerable number were in the first wave of Francisco Pizarro's adventurers. African slaves were making their initial appearance in the Río de la Plata area in 1534, and an undetermined number accompanied Diego de Almagro when he entered Chile two years later. In 1540 Francisco Vásquez de

Coronado took both black and Indian slaves into what is presently the southwestern United States on his search for the gold-filled cities of Cíbola. In short, roughly forty years after their probable arrival in 1502, African slaves had been taken to all the areas under Spanish control, usually appearing simultaneously with the Iberian conqueror.

The presence of the black slave, however, is only half the story. Equally noteworthy was the assistance, especially in the initial phases, given by the *bozales* and *ladinos* in helping the Spaniard to dominate the Indian. The African functioned not only as domestic and transporter but also as gun bearer, soldier, and scout. In the latter capacity, easily the best-known black is the celebrated Estebanico. One of the few survivors of Pánfilo de Narváez's ill-fated Florida expedition in 1528, this resourceful individual and three whites completed an eight-year transcontinental hike from Florida to Mexico City. This feat won Estebanico some notoriety, but it is unlikely that he ever obtained his freedom. His luck appears to have run out when, acting as a guide for Friar Marcos de Niza in 1538, he was killed by Zuni Indians in a small village on the upper Río Grande (contemporary New Mexico).[32]

Much more successful than Estebanico was the slave Juan Valiente. With the permission of his owner, Alonso Valiente, Juan joined Pedro de Alvarado's army as it was moving from Guatemala to Peru in 1534. This black man distinguished himself in Chile with Almagro in 1536 and once again with Pedro de Valdivia four years later. Valiente was undoubtedly a fierce fighter, for, as a result of his exploits in battles against the Araucanian Indians in 1546, Valdivia, then governor of Chile, rewarded him with an estate near the capital of Santiago. Juan subsequently married Juana de Valdivia, the governor's ex-slave in 1548, and two years later he became the first known Negroid to receive a fief of tribute-paying Indians.[33] Juan had little time to enjoy his good fortune, for he was killed along with his benefactor by the Araucanian Indians in the battle at Tucapel in 1553.

The irony of this saga was that, landlord or not, Juan Valiente was still a slave. In 1550 he had hired Esteban de Sosa, a

Spanish official, to negotiate with his old master for the purchase of his freedom. Sosa took the money, but he did little else before returning to Europe. Even before Juan was killed, Alonso Valiente had learned of his whereabouts and initiated legal proceedings to reclaim both the slave and whatever property he might have accumulated.[34] In a condensed fashion, the story of Juan Valiente mirrors the general position of the African in Spanish America: He might garner fame and fortune, but the stigma of his origin was always upon him. No matter how important he might become, there was always a Spaniard ready, willing, and able to put him in his place.

THE BLACK SLAVE AS
INDISPENSABLE LABORER

The *ladinos* who accompanied Governor Nicolás Ovando to Hispaniola in 1502 were probably all house slaves. Nevertheless, when King Ferdinand dispatched one hundred more to the island, he ordered that they be used chiefly in the mines. Africans were likewise pressed into service in the silver deposits in Zacatecas and Durango in Mexico, in the gold diggings in the mountains of Honduras, and in the Cauca River Valley of Colombia. For hundreds of years, black gangs also worked gold lodes in Venezuela, Peru, and even Chile.[35] They managed to escape employment in the silver mines of Potosí (Bolivia) chiefly because the climate on the cool, arid *altiplano*[36] was thought to be inhospitable for them.[37]

As agrarian toilers, the slaves produced the crops that made the *haciendas* and *latifundios* valuable. In Venezuela the product was cacao, while on Peru's south-central coast they raised the grapes and olives that made that area prosperous. Negroid workers tended the wheat fields of Chile for many years, and it is possible that a slave introduced the cultivation of that cereal grain into Mexico.[38] In the sugar-cane fields of Mexico, Colombia, Peru, and the Antilles, thousands upon thousands expended their life energy. It was on these plantations that the daily agricultural regimen was probably the most arduous. The slaves were roused about 5:00 A.M., and the day's labor began. Two meals were generally served, but the intermission allowed while consuming the food was often very brief. Work generally ended about 9:00 P.M., but during the harvest season it might continue until long after midnight.[39]

An indeterminate number of slaves also attained jobs that, though taxing, were not without some compensation. It was the mulatto bastards and *criollos morenos,* for example, who were generally taught to be blacksmiths, cobblers, brick masons, carpenters, or tailors. In Mexico slaves became teamsters, and in Argentina and Uruguay, cowboys. Although forbidden by decree, some Spaniards armed trusted slaves and used them as bodyguards.[40] There were, of course, countless male and female servants who functioned as domestics, performing all manner of cleaning, kitchen, and personal tasks.

Some work performed by slaves was especially debilitating psychologically and/or physically. Many unfortunate captives labored all day in small textile factories in Peru only to find themselves chained all night to their work benches. But these bondmen were doubtless better off than the slaves forced into the indigo dye-processing plants that sprang up in Central America. The stinking bagasse in the steeping vats attracted numerous insects and "menaced the health of man and beast." Concerned over the death and incapacitation of so many indigenous people working in these factories, Madrid banned the employment of Indians in these enterprises in 1563.[41] The royal suggestion that *bozales* be utilized for this work is a superlative illustration of how necessary an official "nigger" was in the Indies and why that person had to be easily identifiable.

Perhaps the most unusual group of all were the slave pearl divers who operated chiefly off the Colombian and Venezuelan coasts. These prisoners were well fed and well housed, but were permanently denied the solace of a wife or concubine, the assumption being that sexual relations would make them more buoyant and less capable of diving to the oyster beds.[42] Those finding extra-large pearls were sometimes able to buy their freedom, but relatively few survived the hazards of diving continuously into shark-infested waters.

Operating under a mixture of good and bad circumstances

were those slaves who were the properties of convents and monasteries, or who were owned by a governmental agency. These bondmen may not have had demanding physical tasks, but since they had no permanent masters, they were completely at the mercy of the slave driver or the manager of the institution that owned them. The private owner of slaves might feel some personal regard for his properties or treat them reasonably well because their death or escape would cost him money; captives held by an institution could hardly expect such consideration.

Finally, there were the female slaves who, by choice or necessity, served their masters as objects of sexual gratification. Probably the most unlucky were those who functioned as public prostitutes, surrendering to their owners the proceeds of their activities. The effective careers of these tortured souls were fortunately of short duration.[43]

The trials and tribulations of enslaved Africans only accentuate the fact that in colonial Spanish America these transplanted peoples performed every kind of labor that the Spanish desired. Under these circumstances, the Indian also came to regard the black as the natural executor of heavy physical labor; particularly in Peru, some of the indigenous people owned large numbers of *varones* and *hembras*.[44] Admittedly, Indian slavery had existed in Spanish America since Queen Isabella's day, but in 1526 and 1601 the crown had specifically ordered the indigenous peoples relieved of mine and factory toil. Disguised forms of involuntary Indian servitude surreptitiously persisted despite these decrees, but after 1609 only the African could be legally enslaved. Highly illuminating was the argument presented by a group of Mexican Indians to Viceroy Manrique de Zúñiga. The natives declared themselves unable to work "in the sugar refinery and perform other difficult and arduous labor which are only for the Negroes and not for the thin and weak Indians."[45]

The insidious nature of this incident lay in its indication of the growing correlation in the minds of all — Spaniard, American Indian, and African — that dark skin and debasing labor went together. Over the centuries, this may have been the greatest of all crimes committed against the New World's Negroid peoples.

THEORY AND PRACTICE OF SLAVE LAW
IN COLONIAL SPANISH AMERICA

According to the *Siete partidas*, a body of laws formulated by the Castilian monarch Alfonso the Wise during the thirteenth century, a slave who married a free person might, as a result of this action, become free himself.[46] In 1526 and 1538, however, royal *cédulas* closed this legal loophole because matrimonial alliances between male slaves and Indian women were producing a plethora of legal tangles and an even greater number of children of mixed blood.[47] These and other previously unforeseen circumstances and changing policy objectives meant that the slave legislation customarily enforced in Spain would not always be applicable in the New World. In order to confront the new situation successfully, the crown issued countless and sometimes contradictory *cédulas* governing almost every aspect of slave life in all parts of Spanish America.

One area for which Spanish officialdom demonstrated an unusual concern was in Afro-Indian relations. Since Negroids were considered depraved and the indigenous people in need of protection, laws were rapidly formulated to limit unsupervised contact between red man and black. The crown ordered that any Negroid slave having relations with an Indian woman be given one hundred lashes. If the culprit were caught a second time, the specific punishment was not defined, but it was to be more painful. Furthermore, masters who allowed their slaves to have Indian concubines were to be fined 100 pesos.[48] Strict though they may sound, the laws emanating from the royal government seem relatively mild when compared to some of the local and viceregal ordinances intended to regulate slave conduct. A 1550 Chilean statute directed that escaped male slaves having sexual relations with Indian women were to suffer the loss of their genitals, a punishment that was customary in Central America.[49] Curiously enough, exactly a decade earlier, Charles I had prohibited the infliction of this barbarity upon bondmen.[50] The fact remains that in this case, as in countless others, local officials simply ignored royal policy guidelines.

A more serious and continuing concern for the Spanish regime in the Indies was that of basic security, or protection from slave violence. A 1535 order by the viceroy of New Spain outlawed the possession of a weapon by any Negroid person, free or slave, while in 1577 and 1592 similar ordinances were proclaimed by the viceroy of Peru and the *cabildo* of Santiago de Chile. Meanwhile, in 1552 a Cartagena statute declared that "at the sound of the trumpet" (i.e., at sundown), all slaves had to be off the streets of the town.[51] By 1600 many other cities and towns had passed similar ordinances. African bondmen were also prohibited by both royal and local statutes from riding horses or going from one place to another without the specific permission of the master or overseer.

In comparison with the laws restraining the slave from performing various acts, Spain's preoccupation with the rights of the slave seems inconsequential. Decrees issued in 1544 and 1648, for example, proclaimed that masters must not work their slaves on Sundays and holidays. The problem is that neither *cédula* provided a specific penalty if owners failed to comply. There was also a vague general decree in 1545 stating that slaves must be well treated, but the crown did not specifically call for steps to be taken to chastise recalcitrant slave holders until 1683. In that year Charles II issued an edict affirming that it was the solemn duty of the owner to provide religious instruction for the slave. He also held that, in a proven case of continued mistreatment, the forced sale of a slave could be ordered. Ten years later still another decree affirmed that since slavery in itself was sufficiently rigorous, colonial officials must punish malevolent and sadistic owners. In addition to these *cédulas*, there would be regional orders issued, such as that dispatched to the *audiencia* of Panama in 1710. Claiming that it had knowledge that slaves were being brutalized for minor offenses, Madrid demanded that the *oidores* stop the perpetration of these cruelties.[52]

There is no evidence, however, that conditions for slaves either improved or deteriorated as a result of these commands.

The facts are that Madrid was far away, and royal officials who sought to indict powerful individuals could easily find themselves in vulnerable positions. Since these well-meaning declarations were not reinforced with supportive legislation, it would not be improper to conclude that they were, to a large extent, noble gestures designed to provide their creators with a sense of moral rectitude.

Easily the most important slave regimen issued prior to the general law of 1789 was the *Código negro carolino* ("Black Code of Charles [III]"), promulgated by the *audiencia* of Santo Domingo in 1785. This colony, which covered roughly two-thirds of the island of Hispaniola, had been in economic doldrums since the latter part of the seventeenth century. Since Spain hoped to encourage large-scale cultivation of sugar cane, the new regulations were intended to facilitate the rapid and efficient utilization of the mass of *bozales* that would eventually be imported for this purpose. The chief magistrate of the *audiencia*, Don Agustín de Emparán y Orbe, conferred with numerous Dominican landlords in an effort to construct a regimen that did not unduly conflict with local traditions. The result was a body of law that was potentially enforceable precisely because it reflected some of the biases of the planters.

Among the *código*'s contents were certain stipulations regarding the rights of slaves:

1. Religious education of the slave had to be provided by the owner.
2. Slaves were to have proper food and decent clothing.
3. A garden plot (*conuco*) was to be provided to the slave as his private property.
4. The slave was not to be interrogated under torture, and mutilation of physical features was prohibited.
5. Slave owners failing to fulfill their obligations toward their slaves were to be penalized.[53]

The most glaring omission in the code was its failure to provide for the right of the slave mother to keep her children. Perhaps the answer to these and other deficiencies lay in two principles of general policy established by the document:

1. All Negroids, both slave and free, "will be humble and respectful to each white person as if each was his master or lord."
2. The establishment of "the most comprehensive subordination" on the part of the slave "toward the white population" was "necessary," for this was to be "the fundamental basis of the internal policy of the colony."

To put it bluntly, all prerogatives granted the slaves were incumbent upon what the whites considered to be good behavior. Were the slaves to become anything except humble, the aura of humanistic concern would promptly disappear. The fundamental aspect of the relationship remained white supremacy.

When, on 31 May 1789 Charles IV of Spain proclaimed the *Código negro español* ("Instructions concerning the Education, Treatment and Occupation of the Slaves"), he was introducing a regimen designed to govern master-slave relationships in the entirety of his American possessions. This code incorporated ideas from both the Santo Domingo statute of 1785 and the French *Code noire* of 1685. Among its provisions were the following:

1. Slaves must be given education in religious matters; the master must provide for this.
2. Slaves must have "Christian and decent clothing."
3. Mutilations of the slaves' bodies were prohibited.
4. Slaves must receive adequate housing.
5. Whippings must henceforth be limited to twenty-five lashes for each penalty.
6. Owners must report the death or escape of the slaves within seventy-two hours after the event occurred.
7. Masters and overseers violating these stipulations could be fined up to 200 pesos for each offense.
8. The office of protector of slaves (*procurador sindico*) was to be created in each urban center to investigate violations and argue the case for the slave in civil court. If a master mistreated a slave, the *procurador síndico* could demand that the slave be sold or, if permanently

injured, supported for life by the master.

9. Officials of the *audiencias* and the Church were to conduct inspections two or three times a year to hear slave complaints and see that the code was enforced.[54]

Despite these beneficial provisions, there were some obvious and seemingly inexplicable omissions. The code failed to outline a general means whereby freedom could be obtained, and it did not prohibit the splitting of slave families. In fact, the 1789 *código* becomes more comprehensible only if placed in context along with such previous acts as the *código negro carolino* of 1785 and the free slave-trade policy promulgated for Caribbean regions in February 1789.[55] On the one hand, the humanistic ideals of the Enlightenment had finally achieved some impact in Iberian ruling circles. At the same time, Spain wanted to emulate the success of the French in Saint-Domingue and the English in Jamaica by creating a sugar-cane producing colony that would enrich the mother country.[56] The second goal was possible only if the potential sugar centers received a massive influx of *bozales*; but a century had passed since the notorious 1685 Council of the Indies report,[57] and African slavery could no longer be so easily countenanced. In an effort to reconcile a burgeoning idealism with a corresponding zeal for wealth, a kind of compromise was struck: The needed *bozales* would be imported, but a determined effort would be made to see that they were treated humanely and kept semisatisfied with their condition.

Normally, the promulgation of a new regimen should have engendered at least a modicum of favorable response, but if it did, the applause was lost in the hurricane of dissent that immediately erupted. Angry protests thundered across the Atlantic from both officials and slavocratic interests in Mexico, Santo Domingo, Louisiana,[58] Venezuela, Cuba, and Colombia. Charles IV was urged either to scrap the new code or to suspend its enforcement until some amendments could be made. Historians are still at odds over the actual colonial execution of the *Código negro español*.[59] The document was received in Chile, but only sporadically enforced there, if at all.[60] The viceroy of the Río de la Plata region declared that the law would be obeyed, but there is no evidence whatsoever that any slave owners were punished for violating the stipulations of the decree.[61] In Cuba, Louisiana, and Venezuela, it appears that the code was never issued in its entirety.[62] As for Panama, Colombia, and Ecuador (Viceroyalty of New Granada), the distinguished historian Jaime Jaramillo Uribe states unequivocally that "this legislation did not modify in any significant manner the life of the Negro slave."[63] To support his conclusion, the author examines a number of legal suits brought after 1789 in which the major contention was that slave owners were mistreating their slaves. Conspicuous is the 1796 case against Casimero Cortés, accused of torturing his slaves and driving them to murder their own children. After a special investigation had been undertaken, the *audiencia* of Bogotá recommended that the mistreatment cease immediately and legal action be taken against the slave owner. Nevertheless, for reasons unexplained, no further action was ever initiated; Cortés neither paid a fine nor lost any of his slaves.[64]

In Santo Domingo between 1790 and 1793, legal action was taken against Don Antonio Coba and Don Pedro Betancourt, both of whom had forced their bondmen to work on Sundays and on holidays. Also brought to court during this period was Don Francisco Herrera, who had punished some of his slaves for leaving his plantation during a holiday by putting them on a starvation diet. It is questionable whether Coba and Betancourt were chastened by the 6-peso fine they received, and the 10 pesos Herrera was forced to pay made the question of law enforcement a horrendous jest.[65]

Just as important, perhaps, was the fact that promulgation of the *código* did little to induce greater respect for the wishes of the bondmen. In 1799 María Polonia, a slave owned by Margarita de Tovar, appealed to Caracas officials, claiming that her mistress refused to allow her to marry José Ramón, a slave owned by Manuel Morón, her former master. Margarita de Tovar refused to sell María Polonia, and while Morón would have repurchased her, he refused to release José Ramón. This deadlocked case dragged on into 1800 when Margarita de Tovar broke the impasse by simply dispatching María Polonia to a rural area far from Caracas. The only known decision of the

Caracas judiciary was that, since Manuel Morón had not paid sales taxes when he sold María Polonia, the court wished to see the record of this transaction. We may presume from the muted nature of the last recorded decision that the star-crossed lovers were never permitted to achieve marital bliss.[66] This incident again illustrates the power of the slaveholder in colonial Spanish America.

After nearly five years of procrastination and faced with widespread noncompliance, the crown issued orders, dated 17 March 1794, suspending the *Código negro español*; but royal colonial officials were secretly enjoined to enforce the provisions when possible, avoiding open conflict at all costs.[67] Then, on 19 November 1794 Charles IV ordered that further consideration of the enforcement of the *código* be suspended until the war with France was over. Extraordinary powers of deduction are hardly necessary to arrive at the conclusion that it was the last time this code would warrant serious discussion in Madrid.[68] In the time-honored fashion, still another unpopular body of laws had been discreetly disposed of.

In the opinion of one scholar who has written on this topic, the 1789 *código* could never have been enforced, but "given more time for the ironing out of loopholes, the *cédula* might have made a greater contribution to the pursuit of humane treatment and justice."[69] This sympathetic assessment has its merits, perhaps, but a great deal more than time would have been needed to implement this code. It appears, rather, that in 1789 Charles IV made the same kind of blunder that Charles I had made in 1542.[70] As an absolute monarch, Charles IV was not obligated to consult with the American colonials before issuing this potentially disruptive *código*. Still, the realities of power necessitated that a wise ruler take such action; this was especially true for Charles IV because he lacked the means to force colonial compliance. Paradoxically enough, in introducing the 1789 free slave-trade decree, the crown had moved with caution, implementing this policy only in stages and making creditable efforts to ascertain whether the new rules were really feasible.[71] The failure to act similarly in the case of this much discussed *código* suggests that Madrid never really understood much about the conditions under which slaves labored in the New World.

Rather than risk a serious confrontation over this embroglio, the crown saved face by beating a strategic retreat. Thereafter, it essentially allowed colonial slaveholders to govern their human properties as they saw fit.

MANUMISSION

Not all Africans remained slaves, for legitimate liberation was a distinct possibility. According to some scholars, not only did the Spaniards manumit many more slaves than either the English or the North Americans did but also the slave system was "open" in that emancipation was within the grasp of the majority of bondmen.[72] Because no empire-wide method existed whereby a slave could legally force a master to free him, however, the ease of manumission under the Spaniards must be considered in specific territories and situations.

Probably the surest route to emancipation lay in the realm of extraordinary service. Many of the Africans who fought with the armies of Pizarro and Almagro in sixteenth-century Peru, for example, subsequently received their freedom in exchange for their participation in battle.[73] When the English attacked Havana in 1762, Captain General Juan del Prado promised emancipation to all slaves who would help defend the city. Also, in Chile and Peru during the seventeenth and eighteenth centuries, slaves who were supervisors[74] over Indian labor gangs were occasionally released from servitude. In 1785 the *Código negro carolino* provided freedom for a slave if he (1) denounced a slave conspiracy; (2) saved a white person's life; or (3) provided thirty years of faithful service.[75]

The possibility that slaves in Spanish America might receive their freedom through the payment of a sum of money goes back at least to the sixteenth century. In 1526 the crown timidly suggested that the emancipation of New World servitors might be accomplished for "20 marks of gold";[76] while smaller sums could obtain the freedom of females and small children. Twelve years later in Peru, a slave couple somehow managed to raise the magnificent sum of 1,800 pesos and purchased their liberty.[77] Fortunately, other slave owners were willing to accept much smaller sums in exchange for letters of liberation issued to eager bondmen. In 1710 a slave in Guatemala bought his freedom for a cash payment of 250 pesos. Between 1810 and 1811 in Cuba, some 954 slaves paid specific sums and became free men. A common procedure in Cuba was *coartación*, or the procurement of freedom by installment payments. If the slave changed masters or was resold, the new owner was supposed to respect the amount already paid.[78] A similar practice seems to have been followed in seventeenth-century Lima (Peru)[79] and in colonial Venezuela also, although in the latter country some owners simply refused to allow slaves to buy their freedom under any circumstances.[80] In contrast, the Dominican *Código negro carolino* specifically limited the master's right to free a slave even when the latter could successfully make the payments.[81] Worst of all were the Colombian slave owners, who are known to have collected the agreed manumission fees and then refused to release the slaves who had completed the payments.[82]

Liberation was also possible "by grace" or fiat of the owner. In eighteenth-century Colombia a black slave belonging to Don Francisco Vélez de Guevara found a gold nugget worth 900 pesos; the Spaniard kept the gold but freed the slave. A time-honored custom was the release of those slave women who served their masters as concubines and the emancipation of the mulatto sons and daughters born from such unions. Some slaveholders, perhaps fearing the wrath of God or simply to show gratitude, provided for the release of slaves in their last will and testament. A despicable practice, but apparently a common one, was the "release" of elderly or ailing slaves.[83] These condemned souls were rarely able to fend for themselves, and they often expired from hunger or exposure. "Abandonment" is a more appropriate term for describing how unprincipled slaveholders avoided the support costs for slaves deemed to be of little further use.

There were also acts of liberation that smacked suspiciously of self-aggrandizement. During the last quarter of the eighteenth century, for example, the Count of Tovar in Venezuela manumitted a large number of slaves and made them tenant farmers on his land. It is likely that this aristocrat believed that he had performed a noble act of charity, and, compared with the actions of some of his contemporaries, perhaps he had. Still, the count could not have been unaware that he had also escaped further responsibility for the welfare of his ex-slaves, and assured himself and his descendants a fixed annual rent that might be paid for centuries.[84]

A circumstance not often considered is that of limited, or conditional, manumissions. The case of Pedro Chacon Arrayo, an eighteenth-century Colombian landlord, typifies one aspect of this practice. As part of his last will and testament he freed two of his slaves, but only if they agreed that they would serve his son until the latter's death.[85] Since neither of the bondmen would probably live that long, the dubious nature of such emancipation is self-evident. The only advantage inherent in this situation was that the descendants of the bondmen in question would most certainly be free. Another form of liberation was based on the condition that the freedman leave the vicinity of his enslavement and never return. Often enough, the ex-slave initially accepted this requirement but later returned to the area. In Venezuela, if not elsewhere, such backsliding could result in imprisonment or permanent exile from the territory.[86] Clearly, some owners feared that the nearby presence of the newly freed man might cause less favored slaves to try to escape.

In Paraguay a highly unique method of semiliberation was long in vogue. Mockingly referred to as *amparo* ("protection, shelter"), slaves manumitted by their masters were taken into custody because they could not pay the annual tribute to the crown, which was fixed at 3 pesos per person. Released to Catholic clergymen and local officials, the supposedly freed persons were forced to work as if they were slaves. In 1749, however, fate smiled upon some of these unfortunates. The governor of Paraguay had become obsessed with the fear that the Albayas Indians were ready to revolt. He moved several hundred Negroid men subject to *amparo* provisions to a strategic location and founded the town of La Emboscada. The new settlers were now truly free – provided they fought the Indians when called upon.[87]

Easily the most bizarre aspect of the manumission question in Spanish America was the possibility of reenslavement. The *Código negro carolino* was quite specific in this regard. A freed black or mulatto who was "in grave default of gratitude to his master, or to the wife or children of his master"[88] might find himself again subject to the rigors of involuntary servitude. Available historical evidence suggests that what became the rule in Santo Domingo had long been local law or custom in Uruguay, Chile, and possibly elsewhere.[89] A classic case was the 1787 Chilean litigation regarding Bernarda, a slave woman, and her sons, Pedro and Antonio, all properties of Pedro José de Cañes. This landlord died and willed that Bernarda and her offspring be immediately set at liberty. Some months later, unfortunately, it was determined that Cañes's debts were 20,000 pesos more than his assets. Bernarda and her sons were seized as "property" and turned over to the creditors of the estate.[90]

Investigations concerning the most common methods of manumission have produced controversial conclusions. A benchmark study undertaken by Professor Frederick Bowser of some 294 cases in Lima (Peru) and 99 others in Mexico City between 1580 and 1650 yielded the data shown in table 2. On the basis of the evidence, Bowser concluded that "freedom was a goal obtained for the most part by women and small children." The largest group in Lima and the second most numerous in Mexico City freed by purchase were children under eight years of age. These were obviously the cheapest to free and the group that produced the least in terms of profitable labor. Of those granted unconditional liberation, only 3.7 percent in Lima and 5 percent in Mexico City were slaves between the ages of 16 and 25.[91] Evidently, any charitable instincts the Spanish slaveholder had were often tempered by economic considerations.

The statistics further indicate that 48.6 percent of those manumitted in Lima and 35.3 percent[92] of those freed in Mexico City earned their freedom through some form of financial payment. These findings are utterly at variance with those of two students of conditions in colonial Uruguay. According to Paulo

Table 2. Examples of slave liberation in Lima and Mexico City

Type of liberation	Lima	Mexico City
Unconditional liberation	101	40
Liberation dependent on future service	50	20
Liberation through payment	119	31
Liberation through future or time payments	24	4
Miscellaneous	5	4
Total	299	99
	(95 males, 199 females)*	(37 males, 60 females)*

Source: Frederick P. Bowser, "The Free Person of Color in Mexico City and Lima: Manumission and Opportunity, 1580–1650," (paper delivered at the Conference on the International Comparison of Systems of Slavery, Rochester, N. Y., 9–11 March 1972), p. 16.
*The total of cases and the number of persons freed do not match because some slaves had multiple conditions of manumission to meet.

de Carvalho Neto, the normal method of liberation for all slaves except mulatto illegitimates was death, a conclusion that Carlos Rama modifies only slightly.[93] The findings of these writers are partially buttressed by Carlos Meléndez, who states that the greater number of manumissions in colonial Costa Rica was obtained without monetary payment.[94]

These differences of opinion only emphasize the fact that conditions in the many regions of the Spanish Indies were invariably different. Lima and Mexico City were the largest and wealthiest cities in Spanish America, and, as Bowser acknowledges, the slaves whose stories he documents were overwhelmingly urban. In the poorer and more rural areas, bondmen would have been less likely to achieve similar integration into the money economy. For them, self-purchase was improbable since it would have been quite difficult either to make time payments or to save a sufficient sum to procure their liberation. A case in point is the policy that was practiced at a charitable institution located in the Chuao Valley of Venezuela. In 1743 records indicate that there were at least 143 slaves resident on this cacao-producing establishment. During the period from 1746 to 1756 letters of liberation were sold for an average of 300 pesos each; exactly 8 bondmen, or 5.5 percent of the number of slaves present in 1743, were able to purchase their freedom.[95]

Not often considered is how peer-group pressure tended to affect or influence the prospects of liberation. The celebrated mestizo author Concolorcovo (Alonso Carrio de la Bandera) pointed out that in the city of Córdoba (Argentina) in the late eighteenth century, slave owners made it a general policy not to free their human properties.[96] Of a more concrete nature is the sad experience of Lorenzo Agudelo, who owned a small gold-mining site in the Cauca River Valley (Colombia). In 1781 he unconditionally emancipated eight bondmen who had faithfully worked his property. This action was considered the work of a lunatic by his fellow mine owners; they had Agudelo arrested and, by court order, permanently exiled to Porto Bello (Panama)![97] In short, many other contingencies besides a slave's ability to pay or a master's benevolent feelings often decided which Africans and how many of them were going to be liberated.

If one accepts the hypothesis that the possibilities and types of liberation were dependent upon a host of variables, the question of whether slavery in Spanish America was an "open" system is little more than an academic exercise. Certain groups of slaves and those having the support of powerful persons had an excellent opportunity to obtain freedom. For a great many others, however, freedom was no more than a theoretical concept; their chances for obtaining a letter of liberation were on a par with those of a ghetto-born black becoming president of the United States. The following conclusions seem practical, given the information available:

1. Urban slaves enjoyed better prospects for gaining their liberty than did rural bondmen.
2. *Criollos morenos* and *ladinos* were much more likely to be emancipated than *bozales*.[98]
3. Mulattoes – especially the bastard offspring of Spanish fathers – often found the door to freedom much easier to unlock than their more darkskinned brethren.[99]

In 1789 Yanes Regalado issued a letter of manumission to his personal slave, María del Carmen. Sometime later in the year, Yanes changed his mind and sold the supposedly free woman to a relative, Juan Regalado. María del Carmen sought to have her letter recognized as valid, but the Caracas court ruled in favor of Juan Regalado.[100] In colonial Spanish America liberation was a gift, not a right, and the masses of Negroids who achieved this goal probably had only one thing in common: luck.

THE QUESTION OF SLAVE TREATMENT

At least since the publication of Sir Harry Johnston's *The Negro in the New World* in 1910, a much discussed issue in historical circles has been whether or not the slave system of servitude in Spanish America was milder or more benign than the one that prevailed in the United States. In addition to Johnston, Frank Tannenbaum, Stanley Elkins, and Herbert L. Klein have taken affirmative positions on this question, while David B. Davis, Marvin Harris, and Gwendolyn Hall have denied the validity of such a conclusion.[101] There is also the case of N. A. Micklejohn and the Colombian Jaime Jaramillo Uribe, who studied the same documents and arrived at antithetical conclusions on this topic.[102]

What has never been established is whether a valid comparison of the two slave systems can really be made at all. The slave system in Spanish America was hardly a static entity. Moreover, any number of factors helped to determine, at least as far as the slave was concerned, whether the system was "good" or otherwise. Two cases involving highly different modes of economic activity best epitomize the contrasting nature of colonial slave society. In the copper mines of Concorote, Venezuela, the work force was established and maintained at 89 male slaves and 25 females, a ratio of almost four to one. During the period from 1639 to 1648 there were a total of 13 births; but during the same period 23 slaves died. Since the birth rate in no way sufficed to cover the losses, the work force was maintained only through the periodic acquisition of fresh *bozales*. Sickness was a constant problem, though death in childbirth and from snake-bite were the preeminent causes of mortality. Liberation was rare, even for skilled technical personnel, and, aside from Holy Week, these slaves enjoyed few leisure periods of more than twenty-four hours.[103]

Such dreadful conditions must be contrasted with those existing on several cattle ranches owned by the Jesuit order around Córdoba (Argentina) between 1754 and 1792.[104] No information is available concerning manumissions, but among the slave personnel, births outnumbered deaths by a considerable margin, and between 1754 and 1767 they even surpassed births among free Negroids.[105] The great difference between Córdoba ranching and the mining operations at Concorote is best demonstrated by the comparative mortality statistics. In a quarter of a century (1768–1792), only 31 slave deaths occurred on the Argentine ranches, an average of 1.28 deaths per year. In the Concorote mines over a nine-year period, the yearly percentage was 2.55, almost precisely double.[106]

These two cases glaringly emphasize the decisive roles played by chance and slave function. House servitors, whether in 1520 or 1800, whether as cooks in a Mexico City town house or as body servants on a Venezuelan cacao plantation, could expect better treatment than the nameless field hand. Slave mistresses enjoyed a relatively pleasant existence as long as they pleased the master and escaped the ire of the master's wife. Slave prostitutes had a grim life, and the aforementioned pearl divers of the Venezuelan coast,[107] given their owner's prohibition of heterosexual activity, may have included an inordinate number of homosexuals in their ranks. It stands to reason that the more agreeable or preferred slave occupations fell to *criollos morenos* and mulattoes, but in the shadow of each of these stood the *bozal* ancestor who had chosen neither his eventual master nor his New World port of disembarkation. Obviously, the Creator smiled more on some of the survivors of the Atlantic passage than on others.

Restating the thesis in another way, occupation and regional environment, not slave law, religious stricture, or some nebulous tradition of beneficence, were probably the critical determinants of slave treatment. The owner might believe that his bondmen possessed an immortal soul, but that was cold comfort if the same master committed him to a mine where one strike from a venemous snake might snuff out his existence.

SLAVERY ON THE EVE OF SPANISH
AMERICAN INDEPENDENCE

Involuntary servitude in Spanish America was a multifaceted institution in which the treatment of those subject to its regimen was highly diverse. It is not strange, therefore, that the slave population fluctuated widely from region to region. The figures in table 3 are estimates rather than exact tabulations, but they represent perhaps the best totals available. In addition, aside from the job of domestic worker, the predominant slave occupations also differed significantly.

Table 3. *Estimated total number of slaves in Spanish America*

State (present-day name)	Total number of slaves	Approx. year of estimate
Argentina		
Province of Buenos Aires	6,372	1810
Province of Córdoba	6,338	1778
Province of Cuyo (Mendoza only)	2,140	1802
Chile	12,000	1778
Colombia	70,000	1800
Cuba	212,000	1811
Ecuador	8,000	1800
Mexico	9,000–10,000	1793
Paraguay	3,945	1782
Peru	89,241	1812
Santo Domingo	30,000	1794
Uruguay (city of Montevideo only)	899	1803
Venezuela	87,800	1800–1810

Sources: Figures for Argentina from Emiliano Endrek, *El mestizaje en Córdoba: Siglo XVIII y principios del XIX* (Córdoba, 1966), p. 12; José Luis Masini, *La esclavitud negra en Mendoza: época independiente* (Mendoza, 1962), p. 10; and Evelyn P. Meiners who provides figures from the

Although roughly 200,000 slaves had been unloaded at such ports as Veracruz, Campeche, and Acapulco (Mexico) between 1595 and 1739,[108] Alexander von Humboldt reported only a meager handful of bondmen left. What seems to have occurred was that the growing free Negroid and *mestizo* population had produced a labor surplus, so that forced labor in Mexico had become a nearly moribund institution. A surprising circumstance is that the few thousand slaves left were not employed as house servants,[109] a phenomenon that readily buttresses the supposition that those bondmen who remained were probably retrained essentially to do only tasks no one else would undertake.

In Central America the chronic inability to get *bozales* cheaply and the deep-seated opposition of local administrators to the heavy importation of *bozales*[110] meant that the free population eventually had to undertake the burden of heavy labor. No solid figures on the number of bondmen inhabiting the region are available, but, as we shall see, slavery would not become totally extinct in the region until at least 1823.

Table 3 (*cont.*)

incomplete census of 1810, "The Negro in the Río de la Plata" [Ph.D. diss., Northwestern University, 1948], chap. iv, p. 23. This assessment is used here because the 1778 census made no clear delineation between free Negroids and slaves. For Chile, Gonzalo Vial Correa, *El africano en el reino de Chile: Ensayo histórico-jurídico* (Santiago, 1957), p. 44. A slightly higher figure (perhaps 15,000 slaves) can be deduced from Domingo Amanátegui Solar, "La trata de negros en Chile," *Revista Chilena de Historia y Geografía* 44, no. 48 (1922): 39. For Colombia and Ecuador, José Manuel Restrepo, *Historia de la revolución de la República de Colombia en la América meridional*, 4 vols. (Besanzon, 1958), 1:xiv. For Cuba, Alexander von Humboldt, *Ensayo político sobre la isla de Cuba*, 2 vols. (Havana, 1930), 1:117. For Mexico, see idem, *Political Essay on the Kingdom of New Spain*, 4 vols. (New York, 1966), 1:236. For Paraguay, Josefina Plá, *Hermano negro: La esclavitud en el Paraguay* (Madrid, 1972), p. 36. For Peru, Fredrick B. Pike, *The Modern History of Peru* (London, 1967), p. 14. For Santo Domingo, Carlos Larrazábal Blanco, *Los negros y la esclavitud en Santo Domingo* (Santo Domingo, 1967), p. 184. For Uruguay, Ildefonso Pereda Valdés, *Negros esclavos y negros libres: Esquema de una sociedad esclavista y aporte del negro en nuestra formación nacional* (Montevideo, 1941), p. 16. For Venezuela, Federico Brito Figueroa, *Estructura económica de Venezuela colonial* (Caracas, 1963), p. 58.

In the Caribbean, Cuba had only 38,879 slaves (22.8 percent of the population) in 1774, but by 1811 a survey revealed that the number had ballooned to 212,000. This astronomical increase was an accurate indication of the progress of the vast socioeconomic change transpiring on the island. A few of the bondmen imported saw service as urban laborers, but the mass of freshly obtained *bozales* went directly into the rapidly expanding sugar-cane monoculture. This transformation of Cuba would compensate Spain for the failure of Santo Domingo to develop in the same fashion.

On the South American continent, at least three different patterns were emerging. According to the 1778 census, better than 60 percent of all the slaves in what is presently Colombia and Panama were involved in gold-mining pursuits. Organized into gangs (*cuadrillas*) of 6 to 100 men, these bondmen "were clad in breechcloths or rags, fed a minimum ration of plantains and salt meat, and frequently weakened by disease."[111] Although forced to do some of the most excruciating labor performed by slaves anywhere in the Americas, these luckless souls were the most important producers of the basic source of wealth for almost three centuries.[112]

On the Caribbean coast of Colombia, Ecuador, and Venezuela, sugar-cane and cacao plantations continued to require large numbers of forced laborers, but, in a sense, the demand for fresh *bozales* had already peaked. This was not the case in Peru, where a reported 41,000 slaves in 1791 had purportedly doubled in a generation. As a result of the extension of the free slave-trade policy to the Viceroyalty of Peru, the importation of *bozales* had risen enormously, and between 1790 and 1802 over 65,000 probably entered.[113] Since it was still believed that Indians and *mestizos* could not operate effectively in the hot, humid coastal lowlands, the overwhelming majority of these newcomers were sold to owners of Pacific coastal sugar-cane and fruit-producing plantations.

Whereas the slave work force was increasing rapidly in Peru, in Chile black and mulatto bondmen had increasingly been restricted to the position of house servants. The cost of *bozales* had always been high in Chile,[114] and the long ribbonlike country had never been one of Spain's richer colonies. Once there was a sufficient number of Indians and *mestizos* to perform the agricultural and mining labor needed, the eventual disappearance of the African slave was assured. Even so, the 12,000 or so bondmen left represented half of the total Negroid population.[115]

Difficult to analyze are the conditions under which slaves labored in Argentina, Uruguay, and Paraguay. Aside from domestic service, slaves did not dominate any particular industry or occupation and there were no mines or plantations, but the total of servitors in Mendoza (1802) and Córdoba (1778) represented 16 percent and 14.3 percent of their respective total populations.[116] These percentages take on weight particularly when one considers that the 87,000 slaves reported in Venezuela were allegedly less than 10 percent of the aggregate number of inhabitants.[117] Finally, there is the case of Paraguay, where 40 percent of all Negroids were bondmen. They performed a wide variety of jobs in that country, but perhaps the most striking consideration is that a slight majority of the reported servitors were females.[118]

In scrutinizing the situations and developments described in this section, it appears that by the beginning of the nineteenth century in Spanish America slavery was necessary and unnecessary at the same time. In Central America, Mexico, and Chile, anachronistic elements might struggle to keep the system alive, but, because other parties could now be found to perform the labor needed, there was no need for new and expensive *bozales*. In contrast, in the Colombian gold fields and mines, the Cuban cane fields, and the coastal plantations of Peru, Colombia, Venezuela, and Ecuador, the slave still performed a function that was needed, although in differing degrees. In these areas, until another labor source was found, involuntary servitude remained an imperative.

4
Slave Rebellions and Negroid Resistance

SLAVE PUNISHMENTS

In Spanish America the lash, the stock, detention, and deprivation were standard means by which unruly and defiant slaves
were kept in line. Some masters were known to have whipped
their bondmen to death, while others continued to mutilate
their dusky properties with hot branding irons even after the
crown had prohibited this act.[1] Worst of all were the vengeful
sadists who made their slaves eat excrement and drink urine.[2]
We can only conclude that those who perpetrated these physical
and psychic horrors must have been either oblivious to the prospect of retribution or convinced that the legal authorities would
not consider their actions as criminal in nature. Here again, the
de facto power of the slave owners in the Spanish Indies is
vividly evidenced.

When the slave, however, broke a town ordinance or violated
some royal prohibition, retribution was supposed to be adminis-
tered by local or viceregal authorities. Witness the following
incidents:

1. On 1 September 1540 Pedro Gilafo was apprehended
near the town of Orisco (Costa Rica). He had fled his master and was thought to have been in the company of "war-
like Indians" for the previous twenty days. Local officials
had him boiled alive.[3]
2. A bondman named Domingo resisted a police patrol
that caught him shortly after dark outside the walls of the
town of Montevideo (circa 1754). Domingo was dragged

through the streets and then drawn and quartered. His "unclean parts" were cut from his body, and what was left of him was thrown into the Rio de la Plata.[4]

3. In 1787 and 1788 four white women reported themselves to have been approached, or propositioned, by a "Negro horseman." A twenty-year-old servitor owned by the *La Merced* Convent was eventually identified as the elusive casanova. He was originally sentenced to death, but in his defense it was argued that he was underage and had committed no crime; at best, he had only contemplated one. Finally, on 10 April 1790 the original sentence was reduced to 200 lashes, all of which were to be given in various public places after a full reading of the slave's transgressions.[5]

In the first case noted, Pedro Gilafo was executed even though the authorities were not absolutely certain where he had been, while in the third case, the purported crime was hardly more than a misdemeanor. The conclusion that can be drawn is that slave punishment, as dispensed by legal authorities, was primarily intended to terrorize others sharing the same status.[6] As a result, some slaves were overawed and, believing rebellion to be futile, submitted to their fate. Some committed suicide and others even killed their children rather than allow them to experience a lifetime of frustration and toil.[7] But there were others who, when presented with the opportunity to escape from bondage, seized it unhesitantly.

SPANISH POLICY AND FUGITIVE SLAVES

The hot, humid lowlands of the Caribbean and Pacific coasts were regions that the Spaniards did not find hospitable; for that reason, blacks seeking refuge in the swamps, jungles, and heavily foliated coastal areas had a fair chance of avoiding capture. Others made good their escape by climbing high up the densely covered mountain slopes common to the equatorial regions. Some fugitives united in order to form independent villages where they raised foodstuffs and governed themselves, desiring nothing other than peace and security from reenslavement. A few ex-bondmen organized themselves with much more aggressive intentions. They attacked pack trains, Indian villages, and *haciendas*, and often cooperated with French or English corsairs in raids on Spanish towns. The armed fugitive, or, as the Spaniards called him, *el cimarrón*, was thus born.

The first regulations specifically dealing with these Negroid defiers of Spanish authority were the work of Francisco Pizarro in Peru in 1536. Royal *cédulas* affecting both escapees and *cimarrones* appeared in 1551 and 1578. These ordered various punishments for different crimes, as illustrated in table 4. Although these penalties seem harsh, they were generally milder than regional statutes governing the same situations. According to a series of orders published by the governor of Chile in 1557, escaped slaves were liable to suffer mutilation of the feet, the loss of ears, or castration.[8] A slave code promulgated in Santo Domingo (1528) explicitly established that a slave absent for fifteen days without permission was to receive 100 lashes, and, in addition, a 20-pound weight was to be attached to his leg for twelve months. According to the same regulations, free blacks or mulattoes aiding escaped slaves were to receive 200 lashes for their efforts.[9] Different forms of chastisement for free persons aiding slaves were put into effect in other areas. In 1679 in Antioquia (Colombia), a free mulatto convicted of this offense was ordered to pay court costs plus the equivalent of fifteen months of slave labor to the aggrieved owner.[10] Almost a century later, in 1776, three freed blacks in Venezuela were accused of helping over thirty slaves escape from a plantation. This trio was jailed, probably tortured until they confessed, and then dispossessed of all their earthly goods. Finally, they were exiled under guard to Mexico and sentenced to permanent imprisonment if they ever set foot on Venezuelan soil again.[11]

Given the power of the slaveocracy in Spanish America, escaped bondmen were less likely to experience the full weight of these stringent penalties than free persons who aided them. Owners of African properties in Santo Domingo even protested the harsh penalties prescribed in the 1528 slave code, and in 1542 and 1544 the castigations laid down were significantly

Table 4. *Slave punishments in colonial Spanish America*

Situation	Punishment
1. A slave gone from his residence up to four days.	50 lashes
2. A slave gone from his residence up to eight days or caught more than one league from his home.	100 lashes, and the fastening of a 12-pound iron weight to his leg for two months; if he removed the weight before the two months were up, the period of punishment was doubled.
3. A slave gone more than four months but not identified as a member of a band of *cimarrones*.	at least 100 lashes
4. A slave who escaped a second time and was gone for more than four months.	exile
5. An escaped slave identified as having been in the company of *cimarrones*.	200 lashes (virtually certain death)
6. A slave who had spent six months with a band of *cimarrones* or who had committed some other "crime" in company with these escapees.	death
7. A *cimarrón* caught stealing or bearing arms.	death

Sources: Rolando Mellafe, *La introducción de la esclavitud negra en Chile: Tráfico y rutas* (Santiago, 1959), p. 86; Jaime Jaramillo Uribe, "Esclavos y señores en la sociedad colombiano del siglo XVIII," *Anuario Colombiano de Historia Social y de la Cultura* 1, no. 1 (1963): 22.

reduced.[12] The problem there and elsewhere was that unless the owner bore the slave a grudge, he was loathe to see a valuable property possibly crippled. But a bondman who had fled once, even if treated kindly, might certainly choose to run away again. As a result, some owners, when informed that their fugitive properties had been apprehended, preferred to put the slave up for sale and buy a fresh (and supposedly more malleable) *bozal* with the money received. It may even be that skilled bondmen realized that they would not suffer severe physical punishment and ran off simply to force their present owners to sell them to someone else.[13] In any event, the profusion of laws and regulations that theoretically governed the disciplining of runaways became, in practice, simple guidelines that the local authorities and slave owners reshaped to fit their peculiar circumstances.

In the case of known *cimarrones*, however, the picture was rather different. The *cédulas* of 1551 and 1558 proclaimed that if any Negroid person, free or slave, gave food or drink to a *cimarrón*, the punishment was death or the same penalty meted out to the captured fugitive. In contrast, a Spaniard providing the same assistance was to suffer only the loss of half his worldly goods the first time and banishment from Spanish America the second time.[14] The inequity of these decrees is self-evident, but the overriding concern was the menace that *cimarrones* represented and the probability that they would most likely seek assistance from persons whose background and skin color were similar to their own.

Anti-*cimarrón* campaigns, when conducted energetically, tended to resemble the ferocious antiguerrilla or search-and-destroy operations of the twentieth century. In one instance on the isle of Hispaniola, a band of escaped slaves under Diego del Campo raided plantations and ambushed militia forces very successfully from at least 1542 until 1546. Captured by the Spanish, the *cimarrones* were hung, but not before each had been virtually roasted to death over an open fire.[15] Roughly a decade later, another group of escaped slaves turned bandits was captured by Spanish forces after a stiff campaign on the Isthmus of Panama. Taken to the main square in the city of Nombre de Dios, they were fitted with linked iron collars and wild dogs were then unleashed upon them.[16]

The failure of these diabolical punishments to eradicate *cimarrón* activity can be attributed to several factors. The campaigns were expensive, and special taxes were supposed to be collected in order to provide for militiamen and a system of paid informers who could ferret out the hiding places of the renegades. But, as in countless other cases, the taxes were only sporadically collected, which meant that energetic anti-*cimarrón* campaigns were infrequent. Moreover, sufficient forces were rarely available to complete the task, especially in areas like Venezuela, where in 1800 there were an estimated 30,000 escaped slaves and *cimarrones*.[17] In view of the gap between the draconian nature of the law and the lackadaisical nature of the system of apprehension, the actual intent of Spanish policy would seem to have been the harassment rather than the total elimination of *cimarronaje*.

SLAVE RESISTANCE IN COLONIAL SPANISH AMERICA

Even more menacing than the continuing problem of *cimarrón* attack was the danger of a mass slave insurrection. In the United States, the conspiracies of Nat Turner and Gabriel Prosser have been analyzed and even romanticized, probably because of the relative scarcity of examples of large-scale revolt in that country. The situation was different in Spanish America, where the prospect of uprisings caused the crown to issue special regulations for such contingencies. A 1619 *cédula* dictated that in case of "general rebellion, sedition, or plunder," legal processes need not be followed; ring leaders and their cohorts, of whatever race or color, were to be summarily dealt with by royal officials.[18]

Santo Domingo

What is generally considered to be the first major insurrection of African slaves took place on the island of Hispaniola from 25 to 28 December 1522. Some forty slaves, working at the sugar mill on the plantation of the governor, Admiral Diego Columbus (a son of the explorer), conspired with other blacks working on nearby establishments. On Christmas night the slaves attacked, killing at least nine of the whites on nearby plantations. Columbus was not in his *hacienda*, and, as soon as he heard of the revolt, he took up a defensive position outside the city of

Santo Domingo. Moving rapidly on 28 December 1522, a mixed Spanish and Indian force was assembled under Melchor de Castro; it defeated the rebellious slaves in a pitched battle in which six more whites lost their lives. Many of the Africans fled to the hills of the interior to escape capture, but they were hunted down by Indian laborers under Pedro Ortiz de Matringo. Diego Columbus reported to the royal government early in 1523 that if the rebellion had not been quickly scotched, it could not have been smashed without "much time and many Christian lives."[19]

Mexico

One of the many royal decrees almost totally ignored by the Spanish *conquistadores* was the *cédula* of 6 September 1521, which prohibited the movement of the African slaves into previously unexplored areas. The crown apparently had a fair idea of what the black bondmen would do if given an opportunity, and Hernan Cortés soon found out, for by 1523 *cimarrón* activity was already reported in the Mexico City area. The first general uprising was masterminded by a group of *ladino* slaves recently shipped from the Antilles. Planning the event for midnight, 24 September, 1537, these men intended to murder all the whites, rule the Indians and *mestizos*, and establish an African state in the New World. The plot narrowly misfired. A few hours before midnight, a slave of Viceroy Antonio de Mendoza informed his master of the impending rebellion. Driven by a "demonical fervor,"[20] Mendoza slaughtered an undetermined number of Africans and personally presided over some of the torture sessions.

Implicated Negroids sought protection in nearby Indian villages, but there was a price on their heads. The natives killed at least five and captured a score of others. Viceroy Mendoza subsequently sought to terminate African importation into New Spain, but the discovery of silver mines in Zacatecas in 1546 quickly frustrated that initiative. There were to be more African slaves imported and, as a consequence, more uprisings.

Significant slave rebellions occurred in Mexico in 1546, 1570, 1608, and 1670. In 1609 a plot was suspected, and the viceroy had many slaves lashed in an effort to discover the time and place of the suspected insurrection. In 1612 the fear of a slave insurrection in Mexico City and Puebla became so great that the towns surrounding these cities canceled all Holy Week ceremonies, parades, and processions. The *audiencia* at Mexico City struck back immediately after Easter Sunday. Thirty-six blacks and mulattoes believed to be conspirators were hung in the main square of the city. Later, their heads were removed and put on poles as a grim warning to potential rebels.[21]

Easily the best-known *cimarrón* in Mexican history was Ȳanga (or Nȳanga), who claimed to be a Congolese prince. Operating in the highlands of what is today east central Veracruz state, Ȳanga and his band regularly attacked traffic on the Mexico City–Veracruz highway and raided the *haciendas* in the area. His outspoken second-in-command, Francisco Angola, insisted that the attacks were justified, for Negroids had every right "to liberate themselves from the cruelty of the Spanish, who without any right pretend to be determiners of our liberty."[22]

Naturally, the Spaniards were in no mood to exchange rhetoric with a group of pugnacious ex-slaves. Beginning in 1609 a series of anti-*cimarrón* campaigns were undertaken, but not until 1611 were Ȳanga's cohorts finally defeated. Viceroy Don Luis de Velasco was so impressed with the stamina and courage of his captives that he conceded them their freedom as long as they remained in peace, took in no new fugitives, and obeyed the laws of Philip III. Eventually, in 1612 a settlement was founded for them, the town of San Lorenzo de los Negros de Córdoba.[23]

Over a century later, in the same general vicinity of Veracruz state, slave uprisings in sugar mills around the town of Córdoba (1725 and 1735) culminated in the mass flight of bondmen and a sudden burgeoning of *cimarrón* activity. The attacks by these escaped blacks on pack trains, sugar mills, small towns, and plantations became serious enough to warrant the raising of five different expeditions between 1748 and 1759, all aimed at liquidating the *cimarrones* of the region. None of these forces enjoyed even a modicum of success, and, when war between Spain and England broke out in 1759, the assembled forces had to be diverted elsewhere.

The enemy outside the gate was deemed more dangerous, and

the authorities decided to negotiate with the defiant blacks. In exchange for bearing arms against Great Britain, the acknowledgment of Charles III as sovereign, and the acceptance of the Catholic church as their own, Spain promised a general amnesty, the creation of a semiautonomous settlement, and free land. This arrangement was accepted by Fernando Manuel, leader of the large band of *cimarrones*, but only after a pitched battle in which those who had sought the rejection of the peace package were vanquished.[24]

The ex-*cimarrones* helped to beat off the English attack on the port of Veracruz in 1762, and seven years later the town of Señora de Guadalupe de los Morenos de Amapá was officially chartered.[25] The town's chaplain, José Antonio Navarro, wrote that as a result of the town's founding "the [Córdoba] countryside is now free of their [*cimarrones*] outrages" and that "sugar mill slaves are now more secure in their servitude."[26] Thus it was that in a century and a half two autonomous towns of ex-*cimarrones* were founded in the same general region. The employment of conciliatory tactics as opposed to iron-fist techniques had proven successful, but the irony of the situation was that the 1612 example had been studiously ignored until the threat of a British attack forced an reappraisal of the situation.

Meanwhile, on the other coast, especially during the seventeenth and eighteenth centuries, slaves fleeing the Pacific Ocean ports of Guatulco and Acapulco set up *palenques* in the coastal highlands of the *costa chica*.[27] Despite a number of anti-*cimarrón* campaigns conducted over almost two centuries, these settlements persisted through the end of slavery in 1829. The African fugitives preferred not to mix with the Indians, and their descendants can still be found in the contemporary Mexican state of Guerrero.[28]

Writing in 1951, the Mexican scholar Jorge Fernando Iturribarria would argue that at least during the sixteenth and seventeenth centuries the condition of the Negroids was "worse than that of the Indians."[29] The numerous plots plus the continuing persistence of *cimarrón* activity suggest that among captives of African blood there was a strong inclination not to accept the status quo as a permanent condition.

Central America

Although the first rebellion of African slaves in Central America occurred in the mines near San Pedro (Honduras) in 1548, the most significant movement led by Negroids took place in the Caribbean lowlands of the so-called Mosquito coast. This region, which extends roughly 300 miles from Guatemala south to Nicaragua, was settled by Englishmen who established themselves near Cape Gracias a Dios (Honduras) in 1633. The British brought slaves with them, and these Africans, plus escaping bondmen from both Jamaica and Spanish settlements in the interior tablelands, intermarried with the Sumus Indians who had long inhabited the region. After half a century, there gradually emerged the *sambo-mosquitos* ("Afro-Indians of the Mosquito coast"), who soon outnumbered both the unmiscegenated blacks and Indians.[30]

Around 1700 the Spanish became increasingly concerned about the British settlements on the Central American coast and attempted to destroy them. There were less than 1,000 English settlers in the area, and they depended upon an alliance among themselves and the *sambo-mosquito* clans for survival. Having shrewdly acknowledged the nominal independence of the *sambo-mosquitos* in 1687, the British kept the alliance alive by supplying their part-African allies with guns and liquor. Although several major campaigns were conducted through 1786, the Spanish were unable to consolidate a hold on the Mosquito coast, and the Afro-Indian clans remained their implacable enemies.[31] By terms of a convention signed in 1786, Great Britain agreed to limit its holdings to the area covering the contemporary nation of Belize, but Spain still could not subdue the *sambo-mosquitos* in Honduras and Nicaragua. A few of their descendants continue to inhabit this region.

Between 1612 and 1620 royal officials in Central America made at least three efforts to prevent the further introduction of African *bozales*. These administrators protested to Madrid that the blacks were prone to disobedience and inordinately capable of causing difficulties if they escaped and established bases and camps on the Caribbean coast.[32] With the advantage of near perfect hindsight, one may conclude that although these bureaucrats did not specifically envisage a *sambo-mosquito* warrior, their fears proved well grounded.

Colombia

Settled in 1525, Santa Marta was the first Colombian town founded by the Spanish. Five years later it was the first town completely destroyed as a result of a slave rebellion. It was rebuilt in 1531, but another uprising took place there in 1550. The most spectacular challenges to Spanish authority, however, occurred in the interior, far from this Caribbean coastal port. An eighteenth-century Spanish royal official in the Viceroyalty of New Granada noted that "there are no royal taxes, commerce or special interests that do not depend and obtain stability from the gold of the mines of this viceroyalty."[33] In the valleys and mountains of the southwestern part of the region, thousands of *bozales* gave their lives gathering the precious yellow metal that financed Spain's European adventures. Nevertheless, many slaves were unprepared to accept a slow death in the mines without making some effort to regain control over their lives. In 1545, for example, a group of blacks escaped from a mine in the present-day department of Popayán. They seized the town of Tofeme, killed twenty whites, and carried off 250 Indian hostages to the mountains.[34] Other small uprisings took place in the Popayán area in 1555 and 1556, and in 1598 about 4,000 slaves wrecked the mines near the town of Zaragoza. Described as the "richest and best gold mines discovered in the Indies," their incapacitation was a severe blow to the Spanish royal treasury. One year later Juan Meléndez de Valdés, commanding a force of Spanish regular-army veterans, reoccupied the mines. All the slaves recaptured in the campaign were swiftly and unceremoniously liquidated.[35]

Fortunately, some slaves who fled the mines experienced better fortune. In 1732 a *palenque* was formed by fugitive slaves near the town of Castillo, again in Popayán. Efforts by the local militia to destroy the encampment proved fruitless, and the provincial authorities subsequently declared a general amnesty for the settlement's inhabitants. It was also agreed that new fugitives would be barred from entry, but this condition was never enforced.[36] As a result, in 1745 local troops undertook a new campaign against this same *palenque*. They succeeded in destroying its buildings, but many of the fugitives escaped, eventually forming still other settlements.

Probably the most famous *palenque* was that of San Basilio, established near the city of Cartagena. In about 1599 or 1600 slaves under Dioniso (or Domingo) Bioho fled the city and established a veritable fortress in the highlands behind it. Crowning himself King Benkos, Dionisio Bioho led attacks on nearby *haciendas* and terrorized Spanish travelers attempting to journey inland from Cartagena. A number of expeditions against the *palenque* failed miserably, and in 1612 and 1613, therefore, Governor Diego Fernández de Velasco offered amnesty and freedom to all those who would abandon it. Among those who did was King Benkos, who, in contradiction of royal decrees, demanded and received the right "to dress like a Spaniard, with sword and dagger."[37] Unfortunately, the black chieftain's days of glory were short-lived. A new slave revolt shook Cartagena in 1619, and Governor García Girón arbitrarily imprisoned and hanged Benkos.

Around 1790 a Captain Latorre was trying to survey a road across the highlands from Cartagena into the interior when he came into contact with Negroids, many of whom were descendants of the *palenqueros* of San Basilio who had not accepted amnesty in 1612 or 1613. A number of bloody battles ensued before a settlement was reached. The blacks agreed to accept royal authority, but they would continue to select their own leaders, and the only white man allowed into the village would be a priest. All told, the *palenqueros* from the original settlement of San Basilio had remained completely independent for almost two centuries, making them probably the longest functioning semiindependent group of Africans in Spanish America.[38]

The story of slave resistance to oppression is summed up, perhaps, in an incident that took place on the ranch of one Juan Martín de Setuain about 1795. When the slaves of this Spaniard fled *en masse* from his property, he sent an emissary to cajole them into returning. But the angry blacks resolved "to give their heads before serving any white man."[39] We do not know whether these slaves were forced to make good on their oaths, but their bitter response suggests that master–slave relations in Colombia were hardly of the nature that apologists for slavery throughout the Americas have striven to portray.

Venezuela

The importation of African slaves into Venezuela began in about 1530, when an unknown number of *bozales* was shipped to the mines of Buria (near the present city of Barquisimeto). Twenty-two years later a slave of *ladino* parentage named Miguel led a rebellion that shut down the mines. Gathering together some 800 blacks, mulattoes, and *zambos*, Miguel erected a series of rocky retreats, declared himself king, and created a court. For over two years he conducted a clever campaign against nearby Spanish settlements, stealing cattle, freeing other slaves, holding white hostages for ransom, and generally attempting to extend his control over the territory.

Militia forces were gathered from as far away as Santa Marta (Colombia) in order to capture King Miguel, but the latter's luck held until 1555, when he was killed in a disastrous attack on the city of Barquisimeto. Prior to this assault, Miguel had sought to build up his forces by accepting Indian recruits, but with the stipulation that they darken their faces in order to look like blacks! Ironically enough, following the debacle at Barquisimeto, the Spanish, led by Diego de Losado, lost no time hiring these same Indians to hunt down the remnant of Miguel's shattered band.[40]

Nevertheless, military victory utterly failed to bring about a relaxation of tensions. Near the old mines at Buria, fresh gold strikes were made in 1560. New gangs of *bozales* were imported to work them, and many of these, in the spirit of their predecessors, fled the scene of their enslavement. Efforts made to press the Indians into service soon caused them also to resist the Spanish. Quite discouraged, Governor Arias Vaca wrote to Philip III in 1600, complaining that for "forty years the province of Nirgua is disturbed and in rebellion."[41] Because his

forces were too weak to win a decisive victory, Governor Arias
Vaca declared a general amnesty for all escaped slaves in the
province. He further ordered that as long as the blacks swore
allegiance to the king, they could live in a semiindependent
community that would be under their control.

In 1601 the town of Nirgua was founded. During the next
two hundred years, blacks, mulattoes, and Indians intermingled,
with the result that the unmixed African strain gradually disappeared. Early in the nineteenth century, Baron Alexander von
Humboldt would note the continued existence of the town of
Nirgua, derisively referred to by the Spanish as the "Republic of
Zambos and Mulattoes." No Spaniard had lived there for some
time, and none wished to remain in a town controlled by nonwhites.[42]

The sparsely settled areas of Venezuela and the endless plains
of the south and southwest provided ample space for the establishment of *cumbes*. Commenting on the situation at the end of
the seventeenth century, the contemporary Venezuelan scholar
Miguel Acosta Saignes is most succinct: "They [*cimarrones*]
were everywhere."[43] In 1716 the crown ordered a renewed effort to capture *cimarrones* and break up *cumbes* because it had
come to the attention of Philip V that white renegades had
joined the fugitive groups at large in the countryside. Although
the new offensive enjoyed some success, in 1720 José de Oli-
varriaga reported that there were at least 20,000 *cimarrones*
organized in *cumbes* scattered throughout the territory.

The last major anti-*cimarrón* operations were conducted
around the city of Caracas following the discovery of a slave
insurrection plot in June 1794. More than 300 escapees were
apprehended, some of whom had been at liberty for over seven
years. But this achievement by the local militia forces was of
little import. A reasonable estimate put the number of *cimarrones* at large in Venezuela around 1800 at "roughly 30,000."[44]

Curiously enough, the most widespread racial conflict of the
eighteenth century broke out not in a mining region, but in the
cacao-producing Yaracuy Valley.[45] The origins of this eruption
of violence lay in the 1728 foundation of the Guipúzcoa
(Caracas) Company and Philip V's award of a monopoly over

the Venezuelan cacao trade to this organization. For years, despite the fact that the trade was absolutely illegal, plantation lords in the Yaracuy Valley had shipped their produce to the Dutch on the isle of Curaçao. The persons making a livelihood transporting the produce down river to Dutch schooners or on to Curaçao were free Negroids, fugitive slaves, and a few Indians. It was perhaps to be expected, then, that open warfare would break out when Caracas Company officials set up posts along the Yaracuy in 1730 and attempted to halt the contraband traffic.

Rapidly emerging as the leader of this struggle against the Spanish monopolists was a young *zambo*, Andrés López de Rosario (*nom de guerre*, Juan Andresote). His band of rebels, composed chiefly of free Negroids, escaped slaves, and a small number of Indians, was supplied by the Dutch and enjoyed the sympathetic support of the white plantation owners, for the Dutch paid them better prices than the Caracas Company. Initially, the royal governor, Sebastián García de la Torre, did little more than denounce Andresote as an outlaw. But when a special force had been specifically assembled to capture him, conflict broke loose. On 26 January 1732, near the town of Cabria, Andresote ambushed and defeated the 250-man force. Only 44 white soldiers escaped, and many of the 150 forceably conscripted blacks, mulattoes, and *zambos* who "shared with Andrés the aspirations of the movement" simply switched sides.[46]

This victory proved to be the high point of Andresote's military career. The *hacendados* in the Yaracuy Valley, however, began to fear that his fame and success might spark slave rebellions, and they tended to withdraw their support. In addition, in February 1732 García de la Torre entered the region himself, leading a force of 1,500 men. After a few skirmishes, Andresote boarded a Dutch schooner and fled to Curaçao. His forces melted away before Spanish pressure, but they established strongholds in the forests and hills from which they regularly sallied to attack company officials and small detachments of troops.

Instead of a set-piece battle, the Spaniards were now confronted with a guerrilla campaign that had no immediate end in sight. At the instigation of García de la Torre, Bishop Félix de

Valverde dispatched two Capuchin monks into the troubled region. After months of patient negotiation, *padres* Salvador de Gádiz and Tomás de Pons convinced approximately 158 ex-rebels and *cimarrones* to give up their arms in exchange for a general pardon, which was extended by García de la Torre and Bishop Valverde on 15 January 1733.

Unfortunately, the agreement that was reached began to break down immediately. Local government officials ignored the amnesty and began seizing some of the surrendering parties as fugitive slaves. But the man who really scotched the plan for pardon was Martín Lardizábal, the *juez pesquisador* ("special investigative prosecutor"). The Caracas Company had been increasingly displeased with the governor's conciliatory policies, and since company officials had the ear of the crown, they persuaded Madrid to dispatch a *juez pesquisador* to Caracas. When, in February 1733 there were fresh attacks on company posts in the Yaracuy Valley, Lardizábal deposed García de la Torre and voided the short-lived policy of amnesty. Bishop Valverde attempted to sidetrack Lardizábal, but, in the power struggle that ensued, Madrid ordered the cleric to limit the scope of his interests to the salvation of obedient souls.

Starting in July 1733, a full-scale extermination campaign was executed along the Yaracuy. José Francisco, brother of Andresote, was captured and permanently incarcerated. Another of the latter's henchmen, José Cordero, was imprisoned for life in Spain. Eight persons reputed to have been ringleaders under Andresote (five blacks, one mulatto, and two Indians) were dispatched to the gallows. An unknown number of the fugitive slaves, *cimarrones*, and free Negroids seized on suspicion "were killed under the *ley de fuga* ... simply hung, or killed with a sword.[47]

The Andresote rebellion was ultimately drowned in blood. Within three generations, however, another *zambo* unfurled the banner of popular revolt. This Afro-Indian was José Leonardo Chirinos, and the site of his insurrectionary activities was, appropriately enough, the town of Coro, scene of the first slave uprising in Venezuela (1532).[48] To comprehend the ideological and historical considerations that sparked this incident, it is necessary to recall that between 1789 and 1792 the *Código negro* had been decreed, and both the French and Haitian revolutions had broken out. Like innumerable Negroids in Venezuela, José Chirinos heard garbled reports about the *código*. He came to believe that Charles IV had actually freed the slaves, but that a cabal of slave owners and colonial officials had prevented the public proclamation of the royal decree. Encouraged in his beliefs and fantasies by José Caridad González, a free black who was believed to possess magical powers, the *zambo* intended not only to free the slaves in and around Coro, but to declare a "French Republic" based on the principle of human equality. Chirinos naïvely thought that the events that had transpired in France from 1789 to 1793 signaled its determination to aid similar revolutionary causes around the world. This would-be liberator was banking on the dispatch of military assistance by French corsairs, who many in Venezuela believed were lurking somewhere off the Caribbean coast. His delusions were nourished by the assurances of González, who claimed to be in touch with these French "freedom fighters." Once the uprising was underway, however, his cohort mysteriously disappeared, and Chirinos soon discovered that González's French connections were as bogus as his proclaimed magical powers.

When José Chirinos began to execute his plans, 55 percent of the population of the Coro district were African in origin – full-blooded or in part – and nearly 10 percent were enslaved. On 10 May 1795 perhaps a dozen whites were killed and several *haciendas* burned to the ground. These events caused a large number of free blacks, mulattoes, *zambos*, and Indians to join the movement. The surviving whites barricaded themselves in a church, and although the *zambo*'s forces attacked for two days (11 and 12 May), they failed to capture the edifice. Toward the end of the second day, militia troops began arriving, and the insurrection promptly collapsed.

Spanish forces, especially those led by Mariano Ramírez Valderraín, displayed unusual vigor in chasing the disheartened rebels, and this leader even enlisted the aid of Indian groups to hunt down fleeing Negroids. By 15 June about 171 persons had been executed, and 20 other blacks, mulattoes, and Indians had been sentenced to ten years of hard labor. Thirty-three blacks and mulattoes, both free and slave, were incarcerated for indefinite periods at Puerto Cabello, and José Leonardo Chirinos was finally captured in August. Tortured for some time by Ramírez Valderrain, he was held incommunicado and then executed on 10 December 1796.[49]

Royal officials reported to Madrid that this courageous but pitifully planned crusade was simply another unsuccessful slave uprising.[50] Nevertheless, the whites on the spot undoubtedly realized that, in addition to the slaves, many free Negroids no longer were willing to accept their socioeconomic status.

Ecuador

Almost from the time that Spaniards began importing Africans to work the Cauca River gold diggings in Colombia, blacks managed to escape; a few sought refuge among the Manabi and Mantux Indian tribes of the tropical coast of northwestern Ecuador. The *zambo* descendants of these blacks and Indians became tribal leaders and created a major Pacific-coast headquarters known as El Portete.[51]

This particular settlement acted as a kind of beacon, attracting other bondmen who chose to flee rather than accept a living death panning the streams of southern Colombia for gold dust. It also attracted the attention of the Spaniards, not only because it was a haven for fugitive slaves but also because it was an ideal base for ships sailing between Panama and Peru. Occasional Spanish vessels in trouble attempted to land at El Portete but were driven away by the attacks of the *zambo*-led tribesmen. In 1556, therefore, Gil Ramírez Dávalos, governor of the *audiencia* of Quito, began sending troops to smash the troublesome Afro-Indians and seize the town. He succeeded in capturing the settlement, but the rebels reverted to guerrilla tactics. The troops holding El Portete fell victim to malaria and other tropical diseases at an alarming rate and eventually evacuated the area.

Subsequent efforts to subdue the Afro-Indians failed, and Francisco Arias de Herrera broke the stalemate in 1598 by drawing up a compact with the *zambo* leaders in which the latter agreed to accept the nominal suzerainty of the king of Spain.[52] For all practical purposes, however, they remained autonomous.

This was not to be the final example of African-controlled Indian groups resisting Spanish domination in northwest Ecuador. In 1650 a slave ship proceeding from Panama foundered in a storm off Cape Francisco. Two dozen slaves managed to scramble ashore, murdered the Spaniards who survived the wreck, and somehow established themselves as rulers among the local Indians and *zambos*. Eventually emerging as chief of these liberated blacks was the *ladino* Alonso de Illescas. Later, thanks largely to good fortune and a combination of resourcefulness and ruthlessness, he established himself as suzerain over all Negroids and Indians in the present-day provinces of Esmeraldas, Imbabura, and Pinchincha.[53] Illescas also battled to a standstill the infrequent Spanish expeditions sent into his domain. Not until early in the eighteenth century, when Pedro Vicente Maldonado y Sotomayor cut a trail from the mountain capital of Quito to the northwestern coast of Ecuador, would Spain exercise more than shadowy authority over the region.

Listed in table 5 is a record of other significant slave rebellions that transpired in colonial Spanish America. While not as dramatic, perhaps, as those already discussed, they do merit consideration and further demonstrate the nature and intensity of slave discontent.

BLACKS VERSUS INDIANS

Perhaps the most decisive move in Francisco Pizarro's campaign to conquer the Inca Empire was his capture of the reigning Inca, Atahualpa, at Caxamarca in 1532. After demanding and receiving millions in gold as ransom, Pizarro had Atahualpa garroted in 1533, and, in order to maintain a semblance of indigenous authority, he put Manco Capac, a younger half-brother of Atahualpa, on the throne. In 1536, however, the latter turned on the Spaniards and established a stronghold in the Andes where he held court and launched campaigns intended to destroy the European invaders. In an effort to initiate negotiations for a

Table 5. *Other significant cimarrón campaigns and slave rebellions in colonial Spanish America*

Year	Place	Event
1533	Cuba	An uprising of black slaves occurred in the mines of Jobabo. Four of the leaders of the rebellion were hung, drawn, and quartered, and their heads were put on stakes.
1545–1548	Hispaniola (Santo Domingo)	This was the period of the "War of the Negroes." Bloody battles were fought between Spanish-led forces and *cimarrones*. The most important fugitive, Diego de Campo, had been at large since 1536 and was feared throughout the land. Captured in 1546, he joined the Spaniards and subsequently made short work of other *cimarrones*.
1552–1582	Panama	*Cimarrones* operating from the San Blas Mountains in the isthmus attacked Spanish mule trains carrying either silver and other goods eastward to Porto Bello, or slaves and imported wares westward to Panama City. One group, led by King Ballano, caused serious difficulties until the leader was captured, castrated, and released in 1553. King Ballano then was pardoned, but he later formed another group of raiders that operated successfully until he was recaptured in 1558. His eventual fate is still disputed. Other groups, led by Luis de Mozambique and Antón Mandinga, continued to disrupt isthmus traffic until Madrid issued a general pardon for Panamanian *cimarrones*. These reformed rebels and their supporters were then settled in two towns, Santiago del Príncipe (1579) and Santa Cruz de la Real (1582).

Table 5 (cont.)

Year	Place	Event
1578	Peru	When Francis Drake attacked the city of Lima, the slaves revolted.
1647	Chile	Following an earthquake, an Afro-Indian rebellion was feared in Santiago, as about 400 slaves united behind one of their number who claimed to be of African royalty. The Spanish dispersed the slaves and hung the black leader.
1726	Cuba	As an English fleet maneuvered near Havana, slaves southwest of the city revolted and burned the sugar mills and other buildings owned by the Conde de Casa Bayona. Two companies of mounted militia plus other troops were necessary to subdue the rebels.
1749	Venezuela	Spanish officials discovered a plot involving slaves in Caracas, other plots on ranches near the city, and fugitive slaves and *cimarrones* living in independent settlements in the mountains. On the feast of St. John the Baptist (June 24), the slaves were to rise, murder all the whites, and take over control of the town. Under torture, a slave confessed that another bondman, Manuel Espinosa, was the mastermind behind the rebellion. Several rebels were executed in June 1750, and ten other leaders received heavy lashings, physical mutilations and jail sentences.
1755	Panama	A slave conspiracy was reported by the *alcalde* (chief magistrate) of Porto Bello. Four of the ringleaders were hung, drawn, and quartered.
1763–1764	Peru	*Cimarrones* operating in the Carabayllo Valley near Lima made some roads un-

Table 5 (cont.)

Year	Place	Event
		safe for public traffic. A large military force led by Pablo Sáenz de Bustamonte, including sixty men from the viceroy's personal guard, finally crushed the fugitive blacks, executing those considered the most culpable.
1795	Argentina	Slaves believed that the 1789 *Código negro* had freed them. When reality did not reflect the terms of the *código*, bondmen in Buenos Aires went on a general strike that was broken up after three days.
1713–1798	Cuba	Slaves in the copper mines at Jobabo rose up in 1713 and continued to do so sporadically until they were ordered freed in 1798.
1803	Uruguay	Twenty black males, all but a few of them slaves, met secretly and agreed to flee Montevideo. Taking their women, children, and possessions, they established an independent settlement on a small island in the River Yy (or Yi). Attacked by militia forces near the town of Villa de la Concepción de Minas (about 100 miles northeast of Montevideo), the blacks resisted but were all captured and reenslaved.
1804	Chile	Slaves seized a ship (*La Prueba*) going from Valparaiso to Callao (Peru). They killed 24 of the 36 white passengers and attempted to sail for Africa. On the way they encountered the *Perseverance*, commanded by a Captain Delano of the United States, who recaptured their vessel. Nine blacks were condemned to death, their heads later being placed on stakes.

truce in 1540, Pizarro dispatched a trusted black with a couple of horses and other gifts to Manco Capac's mountain headquarters. The Inca kept the gifts but ordered the black man executed.[54] In 1556 a negro slave woman was captured by a band of Araucanian Indians when the latter seized the town of Valdivia (Chile). These natives had apparently never seen an African woman before, for they tied her to a tree and attempted to rub off her skin pigmentation. Once they determined that the dark color could not be removed, the natives skinned the woman alive and stuffed her skin with straw.[55] These incidents emphasize the fact that Afro-Indian relations were often characterized by a good deal of antipathy.

Royal policy and romantic preconceptions aside, the basic source of black–red discord probably lay in the initial encounters. The Africans, as servants and sometimes fighting companions of the Spanish in Mexico, Peru and Chile, were to the Indian simply *conquistadores* of another color.[56] Recall Juan Valiente, Estebanico, or the fugitive slaves at Tafeme, Colombia in 1545: Each of these fought the Indians, took their women, or used the indigenous people as hostages or servants. King Miguel in Venezuela insisted that the Indians in his band appear black, while a sixteenth-century Negroid extortion network (*La recontoneria*)[57] consistently stripped the Indians of the profits the latter accumulated by selling produce on the streets of Mexico City.

Treatment of Negroids by the indigenous peoples was likewise harsh. Under the Spanish system, no black or mulatto could have an Indian servant, but Indians could and did have Africans as slaves. Moreover, Indians had cooperated with the Spaniards and hunted down rebellious blacks in Hispaniola in 1522, after the Mexico City conspiracy of 1537, and following both King Miguel's debacle and the Coro insurrection of 1795. Furthermore, once the natives came to understand that the Spaniards regarded the African as an inferior being, they were often prone to adopt the same attitude. Witness the testimony in Chile of an Araucanian Indian known as Albea. This individual, when captured and interrogated by the Spanish about 1570, declared that his people fought the whites "because we fear with reason that [by] allowing the Spaniards to establish themselves securely in our lands, we become more prisoners ... than the Negroes."[58]

Naturally Africans and Indians did sometimes unite in an effort to gain some political end, and the very existence of the *sambo-mosquitos* is proof that such alliances were often viewed as being mutually advantageous. Similarly, in the *comunero* revolt of 1780,[59] or in the assorted urban riots that occasionally plagued New World cities, mulattoes, *zambos*, blacks, and Indians closed ranks in a crusade of the poor against the rich.[60] The problem was that the goals of the nonwhite races were not always harmonious. In 1780, for example, when Tupac Amaru II launched a rebellion that shook Spain's hegemony in Peru to its foundations, he did nothing to encourage the Negroid element to rally to his cause. This Indian leader had announced that he intended to remove from his homeland all traces of Iberian influence and reintroduce pre-Colombian economic, political, and social practices. But since the Africans had arrived with the Spaniards, they had as much at stake if Inca rule was reestablished as the Spaniards did; not surprisingly, they cast their lot with the stronger party.[61]

AN ANALYSIS OF SPANISH POLICY
AND NEGROID REBELLIOUSNESS

At first glance, Spanish policy toward rebellious Africans reveals almost nothing in the way of consistency. A few *cimarrones* were barbarously executed, but sometimes they were granted amnesty. A steady stream of royal *cédulas* was issued, but, as usual, the crown had extremely little control over how these laws were enforced in its American possessions. Anti-*cimarrón* operations were undertaken, but hardly with the endurance or energy that would have been necessary had the intent been the total elimination of this menace.[62] On the endemic nature of the problem and the Spanish response to it, José Saco provides the enlightening observation that "neither the conspiracies, nor the uprisings ... were enough to slack the thirst for Negroes which the colonists had."[63] The controlling contingency throughout the colonial period was the need for slave labor in order to exploit as extensively as possible the New World's mineral and agrarian treasures. In exchange for profit, the crown, the mine holder, the plantation owner, and other exploiters tacitly accepted the prospect of occasional rebellions and the moderate frequency of *cimarrón* activity. Naturally, many slaves would escape, but as long as more *bozales* were available, the labor question was basically solved. It was therefore up to the regional bureaucracy to employ the tactics necessary to ensure that the solution reached remained a viable one. Ironically enough, this was probably the only strategy that could have succeeded, given the vastness and diversity of the Spanish Indies, the prohibitive cost that a more militant approach would have necessitated, and Madrid's constant involvement in expensive European conflicts.

But if the Spanish response to black insurrectionary activity varied considerably, so did the motivations for the revolts themselves. Some of the uprisings mentioned and described in this chapter were really spontaneous reactions induced by such things as the sudden increase of work loads or the rapid deterioration in the quality of the food. In such instances, the amelioration of some grievance rather than the attainment of liberation was usually the most pressing goal. Quite different were those premeditated acts of defiance and rebellion aimed at achieving some radical restructuring of the social order. Hypothetically, such episodes can be divided into three general but not mutually exclusive categories:

1. The 1537 Mexico City plot, the 1552 to 1555 war of King Miguel, and the 1749 Caracas slave intrigue were endeavors aimed at destroying Spanish political control in those areas of the New World where the incidents took place. Although the total extermination of the white population or the complete extirpation of Spanish culture were not necessarily intended, the establishment of black dominance was a *sine qua non*.

2. The long-lived *palenque* in San Basilio, the Venezuelan "Republic of Nirgua," and the 1804 River Yi saga in Uru-

guay represented attempts to create semiautonomous African polities in the New World. The subjugation of the Spaniards was not envisioned, but the separation of the races was deemed to be a viable goal. Based upon a similar rationale were the decisions of the followers of Ỹanga in seventeenth-century Mexico and of Manuel Fernando one hundred and fifty years later. In both cases, the ex-*cimarrones* could pledge allegiance to the Spanish crown as long as amnesty was total and the blacks were left in control of their local affairs. This tenuous kind of coexistence was probably not preferred by either group, but perpetual struggle was deemed even less desirable.

3. Differing in many aspects from either of the other categories were the Juan Andresote and José Chirinos uprisings. In the former case, especially in the instance where the free blacks and mulattoes changed sides and joined Andresote (after the 26 January 1732 ambush), one can discern a yearning on the part of the Negroid peoples for an upgrading of their second-class status. Much more explicit in this regard is the sad but somehow appealing tale of José Chirinos. The *zambo* wanted to end slavery, but he obviously did not desire the destruction of Spanish society nor the separation of the Negroid peoples into self-contained segregated units. In his own naïve way, José Chirinos sought the extension of the privileges enjoyed by Spaniards to all persons in colonial Venezuela. If the Spaniards had been prepared to concede a reasonable "piece of the action" to the nonwhites, José Chirinos could have accepted them the way he had expected to receive the French – as brothers.

Another consideration that this recounting of slave activity also raises to the forefront is that of leadership. Ỹanga in Mexico and King Benkos in Colombia were African-born, but King Miguel in Venezuela and Alfonso de Illescas in Ecuador were European-born *ladinos*, while Juan Andresote and José Chirinos were free *zambos*. The point is that the leadership of New World insurgencies cannot simplistically be attributed to any particular group of persons of African ancestry. In addition, the participation of a conspicuous number of free Negroids in those struggles indicates that many of them came to feel an extreme sense of frustration because of their restricted position in colonial Spanish America.

5

Free Negroids in
Colonial Spanish America

THE SOCIETY OF *CASTAS*

In establishing and consolidating its imperial rule, Spain attempted to graft upon its colonies the ideas and institutions then prevalent in the kingdom of Castile. Among these was the concept of "purity of blood," which maintained that bloodlines were infallible determinants of physical beauty and psychic character. Logically, then, those of "unclean" origins were carriers of biological deficiencies and were unfit to occupy positions of moral and political authority.[1] In Spain this notion referred to Moors and Jews. In the New World, however, the concept condemned people of mixed blood in general and African ancestry in particular. Few unmarried European women came to the colonies, and Spanish males enjoyed virtually unlimited access to the mass of African and Indian females. Furthermore, African males, whatever their status, also sought the sexual favors of the indigenous women, especially when those of their own race were unavailable. The net result was a rapid growth in the number of Euro-Africans (*mulatos*), Euro-Indians (*mestizos*), and Afro-Indians (*zambos*). They were generally not European in appearance, and in the Spanish Indies, mixed blood became synonymous with flawed character and illegitimate origins. These circumstances made miscegenated persons the pariahs of the social system.

Although the Spanish government did virtually nothing to prevent white males from taking the Indian and African women they pleased, it was profoundly irritated by the appearance and the growing number of persons who were neither white Spaniards, black slaves, nor pure Indians. In 1543 Charles I even attempted to legislate the Afro-Indian out of existence, a step nearly as futile as ordering a dehydrated man not to drink water. This action proved to be the last attempt on the part of the crown to regulate concupiscence by *cédula*. Thereafter, the *mestizos*, mulattoes, and *zambos* were lumped into one general category, slightly superior to that of the slave, and dubbed *castas*.

Of course, nobody wanted to be considered a *casta*, and requests for exemption from this status were heard at court within the first three decades after Columbus's landing. *Conquistadores* like Pedro de Alvarado wanted their bastard heirs declared legitimate Spaniards, and they had enough of those magic persuaders – money and influence – to get their way. No one has ever explained how a royal declaration cleansed the blood of an innately vice-ridden *casta*, but this is only one example of a whole system that was riddled with logical inconsistencies. All *mestizos*, it should be noted, were recognized as *gente de razón* ("persons of reason"), but *zambos* and mulattoes were not.[2] More significantly, all blacks were considered *castas* even if they had no mixed blood, for African origin was *per se* deemed debilitating. For blacks, mulattoes, and *zambos*, there was to be neither civil nor religious office, and various fields of commercial endeavor were also closed to them.

As the general process of miscegenation inexorably continued, there came into being all manner of African, Spanish, and Indian mixtures. The royal government made little effort to delineate their ranks, but not so the *criollos*, or American-born persons of Spanish blood. Since the *criollos* suffered discrimination at the hands of the European-born Spaniards, they were considerably more apprehensive about the possibility of persons with mixed blood passing into their ranks. It was the *criollos* who were probably most responsible for the development of a hierarchy of types based on the alleged quantity of Spanish blood each possessed. Particularly because of the philosophical and psychological assumptions implied in these rankings, the titles and methods of categorization are worthy of scrutiny.

THE DETERMINATION OF THE *CASTAS*

The primary distinction of types established by white theorists was one of race and/or color, although occasionally a convoluted logic was exercised in order to justify making additional distinctions. A book written in about 1805 by the prominent Peruvian physician Hipólito Uñanue (1755–1833), included a classification scheme long accepted informally in the Viceroyalty of Peru (see table 6).

Table 6. *A Peruvian scale for Casta improvement*

Man	Woman	Offspring (male)	Degree of mixture
White	*Negra*	*Mulato*	1/2 black and 1/2 white
White	*Mulata*	*Cuarterón*	1/4 black and 3/4 white
White	*Cuarterona*	*Quinterón*	1/8 black and 7/8 white
White	*Quinterona*	White	1/16 black and 15/16 white

Source: José Antonio Saco, *Historia de la esclavitud de la raza africana en el Nuevo Mundo y en especial en los países américo-hispanos,* 4 vols. (Havana, 1938), 2:66.

There is at least one obvious inconsistency in this design: Why, for example, was a *quinterón* so called? If a person was seven-eighths white, should he not have been termed a *septerón*? Or, if his African ancestry was the issue, why was he not called an *octarón* ("octaroon")? In any case, the real significance of this classification plan was that it suggested how, under certain circumstances, mulattoes could eventually be "cleansed" and conceivably amalgamated with the white ruling group.

Just as one could become whiter, there was also the possibility of retrogression. The scheme reproduced by Uñanue also included a *salta atrás*, or "throwback" category. All the unions listed in table 7 were placed in the *salta atrás* category because in each of them African blood predominated. Only when the degree of white ancestry increased was an individual of mixed blood believed to be "progressing."

Table 7. *A Peruvian scale for Casta retrogression*

Man	Woman	Offspring (male)	Degree of mixture
Negro	Mulata	Zambo*	3/4 black and 1/4 white
Negro	Zamba	Zambo prieto	7/8 black and 1/8 white
Negro	Zamba prieta	Negro	15/16 black and 1/16 white

Source: José Antonio Saco, *Historia de la esclavitud de la raza africana en el Nuevo Mundo y en especial en los países américo-hispanos*, 4 vols. (Havana, 1938), 2:67.

*Uñanue's reference to a *zambo* as a black–mulatto combination simply demonstrates that in each viceregal jurisdiction there existed euphemisms that often meant something else in another viceroyalty. Along these same lines, James Lockhart records that, at least until 1560, Afro-Indian crosses in Peru were called mulattoes (*Spanish Peru: 1532–1560, A Colonial Society* [Madison, 1968], p. 176).

Another system of color classification is presented in the works of both Rolando Mellafe and Gonzalo Aguirre Beltrán (see table 8).

Table 8. *A Mexican Casta classification system*

Man	Woman	Offspring (male)	Mixture
White	Negra	Mulato blanco	½ white and ½ black
White	Mulata blanca	Mulato morisco	¾ white and ¼ black
Negro	India	Mulato pardo	½ black and ½ Indian
Mulato pardo	India	Mulato lobo ("wolf")	¼ black and ¾ Indian
Mestizo	Mulata parda	Mestizo pardo (coyote)	¼ black, ¼ white, and ½ Indian
Mestizo	Negra	Mestizo prieto	½ black, ¼ white, and ¼ Indian

Sources: Rolando Mellafe, *La esclavitud en Hispano-América* (Buenos Aires, 1964), pp. 87–89; Gonzalo Aguirre Beltrán, *Población negra de México, 1519–1810: Estudio etnohistórico* (Mexico, D.F., 1946), pp. 165–72.

As evidenced by Aguirre Beltrán and Edgar Love, this system was often employed by administrative and church officials in colonial Mexico.[3] It represented a different approach from the semiesoteric arrangements found in Uñanue's scheme since no hypothetical possibility for becoming "white" was included. At the same time, the terminology spotlights the carelessly concealed contempt in which Afro-Indian *castas* were held: *lobo*, or "wolf"; *coyote*, or "prairie wolf." Furthermore, the most common crossing, the *mulato pardo*, was better known in different parts of Mexico by a number of equally ungratifying sobriquets: *loro*, or "parrot"; *cambujo*, or "donkey"; *cocho*, or "dirty"; "a pig." We may assume that, presented with an opportunity, *lobos*, *coyotes*, and *mulatos pardos* would do their best to be known as something other than what they were.

The system of nomenclature embodying at once both the greatest whimsy and the most formidable logical development (twisted though it may be) is preserved in the collection of the Museo Nacional de México (see table 9).

Table 9. *Mexican Casta classification system from the Museo Nacional de México*

Male	Female	Offspring (male)
Spaniard	India	Mestizo
Spaniard	Mestiza	Castizo
Castizo	Española ("Spanish woman")	Spaniard
Spaniard	Negra	Mulato
Spaniard	Mulata	Morisco
Morisco	Española	Chino
Chino	India	Salto atrás ("throwback")
Salto atrás	Mulata	Lobo ("wolf")
Lobo	China	Gíbaro
Gíbaro	Mulata	Alborazado ("braying mule")
Alborazado	Negra	Cambujo ("donkey")
Cambujo	India	Zambaigo
Zambaigo	Loba	Calpa Mulato
Calpa mulato	Cambuja	Tente en el aire ("hung up in the air")
Tente en el aire	Mulata	No te entiendo ("I don't know what you are")
No te entiendo	India	Torna atrás ("turnaround")

Source: Nicolás León, *Las castas del México colonial o Nueva España* (Mexico, D.F., 1924), p. 42.

Obviously, no person was ever referred to as a *torna atrás, no te entiendo*, or *tente en el aire*, except behind his back. One gains the impression that this system was really a tongue-in-cheek affair, an exercise perhaps concocted by university students during an evening of immoderate drinking. Interestingly enough, the offspring of a *castizo* (7/8 white, 1/8 Indian) and a Spanish woman (*española*) becomes a "Spaniard." In contrast, the issue of a *morisco* (7/8 white, 1/8 black) and a Spanish woman becomes a *chino*! That this designation was supposed to denote persons of Afro-Indian ancestry does not seem to have troubled the creators of the scheme.[4] As in the racial classification system referred to by Mellafe and Aguirre Beltrán, the message is explicit: Euro-Indian mixtures could theoretically become "white," but persons who possessed any Negroid blood whatsoever could not.

Regional systems of nomenclature less comprehensive than that of the collection of the Museo Nacional were developed, and, as could be expected, each of these possessed special idiosyncracies. The one that functioned in Costa Rica provides an excellent case in point. On baptismal records an Afro-Indian offspring was considered a *zambo de mestizo* if he was living with his Indian parent and a *zambo de mulato* if his residence was with a Negroid relation. Civil records there, especially in the eighteenth century, refer to many mulattoes as *pardos, pardos loros* (roughly, "brown-skinned persons"), and *pardos atezados* (very darkskinned persons). These were really courtesy designations since many *castas* felt that the term *mulato* was insulting. Colonial Costa Rican baptismal records occasionally list a person of mixed blood as an *octarón* or *octarona*, but precisely what was understood by this designation was never made clear. In a few instances, a person was described on his baptismal record as a "white mulatto" (*mulato blanco*), which seems to have meant that he possessed Caucasian features, but that the Negroid parent was probably known to the priest.[5] In any event, the white mulatto knew better than to attempt to compete for the desirable political, religious, and administrative positions because acquisition of these sinecures required proof of "cleanliness of blood."

The irrational and invidious nature of these systems of socio-racial nomenclature should not blind the reader to their general acceptance by the Indian and African populace and to the effects that they had in reinforcing certain basic principles accepted by the society. Two eighteenth-century travelers to Colombia, Jorge Juan and Antonio de Ulloa, pointed out that in that region "every person is so jealous of the order of their tribe or caste that if, through inadvertence, you call them a degree lower than what they actually are, they are highly offended, never suffering themselves to be deprived of so valuable a gift."[6] The scholarly Alexander von Humboldt, reporting on Mexico in 1803 and 1804, observed that "in a country governed by whites, the families reputed to have the least mixture of Negro or mulatto blood are also naturally the most honored ... it becomes, consequently, a very interesting business for the public vanity to estimate accurately the fractions of European blood which belong to the different castes."[7]

Much as all proverbial roads led to Rome, success in Spanish American colonial society was dependent upon one's whiteness. *Quinterones*, therefore, announced that they were whites; *cuarterones* stated loudly that they were *quinterones* or, if possible, whites. Most of the mulattoes were too dark to deceive anyone, but they resented it when lighter-complexioned Negroids acted in a haughty fashion toward them. Still, these swarthy-skinned folk could take comfort in the knowledge that they were not completely of African origin; there was always the black who had no white blood and was therefore lower in status than they.

Naturally, ranking people in terms of their proximity to a white appearance helped to make individuals of dark pigmentation despise their African origins. Furthermore, civil officials in some areas passed laws and ordinances that by their nature were designed to drive a wedge between blacks and lighter-complexioned Negroids. In Santo Domingo the *Código negro carolino* of 1785 established that freed blacks and mulattoes could not be rented homes in towns but should be forced to reside with a "known master"; this rule could be suspended, however, for *tercerones* and *cuarterones*. Still another part of this statute ordered that any freed black or mulatto showing disrespect toward a white person was to receive 25 lashes; these were to be given publicly, thereby reinforcing the shame and fear of the person punished. *Tercerones* and *cuarterones* convicted of this transgression were to receive no physical punishment, but merely four days in jail and a 25-peso fine.[8] Evidence of the same kind of differentiation is found in colonial Uruguay. The general practice there was to make distinctions between *morenos* ("blacks") and *pardos* ("mulattoes"), not between freedmen and slaves. A prime model of the prevailing attitude was the acts passed by the *cabildo* of Montevideo in May 1760. These regulations established that semiskilled trades such as those of cobbler and tailor were to be opened to *pardos*; *morenos*, in contrast, were to be shunted off into those occupations for which physical exertion was the primary requisite.[9]

As early as 1615, the viceroy of Peru, Don Juan de Mendoza y Luna, reported to Philip III that the numerical superiority of Indians and Africans made the "division of the nations [i.e., *castas*]" an "indispensable element" in the operation of colonial government.[10] It was no accident, therefore, that Peruvian viceroys made it a policy to receive groups of Indians in one office, Spaniards in another, and *castas* in still a third. A further example is found in the *Código negro carolino*, whose authors observed that *cuarterones* and *quinterones* "never mixed with Negroes (whom they regard with disdain) in their uprisings, flights and struggles against the state, and are the strongest prop of public authority."[11] The application of divide-and-conquer tactics was, of course, limited to those areas where the Negroid population was so large that being considered a *cuarterón* or person of another racial mixture did make a difference. Still, insofar as New World administrators were able to use the social-classification system to perpetuate a hostility among the different castes, The overall colonial control of Spain was strengthened.

Published estimates concerning the number of free persons of full or partial African ancestry in eighteenth and early nineteenth-century Spanish America are listed in table 10.

Table 10. *Estimated totals of free Negroids in colonial Spanish America*

	Year	Total	Comment
Argentina			
Buenos Aires	1810	503	Figure for city only.
Córdoba	1778	14,892*	Figure for city and province.
Mendoza	1802	4,092*	Figure for city and province.
Chile	1778	13,000–15,000	
Colombia–Panama	1800	140,000	
Costa Rica	1801	8,925	
Cuba	1811	114,000	
Ecuador	1800	42,000	
Guatemala	1740–1743	6,040	Listed as mulattoes in Guatemala City and surrounding area.
Mexico	1810	624,461	Chiefly *zambos* and mulattoes.
Paraguay	1782	6,893	
Peru	1791	41,256	
Santo Domingo	1795	38,000	
Uruguay	1803	899	
Venezuela	1800	440,000	

Sources: For the Buenos Aires figure, see Evelyn P. Meiners, "The Negro in the Río de la Plata," (Ph.D. diss., Northwestern University, 1948), chap. iv, pp. 10–23; for Córdoba and Mendoza, Emiliano Endrek, *El mestizaje en Córdoba: Siglo XVIII y principios del XIX* (Córdoba, 1966), p. 12; and José Luis Masini, *La esclavitud negra en Mendoza: Época independiente* (Mendoza, 1962), p. 10; for Chile, Gonzalo Vial Correa, *El africano en el reino de Chile: Ensayo histórico-jurídico* (Santiago, 1957), p. 44; for Colombia–Panama and Ecuador, José Manuel Restrepo, *Historia de la revolución de la República de Colombia en la América meridional*, 4 vols. (Besanzon, 1958), 1:xiv; for Costa Rica, *Monografía de la población de la República de Costa Rica en el siglo XIX*, Ministerio de Economía y Hacienda, Dirección General de Estadística y Censos (San José, 1951), pp. 3–4; for Cuba, Alexander von Humboldt, *Ensayo político sobre la isla de Cuba*, 2 vols. (Havana, 1930), 1:114; for Guatemala, Chester L. Jones, *Guatemala, Past and Present* (Minneapolis, 1940), pp. 141–43; for Mexico, Gonzalo Aguirre Beltrán, *Población negra de México, 1519–1810: Estudio etnohis-*

THE CHURCH AND THE *CASTAS*

A royal *cédula* promulgated in 1538 prescribed that "the slaves, free Negroes, and mulattoes be instructed in the Holy Catholic faith."[12] Churchmen took this decree seriously, but the instruction was generally limited to the elementary concepts of Catholic dogma. Many slave owners were loathe to allow their slaves to have anything more than the most rudimentary religious instruction; overall, the quality of religious instruction was consistent only in its diversity.

The Church itself represented one of the largest slave holding entities in Spanish America, with monasteries and individual ecclesiastics owning numerous bondmen. The Jesuits were the largest holders of Africans in Chile until their order was suppressed in 1767.[13] These followers of Ignatius Loyola were said to support their slaves even after they were too old to work, but whether other ecclesiastical orders did likewise has never been established.

In responding to the needs of the free blacks and mulattoes, the Catholic church operated within the bounds of the racial-separation policy the Spanish promoted. Ideally, it dispensed the sacraments of Baptism, Penance, and Holy Communion and did not oppose marriage between Africans and Spaniards unless the alliance was in violation of the civil law. Priests dutifully recorded in the parish registry books not only the racial origins of newborn *castas*, but also their particular subspecie based on the socioracial nomenclature prevalent in the region.

tórico (Mexico, D.F., 1946), p. 237; for Paraguay, Josefina Plá, *Hermano negro: La esclavitud en el Paraguay* (Madrid, 1972), p. 36; for Peru, Fernando Romero, "The Slave Trade and the Negro in South America," *Hispanic American Historical Review* 24 (August 1944): 378; for Santo Domingo, Carlos Larrazábal Blanco, *Los negros y la esclavitud en Santo Domingo* (Santo Domingo, 1967), p. 184; for Uruguay, Ildefonso Pereda Valdés, *Negros esclavos y negros libres: Esquema de una sociedad esclavista y aporte del negro en nuestra formación nacional* (Montevideo, 1941), p. 16; and for Venezuela, Federico Brito Figueroa, *Estructura económica de Venezuela colonial* (Caracas, 1963), p. 58.

*Figure probably includes some *mestizos* as well as blacks, mulattoes and *zambos*.

The Church acted most effectively in satisfying the social and psychological needs of racially mixed peoples in its sponsorship of *cofradías*.[14] The organization of these groups tended to reflect the segregated societal pattern that the Spanish government favored for its New World possessions. Possibly the first of these auxiliaries formed was the *Cofradía de Juan Bautista* ("Brotherhood of John the Baptist"), established in 1602 in Santo Domingo and restricted in its membership to American-born free blacks. Other associations limited their enrollments to mulattoes, or, like the *Cofradía de San Cosme y San Damián* ("Brotherhood of St. Cosmas and St. Damian"), accepted both freedmen and slaves but excluded persons on the basis of African geographic origin.[15] American *cofradías* usually obtained or built a chapel in a wing of some larger church, and there they held meetings and religious services. They provided burial arrangements and economic assistance for their members and held gala parades and dances on the annual feast day of their patrons. In addition, a few groups, like the *Cofradía de Nuestra Señora de Belén* ("Brotherhood of Our Lady of Bethlehem") in Santiago (Chile) provided free meals for imprisoned *castas*.[16] Widespread too was a practice followed by the *Cofradía del Rosario* ("Brotherhood of the Rosary"), a mulatto association in Córdoba (Argentina), which, in parades, always carried icons of the Blessed Virgin Mary, painted with black or brown skin and Negroid features.[17]

Gradually, some churchmen came to view the *cofradías* rather ambivalently, arguing that the social aspect of these fraternities had eclipsed their religious function. This objection was valid in many instances. The fraternal needs of the subject people were real, however, and since the Spaniards provided almost no other outlets, it was natural that the *cofradías* came to fill the void.

Although all persons of African blood were technically considered "New Christians" and incapable of rational cognition owing to their supposedly defective origins, they still found themselves subject to the long arm of the Holy Office of the Inquisition. As intellectual novices, Negroids were not prosecuted for heresy, but blasphemy and the black arts of witchcraft and sorcery were seen as their particular transgressions. In general, accused persons falling into the clutches of the inquisitors could expect neither tolerance nor compassion. In 1581 Hernando Maravilla, a slave in Santiago declared his disbelief in the Christian God, h:s discipleship with the Devil, and his disdain for the local bishop. The inquisitors made short work of this unfortunate black, ordering him to be muzzled and sentenced to 400 lashes.[18] The protectors of public morality did not become more tenderhearted with the passage of time. In 1737 in the same city, a fifty-year-old slave, María de Silva, was convicted of casting "love spells"; as part of her sentence, she was whipped and sentenced to ten years' hard labor on the frontier in southern Chile.[19]

Free Negroids did not fare much better. In about 1600 a Peruvian *zamba*, Juana de Castenada, was whipped for being a witch. Twenty-five years later, a *mulata*, Morin Martínez, was arrested on a similar charge, but her fate remains unknown.[20] Badly treated was Francisco Rodríguez, a *zambo* who was tried in 1646 in Mexico City for "having made a pact with the devil to render him adoration." In return, Rodriguez was to have obtained power "to be able to fight a thousand men [and] to win all the women he wanted." This poor soul would need the strength of Samson, however, for the tribunal sentenced him to 200 lashes and a turn at the oars as a galley slave.[21]

At times, the fury of the tribunal seems to have been directed at those Negroids whose "crime" was that they had somehow succeeded against the odds. Consider the case of Diego López, a mulatto slave born in 1591. Attached to a hospital, López learned the art of barber–surgeon and earned enough money to buy his freedom. He enjoyed a successful practice until he was seized on 5 January 1633 after nine women (all under twenty-five years old) had accused him of casting spells and being a sorcerer. In the first three hearings, López denied all charges, but the inquisitors kept him sequestered in a special jail, and at his fourth hearing he confessed. Over three years later (1 June 1636), an *auto da fé*[22] was celebrated in Cartagena; among those publicly confessing their guilt was Diego López, who was sentenced to "perpetual imprisonment" and 200 lashes.[23] In contrast, concern over the growth of Negroid witches and warlocks never caused frenzied investigations in Argentina, and prior to 1790 only one Negroid suspect was punished by inquisitional proceedings in Uruguay.[24] As with all other colonial institutions, the execution and implementation of policy varied dramatically from region to region.

The basic problem for the Spaniards was lack of control over the religious tendencies of slaves and their descendants. As long as fresh *bozales* were imported and dispatched to all the regions of the Indies, there would never be enough inquisitional committees to oversee them. There also seems to have been a constant shortage of priests in the rural regions of the Indies.[25] In addition, such practices as the personification of natural forces, ancestor worship, and the perception of multiple deities were basic to the religious experience of western Africa. A few hours of catechism, the pouring of baptismal waters, and the threat of possible torture were simply not going to eradicate this background. Indeed, it would have been astonishing had the Negroid peoples totally rejected the religious concerns of their ancestors and unconditionally embraced those of their dominators; they were more likely to mix them conveniently together. Blacks and mulattoes went to Mass and outwardly conformed, but as can be gleaned from the previously cited cases, many who carried rosaries in one hand also had a magic charm or mystical talisman in their pocket.

Because the priesthood was considered to be one of the most exemplary positions available in colonial Spanish America, the policy of the Church toward admitting people of African origin to the ranks of the clergy deserves special consideration. For half of the sixteenth century, the ordination of any person of "impure blood" was absolutely prohibited. There developed, however, a growing need for priests who spoke both Spanish and the assorted Indian tongues. Bowing to the demands of expediency in 1558, the royal government authorized *mestizos* of legitimate birth to receive training as clerics.[26] But the exemption of the *mestizo* did not mean that conditions had improved for Negroid people.

Not until the bishop of Santo Domingo reported that there were almost no whites who wished to enter the seminaries did

Madrid agree (1707) to allow men "who have some [blood] line mixed with mulattoes" to receive Holy Orders. This reversal of past policy was to be allowed only in Santo Domingo, and the mulatto priests were to be assigned to lowly positions and not made eligible for promotion.[27] Furthermore, in 1723 the king directed the bishop of Santo Domingo to be even more discriminatory in the selection of light-skinned mulattoes for seminary training. Nonetheless, once the barrier had been breached, it could never be fully restored; a number of mulatto priests were ordained in Santo Domingo, and at least one curate of mixed blood, Nicolás de Aguilar, was appointed canon at the cathedral in the capital.[28]

For the other regions of South America, crown and church policy remained unchanged. Instructions and *cédulas* sent to civil and ecclesiastical officials in 1709, 1760, and 1772 reiterated the longstanding interdiction against the entry into the priesthood of blacks, mulattoes, and *zambos*. Still, as in so many other instances, the official position fails to provide an accurate picture of the true situation. The Mexican patriot José María Morelos y Pavón (born 1779), for example, was apparently a *mulato pardo* (1/2 black and 1/2 Indian); nevertheless, he received Holy Orders. The baptismal register in his village reveals that, while he had originally been designated a "mulatto," the register was somehow changed to read "white."[29] Perhaps the payment of a sum of money by his parents or the pleadings of an ambitious mother made the difference. The pity was that blacks, mulattoes, and *zambos* were expected to observe Catholic dogma, but unless they hid or denied their African origin, entrance into the clergy was most likely to be refused them.

A relatively impartial assessment of the Church's treatment of people of mixed blood is possible only if its general position in colonial Spanish America is understood. Critical in this connection is the *patronato real* granted by Pope Julius II to the monarchs of Spain in 1508. Armed with these powers, the successors of Ferdinand and Isabella intervened in religious affairs whenever royal prerogatives seemed effected. The Catholic church in Spanish America was a state organ, different from the

Casa de Contratación, but nevertheless an arm of the crown. If Spanish policy called for the separation of the races, it was not the Church's place to support a contradictory initiative. Pacification and Christianization, not disruption, became the primary ecclesiastical missions. People of mixed blood may have been unjustly treated, but the redress of grievances would have to occur in the life beyond.

To be sure, there is still another, more ironic side of the picture. Consider the case of Martín de Porres, a free Peruvian mulatto, who in the eighteenth century became a lay brother in the Dominican order. Aside from Saint Rose of Lima, a *criolla*, Porres is the only other Spanish American canonized (1962) by the Catholic church. Still, this holy man, who allegedly worked miracles, given his half-breed origins, would never have been allowed to become a priest.

THE PROBLEM OF INTERMARRIAGE

The laws

The belief long prevalent both north and south of the Río Grande has been that the mixed biological character of the Latin American is proof that the racial hatreds characterizing Anglo-Saxon America were nonexistent or greatly muted in the Spanish and Portuguese-dominated zones.[30] A comprehensive examination of intermarriage as practiced in colonial Spanish America does little to justify such a premise. In 1514 Spain sanctioned white–Indian alliances, but treatment of the Negroid was another story. *Cédulas* issued in 1527 and 1541 suggested rather emphatically that Africans should be encouraged to unite only with other Africans, although no specific legal obstacle was placed in the path of Afro-Spaniard alliances until 1687. At that time, administrative officials in Santo Domingo had become increasingly alarmed because an undetermined number of Spanish military officers stationed on the island had married black and mulatto women. Madrid therefore decreed that officers might marry whom they pleased, but if they chose women of Negroid origin, they jeopardized all future promotion.[31] This move was apparently effective since the "rash" of interracial alliances involving commissioned military personnel soon came to an end.

This was a limited step since only Santo Domingo was involved, but it was to be followed by more sweeping changes roughly a century later. Charles III issued a statute in 1776 governing marriages in Spain and applied its provisions to his American possessions in April 1778. This new sanction legally established that parents could prevent the marriage of any of their offspring under the age of twenty-five to a person lacking "clean blood." Thereafter, if parents or legal guardians objected to a marriage on the grounds that the prospective son-in-law or daughter-in-law had mixed origins, the courts would have to settle the issue before any marital ceremony could transpire. The law specifically exempted from its jurisdiction parents who were "mulattoes, Negroes, *coyotes*, and individuals of the *castas* and similar races," the assumption being that persons of such low origins had no heritage to protect.[32]

The 1778 law was somewhat contradictory since it also established that black and mulatto officers of the militia, as well as those *castas* mysteriously described as "distinguished from the rest by their reputation," were subject to the strictures of this regulation.[33] The royal acknowledgment that some persons of African origin were deserving of merit caused consternation in some regions. Almost immediately, colonial officials in Chile and Mexico argued that Indians and legitimate *mestizos* should come under the strictures of this edict; *cédulas* issued in 1780 and 1790 sanctioned this position. Still another decree promulgated in 1803 reiterated the essentials of the laws of 1778, 1780, and 1790, but the ultimate *cédula* issued by Charles IV in this regard (15 October 1805) was even more pointed. Addressing itself to the question of "marriage between people of distinguished quality and Negro women and other *castas*," it commanded that Spaniards, Indians, and legitimate *mestizos* contemplating possible union with such lowly females must receive permission from either the viceroy or the *audiencia*.[34]

On its face, this last decree governing matrimonial practices seems no more restrictive than the others issued since 1778, but colonial administrators apparently thought otherwise. Upon receiving this *cédula*, Viceroy Nicolás Sobremonte, who had requested that the crown take this step, publicly asserted that in Buenos Aires dispensations from the terms of the *cédula* would not be granted.[35] Not so vocal but just as obdurate were the *audiencia* judges in the Captaincy General of Caracas. In July 1804 María del Carmen Correa first sought permission to marry a mulatto medical surgeon, Juan Josef Ximénez. First the parents of María del Carmen and then the *audiencia* had vetoed the proposed match, but the lovers appealed to Madrid for a final decision. In its reply of 26 August 1806, the Council of the Indies took note of the fact that the mulatto was a noted surgeon who had acted as medical officer in a local *pardo* militia battalion. It found him "honorable" and "virtuous," but it decided not to interfere.[36]

The 1778 sanction had prevented whites under twenty-five from marrying without parental consent; now the 1805 decree provided legal methodology for preventing those over the age limit from entering into unions that the government might consider embarrassing. What was most disturbing, however, was the laissez-faire attitude adopted by Madrid in regard to the enforcement of this decree. The 1778 law had acknowledged that some Negroids were to be included among the favored folk in the Indies, but colonial officials acted as if they thought the 1805 decree banned interracial marriage, a conviction Madrid took no steps to correct. Much as in the case of the 1789 *Código negro español*, the Spanish government dimly perceived that it must take into consideration the needs and desires of all the population in formulating its policies. At the same time, practicality demanded that the wishes of the whites in the Americas remain paramount. Thus, if the price of nonconflict was the sacrifice of Negroid rights, that was what eventually would happen.

Societal attitudes

Even before the promulgation of new marital regulations in the eighteenth century, the total number of marriages between whites and persons of any discernible African ancestry was a

miniscule percentage of the total number of marriages contracted.[37] Concerning this situation, one observer wrote that
during the last quarter of the eighteenth century

> if a young man attempted to contract matrimony with a
> woman who was suspected or about whom it was said that
> she had black or mixed heritage, even if it be of remote
> origins, from this would arise the discrediting of families
> by others, disunion, perpetual enmities, law-suits and evils
> without end.

Additional evidence reinforces the veracity of this conclusion.
In 1811 in the city of Córdoba, for example, a marriage between a Spanish woman and a black, Manuel Rodríguez, took
place, but it was almost immediately annulled. In fact, the Negroid party was thereupon jailed for having given in to his im-
pulses.[39]

Further research buttresses the conclusion that intermarriage
in the Río de la Plata region was exceedingly rare. The town of
Chascomús[40] was founded in 1779, and by 1800 from 250 to
300 persons lived within its general environs; one-fourth to one-
third of this population was black or mulatto, and perhaps two-
fifths of that was enslaved.[41] Complete parish records for the
town date from 1804, and the *Libro de matrimonios* ("Book of
Marriage Records") notes that, during the period from 1804 to
1826, 236 weddings were performed. In exactly three of these
(1.27 percent), a Negroid person married someone of another
race.[42] Even if it is argued that ten times this number of mixed
nuptial ties took place in other Spanish American parishes, it
would still be manifest that licit wedlock was an inconsequential means for the mixing of African and white blood.

But if, as the data suggest, church-sanctioned alliances between Negroid persons and those of other races were decidedly
uncommon, why was there such a mushrooming opposition to
such unions? It would seem that the general economic upsurge
in the last half of the eighteenth century in much of Spanish
America may well have been responsible for the growing interracial friction. While the *criollos* seem to have profited greatly,
a few persons of mixed blood were also able to break the lock-

step imposed by ancestry. For such people, especially those with light skin or some Caucasian features, all that was needed for the final leap into the ranks of the dominant class was a white mate. The suspicion is strong that the fears engendered by this rise in status, rather than an actual increase in white–Negroid nuptials, was the factor that most frightened the *criollos*.

Another aspect of the intermarriage question was the fanatical opposition of some administrators and clergymen to Afro-Indian matches. These defenders of the indigenous tribes took the view that the African was debauched and that the innocent, naïve Indian required their protection. Furthermore, the issue of such matings, the *zambo*, was hardly held in societal esteem. According to the French observer Dauxion-Lavaysse,

> in the metropolis [Caracas] the word *zambo* is synonymous with idler, liar . . . thief, villain, assassin. These individuals are born of clandestine and adulterous unions, of natives who have contracted only the vices of civilization, and of African slaves: what can be expected of children born of such parents.[43]

During the sixteenth century in Mexico City, Viceroy Martín Enriquez called upon Philip II either to prohibit Afro-Indian marriages, or to declare that the *zambo* offspring of such unions would automatically be classified as slaves. But, since the king took no steps in this regard, it became the duty of the self-appointed Indian protectors to take the requisite actions. Particularly in Mexico, the belief that the Indian required defenders against black or mulatto exploiters seems to have been widespread. In 1769 Archbishop Lorenzana of Mexico City called upon the Indians to marry their daughters to Spaniards or Indians, but not to blacks, mulattoes, or *zambos*.[44] Then, in 1784 the *audiencia* of Mexico City instructed parish priests to alert the Indians to the "serious harm" that would befall them if they married Negroid persons. Indigenous men and women who insisted upon contracting such alliances were to be informed that their descendants would be "incapable of obtaining [even] municipal positions of honor."[45]

Colonial Spanish America did become miscegenated, but the easy access that white men had to African and Indian women was the paramount reason for the wide variety of racial admixtures that eventually emerged. To the dominant race, the black and red women were sexual objects rather than persons, and Negroid males, aping the master class, did their best to perpetuate a practice by which illegitimacy bred more and more of the same.

THE EDUCATIONAL PLIGHT OF
THE NEGROID *CASTAS*

While special schools were built for the Indians as early as the sixteenth century, the problem faced by people of African origin is exemplified in the charter of two orphanages founded by José Antonio de Alberto, bishop of Córdoba (Argentina), in 1782. Each institution was to accommodate 200 persons and provide them with as complete an education as available resources would permit. The school for girls was to allow 4 percent of the enrollment to be *mulatas*, while its counterpart for males could permit 10 percent of its constituency to be "of the low race of Negro slaves, *mulato* or *zambo* [sic]." In addition, the bishop stipulated that the nonwhites were to act as servants to the whites, and they were not to study the same curriculum.[46]

In the city of Buenos Aires in 1810, a *cabildo* ordinance declared that the primary schools were closed to "Negroes, *zambos*, mulattoes, and *cuarterones*," while similar restrictions seem to have been in effect throughout Colombia during the colonial period.[47] One of the more conspicuous attempts to change this situation occurred in March 1810, when another bishop of Córdoba, Rodrigo Antonio de Orellana, sought to open a primary school for *pardos* on the grounds of the university. As this prelate was also rector of the institution, his decision would have been final had not the faculty provided implacable opposition. The learned professors informed the bishop that, while his motives were commendable, the presence of the *castas* in the general proximity of the university would have detrimental effects upon scholarship and decorum; on this note, the matter rested.[48]

At the university level, royal decrees beginning in 1688 forbade the matriculation of all people having any African blood. In addition, specific *cédulas* barred their entry into the universities at Lima, Mexico City, and Havana. Still, in 1801 one of the applicants for the vacant chair of philosophy at the seminary of San Carlos (Colombia) was a mulatto named Juan Carrecedo. He was immediately denounced by a rival aspirant, José Sotomayor, who argued that "the laws of the *colegio* [San Carlos] require the indispensable circumstances of descending from Spanish parents, clean of all evil race." Sotomayor insisted that since Carrecedo's mother had been an "illegitimate Negro woman," his academic achievement was not enough to qualify him for the position. The resolution of the imbroglio is not clear since the seminary did not state on what grounds its final decision was made. Juan Carrecedo did not receive the appointment, but even to be a contestant, he necessarily had to have earned a university degree.[49]

Once again, we hear the same old refrain: The implementation of royal laws in the Indies was uniform only in its lack of uniformity. Several wealthy mulattoes like Sebastián López Ruiz attended the university at Bogotá, and a few of their counterparts in Santo Domingo gained entry to the university there.[50] Since after 1688 university applicants had to present a *limpieza de sangre* ("purity of blood") certificate in order to matriculate, the presence of these persons of mixed blood suggests that money and/or the influence of some governmental functionary were often powerful and instantaneous blood purifiers.

Dimly discernible in this study of strife and striving is the existence of a kind of nebulous royal policy regarding the education of *castas*. Madrid hardly favored it, and the American-born whites were adamantly opposed to the emergence of a mulatto elite that might compete with their own sons for the limited number of civil and clerical appointments available. But, in certain geographical areas where mulattoes were very numerous, or in the case of a particularly light-skinned individual supported by a powerful Spaniard, the necessary legal fiction could be manufactured and required credentials provided. Without question, though, the number of exceptions had to be small, and when these aroused virulent white opposition, as we shall see, the crown did not hesitate to beat a hasty retreat.

Education represented the key to upward mobility in what was indisputably a restrictive social system. Bearing this fact in mind, it is quite logical that the only person reputed to have been publicly whipped simply because he knew how to read and write was a mulatto.[51]

OPPRESSION, TRIBUTE, AND MILITARY SERVICE

A curious, brutal, but effective mélange of methods was used by the Spaniards in order to maintain the caste system they had created. One of the victims was Andrés Solís, a man described as a *cuarterón*. When this gentleman was appointed to a secretarial position in the colonial administration in Colombia in 1686, the governor of Cartagena had him dismissed immediately. The governor reported his action to the king and stated that royal command prohibited persons without "clean blood" from holding any positions in the colonial government. Another royal *cédula* was then circulated in Colombia stating that proof of "cleanliness of blood, life, and customs" had to be first demonstrated before any public servant could fill a position.[52]

The tragic tale of another freed black also illustrates one of the more anomalous means by which persons of mixed blood could be prevented from advancing too high up the social ladder. In 1785 Lieutenant Rafael María Castellano appointed Juan Morelos tax collector in the town of Saucé (Argentina). Perhaps the zeal with which the Negroid executed his task inspired the desire for revenge. At any rate, the governor of the province soon received a general letter from the townspeople reporting that Morelos had taken to calling himself *Don Juan*; an insulting situation, since no person so darkly pigmented could have this title of nobility! The governor apparently found the argument logical, for Morelos was dismissed posthaste.[53]

Another area in which the Spanish strove vigorously to establish universally recognizable distinctions was in the matter of wearing apparel for the various female *castas*. Royal decrees in 1551 and 1571 barred all women of African blood from wearing gold jewelry, silk dresses, pearls, and *mantos*.[54] Only if a *negra, zamba,* or *mulata* should marry a Spaniard could she wear gold earrings with pearls, a small pearl necklace, or "on her skirt a fringe of velvet."[55] Attempts to enforce such unreasonable standards were bound to engender bitter conflicts. During the late seventeenth century, the viceroy of Peru initiated a crusade in the city of Lima, and numerous *mulatas* received assorted punishments and fines until they appeared in apparel more representative of their social status.

On at least one occasion, the wearing-apparel conflict was settled with a malicious savagery peculiarly characteristic of those determined to mete out more personal forms of "justice." The town council of Córdoba twice warned Eugenia Montilla (1746 and 1750) that she was not to wear silk dresses or a *manto* in public. This *mulata* was married to a Spaniard, and she apparently believed that her husband's power and influence would shield her from the wrath of the local officials. Unfortunately, she failed to reckon with feminine fury. Invited to the home of a supposedly friendly Spanish lady, Eugenia discovered too late that she had wandered into a trap. A group of angry white women stripped her, had their slaves beat her, burned her silk dress, and then clothed her in garments "corresponding to her birth."[56] Her spirit broken, Eugenia Montilla fled the town.

It is undeniable that the Spanish government fostered a policy of residential segregation,[57] but its initial intent had been to protect the Indian from possible European corruption and exploitation. In the case of the *castas*, the premise was reversed; the whites wished to protect themselves (and their Indian wards) from the dissolute and essentially degenerate Negroids. As early as 1537, the town of Tianguey (Guatemala) had banned the unauthorized entry of any black, mulatto, or *zambo*, on pain of 100 lashes.[58] In Buenos Aires free Negroids were confined to suburban districts, which they were allowed to govern autonomously, but, in exchange, they were not to encroach upon white residential areas.[59] Slightly different was the situation in Cartago, the colonial capital of Costa Rica, where a special section was set aside for the settlement of blacks, mulattoes, and "low mestizos." The *castas* were allowed a measure of self-governance in the affairs of their segregated *barrio*, but the Cartago city council could and did reverse decisions that the whites considered unwise.[60]

Distinctly more antagonistic was the raft of declarations and local ordinances serving as constant reminders to Negroids that release from slavery did not carry in its train equality with the Spaniard. A 1768 Santo Domingo statute prohibited the sale of lands to *libertos negros* ("freed blacks"),[61] while in 1746 the bishop of Buenos Aires published an edict condemning African dances, which he deemed immoral. Eventually, ordinances prohibiting or restricting parades, African dances, and public *fiestas* sponsored by Negroid fraternal organizations were passed in Buenos Aires (1778), Asunción (1782), and Montevideo (1807).[62] Even more inimical were proscriptions like that issued in 1801 by a Colonel Ramón Castillo, which barred from membership in the Buenos Aires *Sociedad patriótica* ("Patriotic Society") all "Negroes, mulattoes, *chinos, zambos, cuarterones*" – and even *mestizos* of legitimate birth. This officer doggedly defended his order, insisting that being too permissive with that multitude "having and reputed [to have] vile and infamous origins is extremely dangerous both to the religion and to the state."[63] This reply caused enormous repercussions, and a number of indignant *mestizos*, claiming that the 1780 and 1790 *cédulas* confirmed that they possessed clean blood, threatened legal and other actions. Eventually a number of Indo-European mixed bloods were admitted to this prestigious social assemblage, but persons of Negroid origins remained excluded.[64]

The very existence of these rules and regulations attests to the pervasiveness of racism in Spanish America. The examples cited also suggest the existence of an implicit but widely perceived dualism in colonial society. Despite the law, a few persons of doubtful Spanish ancestry probably purchased land in Santo Domingo after 1768, and several fair-complexioned mulattoes may possibly have lived in the white residential zone in Cartago. But for a black, a mulatto who lacked straight hair, or a person of mixed blood whose black-skinned relatives were commonly known, the credibility gap was just too great. For them the laws could be oppressive as their wording suggests, and the rage felt by these people toward mulattoes who successfully passed for white must have been vitriolic.

Although the free people of African descent were expected not to encroach upon the special preserves of the Spanish population, they were still expected to pay tribute as vassals of the king of Spain. Orders to this effect had been issued by Madrid in 1572, 1573, and 1577, the last one setting the payable tax at "one mark of silver per year, per head."[65] Nevertheless, the rate of payment could be adjusted according to the wealth of the Negroid peoples living in a region, which is to say that both the efficiency of collection and the amounts collected varied rather widely. In Chile in 1696 the *audiencia* of Santiago ordered all free Negroids to pay 1.5 pesos annually if they owned any property or were herdsmen; all others were to pay 1 peso per year. This proclamation apparently failed to achieve the desired results, because in 1699 the same agency threatened those who refused to pay with reenslavement.[66] This situation should be compared with that in Paraguay, where governing officials did not collect tribute since the practice of *amparo*[67] proved much more lucrative. Efforts to collect the tribute in eighteenth-century Venezuela caused large-scale flights into *cumbes* and isolated villages, while in Central America, royal officials tacitly gave up trying to levy such taxes after 1769.[68]

A common means of tribute payment by many blacks and mulattoes was through service in local militia units. Spain rarely could dispatch many regular military units to the New World, so the armed forces that fought the unpacified Indians, patrolled the frontiers, put down slave rebellions, and fought *cimarrones* and pirates were invariably militia formations. In Central America blacks and mulattoes had entered such units in 1615. An all-Negroid artillery company was formed for the defense of Cartagena in 1619, and thereafter segregated companies of *pardos* ("mulattoes") and *morenos* ("blacks") were formed in all the regions of Spain's far-flung empire. Many of the men who initially enrolled in these outfits stayed on, for the military occupation was one of the few in which Negroids could encounter a degree of acceptance. Also, all troops were subject to the *fuero militar*, and this allowed Negroid troops to escape the jurisdiction of prejudiced civilian authorities.

The black or mulatto as foot soldier or noncommissioned officer was easily accepted by colonial society, but the appointment and promotion of Negroid commissioned officers was prohibited by royal *cédulas* in 1643 and 1648.[69] As one might expect, the needs of imperial defense soon overrode all philosophical qualms Madrid might have had about allowing Negroids to command *pardo* and *moreno* units. As a result, in 1678 Vicente Méndez became the first mulatto to reach the rank of captain in the militia in Panama. Others would eventually reach higher positions in Cuba and Santo Domingo, but none exceeded that rank in Chile or Venezuela. In Argentina and Uruguay, no acknowledged Negroid held commissioned officer status prior to 1810.[70]

As officers, blacks and mulattoes were often ignored by their counterparts in white units, and the noncommissioned officers and lower ranks regularly received stringent punishments for minor crimes. Especially in Peru, the *fuero militar* itself was occasionally ignored, and Negroid militia officers were thrown into civilian jails and tried by civil judges. *Criollo* anxiety over what one observer succinctly summarizes as the "*pardo* social issue" prevented the Peruvian militia from ever cooperating as a unified interest group.[71] But particularly after the Seven Years' War in Europe, Spain tended to lean on the military units formed in the colonies for defense against possible British attack. Those Negroids who provided for the defense of Spain's imperial holdings could no longer be officially denigrated as dissolute and dishonorable men, a factor recognized by Charles III when, in the October 1778 Pragmatic Sanction, he listed militia officers as honorable men whose lineage was to be protected.

Outside of military service, the prospects of breaking the lockstep of perpetual poverty and attaining some social advancement remained quite limited. Specialized guilds such as those of the silversmiths and the printers banned Negroid membership, but blacks and mulattoes found their niche as carpenters, blacksmiths, brick masons, and tailors. By 1800 the mass of general artisans in Venezuela were mulattoes, and in Peru, a few of the master weavers were also of mixed blood.[72] As peddlers and owners of small businesses, a few free Negroids became relatively wealthy, especially in Panama and Costa Rica.[73] Nevertheless, extensive penetration into the lower echelons of the tabooed governmental ranks was accomplished only in Panama and Santo Domingo, regions where mulattoes formed the overwhelming majority of the population. In the former region, they were appointed as public secretaries, while in the latter, the scarcity of whites permitted the appointment of "free mulattoes" to a multiplicity of petty administrative posts.[74]

In evaluating the experience of the free black or mulatto in colonial Spanish America, an incident reported by Baron Alexander von Humboldt provides crucial insight. Crossing the interior of Venezuela during the early 1800s, he encountered a *zambo* who referred to himself as a white man. The Afro-Indian had adopted the position that any person of refinement and culture became "white," a supposition that the German naturalist emphatically considered erroneous.[75] Obviously, for many free Negroids, illusions and fantasies were all that made life palatable. As we shall see, however, situations sometimes developed where pretense and quiescence ceased to be acceptable alternatives.

FREE-NEGROID RESISTANCE TO
THE CASTE SYSTEM

Without doubt, the majority of the freed Negroids continued to show deference toward the whites they encountered and accepted their positions as second-class citizens. But on several occasions during the three centuries of Spanish rule, the nonenslaved blacks, mulattoes, and *zambos* threw off their submissive demeanor and publicly manifested their resistance as a unified racial group. On 7 February 1775, for example, numerous Negroids in the city of Lima dressed as city government officials and paraded with a flag on which a chain was drawn to symbolize both the suffering of their enslaved brothers and their own semifree status. The *cabildo* initially declared this demonstration to be treasonous, but the unsettled conditions of the viceroyalty and, perhaps, the audacity of the blacks and mulattoes won for them a conditional reprieve. No formal action was taken, but the Negroids were warned that another such challenge to authority would earn appropriate retribution for the participants.[76]

The most vexing defiance and, at the same time, the most distinctive exhibition of racial consciousness among the free blacks and mulattoes in Peru was the Lambayeque Rebellion of 1779. Three years before the Viceroyalty of the Rio de la Plata had been formed, and the silver mines in Bolivia were transferred to the new administrative unit's jurisdiction. The fiscal position of the Viceroyalty of Peru slumped accordingly, and a *visitador*, José Antonio de Areche, was dispatched by Madrid to attempt the resuscitation of Peru's ailing treasury. In 1779 this official instituted a military tax and levied it upon free Negroids, the ostensible basis for his actions being the fact that Spain and Great Britain had begun hostilities during the year.[77] A registration of these taxpayers was also attempted in an effort to identify potential conscripts, but when Viceroy Manuel de Guiver called upon the blacks and mulattoes to join the militia units, few responded. In October 1779 Guiver blasted their refusal to enlist as "prejudicial and criminal" and threatened that those who failed to enter the service, once they were called up, faced the suspension of their citizenship rights.[78]

It was against this background that the Lambayeque incident transpired. In November of the same year, a white militia captain, Juan de O'Kelly, was dispatched to Lambayeque to institute collection of the new military tax. He met with two mulattoes of the local militia, Captain Celedino Oliva and Lieutenant Manuel Bejerano, and explained to the Negroid townsmen why the money was needed, saying that it was not really a tax, but a "donation." Under the urgings of the mulatto officers, however, the townspeople forwarded a written reply to O'Kelly stating that they considered the requested impost a "violation of the rights of the people;" they also insisted that the tax was a form of tribute, and, in their experience, only Indians had been forced to provide that form of payment.[79]

O'Kelly was displeased with this reply and wrote to *visitador* Areche suggesting that Oliva and Bejerano be cashiered since they had refused to remove their hats in O'Kelly's presence and displayed a general attitude of insolence toward a white person. Areche definitely hoped to smash the defiant protestors, but the Indian unrest that would culminate in the Tupac Amaru Rebellion of 1780 had already reached dangerous proportions, and troops simply could not be spared in order to "bring these miserable people to their senses" [Areche's comment]. Oliva and Bejerano were given official reprimands, but the need for the *pardo* and *moreno* fighting units precluded the assignment of a punishment that might engender further disaffection from the royal cause. Negroid unity and the threatening Indian problem had produced for the Lambayeque townspeople a victory they might long savor.[80]

When not pressed by other considerations, however, the Spaniards did not hesitate to crush Negroids whose intransigence was considered menacing. One such incident resulted from the hostilities between France and Spain that began in 1793. In the New World, the island of Hispaniola became the primary scene of Franco-Spanish conflict. This struggle was further complicated by the fact that the black slaves on the French third of the island (the colony of Saint Domingue) had rebelled in 1791, and some of them had crossed over into Spanish territory where they fought against the forces of both European states. Convinced that some of these fugitives could be effectively employed against the French, the Spanish governor recruited a band, led by a black named Juan Francisco, to carry out guerrilla raids. The group's members were pardoned of all crimes committed against Spaniards and were given salaries and arms; Juan Francisco was made a general.

These black irregulars fought effectively for Spain, but the war in Europe had gone disastrously; in the Treaty of Basel (1795), France obtained the entirety of Hispaniola. As a reward for distinguished service, Charles IV allowed Juan Francisco and 780 of his cohorts to migrate to Cuba. The arrival of these blacks frightened and angered officials in Havana, who warned Madrid that the very presence of these ex-slaves-turned-guerrillas would make Cuban Negroids more difficult to control. The social climate of the Pearl of the Antilles also failed to enthrall Juan Francisco, and following a royal suggestion that they find a more palatable sanctuary in Central America, he and 307 of his followers agreed to move to Trujillo (Honduras). Almost immediately the governor there began complaining that the presence of these swaggering blacks represented a threat to the social order; still, in 1797 Juan Francisco's troops helped to defeat an English attack upon the town. Trujillo's royal officials reported favorably on the fighting prowess of the blacks, but continued to insist that the social situation was becoming increasingly unmanageable because of the presence of the "new citizens."

Charles IV finally came to the conclusion that these ex-slaves had outlived their usefulness and could now be dispensed with. Special orders were dispatched to the governor of Trujillo ordering that Juan Francisco and his men be stripped of "the complex of equality that they had formed in their battles with white men." They were to be disarmed "with caution and divided into small groups," the young men in particular to be shipped to Nicaragua and El Salvador where "they may rapidly be absorbed."[81] Naturally, the leader of the ex-slaves resented the governor's efforts to divide his followers, but once disarmed, there was little that he could do to prevent the execution of these orders. The end came in 1806 when the captain general of Guatemala ordered the cancellation of the lifetime pension that the crown had awarded to Juan Francisco. He traveled to Guatemala City to personally protest this breach of faith, but to no avail. Disgusted and embittered, the black leader and an unknown number of followers migrated to Port-au-Prince (Haiti).[82]

What the Juan Francisco story duly emphasizes is that those blacks and mulattoes who would not accept their lowly positions had little choice except exile or operation outside the law. Many free Negroids were not prepared to go to that extreme, but they could and did intermittently serve notice that they possessed rights that the Spaniards could not ignore with impunity.

BLACK "WHITE MEN" IN SPANISH AMERICA

In stipulating that militia officers and other blacks and mulattoes of repute were bound by his 1778 marital decree, Charles III strove to hinder marriage between Negroid and white persons while paradoxically establishing that certain persons of African origin were first-class citizens. This new attitude became more pronounced in 1783, with the king arguing that, through his fiat, a person of impure origin could be declared cleansed. Soon thereafter, the kings of Spain began granting certificates, called *cédulas de gracias al sacar*, to individuals of African heritage. With the promulgation of a new law on 10 February 1795, legal whiteness was put on a strictly commercial basis. Five hundred pesos obtained for the purchaser a "dispensation from the quality of [being] *pardo*," while for 800 pesos, one could be liberated from the "quality of [being] *quinterón*." Six years later, on 3 August 1801, the prices for the change of classification from *pardo* or *quinterón* to white were raised to 700 and 1,000 pesos, respectively.[83]

At such prices, no more than a few thousand Negroid people – if indeed that many – could afford the purchase of these legal exemptions. There is also some question as to how much "whiteness" was actually being purchased, but for those who could pay the price, otherwise unattainable benefits were at times forthcoming. One of the first purchasers of a *gracias al sacar* certificate was Pedro de Antonio de Azarza, a militia captain stationed in Porto Bello. Azarza wanted his son, Josef, admitted to the University of Bogotá, but the school officials, citing past *cédulas*, argued that the matriculation of persons of mixed blood was prohibited. On 16 March 1797 the Spanish government issued a second certificate to Josef de Azarza, which allowed him to enter the university as a legally white person.[84]

In opening the door to higher education for Captain Pedro de Azarza's eldest son, Madrid specifically stated that this dispensa-

tion would not be extended to other children in the family, and
the decreed entry into the school at Bogotá was not to "serve as
a precedent."[85] This disclaimer was fortuitous, for although the
crown would allow José Manuel Valdés (a man of mulatto–Indian origin) to enter the University of Lima in 1807,[86] an attempt to liberalize the situation in Venezuela would end igno-
miniously.

When Spain had announced the initiation of the *gracias al
sacar* program in February 1795, the city council of Caracas
reacted in choleric fashion:

> How could the . . . white inhabitants of this Province
> possibly admit to their side [as equal] . . . a Mulatto de-
> scended from their own or their father's slaves . . . a
> Mulatto whose relatives find themselves in actual servi-
> tude, a Mulatto whose origin is stained by a long series
> of bastardies and turpitude.[87]

The concern of the councilmen of this Indies governmental
body was patently evident; they simply did not want mulattoes
to become eligible to enjoy the socioeconomic prerogatives that
up to that time had been reserved for those considered white.
Cabildo members clearly believed that some mulattoes would
make haste to avail themselves of the advantages that the new
racial policy provided, and these fears had some basis in fact. In
1796 Diego Mexías de Bejerano, a mulatto doctor, became the
first Afro-Venezuelan to purchase one of the controversial certificates. Because of the procrastination and legal maneuvering
on the part of local officials, it was not until 1801 that Diego
received the document that legally cleansed him of his ancestral
deficiencies. Two years later, on the strength of his father's
dispensation, Lorenzo Mexías de Bejerano applied to enter the
University of Caracas. School officials unanimously rejected his
application, citing the fact that he was not "of clean birth and
purely European origin." In addition, on 20 October 1803 the
faculty of the university forwarded to Charles IV a heated letter
insisting that the very enrollment of the mulatto would cause
the institution to be "eternally ruined."[88] To its credit, Madrid
remained unimpressed by these dire predictions of academic

calamity, and, in a *cédula* dated 7 April 1805, it ordered Lorenzo Mexías de Bejerano immediately enrolled in the faculty of
philosophy.[89] For a change, it seemed that justice had triumphed over bigotry.

But had it really? The decree specifically restricted the advancement of *pardos* to the "middle clerical level."[90] Also, the
young mulatto's hopes of attaining the priesthood were rudely
shattered when Archbishop Francisco de Ibarra, the university
rector, denied enrollment in the school to "the mulattoes Lorenzo Mexías de Bejerano and Domingo Arévalo." Ibarra informed Madrid that to allow these Negroids to become priests
(which seems to have been their intention) would inevitably
result in the "absolute collapse of the honor and esteem" in
which the people supposedly held their clergy. This cleric added
vicious insult to injury by affirming categorically that "there are
no mulattoes worthy of the priesthood."[91]

Naturally, the Mexías de Bejerano family sought legal redress,
and the crown was once again drawn into the fray. We cannot
know what pressures were exerted behind the scenes, but
Madrid suddenly decided that it had done enough for the em-
battled mulattoes. On 6 July 1806 the Council of the Indies
declared that, although the *gracias al sacar* certificate changed
the status of Diego Mexías de Bejerano, the privileges granted
"were not to extend to his children."[92] Furthermore, the ca-
nons and statutes of the University of Caracas were to remain
"inviolate."[93] Since this institution did not formally discard the
limpieza de sangre entry requirement until 1822,[94] we may assume that Lorenzo never did earn academic credits at the university of his choice.

Among other things, this particular case clearly demonstrates
that purchasing a *gracias al sacar* certificate did not necessarily
grant the same rights in every region. There also seems to have
been a question as to which Negroid people could buy these
documents. One finds that in the Río de la Plata area only very
fair-complexioned Negroids (i.e., *cuarterón, quinterón*) were
able to buy the certificates; the rest were considered "totally
irredeemable."[95] If this is a valid assessment of the situation, the
gracias al sacar program is correctly described as a plan whereby

only Negroid persons possessed of wealth and light skin could become the legal equals of American-born Spaniards.

In initiating the sale of *gracias al sacar* writs in 1795, the aims of the crown seem to have been the following:

1. To reward successful Negroids and thereby prevent their possible subversion
2. To remove from the ranks of the blacks, mulattoes, and *zambos* potential revolutionary leaders
3. To create a group of faithful citizens who might act as a counterpoise to the increasingly restive *criollos*
4. To obtain needed funds

No figures are available citing how many of these documents were purchased, and the program was not in effect long enough for a comprehensive judgment to be made as to whether the stated goals could have been achieved. It obviously failed to produce social equality, as seen in the previously discussed Mexías de Bejerano case, which gives indisputable evidence of the implacable opposition of the *criollos* in Venezuela. Elsewhere the program succeeded in temporarily galvanizing both *criollos* and European-born whites to join against mulatto arrivistes.[96]

Only in one area did the *gracias al sacar* certificate provide the expected benefits. An observer in Caracas (Venezuela) in the early nineteenth century recorded that, after a Negroid male purchased the document in question, the women in his family began to wear *mantos* to church services. White women did not seem to be highly scandalized by this social innovation, one reason being black or mulatto women whose families did not purchase these certificates dared not to take similar liberties.[97] Bearing this situation in mind, the *gracias al sacar* writ may be characterized not as a pass to the reserved seats, but a ticket into the bleachers from where the black or mulatto bearer could sneer disdainfully at other Negroids unable to enter the stadium.

THE DEATH OF THE SYSTEM OF *CASTAS*

For almost three hundred years, the Spanish court treated its American vassals who possessed some degree of African blood as second-class citizens against whom the other elements of the population had to be safeguarded. A partial change in attitude had occurred during the last quarter of the eighteenth century, but not until 1806 did the Council of the Indies propose a general modification in the civil status of blacks, mulattoes, and *zambos*. The *gracias al sacar* scheme was judged to be less than satisfactory in its effects, and the council recommended that in the future very few of these exemptions be given. The real problem, in the opinion of the councillors, was that the mass of free Negroid peoples wanted legal and social equality with the whites. Unless they were conceded such parity, His Most Catholic Majesty's American dominions would eventually be faced with the specter of bloody revolt.

Was the Council of the Indies suggesting that the crown strike for social justice, *coûte que coûte*? Hardly. It offered instead a scheme guaranteed to ease the inevitable drift toward social democracy, while simultaneously keeping the mulattoes, *zambos*, and blacks divided and thereby manageable. From then on, a person with any degree of African blood would become the legal equal of a *criollo* if he could prove his descendancy back through four generations of relatives born in wedlock. Millions would be unable to meet this requirement, but those with three generations of legitimate ancestors would know that their unborn children would someday become equal, and so on down the line. Also, the *criollos* might possibly be mollified because race parity would come in stages, and not with one dynamic shock, as in the French Revolution. Everyone still had someone to look down upon since the council's proposal wisely avoided the question of the emancipation of the slave.[98]

This rather innocuous proposal was never adopted by either Charles IV or his eventual successor, Ferdinand VII, but that factor does not diminish the historical importance of the document. Despite the occasional lapses into the insulting and bombastic language of old, the Council of the Indies had finally admitted that a major effort would have to be undertaken in order to incorporate the *castas* into the mainstream of colonial society. But having recognized the need for the introduction of massive social changes, there was no indication that Spain had either the will, the energy, or the power to accomplish them. Obviously, any upgrading of the position of the Negroid castes would engender militant opposition on the part of the *criollos*, and their disaffection was something Madrid could not afford. Spain was damned if it did, and damned if it didn't. Ironically enough, the wars of independence from 1810 to 1825 served as a means to get the mother country off the hook.

6

Negroid Soldiers in the
Wars of Independence

THE ORIGINS OF THE CONFLICT

Spanish America and the thirteen mainland colonies governed by Great Britain were different entities, but the essential problem that both imperial powers faced was strikingly similar: How could the colonial demand for greater autonomy be reconciled with the need for centralized administrative control and procedure? Ultimately, neither European power succeeded in conciliating the colonials, whose attitudes may have been partially dictated by their perception of the mother country. As a result of its victory in the Seven Years' War (1756–1763), Great Britain had virtually eliminated France as a colonial competitor in the Americas. With its awesome economic power and the Royal Navy as its durable ace-in-the-hole, Great Britain could have enforced the tax acts passed between 1764 and 1774. Spain, in contrast, had been slipping steadily for almost two centuries. It had yielded Santo Domingo to France in 1795, Trinidad to Britain in 1797, and the Louisiana Territory to Napoleon in 1801. Spain had issued hundreds of decrees governing such things as the slave trade, and these had been broken with impunity. Thus, while Yankees in the thirteen colonies had good reason to respect the resourcefulness of the British lion, *criollos* found the wrath of the Spanish "paper tiger" tolerable for over three decades after 1776.

Eventually some *criollos* tired of this salutary ineptitude, and, having drunk deeply of the ideas of the Enlightenment, they deemed themselves capable of running their own affairs. In keeping with the ideals of the French Revolution, the *criollos* mouthed the watchwords of fraternity and equality, although socioeconomic parity with the *castas* and Indians was not a contingency they considered favorable. What the new ideas emanating from France, Britain, and the United States seemed to imply to them was that society could be beneficially reconstructed by those who chose to undertake such a task. If the Yankees and French could do it, why not the *criollos*?

As one might expect, there were also a host of political and economic considerations that aggravated colonial discontent. Royal efforts to collect new taxes had resulted in angry uprisings (such as the 1780 *comunero* revolt), and the institution of the intendant system[1] had increased royal control over American activities. Under Charles III and Charles IV, there had been a liberalization of Indies commercial restrictions, but this development had produced mixed results, in that

> the markets of Peru, Chile, and the Río de la Plata were saturated, and while this lowered prices for the consumers, it ruined many local merchants and drained the colonies of their money. From all South America, cries arose that the Metropolis restrain itself.[2]

It was impossible for Spain to have evolved a commercial policy that would have pleased all its heterogeneous Indies interests, and this became the crux of the problem. *Criollo* economic interests in the Río de la Plata region were not in the least concerned with what kind of policy their counterparts in Venezuela or Mexico might desire. And, of course, each group knew better than Madrid what kinds of policies should have been promulgated for its particular area.

Another basic bone of contention was the growing rivalry between European and American-born whites over occupation and control of the upper-level administrative and religious positions in Spanish America. Of some 170 viceroys appointed between 1535 and 1813, only four had been born on the western side of the Atlantic.[3] Furthermore, the vast majority of the

more prestigious governmental posts had long been monopo-
lized by Iberian-born whites. Concerning clerical posts, violent
and un-Christian feuds between *criollos* and Spanish churchmen
had long been a serious problem,[4] and less than 15 percent (105
of 705) of the bishops appointed in three centuries had been
born in the Americas.[5]

The exclusion of the *criollos* from positions at the peak of
the religious and political pyramids should not, however, obscure the fact that during the eighteenth century they had come
to dominate at least the middle level of administration in the
colonial bureaucracy. Perhaps Jaime Eyzaguirre assessed the situation better than he realized when he wrote that "they aspired
not merely to the majority of offices in their respective provinces, but to all of them."[6] Add to this conclusion the one made
by Alexander von Humboldt that "the most miserable European, without education and without intellectual culturation,
thinks himself superior to the whites born in the new continent,"[7] and we have the basis for a struggle that sooner or later
would have laid the Spanish Empire low.

But the many and varied *criollo* grievances were not in themselves sufficient to spark the conflagration that erupted in 1810.
Since its crushing defeat at the hands of the French in 1795,
Spain had been the cockboat inextricably tied to the French
man-of-war. Finally, Napoleon Bonaparte decided that he could
do without the feeble and fumbling Bourbon regime in Madrid.
In March 1808 Charles IV abdicated the throne in favor of his
son, Ferdinand VII; three months later, by means of a clever
ruse, Bonaparte seized Charles and Ferdinand and made them
both renounce the throne. He then dispatched his brother to
Madrid, and by the grace of 100,000 French bayonets, Joseph
Bonaparte became king of Spain.

This brazen act had a paralyzing effect upon Spanish colonial
administration, for although Joseph Bonaparte could remove
officials loyal to the deposed Bourbons, the replacements he
dispatched were often driven from office by colonial mobs pro-
claiming their undying fealty to Ferdinand VII. In Spain itself
in September 1808, there arose the *Junta suprema gobernativa*

del Reino ("Supreme Governing Committee of the Kingdom"), which claimed to rule in the captive king's name and sought to keep the colonies in line, issuing a steady stream of decrees and sending new officials to Spanish America. French forces, however, chased the Junta into Seville, and it temporarily disbanded when they entered the town in April 1810.

The arrival of news of this event triggered decisive action. Between May and September 1810 *criollo* rebels established governing juntas of their own in Buenos Aires, Santiago, Bogotá, Quito, and Caracas. In their view, with the disappearance of legitimate government (the Junta suprema), political power reverted to the "people" – and new leadership knew precisely what the people wanted.[8] When Ferdinand VII finally returned to power in 1814, this great charade came to an end, but the new governments had already been given sufficient time to begin functioning politically.

Why these independence struggles lasted almost fifteen years can be a puzzling matter, especially considering that as of 1800 there were allegedly 2,924,702 *criollos* in Spanish America as compared to 153,405 Iberian-born whites.[9] Furthermore, the reinstated king, although he could send few troops to Spanish America, dispatched virtually none at all during the critical period from 1820 to 1823. Naturally local issues and the conflicts already discussed played a decisive role in the longevity and persistence of these wars, but another reason was the indifference and hostility of many *criollos* to the independence struggles being waged by Simón Bolívar, José de San Martín, and the other liberation leaders. Thus, the conflicts from 1810 to 1825 were often civil wars in which *criollo* revolutionaries triumphed over forces sometimes led by *criollo* loyalists.

Hesitantly at first, but with decreasing reluctance, both sides recruited the Negroid masses into their armed forces. Most of these troops had only a hazy idea of what they were fighting about, and few realized that neither side was an advocate of social revolution. Some changes would eventually ensue, but heavy casualties among black and mulatto males would have deleterious effects.

THE WARS IN SOUTHERN SOUTH AMERICA

The English invasions: a rehearsal
for things to come

In 1806 an English fleet commanded by Sir Home Riggs
Popham reached La Plata estuary and on 25 June 1806 disembarked a 1,500 man force commanded by General William C.
Beresford. The Spanish viceroy, the Marquis de Sobremonte,
departed with indecent haste, and on 27 June the British occupied the city of Buenos Aires. The triumph of the redcoats was
greeted despondently by the *criollo* and European populace,
but the slaves concluded that their hour had come; large numbers abandoned the homes of their masters or simply refused to
work. Believing that the social order was about to collapse,
several leading families sent Juan Martín Pueyrredón, future Argentine patriot, to ask that the British order the slaves to submit.

At least since the Reformation, England and Spain had been
traditional enemies, but the specter of a slave uprising brought
the victor and vanquished immediately together. General Beresford promptly issued an order declaring that all bondmen remain "in the same status in which they had previously been,
without any variation."[10] If any subsequent indications of vagrancy or disobedience on the part of the slaves occurred, Beresford promised to mete out " 'the most rigorous penalties that I
have the power to impose.' "[11] Writing about those turbulent
days to a friend (3 July 1806), Pueyrredón summed up the
situation tensely: "The slaves wanted to proclaim their emancipation, but the movement was thwarted in time."[12]

Two months later, a secretly assembled force led by Pueyrredón and Santiago Liniers surprised the British and forced their
surrender. Word of Beresford's discomfiture reached London,
and a 12,000 man force under General Whitelocke was dispatched to teach the upstarts in Buenos Aires a lesson. The
British force reached the Río de la Plata region in February and
quickly seized the city of Montevideo. But not until June did
Whitelocke move on Buenos Aires, and, upon entering the city

proper, his troops came under violent assault from all sides. In addition to the *pardo* and *moreno* militia units, the grimly resolved citizenry had even armed the slaves. Hot lead, stones, and boiling water descended upon the British as they recklessly tried to force their way up the narrow streets. After only one day's fighting, but with over 3,000 of his troops killed or captured, a demoralized Whitelocke asked for truce terms. On 12 September 1807 officials in Buenos Aires paid official homage to those blacks and mulattoes who had helped to defend the city. A square was renamed Plaza de la Fidelidad ("Fidelity Square"), and, of 686 slaves who had taken part in the battle, seventy were formally emancipated.[13]

Historians have recorded that, as a result of the struggles in 1806 and 1807, the *criollos* gained new confidence in themselves, for they had twice overwhelmed a foreign enemy without any assistance from Madrid. Just as important in the long run, they had also discovered that, if the need arose, the black and mulatto population could be effectively mobilized and transformed into a dependable fighting force. Of course, the American-born whites were not the only parties who could draw a few conclusions from these two memorable episodes. The refusal to work in June 1806 and Beresford's stringent ultimatum again spotlighted the fact that the whites would tolerate no move by the slaves to significantly alter the social status quo. But if blacks and mulattoes could make themselves invaluable to one side in a struggle between white groups, emancipation and bountiful booty might eventually be forthcoming.

The role of blacks and mulattoes in southern South America

During the independence struggles from 1810 to 1820 in the Río de la Plata region, Negroid troops were very much in evidence. Quite conspicuous were the ninth and tenth regiments of *pardos* and *morenos*, formed in Buenos Aires and led by white officers. These units were often "the last to be fed, and the first ones in dangerous positions,"[14] but their fighting prowess made them well known in northwestern Argentina and southern Bolivia. Unfortunately, the conduct of some of the troops engendered a great deal of criticism among certain army commanders. Possibly the most outspoken of these was the Argentine revolutionary hero, Manuel Belgrano, who insisted that "the Negroes and mulattoes are a rabble that is as cowardly as it is bloodthirsty." In his view, if black and mulatto troops could be made to function effectively at all, it was because of the tenacity and patience of their "white commanding officers."[15] Other leaders may have agreed with Belgrano, but since Negroid cannon fodder was often all that was readily available, the manifestation of a more pragmatic attitude became necessary.

Having discovered in 1806 and 1807 that, in exchange for freedom, slaves could be transformed into valiant warriors, it is not surprising that Argentine patriots would devise tactics that allowed them to tap this manpower reservoir. On 31 May 1813 a national assembly, purportedly meeting in Buenos Aires to draw up a constitution, approved a law whereby slave masters would be obliged to sell their male properties in return for compensation. Thanks to this legislative maneuver, over 1,000 slaves were obtained in Buenos Aires province alone.[16] Nevertheless, by September 1816 the need for fresh troops sparked a call for the drafting of more bondmen. On this occasion, slaves owned by churches, clergymen, and European Spaniards who had not taken out citizenship papers became the primary targets; at least 576 were conscripted.[17] The former owners received cash or a promissory note, while the slaves received a uniform and a gun. The latter also were promised freedom after five years' service, but, given the likelihood that they might also be killed, maimed, or badly wounded, the terms of induction were anything but generous.

After the Argentine patriots pioneered the idea, others soon rushed to board the bandwagon. On 29 August 1814 the Chilean rebel government decreed that all male slaves capable of bearing arms and enlisting in the army were "free from that instant." Owners of these bondmen were to be paid for the loss of their properties, but those masters who "concealed slaves" were to be deprived of half their estate and suffer two years' exile.[18] It appears that some owners chose to cooperate, but many of their slaves did not. This reluctance induced the promulgation of still another decree on 4 September 1814. The new law threatened those slaves who failed to report for military induction with 100 lashes and "perpetual slavery at the judgment of the government."[19]

Spanish loyalist forces moving down from Peru crushed the Chilean rebels at the Battle of Rancagua (1 and 2 October 1814), but forcibly conscripted ex-slave soldiers would soon be entering Chile from another direction. As early as 1813, slave owners in the Argentine provinces of Córdoba and Cuyo[20] had been asked to enlist their slaves in the local militia in return for financial compensation. These masters reacted negatively to such requests, and on 16 January 1815 a governmental decree was issued demanding compliance. All male slaves between the ages of eleven and thirty were eligible for this draft, and those examined and accepted for service would be paid for by the revolutionary government.[21] But because this law also failed to elicit an affirmative response from the slavocrats, General José de San Martín finally took matters into his own hands. Since he was also governor of Cuyo, he issued a confiscatory order on 2 September 1816 that allowed special detachments to seize immediately any slave thought to be physically capable of serving as a soldier. Owners were to be paid off in scrip and promissory notes. By means of these tactics, an additional 710 slaves were rapidly placed under arms. When the Army of the Andes finally took the field late in 1816, among its 4,500 troops were the seventh and eighth regiments of *pardos* and *morenos*, which included roughly 1,554 ex-slave infantry men.[22]

Although San Martín considered these Negroid troops basically deficient in their mental capabilities, he nevertheless praised their valor, commenting that "the best infantry soldier that we have is the Negro and the mulatto."[23] Still, the commander of the Army of the Andes scrupulously maintained segregated units for "military reasons and due to the pressure of the social environment."[24] Furthermore, he was not above using psychological deception in order to elicit the final ounce of effort from his *pardo* and *moreno* units. Before the decisive Battle of Maipú (Chile) in 1818, he informed them that if the Spaniards were ultimately victorious, all survivors of African descent would be reenslaved. This fabrication appears to have paid dividends. Four hundred blacks and mulattoes were killed or wounded at Maipú, and their commander-in-chief subsequently acknowledged the decisive role they played in that struggle.[25]

Meanwhile, in the Banda Oriental (the Eastern Republic of Uruguay after 1830), the father of that nation, José Artigas, was putting together a military force composed in large part of blacks and mulattoes. A special battalion of ex-slaves, *los libertos orientales* ("the freedmen of the Banda Oriental"), saw almost continuous service from 1816 until 1820, while another group, the sixth regiment of *pardos* and *morenos*, gained glory as a result of a bayonet charge in the Battle of El Cerrito in 1812. But some of these same troops were also known to have switched sides. In 1817 a Brazilian army entered Uruguay and promised freedom "someday" to all "armed slaves lacking occupation" who would enlist under its banner.[26] This pledge may not seem particularly enticing to twentieth-century readers, but at least one hundred of Artigas's Negroid troops chose to seek employment with the Brazilians. Even so, when Artigas fled to Paraguay in 1820 after many defeats, virtually his only supporters were black and mulatto troops. His last companion was a black soldier named Antonio Ledesma, better known in Uruguayan history as the "faithful Arsena."

Despite the critical role played by the *pardo* and *moreno* units in succoring the birth of political independence in Chile and the Río de la Plata countries, the general attitude toward Negroid people hardly changed at all. What the *criollo* rebels in southern Spanish America set out to do was to destroy Spanish authority and place themselves in power. Upgrading the position of the resident Indian and Negroid populations had never been intended, and, in the end, it did not occur. To be sure, those able to throw off the yoke of slavery improved their position, but many who sought to do so failed to survive the rugged military campaigns in which they participated. Some, like the Negroid troops that fought with San Martín from 1816 through 1823, wound up stranded in Peru and never saw their homeland again.[27]

It has been estimated that one-third of the entire black and mulatto male population in the United Provinces of the Río de la Plata saw service during the independence struggle,[28] but not one among them rose above the rank of captain until after 1820. By that time, Chile was liberated, and the continuing conflict had degenerated into efforts by Buenos Aires to dominate the other Argentine provinces or drive the Brazilians from the Banda Oriental. Perhaps three mulattoes subsequently reached the rank of colonel. The most famous of these was Lorenzo Barcala, known because of his exploits as "the black *caballero*."[29] The only man of known African ancestry who emerged on the diplomatic or governmental level was José Bernardo Monteagudo. This controversial figure, an avowed early patriot, hatchetman, fop, and lodge brother of San Martín, rose to the rank of Peruvian minister of War and Navy (1822) before an assassin's blade cut him down in a Lima (Peru) alley. Recent historical scholarship has persuasively demonstrated that Monteagudo had a mulatto ancestor.[30] His diligent efforts to conceal this origin give credence to the assumption that the wars of independence provided the identifiable Negroids with only a limited opportunity for sociopolitical ascent.

In attempting to determine the reaction of blacks and mulattoes to the revolutionary struggle in southern South America, the lives of two soldiers, the semimythical Falucho[31] and the previously mentioned Colonel Lorenzo Barcala, loom large as contrasting examples. The first man, usually presented as a black, was one of the troops abandoned by San Martín in Peru. He opposed a budding counterrevolt among the disgruntled troops and gave his life shouting his implacable opposition to Spanish tyranny.[32] There is no question about the existence of Lorenzo Barcala, a figure mentioned for his military exploits in Argentine historical tracts. After being promoted to the rank of captain in 1820, Barcala fought against the Brazilians in the Banda Oriental (1825–1828), with the Argentine Unitarians against the Argentine Federalists (1829–1831), with the Federalists against the Unitarians (1833–1834), and again with Federalist forces against the Indians (1835). Unfortunately, during this last campaign, his complicity in an officers' cabal intended

to depose Juan Manuel Rosas[33] was discovered, and Barcala paid
with his life.[34] One is tempted to conclude that a major reason
the colonel was executed was that the cause always nearest his
heart was that of gaining power and glory for himself.

Today in Plaza Palermo in Buenos Aires there stands a magnificent statue of Falucho, and the placard under it states that
he "lost his life because he did not wish to render honor to a
flag against which he had always fought." As for Lorenzo Barcala, his name is found in the thick tomes favored by historians,
but hardly anywhere else. Most people would agree – at least in
the abstract – that those who gave unstintingly of themselves
are the persons who ought to be most fondly commemorated. If
we assume that Falucho actually lived, then the de facto situation is exactly as it ought to be.

Still, this issue can and should be approached from a different angle. Recall that the great military heroes of the independence, Belgrano and San Martín, considered the black and mulatto soldiers to be, at the very least, mentally deficient. Furthermore, while the *Reglamento provisorio de 3 de diciembre
de 1817, dictado por el congreso general constituyente* ("Provisional Ordinance of 3 December 1817, Dictated by the General
Constituent Congress") called upon the "African or free *pardo*"
to submit to militia induction in case of national emergency,[35]
the same document specifically limited Negroid suffrage and all
but eliminated the possibility of their holding political office.[36]
In those days, a simple soldier like Falucho would not have
been allowed to vote no matter what the color of his skin, but
for the upwardly mobile Barcala, the fact that the law discrimi-
nated against people of his racial background could have had a
much more potent effect on his attitudes toward both his country and its leaders. Finally, there is the fact that Barcala never
seems to have commanded anything other than *pardo* and *moreno* units, a situation that was perpetuated because provincial
laws strictly maintained this barrier even after independence.[37]
All of this raises a weighty question: Should an individual
pledge his unconditional loyalty to a nation or cause if equality
is specifically denied to his race?

THE WARS OF INDEPENDENCE IN
NORTHERN SOUTH AMERICA

The *criollos* change their minds

When in April 1810 definite news reached Caracas of the imminent collapse of the Junta suprema in Seville, the patriot party
took action. On the nineteenth of the month it deposed Captain
General Vicente Emperán and all the European administrators
and judges. According to two respected historians, these *criollos*
moved with celerity because "they . . . had to seize the opportunity of independence not only to take power from Spain, but
above all to prevent the *pardos* from taking it."[38] Thus, the
mobilization of large numbers of blacks, *zambos*, and mulattoes, as had occurred in the Río de la Plata region, was not
deemed a desirable option in Venezuela. By default, therefore,
this source of manpower passed uncontested to the royalists. In
the autumn of 1813 a Spanish officer, Tomás Boves, began
organizing the *llaneros*[39] and turned them to attacking the revolutionaries. These Venezuelan equivalents of the Argentine *gauchos* first intimidated and then utterly defeated the patriots led
by Francisco de Miranda and Simón Bolívar.

Boves proved himself a clever practitioner of psychological
warfare, for in addition to engaging the *llaneros*, he declared the
slaves held by the patriots freed. Nevertheless, the rising consciousness of power on the part of the black and mulatto
peoples was also viewed with growing apprehension by other
Spanish commanders. Captain General Francisco Montalvo of
Venezuela informed his superiors that the Negroid troops in his
armies were hardly fervent supporters of Spanish sovereignty.
According to him, the

> *zambos* and mulattoes [are] now fighting to destroy the
> white *criollos*, their masters. . . . It will not take long
> before they start to destroy the white Europeans, who are
> also their masters.[40]

Montalvo argued that the loyalty of these *castas* could be maintained only by granting large numbers of *gracias al sacar* certifi-

cates, or discovering some discreet method whereby the Negroids could somehow count themselves as white.

The logic of this analysis went unquestioned in Madrid, but the proposed remedies were too drastic for Ferdinand VII to accept. The king wished to destroy the *criollo* revolutionaries, but if a social revolution was to be the price, he did not intend to pay it. After 1814 crown policy was based on the assumption that European troops would be dispatched to crush the *criollos*, thereby making the widespread use of *castas* unnecessary.[41]

Ferdinand's decision proved an unmitigated disaster, for the royal troops he hoped to dispatch were never available in the number needed. Indeed, in 1820 troops about to be embarked for America revolted and forced the king to accept a modified version of the Constitution of 1812. Included in the new fundamental law, but aimed primarily at the American colonies, was a declaration that established that "the rights of citizenship" were not to be extended to any person who possessed "on whatever side . . . African origins."[42] If nothing else, the Spanish government was consistent: It never planned to defeat the revolutionaries by catering to the Negroid peoples.

Sharing the aversion for the blacks and mulattoes, and morbidly afraid of what they might do, were the Venezuelan *criollos*. In 1813, for example, Simón Bolívar had condemned in the harshest language the royalist use of *castas* "to make war on white patriots."[43] But after two vain attempts to overthrow Spanish rule, Bolívar had to face the fact that victory for his cause necessitated the utilization of the Negroid masses; he would just have to open Pandora's box and take his chances.

It cannot be determined exactly when the Liberator decided to arm those he distrusted, but, immediately upon landing in Venezuela to begin his third campaign in 1816, he called for the creation of a special battalion of blacks, mulattoes, and *zambos*. He then declared all slaves between fourteen and sixty eligible to join his army, and in 1817 he secured the loyalty of the *llanero* chieftain, José Antonio Páez. In recruiting large numbers of Negroids to fight the royalists, Bolívar had no illusions about the cause of his sudden success in this regard. The attitude of Pedro Comejo, personal bodyguard of José Antonio Páez and known in Venezuelan history as "the first negro," probably typified that of the average black or mulatto soldier:

> I had noted that everybody went to war without a shirt and without a *peseta*, and came back afterward dressed in a fine uniform and with money in his purse. So I wanted to go and seek my fortune and more than anything else to get silver.[44]

Bolívar had learned what Montalvo knew: If the price was right or the rewards substantial enough, most Negroid troops did not care what the war was about.[45]

Bolívar and the racial question

In coming to grips with the racial problem, the patriots gradually managed to evolve a formula that worked effectively until the cessation of hostilities against Spain in 1824 and 1825. The promotion of some Negroids to positions of military importance had to be conceded, but the principle of white supremacy remained preeminent. A case in point is the execution of the mulatto Manuel de Piar in October 1817, on Bolívar's orders. Piar had been made a general, but he also had plotted to replace the Liberator as chief of the patriot army. In this respect, it must be stressed that he was hardly different from Santiago Mariño and other white officers. Piar was considered dangerous, however, chiefly because of his "hatred of the white race" and his alleged intention of initiating a "slave or race war."[46] Mariño was also guilty of conspiracy and conceivably could have been liquidated, but "Piar, a mulatto and a foreigner was a better victim to Bolívar's assumption of authority."[47]

Other forms of racial friction also plagued the heterogeneous forces that Bolívar managed to assemble. Foreign volunteers from Great Britain, France, and the Germanies spoke disparagingly of the lower patriot ranks, the majority of which appeared to be composed of "young negroes and mulattoes, most of them mere boys seemingly not more than thirteen or fourteen years old, tottering under the weight of their muskets."[48] When Bolívar moved the focus of his operation from Venezuela to Colombia in 1819, a fierce controversy developed over the need to obtain slaves in the latter country for military service. Owners were markedly reluctant to release their properties, but Bolívar was adamant: "In Venezuela I saw the free population die and only the enslaved lived. I do not know whether this is politic, but unless we make use of the slaves of Cundinamarca, the same thing will happen again."[49] Five thousand bondmen were allegedly recruited or conscripted into the patriot forces between 1819 and 1821. Apparently *El Libertador* did not want too many whites to die nor too many blacks to live, and his apprehensions in this regard were shared by other leaders as well. After Bolívar's victory at Carabobo in 1821, patriot control in Venezuela and most of Colombia was, in essence, assured. Judging this development exceedingly fortuitous, Juan Antonio Páez, *Jefe Civil y Militar del Estado de Venezuela*, secretly conspired to have the black and mulatto army officers in his territory transferred to the new battle zone in southern Colombia and Ecuador.[50] Negroid leaders were needed as long as there was fighting to be done, but the sociopolitical questions that emerged in the wake of victory were to be settled exclusively by the *criollos*.

A wealth of books about the life of Bolívar has appeared in both English and Spanish, but his racial views have rarely been awarded even a cursory examination. Certainly they are complex, but they hardly substantiate his image as an altruistic patriot. In 1816, for example, Bolívar accepted military assistance from President Pétion of Haiti and promised to abolish slavery if he was ultimately victorious.[51] As president of Gran Colombia,[52] Bolívar was partially able to fulfill his promise, but he opposed the establishment of diplomatic relations with Haiti, claiming (without much evidence) that the latter government was attempting to "foment racial conflict" on the mainland.[53] He considered the black slave to be a "child," and the revolt of Negroid people to be "a thousand times worse than a Spanish invasion."[54] Ruefully commenting in 1825 on the activities of Admiral José Padilla, a mulatto whom he believed to be working to achieve political power, Bolívar wrote that

> equality under the law is not enough in view of the [Negroid] people's current mood. They want absolute equality

on both public and social levels. After that, they will
demand that the darker skinned elements should rule [i.e.,
pardocracia]. This will ultimately lead to the extermination of the privileged class.[55]

As a member of this privileged class, Bolívar wrote on still
another occasion that he had not defeated the Spaniards so that
there would be government by the *pardocracia*.[56] Gradually,
however, it became increasingly difficult to hold the quarrel-
some elements of Gran Colombia together, and on 8 August
1826 Bolívar pessimistically wrote to Páez that

> we shall not speak of the democrats and fanatics, and we
> shall say nothing of the persons of color, for to enter
> the bottomless abyss of these problems is to bury reason
> therein as in the house of death. . . . Believe me, my
> dear General, a great volcano lies at our feet, and its
> rumblings are not rhetorical, – they are physical and very
> real. . . . Consider, my General, who shall restrain the
> oppressed classes? Slavery will break its yoke, each shade
> of complexion will seek mastery.[57]

In keeping with his despondent conviction "that anyone with
a white skin will be fortunate to escape" the race war he sometimes considered inevitable,[58] Bolívar continued to maintain a
vigilance in regard to those Negroids he perceived to be dangerous troublemakers. In 1825 he sanctioned the execution of the
black-skinned Colonel Leonardo Infante, and four years later he
ordered the death of Admiral José Padilla. In both cases, the
real or fancied belief that these men were advocating the rule of
the *pardocracia* was the basic reason for their liquidations.[59]

Yet, it was not in the executions or the angry and morbid
denunciations that the depth and scope of the racial fear was
best dramatized, but in the semisecret communications between
leaders. In a letter written to Bolívar by General Bartalomé
Salom in 1826, the latter complained vigorously about the
twenty-four officers he described as *pardos* who had been detailed to his headquarters. Salom wished to send them elsewhere
since they were "given to bad habits" and their presence was

not desired "in any part of the Republic."[60] We cannot determine how long these mulattoes had been at General Salom's headquarters, and the charges presented do not indicate whether they had actually committed punishable crimes. But at one time or another, the revolutionaries had seen fit to commission these men, and they probably had risked their lives so that Gran Colombia could be created. With the collapse of Spanish resistance, however, it was apparently time that they be reminded that they were not white.

The *criollo* rebels in northern South America shared the same goals as their brethren in the Río de la Plata region and Chile. Unfortunately for them, the wars lasted too long, there were too many Negroid peoples in the territory, and of those who served in the armed forces too many had to be promoted to positions of authority. In addition, an event transpiring on 9 December 1824 had suggested to the *criollos* that accommodation of some kind would have to be forthcoming. Blacks and mulattoes in the town of Petaré had run amuck, shouting, " 'Kill the whites! Long live the king.' "[61] The riot had been promptly quelled, but what might happen in the future if the angry black masses ever found a clever leader? Absorbing a few mulattoes into the upper class was a thousand times preferable to having some embittered half-caste instigate and organize one hundred incidents like the one just described.

Evidence that some racial maneuvering took place can be discerned from political appointments made both before and after the 1830 splintering of Gran Colombia into the smaller republics of Venezuela, Colombia, and Ecuador. Miguel Peña, who may have been mulatto and whom Bolívar once suspected of currying favor with the Negroid masses,[62] became secretary of Home Affairs in the Venezuelan government of José Antonio Páez (1830). There was also ex-Colonel Remigio Márquez, whose part-African ancestry was evident to all observers. Accused of attempting to provoke racial warfare, Márquez was eventually cleared of all charges in 1824 and allowed to take his seat as a senator in the Gran Colombian congress.[63] Still, the rise of the few did not signal that the dam had given way. In none of the new republics did the *pardocracia* seize power, and no

flood of black and brown office seekers ever materialized. Had
more Negroids thought like Manuel de Piar rather than like
Pedro Comejo, developments along these lines might have come
to pass, thereby justifying Bolívar's fears of racial cataclysm. As
it was, *El Libertador* only demonstrated that forecasting the
future was one of the weaker aspects of his repertoire.

THE WARS OF INDEPENDENCE IN
CENTRAL AMERICA AND MEXICO

In Central America virtually no fighting took place because the
criollos easily displaced the European Spaniards. The absence of
military conflict between the white elements meant that opportunities for social and economic advancement for Negroid persons simply did not develop.

Beginning on 15 September 1810 with the cry "Death to the
gachupines," Father Miguel Hidalgo y Costilla led the Mexican
Indian, *mestizo*, and Negroid masses in a campaign to destroy
both the caste system and Spanish rule. Hidalgo really favored
the rule of the *criollos* once independence had been achieved,
but his dream and reality proved unalterably antagonistic. To
the *zambo*, *mestizo*, or Indian, whites who possessed anything
were the enemy; it hardly mattered at all whether the store or
hacienda they pillaged belonged to a *criollo* or European. The
former paid no better wages and rarely displayed any more
compassion than the latter. The result was that the *criollos*,
many of whom were initially sympathetic to Hidalgo's red,
brown, and black insurgents, soon allied themselves with the
gachupines. The priest's idealistic social revolution was thus
smothered in a hail of bullets; he and several of his lieutenants
were executed on 30 July 1811.[64]

Hidalgo's demise did not terminate the battle for social equality, for early in the struggle the fighting priest had commissioned another cleric, José María Morelos y Pavón, to carry on
the fight in southern Mexico. Morelos, a man of Negroid origin,
considered himself a *criollo*,[65] and prohibited the use among his
followers of such appellations as mulatto, *casta*, and Indian
(November 1810). Even so, he soon encountered divisive racial

problems. In the summer of 1811 two discontented *criollo* officers, Mariano Tabares and David Faro, were charged with attempting "to incite the negroids in Morelos's army to slaughter
the whites."[66] The fighting cleric moved with some dispatch to
have Tabares and Faro shot. Later, on 13 October 1811 this
Afro-Indian, who insisted that his parents were "Spaniards,"
issued the following decree:

> Our system is only intended to invest the political and
> military government that now resides in the Europeans
> [*gachupines*] in the *criollos* instead . . . there is no
> reason for those who used to be called *castas* to try to
> destroy each other, for whites to fight Negroes, or Ne-
> groes to fight natives [Indians]. . . . As the whites are
> the first representatives of the kingdom and the first to
> take up arms . . . the whites . . . should deserve our
> gratitude and not the hatred that one has tried to instill
> against them.[67]

Morelos's call for unity reemphasized what the shrewder members of his army should have seen: The lot of the *zambo*, black,
or mulatto would be improved, but *criollos* would monopolize
the economic and political positions of power. Those who had
contrary ideas could expect to share the fate of Tabares and
Faro. Mexican independence was finally achieved when both
the *gachupines* and *criollos*, concerned over the 1820 revolt that
brought liberal elements to power in Spain, combined to effect
the separation. As in the other regions, they achieved it without
allowing the nonwhites to upset the social status quo.

THE LEGACY OF THE WARS
OF INDEPENDENCE

According to Magnus Mörner, as a result of the wars of independence, "many individuals of more or less dark skin were able to
climb the social ladder because of their military merits, such as
Andrés de Santa Cruz, José Antonio Páez, Vicente Guerrero and
Agustín Gamarra."[68] The Swedish historian points out that
these men all became presidents of their respective countries.

The emphasis given to opportunities for social ascent provided by the wars is justified, but this same mobility was by no means enjoyed by all *castas* "of more or less dark skin." The four figures singled out by Professor Morner were probably *mestizos*,[69] and it should not be forgotten that the rise of these Indo-Europeans and their increasing acceptance predated the 1810 to 1825 conflicts. In order to triumph over the Spaniards and win the support of the American populace, the *criollo* revolutionaries realized that they had to make some concessions, but allowing a *mestizo* in the chief executive's chair was not the same as letting a black man occupy it.

Ultimately, the general advantages stemming from the wars and accruing to the Negroids fall into two general categories. Many blacks and mulattoes were still slaves in 1810, but the assorted conflicts dealt a body blow to slavery. Many slaves simply fled their masters and those who entered military service were not reenslaved. Also, the revolutionaries commandeered bondmen (recall San Martín in 1816), paying the ex-owners in scrip or notes that often proved worthless. Thus, many slaveholders not only lost their properties but also suffered financial reverses that made the replacement of the lost hands extremely difficult. The misfortune for many Negroids was that this despicable institution was not similarly wounded throughout Spain's rebellious colonies. In Central America and Paraguay, for example, independence was effected without prolonged hostilities, a circumstance that meant that, while male slaves may have lived longer in these regions, their prospects of manumission were a good deal dimmer.

The second major gain was constitutional but, given the existing conditions, of little except psychological benefit. In the United States after 1865, the freedman hoped for "forty acres and a mule"; instead he got the fourteenth and fifteenth amendments. Quite likely, the blacks, mulattoes, and *zambos* who fought for Spanish American independence wanted much the same thing: money, manumission, land, and control over their own destinies. What all but a handful received, however, were vague constitutional declarations that ostensibly abolished the caste system and recognized the theoretical principle of human equality.[70] The stroke of the pen brashly announcing the arrival of brotherhood proved incapable of eradicating old antagonisms and prejudices. Mulattoes continued to look upon blacks with disdain, and whites held both to be inferior. No longer could a *zambo* be legally prohibited from running for political office, but indirect methods could be utilized to accomplish the same end.

The caste system had given way to the class system, but the free Negroid could not eat, drink, or wear his newly granted paper equality. The first day of the New Order was almost, but not quite, the same as the last day of the old one.

PART TWO

Since Independence

7

Negroid Peoples in the Rio de la Plata Countries

ARGENTINA

The abolition of slavery: 1813–1852

On 25 May 1810 *criollo* rebels forced a *cabildo abierto* ("open town meeting") in Buenos Aires to declare independence from French-controlled Spain and then established an autonomous junta that was to rule allegedly until Ferdinand VII could regain the throne.[1] Although the city had declared its freedom, the rest of the provinces were slow to follow its example, and armies had to be raised both to convince the reluctant provincials to accept liberation and to drive royalist forces from Bolivia. Meanwhile, in the city of Buenos Aires itself, royalist, liberal, and conservative elements struggled to control the junta or to destroy the power of the faction that happened to be in control. In October 1812 a cabal of liberals led by José de San Martín, Carlos Alvear, and Matías Zapiola seized power and called for the election of a national assembly.[2] Brought into existence chiefly to draft a constitution, the Sovereign Constituent Assembly of the United Provinces began its deliberations on 31 January 1813. Dominated and controlled by men whose intellectual influences stemmed from the Enlightenment and the French Revolution, the assembly wasted little time demonstrating its commitment to national reconstruction. On 3 February it passed a law declaring that all children born to slave women since 31 January and any time thereafter were liberated and were to be known as *libertos*. Two days later, the entry into the nation of additional slaves was declared illegal, an indirect method of prohibiting citizens from participating in the international slave trade.[3] Finally, on 23 May 1813 further legislation was ratified creating a financial agency (*Tesorería Filantrópica*, "Philanthropic Treasury") to aid the *liberto* children of slaves and to provide qualified males with free land for agricultural exploitation.[4]

These steps represented the feasible limit at that time, for had the assembly totally abolished slavery, the owners of bondmen would undoubtedly have withdrawn their support from the revolution and probably prevented the creation of a viable and stable republic. It was necessary, therefore, to include other provisions in the act of 23 May 1813 to reassure the slaveholding interests. One such article established that the *libertos* would have to work uncompensated for their mother's owner until they were fifteen years old, and then for five additional years at 1 peso per month.[5] Obviously, the exigencies of war had caused the rapid dissipation of the idealism that had created the *liberto* system. The emasculated program that survived the amendments of 23 May represented an attempt to please all parties. Compromise efforts like this rarely succeed; this one proved even less successful than most.

Meanwhile, slave owners busied themselves discovering means to render the 1813 legislation null and void. As free persons, *libertos* could not be sold, but owners of these youths were eventually dispatching them to other masters, claiming that they were not selling the *libertos*, but only the "rights of patronage" over their service.[6] Such ill-concealed legal chicanery was never invalidated by Argentine courts, so that the de facto status of the *liberto* remained virtually the same as that of his captive mother.

Not only was the *liberto* law rendered impotent but also, despite the 1813 legislation, fresh shiploads of African captives, euphemistically dubbed "servants," began arriving once again in Buenos Aires harbor. A decree issued by Governor Las Heras on 3 September 1824 denounced this quibbling over terms and again banned the traffic, but it surreptitiously continued.[7] Article 14 of the Trade Treaty signed with Great Britain on 2 February 1825 called for both countries to restrain their citizens from participating in the African slave trade,[8] but, again, nothing of consequence was accomplished. In 1829 Juan Manuel Rosas took office for his first term as governor of Buenos Aires. On 15 October 1831 he took a brazen but admittedly candid step by declaring the law of 3 September 1824 null and void. From then on, "servants" could be imported openly, although slave traders were expected to be somewhat circumspect in their dealings.[9] The succeeding governor, Carlos Viamonte, declared all the previous anti-slave-trade laws to again be in effect, but their enforcement remained a haphazard process. Rosas returned as provincial governor in 1835, and in May 1839 he signed another pact with Great Britain prohibiting Argentine participation in the African slave trade. Despite this accumulation of uncompromising legal statutes, in the words of the Argentine scholar Orlando Carracedo, "the traffic nevertheless persisted."[10]

Meanwhile, in the interior provinces of Córdoba and Mendoza, the creation of a *liberto* class brought with it a raft of difficulties. A law of 6 February 1813 provided that the freed youths were to receive land grants. The execution of this statute would have had a tremendous impact on the existing socioeconomic order, for the sparse census data available suggests that the Negroid population in these provinces was comparatively large.[11] Given the political instability and the racial situation, it is not difficult to understand why the proposed land-grant program was never put into effect.[12]

Politically, *libertos* could best be described as nonpersons. Property and tax requirements would have made it impossible for them to vote in Buenos Aires Province anyway, but a law was promulgated in 1821 in Córdoba absolutely banning their participation in the electoral process.[13] Surprisingly, an 1830 statute extended the franchise to *libertos* in Mendoza Province, but only for certain local elections and with the understanding that their patron did not object.[14] It is highly unlikely, therefore, that prior to 1852 the *liberto* vote in Mendoza proved crucial in any election.

Article 15 of the Argentine Constitution of 1853 banned slavery, and, with the abolition of this institution, the totally discredited *liberto* system also passed into history. Unfortunately, no records are available concerning the number of bondmen freed. The uncompromising language of this statute insisted that "in the Argentine nation there are no slaves," but in the city of Buenos Aires some families continued to enjoy the services of unpaid domestic servants.[15] When the last of these retainers either began receiving a salary or died is, of course, unknown. Article 15 also called for the passage of legislation to indemnify ex-slaveholders, and in 1860 Governor Leiva of Santa Fé Province actually established commissions in order to determine how much ex-owners in his territory should receive from the federal government.[16] Typically, no compensation law was ever passed.

In reviewing this sorry record of the nonenforcement of the *liberto* welfare and slave-trade prohibition laws, one is reminded of the countless inapplicable *cédulas* issued by the kings of Spain over a period of three centuries. Did the delegates who produced the 1813 legislation concerning *libertos* really intend to enforce its provisions? Quite likely they did, but, before laws can be enforced nationally, a federal constitution of sorts, a chief executive, and a national enforcement agency had to be created. Not until 1853 and 1854 were the first two of these provided in a *de jure* manner, and by that time the first *libertos* were at least forty years old. The delegates to the 1813 assembly had probably hoped that a constitution could soon be drawn up and ratified and that there would be a national government shortly thereafter. In the meantime, there were good gestures and hope that righteous men would act accordingly. Overall, this highly unflattering record of noncompliance and evasion gives credence to the theory that in Argentina slavery was never abolished; it literally died of old age.

The free Afro-Argentine: 1813–1852

Although the action taken toward slaves could charitably be described as ambivalent, the overall attitude of the *criollo* revolutionaries toward the free Negroids can only be characterized as distrustful. Blacks and mulattoes had been denied the right to vote for delegates to the 1813 Constituent Assembly,[17] but not until 1817 did those seeking to build a national government reveal their full enmity. In Chapter 3, Article 7 of the *Reglamento provisorio* ("Provisional Constitution"), approved by the General Constituent Congress on 3 December 1817, "those born in the country who had origins by whatever line from Africa" were granted the franchise, but with certain important restrictions. Anyone who was the son of a freeborn father could vote, while political office was open to those who "were of the fourth degree removed" from slavery.[18] The malevolent intent buried in this ambiguous legal jargon becomes evident if the provisions of the law are contrasted with the existing situation. As of 1822 in the city of Buenos Aires and the surrounding area, about one quarter of the population was Negroid, with roughly 45 percent of that group enslaved.[19] Only a small percentage of the free could have proven that their parents had enjoyed the same status, and perhaps one in a thousand could have verified for an electoral commission that his great grandfather had been a free man. Clearly, the Congress did not want Negroids to vote, but it also wanted to maintain the formal trappings of liberty, fraternity, and equality. Article 7 of Chapter 3, like the poll tax and the literacy test prevalent in the southern United States between 1886 and 1964, effectively attained these ends.

On the provincial level, the whites were much less concerned about disguising overt discrimination. The aforementioned 1821 law in Córdoba also banned free Negroids from voting, and, while an 1829 law opened the public schools to the "sons of *pardos*,"[20] efforts to penetrate the barriers to higher education precipitated a twelve-year battle. In 1832 José María Pizarro, a mulatto, brought suit against the University of Córdoba for refusing to admit his son. After almost a year of civil litigation, Governor Benito Otero declared the school open to all who could qualify academically. Nevertheless, on 6 April 1836 university officials obtained a court order allowing them to reject any person who failed to qualify under the "clean blood" provisions of colonial times.[21] The object of this legal maneuver seems to have been the expulsion of Paulino Rafael de Paz, another mulatto who had entered the university and applied to obtain degree status. Paz's application was rejected, but the last battle did not occur until 18 December 1844. At the time, Governor Manuel López signed a decree stating that no more *castas* could be enrolled in the university. Of those already enrolled, none could (1) study civil or common law; (2) complete more than the four-year course in philosophy; or (3) transfer into the four-year course in philosophy if they were not already in it.[22] Not until 8 November 1852 was a law promulgated prohibiting discrimination against nonwhites in public facilities. When mulattoes or blacks actually graduated from the University of Córdoba is unknown, but the Pizarro case accentuates the fact that political independence in Argentina did not bring in its train a fundamental reduction in the degree of the old caste prejudice.

Nevertheless, it was in and around the city of Buenos Aires that the most crucial racial drama was ultimately played out. The overwhelming number of the free Negroid population, by agreement with the authorities, lived in segregated but semiautonomous districts,[23] referred to derisively as *barrios de tambos* ("districts of the drums"). During the 1820s powerful organizations grew up in these districts called *sociedades de morenos africanos* ("societies of black Africans"), and although they were restricted in their membership, these groups provided important benefits to their members. Funds were collected in order to manumit enslaved brethren, educational activities were sponsored for children, and occupational tools were furnished to those members needing them.[24] The most powerful of these societies obtained sites outside their districts where public dances and ceremonies could be held. Whites and mulattoes could always watch such public festivities, but the former were banned from participation, and the latter were usually discouraged.[25]

The more liberal political elements, including celebrated figures like Manuel Belgrano and Bernardino Rivadavia regarded the Negroid population as generally useless,[26] but Juan Manuel Rosas, governor of the province after 1829, thought otherwise. Regularly on Sundays, this sagacious politico visited the *tambos*, making speeches, shaking hands, distributing gifts, and tirelessly voicing his respect for blacks and mulattoes. The seeds of goodwill planted by the governor would soon sprout and provide him with a rich harvest. After 1835 Rosas made himself de facto dictator of all Argentina.[27] From that date until 1852, he would continuously be fighting Indians, European and Latin American opponents, and exiled dissident elements. Black and mulatto troops were a vital element in Rosas's legions, despite the fact that they served in segregated units, a contingency the governor helped to perpetuate. Occasionally their ranks became desperately thin, but Rosas solved this difficulty by decreeing an annual capitation tax and summarily inducting into his forces all free Negroids who lacked the money to pay.[28] In addition, many black and mulatto cooks, porters, and household servants were members of an effective espionage network that allowed Rosas to keep himself attuned to the discontents voiced by middle and upper-class elements.[29] Despite the fact that his ceaseless military campaigning eventually decimated the Negroid male population in Argentina,[30] the collapse of the Rosas dictatorship in February 1852 was not greeted with rejoicing among the black and mulatto citizenry. Under Juan Manuel, they had come to occupy "a place in society".[31] The republican leadership that followed would not need their support and paid them little attention.

The emergence of a national racial philosophy

Even before the ink was dry on the Constitution of 1853, certain native thinkers had begun plotting a national future in which the Afro-Argentines would play virtually no role. In fact, in intellectual and academic circles, an insidious pseudo-scientific racism gradually was sinking deep roots. The assumptions upon which these arguments rested were initially expounded in the writings of Juan Alberdi, Father of the Argentine Constitution.[32] In his *Bases y puntos de partida para la organización política argentina* (*Bases and Points of Departure for Argentine Political Organization*), written in 1852, Alberdi laid down the celebrated maxim, "To govern is to populate." Since he also believed Europe to be "the most civilized land on the globe," the immigration of Europeans was deemed requisite for future national development.[33] The delegates to the constitutional convention unquestionably shared Alberdi's ideological bias, for they had an article written into the final document that began: "The Federal Government shall encourage European immigration."[34] For nonwhites, Alberdi had only words of disdain, claiming that "to populate is not to civilize, but to brutalize, when one populates with Chinese and with [the] Indians of Asia and with Negroes from Africa."[35]

Producing a variation on this theme was Domingo Faustino Sarmiento, author, educator, and president of Argentina between 1868 and 1874. In the 1840s he had argued that the climate and physical terrain of Argentina had exercised a crucial influence upon the formation of the national character.[36] Two generations later, heavily influenced by the Social Darwinist and Positivist views then in vogue, Sarmiento shifted his ground and professed the idea that a nation's biological heritage has a predetermining effect upon its psychic character. An unabashed admirer of the United States, Sarmiento believed that the Anglo-Saxon, unlike the Spaniard, had been wise not to mix his blood with Indians and Africans. Although Sarmiento did not go so far as to condemn him utterly, he held that miscegenated man was an inferior creature. Marshaling these opinions in his 1883 book, *Conflictos y armonías de las razas en América* (*Conflicts and Harmonies among the American Races*), Sarmiento declared that the Afro-Argentine had made no important contribution to the national culture. He further reported, with some satisfaction, that not only was the Negroid Argentinian disappearing, but also "in twenty more years, you will have to go to Brazil" in order to find black-skinned persons.[37] His solution to the nation's racial ills was the same as Alberdi's: Encourage the entry of European immigrants.

A devotee of the theses presented in *Conflictos y armonías* was Carlos Octavio Bunge, whose *Nuestra América: Ensayo de psicología social* (*Our America: Essay of Social Psychology*) originally appeared in 1903. This publication represented the first systematic study of racial types undertaken by an Argentine, although Bunge was hardly what one would call a dispassionate observer. Like Sarmiento, the author of *Nuestra América* was knee-deep in the Positivist doctrines of his epoch. He insisted that "each physical race is [also] a psychic race,"[38] and, hypothesizing from this premise, he sought to determine what psychic traits the African and Indian have contributed to the formulation of the Argentine national character. Bunge roundly denounced the indigenous people, but it was the Afro-Argentine who drew his greatest wrath. He reckoned that the legacy of this "rabble" was "servility," "corruptibility," "vanity," and "swollen ambition" (*hipertesía de la ambición*).[39] Obviously, Argentina did not need blacks and mulattoes, and miscegenation was a catastrophic mistake. Predictably, his recipe for greatness was the continued stimulation of European immigration.

The last but most academically respected of these authors was José Ingenieros, physican, publisher, and, in his prime, supposedly "the most widely read of all writers in Spanish."[40] Convinced of the African's innate inferiority,[41] he argued that the ideas of Alberdi and Sarmiento concerning white supremacy and the need for European immigration were identical, and that Presidents Urquiza, Mitre, and Avellaneda had all been advocates of the same concepts.[42] After the Bolsheviks took power in Russia in 1917, Ingenieros announced his allegiance to the Communist cause.[43] Perhaps he could support a theoretically classless society while advocating white supremacy because there was an ocean between his nation and the Soviet Union.

The theories and arguments of Alberdi, Sarmiento, and the others may seem peculiar in that, even in 1852, Argentina was considered a "white" nation. They become tangible only if it is understood that these authors looked upon most Argentine whites as *mestizos*.[44] Their intention was to create a people who would be physically and culturally interchangeable with the inhabitants of Spain, France, and Italy. This goal achieved national acceptance, and a Europeanized Argentina became a reality. Between 1870 and 1914 the nation welcomed over 2 million immigrants, of whom only about 2 percent were non-Caucasian. On the eve of the First World War, 30.3 percent of the population were foreign-born.[45]

The Afro-Argentine since the
abolition of slavery

The odd man out in this metamorphosis of a people was the Afro-Argentine. Blacks and mulattoes had been good enough to shoulder a rifle from 1810 to 1852, but, in a nation bent on whitening its appearance, Negroids had lost their utility. A kind of tacit agreement that their presence was neither necessary nor desirable may well be the reason that many Argentine scholars have completely ignored the Negroid element in their discussions of post–1852 Argentine national history.[46] As to the disappearance of the darkskinned population after 1852, few records seem to exist except in the state and city of Buenos Aires. From 1825 to 1852 the death rate of the blacks there exceeded the birth rate, and contagious outbreaks such as the yellow fever epidemic of 1871 exacted a terrific toll among blacks and mulattoes in the Buenos Aires urban area.[47] The Constitution of 1853 declared all inhabitants equal,[48] but many bars, cafes, and dance halls in that city continued to refuse Negroid customers; until 1880 a number of theaters unhesitantly prohibited their patronage.[49]

Particularly critical to the Afro-Argentine was the issue of education. On 27 October 1852 a group of Negroid citizens obtained an audience with the governor of Buenos Aires Province and demanded that the separation of white pupils from "students of color" cease. The rector of the University of Buenos Aires, José Barros Pazos, came to their defense, but in 1857, despite continued agitation, black and mulatto students were registered at only two of the twelve public schools in the city.[50] Segregation had been confronted but hardly destroyed; meanwhile, the general public remained totally indifferent, a sure sign that the Negroid element was not held in the highest esteem.

In the face of these indignities, Afro-Argentines published newspapers, such as *La Raza Africana* and *El Proletario*, but none of them lasted for more than five years. A man who articulated much of the frustration and despair experienced was the mulatto intellectual, Horacio Mendizábal, who asked,

Would you be horrified to see a Negro seated as the President of the Republic? And why, if he was as learned as the rest of you, righteous as the best of you? Just because the blood of his veins was browned by the African sun on the forehead of his grandfathers? Would you be horrified to see seated in the benches of the Congress a man that you call with so much disdain "mulatto," just because his forehead is not the same color as yours? If this is what you think, I am ashamed of my country and lament over its ignorance.[51]

Statistics for the city of Buenos Aires in 1887 placed the number of persons of African origin and *chinos* [?] at 8,005, while the second national census in 1895 established the total at 8,000.[52] The *barrio* of Barrancas was their largest residential ghetto, but after 1900 the number of Italians in this district exceeded the total of Negroids. The third national census listed 523 *africanos* as citizens of the nation in 1914.[53] Since that time there has been no census in which information concerning Afro-Argentines has been sought. It is ironic that in 1920 the government could tell how many Japanese immigrants there were in Argentina,[54] but how many black and mulatto citizens there were, nobody seemed to know or care.

Still, the Afro-Argentine has not disappeared entirely. As of 1971 perhaps 3,500 lived in the city of Buenos Aires and its suburbs.[55] Efforts to determine what these persons think about their position in the national society produced some interesting opinions. All but one of the blacks and mulattoes queried denied that racial problems existed. The sole exception, Enrique Nodal, was a mulatto whose son had been refused admission into an exclusive kindergarten (1967). The director explained that to admit a mulatto child might "cast doubts on the quality of the institute." Nodal also reported that a "mixed [racial] couple" had a difficult time since "few parents . . . accept with equanimity [the fact] that their son or daughter is married to a person of color."[56]

A number of Negroids, while careful to point out that they had not personally suffered from discrimination, had curious complaints to record. One gentleman remarked bitterly that Afro-Argentines received "almost automatic identification" as singers, dancers, and musicians. Still another lamented that "we are identified only with the drum." But the most comprehensive and revealing statement came from Professor Héctor Obello. After affirming in impassioned terms that no one had ever raised a question about the color of his skin, he suddenly made the more candid observation that "in our country we are too few to constitute a problem."[57]

In Buenos Aires today one may see a mulatto on the street or even in the lower realms of governmental service,[58] but, for someone searching for a settlement of native Argentine Negroids, a trip into the interior is necessary. Located about sixty-five kilometers southeast of the city of Buenos Aires is the town of Chascomús, where there exists a colony of perhaps ten blacks and over 100 mulattoes.[59] The most heralded attraction in this otherwise nondescript community is the *Capilla de los Negros* ("Chapel of the Blacks"), built in 1835 by the ex-slave Luciano Soler Alsina and made a national historical monument in 1950. Among other artifacts to be found in the old church building is the statue of the black Virgin Mary, reputedly brought from Africa by Christianized slaves over two centuries ago.[60]

The attitude of the Afro-Argentines in the town is representative of the sense of malaise that their status probably causes them to feel. Guardian and caretaker of the shrine is Señora Guillermina Eloísa González de Luis, granddaughter of Luciano Alsina. A spry and witty lady of eighty years, she replied to my salutation of "Good afternoon, I am an Afro-American," with a no-nonsense "I am Afro-Argentine, so what?" She evinced a lively interest in the life styles of persons of African origin in other parts of the Americas but also reported that most of the mulattoes in the town displayed very little interest in the *capilla* or in their Afro-Argentine heritage.[61]

The overall attitude of Señora González de Luis must be contrasted with that of another Chascomús black, Pedro Piñero, who, when asked by a newspaper reporter whether racial prejudice had been experienced by any of the Negroids in the town, replied, "It's better not to talk about these things. . . . I married a white woman and my sons are not Negroes." When the reporter continued to ask questions about racial topics, Piñero "angrily refused to answer."[62]

As a result of European immigration, the Afro-Argentine lost any economic importance he may have had as a laborer; since then, his status has become that of historical curio. Yet, the most important cultural contribution of the Afro-Argentine was not made until after he had become economically irrelevant. Neither the *gauchos* nor Rudolph Valentino created that dance called the "tango"; cultural investigators have now duly demonstrated that it was born of the Afro-Argentine.[63]

URUGUAY

The abolition of slavery: 1825–1853

The Banda Oriental of Uruguay was long an area of contention between Spain and Portugal. In 1814 it fell under the control of the United Provinces of the Río de la Plata, but in 1816 José Artigas, a local statesman and former chief in the United Provinces forces, declared its independence. In 1817 an army from Brazil invaded the area, defeated Artigas, and in 1820 formally annexed the territory, naming it the Cisplatine Province. Not unnaturally, a number of the region's Spanish-speaking inhabitants were dissatisfied with this state of affairs, so on the night of 29 April 1825 a group of these dissidents (known historically as the "thirty-three"), crossed the Río de la Plata from Buenos Aires and began recruiting an army. Their motto was "liberty or death," but, in fact, incorporation of the territory into the United Provinces was their immediate goal; "liberty" should therefore be interpreted as meaning freedom from the Portuguese-speaking Brazilians.

A little-known bit of history is that two of the thirty-three immortals were black slaves: Dionisio Oribe and Joaquín Artigas.[64] After winning a few victories over Brazilian forces, the thirty-three felt strong enough to call a constituent assembly on 7 September 1825. They declared that all persons born to slaves from that date on were freed, but they expected that such magnanimity be repaid with the Negroids' gratitude. The rebels then opened their enlistment rolls to all blacks and mulattoes, whether free or slave.

An assembly representing the United Provinces of the Río de la Plata had been meeting in Buenos Aires, and it now openly moved to provide military assistance for the thirty-three and their followers. Not unexpectedly, Dom Pedro II, the Brazilian emperor, interpreted this action as a threat and declared war on 10 December 1825. During the three-year struggle that followed, both Buenos Aires and Rio de Janeiro appealed to the British government for assistance and mediation. The clever, calculating foreign minister, George Canning, knew well that if he favored either side, British merchants in the less-succored nation would suffer. His conclusion was that a buffer state was the best solution to the problem, and, once both sides had exhausted themselves, his decision prevailed.[65] On 18 July 1830 the Eastern Republic of Uruguay was officially founded.

Interestingly enough, a provisional legislative assembly had begun to act on the slavery issue even before the nation had officially been founded. A law of May 1829 expressly granted freedom to any slave who had personally contributed to the liberation struggle. A free-womb law of 7 September 1825 was written into the national Constitution of 1830 in addition to provisions ending the overseas slave trade and liberating all slaves whose masters had fled to Brazil.[66] In 1837 still another measure placed the blacks and mulattoes (called *libertos*) freed by the 1825 and 1830 provisions under the guardianship of public trustees, who were charged with regulating their conduct and providing material aid. Finally, in 1841 the government ratified a treaty with Great Britain abolishing the external slave trade.

The forgotten men in this flurry of lawmaking were the slaves born prior to 7 September 1825, and those who could not demonstrate that they had actively participated in the conflict from 1825 to 1828. Many Negroid ex-soldiers in the city of Montevideo were not contented with their lot either. Early in May 1832 a planned revolt of slaves, ex-soldiers, and other freed blacks and mulattoes was uncovered by the government. The mastermind behind the plot was a black named Santa Colombo, who had served for some years as military aide-de-camp to the president of the Republic, Fructuoso Rivera. Santa Colombo had planned to seize the fortress in the capital, reduce all whites to a position of vassalage, and establish a state ruled by Afro-Uruguayans. Once the plot was discovered, all the ringleaders were jailed, condemned to death, or, in the case of the slaves, sentenced to 200 lashes.[67] A movement for clemency soon developed, however, since many of those implicated had taken part in the independence struggle. Demonstrating an unusual agility in the use of legal language, the Uruguayan Supreme Court ruled that the convicted blacks and mulattoes were not "responsible persons." Having now established a basis for concluding that the convicted Negroids had not committed a major crime, the death sentences were changed to deportation and jail terms.[68]

As the reader may have come to expect, the ultimate extirpation of slavery in Uruguay came about as a result of another Armageddon. Late in 1842 Fructuoso Rivera (who had recovered the office of president as a result of a coup in 1838) freed all his slaves and then conscripted them into the national army. Modern historians have since established that about 4,000 slaves were introduced into Uruguay from Brazil between 1829 and 1841, their arrival aided and abetted by the sworn defender of the Constitution of 1830, Fructuoso Rivera.[69] The development that caused this tyrant to shift gears and suddenly assume the role of emancipator was that across the river, Juan Manuel Rosas, a more resourceful dictator, was planning Rivera's demise. The latter had aided the Argentine exiles and allied himself with anti-Rosas elements in Argentina. Rosas really planned to reincorporate Uruguay into Argentina, although initially he was supporting the pretentions of Manuel Oribe, the ex-president whom Rivera had unlawfully deposed in 1838. In a decisive battle fought at Arroyo Grande (6 December 1842), Rivera's army was crushed, and its leader sought asylum in Paraguay. On 12 December of that year, Joaquín Suárez, the new president, declared slavery abolished, and all male slaves were drafted into the army "for whatever time that is deemed necessary."[70] Owners whose Negroid properties had been accepted for military service were promised compensation, but the slaveholders of Montevideo (the capital) openly defied the decree. Not until the Rosas–Oribe forces reached the gates of the city in February 1843 did they grudgingly comply.

The seige of Montevideo, possibly not the major but certainly the longest event of what Uruguayans called "The Great War," lasted until 1851. Of the approximately 4,000 defenders who manned the walls of the citadel in 1845 and 1846, at least 690 were slaves conscripted into the third, fourth, and fifth battalions. The Oribe–Rosas force already included blacks and mulattoes from Argentina, but additional Negroid warriors would prove useful. In October 1846 Oribe abolished slavery in Uruguay and then set about drafting all the darkskinned Uruguayan males he could find. In numerous battles, Negroids fought Negroids for no other reason than money and a promise of freedom from either side.

Finally, on 2 May 1853 law 316 proclaimed the total abolition of slavery, but exactly what this piece of legislation accomplished is not easy to determine. The 1837 Guardian Law had been widely ignored, and, despite Suárez's decree of 12 December 1842, not a peso of compensation was ever received by complying slaveholders.[71] The law of 2 May 1853 was in keeping with this syndrome of legislative double cross because it allowed owners to keep *libertos* under sixteen in their power as "wards."[72] Some owners had their slaves detained in basements and other improvised prisons until they could be loaded aboard ships and dispatched to Brazil or Cuba for sale.[73] In addition, newspaper advertisements concerning the sale of bondmen continued to appear months after the May 1853 law had been promulgated.[74] It is therefore impossible to ascertain when all the slaves in Uruguay were liberated, for, unquestionably, a handful continued to be subject to the rigors of involuntary servitude after the Emancipation Law was put into effect. But as long as the mass of the population believed that the institution had been abolished, the law had served its purpose. As in Argentina, slavery seems to have eventually died of old age.

The Afro-Uruguayan since abolition

Prior to 1810 both regional statutes as well as royal *cédulas* prohibited freed Negroids from holding municipal offices, entering the priesthood, or carrying arms. In addition, local law forbade them from inheriting land. On top of these restraints, in 1807 the Montevideo *cabildo* had banned "the public dances of the negroes," an ordinance that Chief of Police Luis Lamas would finally modify in 1839.[75] This magistrate proved somewhat more sympathetic to the needs of the African-oriented portion of the town's population; he allowed "dances with drums" on special church feast days, but under no circumstances could they be continued after 9:00 P.M.[76] After 1853 these restrictive public ordinances were gradually forgotten or discarded, but the Afro-Uruguayan remained essentially a second-class citizen. Note that during the conflict from 1843 to 1851 no Negroids rose above the rank of sergeant in Uruguayan armies. For those who took part in the War of the Triple Alliance against Paraguay (1864–1870), however, positions in the officer corps gradually became available. In 1894 Feliciano González, who had joined the army as a private in 1837, reached the rank of colonel.[77] But he received no further promotion, and, for whatever reason, no other Afro-Uruguayan has managed to attain that rank to this day.

On other fronts, blacks and mulattoes encountered many frustrating difficulties. In 1860 Santiago Botano, the Montevidean chief of police, barred the hiring of Negroids as night watchmen. For many years after 1853 they were informally barred from some restaurants and theaters. Then, in 1878 the prospect of their attendance in public schools caused a rapid rise of tension and turmoil in the capital city. This issue was finally defused by legislative action, but debates on the measure provide a penetrating insight into the development of post-1853 race relations in Uruguay. José Pedro Varela, sponsor of the Primary Education Acts, avoided any discussion of racial friction but pounded away on the theme that education must help remove class differences. His major opponent, Lucas Obes, insisted that his enmity for Afro-Uruguayans was not racial; he merely opposed the integration of a lower social class with a higher one.[78]

These semantic gymnastics reveal that by the late nineteenth century racial prejudice had become a taboo; only class prejudice now existed. The new ethos suggested that Negroids were generally amoral, lazy, and mentally dull. Still, if an individual obtained an education or money, he could rise and would then be acceptable to whites of the same class.[79] In reality though, most blacks and mulattoes were unskilled laborers, a situation that meant that their prospects of social ascension were slim. The class-prejudice argument, like the *buena guerra* rationalization of old, was a logical construct designed to anesthetize otherwise potentially troubled consciences. The moral tragedy is that it succeeded only too well.

In regard to his economic position, the Afro-Uruguayan has made little progress in the twentieth century. A survey taken by the popular magazine *Marcha* in May 1956 noted that of some 14,979 barbers, hotel porters, bus drivers, conductors, guards, and store clerks, exactly eleven were black or mulatto.[80] The same journal established that since 1900 the National University of Uruguay had graduated only two lawyers, one doctor, one pharmacist, and one midwife of African descent.[81] The effects of slavery and the low economic level of their ancestors undoubtedly tended to inculcate in young Negroids the idea that people of their color were always to be in that same position. Nevertheless, this does not wholly explain why there were so few Afro-Uruguayan barbers or bus drivers. The Uruguayan scholar Ildefonso Pereda Valdés seems to have reached a valid conclusion:

> We believe that racial discrimination [is] deeply embedded in our society, with much deeper roots than that which is supposed. . . . It is a barrier which closes to the Negro people of Uruguay their integral development. . . . In Uruguay, concerning the Negro, Jim Crown [sic] is applied despite the guarantees of the laws and constitution.[82]

Afro-Uruguayans have not chosen to accept their lot without protest. Racial unity has traditionally been their response to discrimination. Beginning in 1872 with the publication of the journal *La Conservación*, the emphasis has been on the need to bring together the "collectivity," that is, all the blacks and mulattoes in the country.[83] Although *La Conservación* lasted only three months, another journal, *La Verdad* (*The Truth*), proclaimed between 1911 and 1914 "the necessity of union and the common effort for the realization of the common goal."[84] The most militant example of the Negroid press in Uruguay was *Nuestra Raza* (*Our Race*), first published in 1917, but chiefly in evidence between 1935 and 1948. Incidents of discrimination in housing, transportation, and the public service fields filled its pages. With strident voice, its editors urged that "for the rights of our collectivity . . . unite."[85]

An opportunity to determine just how the concept of the collectivity was really viewed came in 1937, when a group of Afro-Uruguayan intellectuals founded a political party, the *Partido autóctono* ("Indigenous Peoples' Party"), designed to elect Negroids to the national assembly. In the pages of *Nuestra Raza*, the party chieftains made it clear that action on the political front had to be taken because

> all of us know perfectly well that in more than a hundred cases, the approval of an employee or the naming of an official has certainly not depended . . . on the greater or lesser qualification of the candidate . . . but on the greater or lesser pigmentation of this or that one.[86]

The congressional elections of 1937, nevertheless, told an unmistakable story: The *Partido autóctono* met complete disaster at the polls. Today, social clubs like the *Asociación cultural y social uruguayo* ("Uruguayan Cultural and Social Association"), founded in 1941, continue to prosper, demonstrating quite clearly that Negroid Uruguayans feel a need to unite.[87] Politically, however, the collectivity lacks both the consciousness and the courage to cast its votes for those who would defend its rights.

In 1842, 6,000, or 19 percent, of the 31,000 inhabitants of the city of Montevideo were Negroid. Between 1850 and 1930, however, slightly more than 1 million Europeans entered the country.[88] The Afro-Uruguayan has virtually been drowned in this tidal wave of Caucasian blood, a development some Uruguayan politicians must have deemed propitious, for in 1886 they absolutely prohibited the immigration of any person of African origin into the republic.[89] Presently there are perhaps 60,000 blacks and mulattoes in a nation of about 2,800,000 – less than 2 percent.[90] The crowning irony is that, despite this small number, bias against the Afro-Uruguayans has hardly disappeared. A 1956 survey of 694 students between the ages of eleven and twenty-one presents revealing information about their attitudes (see table 11).

Table 11. *Racial attitudes of Uruguayan white students*

A white	If he (she) were black (%)	If he (she) were mulatto (%)
would not marry a person	77	72
would not accept a brother-in-law or sister-in-law	42	39
would not accept a fellow student	14	9
would not invite a person to a birthday party	62	61
would not accept a neighbor	14	12
would not accept a servant	16	13

Source: Paulo de Carvalho Neto, *Estudios afros* (Caracas, 1971), pp. 216–18, 225.

This study may well be the only one of its kind published about the Uruguayan racial situation. Although the figures speak for themselves, they take on an additional significance when we consider that school officials only reluctantly allowed this study to be undertaken, and the majority of the student respondents denied that any racial bias existed in the country.[91] The outstanding Afro-Uruguayan poet Pilar E. Barrios once wrote a poem in which she advised young blacks and mulattoes in this fashion:

And he who would tell you, through sign or gesture
That since you are born of a humble race,

You are therefore an inferior being,
Then demonstrate as evidence
That never was intelligence
At odds with color (of skin)[92]

Unfortunately, the great prejudice in Uruguay seems to be that the white population is loathe to admit that racial prejudice exists. This means that, because of their relatively small number, Afro-Uruguayans may scream, but few will listen to the message that they are trying to get across.

PARAGUAY

The near elimination of the Afro-Paraguayan

It might be assumed that in a region where the Negroid population was quite small during colonial times and where the slaves did not work either in gold mines or on immense sugar plantations, overall racial discrimination was relatively less prevalent. Paraguay was such a country, but the treatment of blacks and mulattoes there does not provide justification for this supposition. The vicious practice of *amparo* plagued free black and mulatto males, while the ownership of land was generally denied to all persons of detectable African origin.[93] A town of blacks and mulattoes, Tobapy, had been founded in 1653, and another, Arequi, was founded before 1800. A third, La Emboscada, had been established as a military outpost in 1740, the provision being that the free Negroids residing there would pay their tribute by acting as soldiers.

National independence was achieved in 1813, chiefly through efforts of José Gaspar Rodríguez de Francia, who proceeded to rule the nation as his personal fief. An opponent of what he conceived as the decadent forces of liberalism, *El Supremo*, as he was called, fortified his frontiers, cut off contact with the neighboring states, and strove to make his nation as self-sufficient as possible. He seized church properties and estates belonging to those landlords who plotted against him. When he died in 1840, the overwhelming number of Paraguayan blacks and mulattoes were still either slaves or subject to some form of *amparo* obligation.

A moderate change transpired under Carlos Antonio López, the strongman who succeeded Rodríguez Francia. As a result of a free-womb law passed in November 1842, after 1 January 1843 all children born of slaves were free and were dubbed "*libertos* of the Republic of Paraguay." Other articles in this general decree required priests to baptize and bury *libertos* free of charge and proclaimed all fugitive slaves entering the country to be liberated.[94] There were, of course, other aspects of the new legislation that were not nearly so benign. *Libertas* were bound to work for their masters until they reached the age of twenty-four; and *libertos*, until the age of twenty-five. In addition, the law said nothing about terminating the old *amparo* practice, and the status of the older slaves remained unchanged.

The critical factor in Paraguay was that, since the National Treasury was the largest owner of estates, the bulk of the slaves and *libertos* really worked for the government. Together with those free Negroids subject to *amparo* requirements, these Afro-Paraguayans tended the state-controlled *yerba maté*[95] farms and cattle ranches. They performed manual labor in national factories and iron smelters and did stevedore and road repair work. As a result, the state achieved important economic gains simply because it possessed this readily available labor force that it did not have to pay.[96]

On state-owned enterprises, the Negroid workers, no matter what their ostensible legal status, were generally categorized as slaves, a revealing indication of the society's true view of the black and mulatto.[97] The health conditions for government-owned properties were generally inferior to those for bondmen working for private owners.[98] Still, given the fact that no Africans had been imported since Rodríguez Francia's time, the growth of the slave population suggests that conditions in Paraguay could not have been too horrendous. By 1864 there were about 20,000 slaves and 24,000 *libertos* and free Negroids in the country, a total that comprised nearly 9 percent of the national population.[99] Considering that 1782 estimates had pegged the region's black and mulatto population at 10 percent of the whole, Afro-Paraguayans were probably holding their own.[100]

Nevertheless, by 1864 Paraguay was the only Spanish American republic where slavery was still a legal institution. Given the past record of events, it should come as no surprise that the ubiquitous diety, Mars, would bear a major responsibility for effecting full and final abolition. Between November 1864 and May 1865 President Francisco Solano López, fearing attack from Brazil and Argentina, became involved in hostilities with these two countries and Uruguay. Manpower requirements were prodigious, and on 6 September 1866 Solano López ordered the drafting of slaves and *libertos*. Even though they had been essentially second-class citizens, the Afro-Paraguayans defended their homeland with a fanaticism matching that exhibited by other societal elements. They were usually made to fight in segregated units, but a few of these formations, like the *nambi-i* (literally, "small ear") battalion, came to be regarded as elite troops.[101]

In January 1869 the capital of Asunción fell, and by the middle of the year, all the major districts of the country were under Brazilian control. The commander of the occupation army, the Count d'Eu, was a firm believer in abolition. Discretion had tempered his statements on this question in his own country, but in a now prostrate Paraguay, he could act as he wished. The newly erected puppet government was ordered to abolish slavery, and on 2 October 1869 it complied by issuing a decree to this effect.[102] At least half the Paraguayan population had succumbed during the conflict,[103] and the Afro-Paraguayan population suffered similar decimation. Old men, women, and under-age *libertos* were probably the only ones left, and no published source has ever hazarded a guess as to the grand total emancipated.

But having reached its demographic nadir, the number of Negroids in Paraguay suddenly began increasing, thanks to a strong stimulus from an unexpected quarter. The Count d'Eu was not the only individual free to act as he pleased in a vanquished nation; the black and mulatto soldiers in the Brazilian Army of Occupation played the historic role of territorial conquerors, and before they departed in 1876 they sired an unusual number of offspring.[104] These mixed-blood illegitimates would probably have been treated as social pariahs except that during the generation after the termination of the Triple Alliance War, the presence of so few able-bodied Paraguayans made looser moral standards prevalent.

During the twentieth century the Afro-Paraguayan seems to have staged a numerical comeback, no small feat considering that since 1903 the issuance of visas to "individuals of the . . . negro race" has been technically illegal.[105] By 1925 there were an estimated 10,000 Afro-Paraguayans, but a semiofficial census dated 31 December 1934 put the black and mulatto population at roughly 31,500 souls.[106] One may question the reliability of this figure, for at that time Paraguay was involved in the Chaco War (1932–1935), another ferocious bloodletting in which thousands of male inhabitants perished. There is, however, no record of any special battalion of Negroid troops; presumably, Afro-Paraguayans fought in this conflict on a par with the other racial groups.

An informal survey printed in 1951 estimated that approximately 3.5 percent of the population in this overwhelmingly Indian and *mestizo* nation possessed some African blood.[107] Only one settlement composed primarily of Negroids is known to be still in existence. This is Laurelty, which was started in 1820 by fifty black and mulatto followers of the vanquished Uruguayan patriot, José Artigas.[108] It is apparent that the hamlet prospered until the destructive Triple Alliance War (1864–1870); presently, it appears to be in the process of dissolution. At least half of the surviving females are married to Bolivians, who were themselves prisoners of war taken by Paraguayan forces in the aforementioned Chaco struggle of the 1930s. Of the other forty-four persons remaining at Laurelty, mulattoes and *zambos* are a clear majority, so that the time of the disappearance of the last black person in the settlement cannot be far off.[109]

As far as most citizens in the capital city are concerned, the total physical assimilation of the Afro-Paraguayan has already occurred. In 1965 I was doing historical research in the diplomatic archives in Asunción. Whenever I entered a store or restaurant or took a collective taxi, I was greeted as a Brazilian. On occasion, I asked the person who greeted me whether or not there were any Negroids in Paraguay, and in every instance I was assured that none now existed. Despite these declarations, I discovered several unmistakably Negroid persons living in a poor section near the Paraguay River. Unfortunately, all attempts to interview them proved fruitless. Every time I managed to get close enough to hail them, they ran away.

8

Negroid Peoples in the Andean States

Emancipation and disappearance
of the Afro-Chilean

On 11 September 1811 the revolutionary government of Chile declared its independence from Spain, but for the nearly 25,000 Chileans of African origin, a more fundamental and decisive change had already occurred. Until the eighteenth century, a good deal of the agricultural and mining labor had been the work of slaves and free Negroids. During the next hundred years, however, Indian and *mestizo* serfs totally replaced the slaves as the work force for the *fundos* of Chile.[1] By the time the Chilean *criollos* announced the separation from Spain, both free and enslaved Negroids had become largely limited to occupations in domestic and urban labor. In the sense that they were no longer irreplaceable workers, their future in the country would have been hazardous whether a political revolution had occurred or not.

A temporary reversal in their importance, however, developed as a result of burgeoning national defense needs. As we have seen, in an effort to stave off reconquest by Spanish troops sent from Peru, the infant Chilean Republic had begun drafting slaves in 1814.[2] When General San Martín crossed the Andes and commenced the final campaign for Chilean freedom in 1817, an uncertain but conspicuous number of Afro-Chileans either joined or were inducted into his forces.[3] Many probably remained under arms when San Martín moved his army north to Peru after the process of Chilean liberation was completed.

AN ESTIMATE of the NEGROID POPULATION in CONTEMPORARY SPANISH AMERICA

The Negroid population has disappeared, or become almost totally amalgamated (1% or less)

A Negroid population exists, but it is a small minority (2-5 % of the population or less)

MEXICO

CUBA SANTO DOMINGO

GUATEMALA
EL SALVADOR

HONDURAS
NICARAGUA

COSTA RICA

PANAMA

COLUMBIA

VENEZUELA

BRAZIL

EQUADOR

PERU

BOLIVIA

PARAGUAY

CHILE

ARGENTINA
URUGUAY

A significant Negroid minority (6-30% exists in these states)

The largest population group in these countries is probably Negroid

On 24 July 1823 the government of Ramón Freire initiated a program for the legal abolition of African slavery. There is no record of the total number of bondmen eventually released, but scholars have generally accepted an estimate of 4,000 persons, most of whom were women, juveniles, and old men.[4] The law of 24 July, however, limited emancipation to slaves who could obtain a certificate of liberation from the local police. The latter were prohibited from issuing this document unless the slave could prove that he had some "honest occupation."[5] Subsequent declarations of emancipation in the Constitutions of 1825 and 1829 and in Article 132 of the Constitution of 1833 (in force until 1925) dropped this condition. Probably, Chile was the first Spanish American state to effect the full abolition of slavery.

The most conspicuous Afro-Chilean to gain prominence after emancipation was the mulatto soldier José Romero. A veteran of the wars of independence, he was promoted to the rank of second lieutenant in 1819. He participated in the civil war that took place from 1829 to 1831 and rose to the rank of *sargento mayor*,[6] eventually commanding the Third Civic Battalion of Santiago. Having served with the victorious conservative forces (*pelucones*, or "big wigs," as they were called), Romero was named an administrative aide to the Chilean Chamber of Deputies in 1832, holding this post until he died in 1858. A memorial statue was later erected in his honor. The notable scholar Guillermo Feliú Cruz has referred to Romero as "the illustrious mulatto."[7] The definite article is quite appropriate because post-independence history does not appear to recognize any other Afro-Chilean of distinction.

According to the historian Francisco Encina, the disappearance of the African from the Chilean scene occurred with "dizzying rapidity."[8] While this conclusion may be accurate, it fails to explain the almost total disinterest of national researchers in the Afro-Chilean since emancipation. Can it truly be said that the Negroid peoples in the national territory have been totally absorbed?[9] It is to be hoped that the Chilean academic community will eventually launch an investigation of this question. Encina's pronouncement aside, there may in fact be a few predominantly Afro-Chilean communities still in existence.[10]

Chilean immigration policy and
national racial preferences

Given the alleged visual disappearance of the Afro-Chilean, possibly the most pertinent question left to ask is whether or not immigrants of African origin could become citizens of that republic. On the negative side, it must be stressed that from the mid-nineteenth century, Chilean governments began supporting a pro-European immigration policy.[11] Although the country proved less successful in its efforts than Argentina, the fundamental assumption was the same: Only European blood could heighten the psychic and physical capabilities of the national population. As recently as 1952, the Department of Immigration in the Ministry of Foreign Affairs announced that one of its fundamental goals was "to perfect the biological condition of the Chilean race."[12] This policy declaration implies that the entry of Negroids who might take up permanent residence is not favored. Indeed, both an internationally known newspaper[13] and an impeccable private source[14] have stated that Chile accepts no immigrants of African blood.

A minimal sense of fairness requires that any positive information concerning this issue be presented as well. There are no racial restrictions mentioned in the Chilean Constitution, and the most recent *Recopilación de reglamentos* (1961) dealing with entry and immigration affairs contains no prohibitions whatsoever regarding race.[15] Furthermore, several years ago I met some Afro-Americans living semipermanently in Santiago and playing on national basketball teams.[16] On the basis of these contacts, a reasonable conclusion might be that, while individual Negroids are allowed to live in Chile, the immigration of groups of unskilled blacks and mulattoes would not be sanctioned.

Such a barrier could be informally enforced and would allow Chile to escape the type of international criticism that has been voiced regarding the "lily white" immigration policy practiced by South Africa and at one time by Australia. A minor diplomatic embroglio did develop, however, when the Chilean government allegedly prevailed upon the United States not to send an Afro-American military attaché to Santiago in November

1973.[17] It can only be hoped that the circumstances as reported in the press were either incorrect or that, for unreported and mitigating reasons, the United States government chose to withdraw the black officer's supposed nomination.

In an ultimate sense, the attitude of the Chilean governments on this question may simply be a reflection of the general attitude of the more influential sectors of the Chilean public. As a black visitor in Chile, I encountered no discriminatory situations. What proved surprising, however, was that Chileans preferred to think of themselves as "white" and their country as "European," although at least half of those I encountered (especially outside of Santiago) displayed varying degrees of Indian ancestry.[18] As long as this kind of preference prevails, there is little reason to believe that Negroid immigrants would find the Republic of Chile a place where they could settle and live comfortably.

BOLIVIA

The Afro-Bolivian presence on the Altiplano

Although the silver mines at Potosí made Bolivia extremely important during the colonial period, the region probably had fewer Negroid residents than any other South American territory settled by Spain. As early as 1554, officials of the Spanish court had concluded that the cold weather and thin air made the Bolivian highlands unhealthy for Africans.[19] Furthermore, the great distance of Potosí from slave ports like Cartagena and Buenos Aires and the difficulty of traveling in the highlands made prices for *bozales* the highest in the New World.[20] A combination of all these factors made the utilization of the local Indian population essential and, incidentally, made hard labor in the Potosí silver mines one of the few tasks that Negroid slaves were spared.

There were jobs for African bondmen to do, however, and in the rich city of Potosí a few thousand served as domestic workers in the homes of wealthy Spaniards.[21] Much as in sixteenth-century Spain, the possession of an expensive black slave was living evidence of the owner's financial status. It is quite likely that these blacks were treated much better than the Indian miners who were worked as beasts of burden and then discarded.[22]

Bolivia, or Upper Peru, as it was often referred to in colonial times, was the last territory liberated by Simón Bolívar's forces. National independence was proclaimed on 6 August 1825, and Marshall Antonio José de Sucre became the first national president. This young military genius (he was *El Libertador*'s most trusted lieutenant) had few illusions about the future of the fledgling nation. One of his most serious problems was the fact that his main source of support was some 2,000 troops from Colombia and Venezuela, many of whom were blacks or mulattoes. The presence of these soldiers caused increasing resentment among the *criollos, mestizos*, and Indians of the Altiplano. An indication of how strained racial relations became can be perceived in the shrewd tactics employed by Agustín Gamarra, the Peruvian president, who invaded Bolivia in 1828. To the cry of "mulattoes, no!"[23] this *caudillo* swiftly occupied the country's major population centers and forced Sucre to resign. Departing the capital city of Chuquisaca for the last time, the ex-president was hurried on his way with shouts of "out with the mulattoes."[24] This was neither the first nor the last time that racist jingoism would be utilized in order to foster unity and encourage resistance against foreign elements. This hostility evinced by Bolivians toward the black and mulatto troops attests to the strength of anti-Negroid prejudice even where Negroids were not numerous.

Article 156 of the Constitution of 1831 stated that "nobody had been born a slave in Bolivia since 6 August 1825."[25] This free-womb law was hardly more than a pious wish, for nothing in the form of enforcement legislation was ever sanctioned. Only after Andrés de Santa Cruz, already president of Bolivia, took power in Peru and formed the Bolivian–Peruvian Confederation (1836) was a treaty signed with Great Britain (5 June

1837) that prohibited Bolivians from participating in the external slave trade. This treaty was never ratified, however, and Santa Cruz's political creation disintegrated two years later.

According to an informal reckoning made in 1846, there were at least 1,391 slaves still present in the country,[26] but the moral aspects of the institution do not seem to have caused either the Bolivian rulers or the populace much concern. Not until 1861 was total abolition decreed,[27] and no information is available concerning the number of persons liberated, or even whether Bolivian slaveholders bothered to obey the law. As in Argentina and Uruguay, all manner of idealistic precepts were decreed or written into the constitutions, but their rigorous enforcement was not envisioned and, given Bolivia's chronic political instability, they were not likely to be effective.

The first national census was completed by the Bolivian government in 1900. It reported that some 3,945 members of the *raza negra* were residents of the country.[28] Included in this group were persons of Afro-Indian blood called *sambos* and described as a "valiant race . . . with an aptitude for music . . . but with a general reputation for perfidity."[29] The census failed to establish what kind of tasks Negroid inhabitants performed in the general labor market, but since slightly more than half of the Afro-Bolivians reported lived in La Paz,[30] domestic and urban service was probably their forte. The census also implied that as a result of miscegenation the Afro-Bolivians were rapidly disappearing, but a study written by a Mexican geographic scholar thirty years later placed the composite number of Negroids in Bolivia at 59,740 souls.[31] Even granting that numerous blacks and mulattoes wandered into eastern Bolivia from Brazil, this astounding increase can hardly be made compatible with the 1900 total. At the same time, nothing can be done to establish the veracity of either of these estimates, for in subsequent censuses, Bolivian officials have presented no data on race.

It is quite likely that several thousand Afro-Bolivians can still be found in this overwhelmingly Indian and *mestizo* nation, but they have not played a substantial role in the national past and are unlikely to do so in the future.

PERU

The struggle for emancipation

Much as in Bolivia, African slaves usually managed to escape the rigors of labor in the mining areas of Peru.[32] They were, instead, put to work on the sugar plantations and fruit orchards near Trujillo and Lima and farther south along the Pacific coastal plain. With the initiation of the free-slave trade in Peru in 1794, the high prices previously charged for *bozales* declined, and by 1812 the number of slaves in Peru had rapidly increased.[33] Unlike the situation in Argentina or Venezuela, independence was imposed from outside, for many *criollos* in Peru displayed little interest in terminating Spanish rule. An army led by José de San Martín reached the country in late August 1820 and finally entered Lima on 12 July 1821. He was named Protector of Peru, and on the twenty-eighth of the month Peruvian independence was declared.

The question of the status of an estimated 40,000 to 50,000 bondmen[34] became a public issue within weeks after San Martín had taken power. On 12 August he declared the descendants of slaves born after 28 July 1821 legally free but subject to the same kind of *liberto* restrictions that had been adopted in Argentina in 1813. Nevertheless, all slaves owned by Spanish royalists were immediately emancipated, as were those who joined the patriot army and "distinguished themselves by their valor."[35] Buttressing this decree was still another, issued on 24 November 1821, which banned further Peruvian participation in the slave trade. Although San Martín departed the country in 1823, the spirit behind his edicts enjoyed a much longer life. Article 152 of the Peruvian Constitution of 1828 declared that "no one is born a slave in the Republic," and "those [foreign slaves] who for any reason tread on Peruvian soil" are free. The high point in antislavery idealism was reached when, in a treaty of 22 September 1829, Peru and Gran Colombia agreed that any of their citizens apprehended in the international slave traffic "would be considered pirates."[36]

The next decades witnessed a spectacular reversal of policy, while civil war reduced the concept of rule by law to the status of a crude joke. Blustering dictators strove desperately to stabilize their regimes by enlisting the financial aid of wealthy interests, and this contingency made the slaveholders nearly omnipotent. After declaring President José Luis Orbegoso deposed on 3 March 1835, for example, General Felipe Salavery issued a decree permitting the resumption of the slave trade. The young rebel soon paid for his audacity with his life, but slave interests seized upon this convenient authorization and began the semi-clandestine importation of slaves from Colombia and Ecuador.[37]

When Agustín Gamarra outmaneuvered several rivals and again seized the presidency in 1839, slave interests were able to obtain new concessions in exchange for contributions to the empty national treasury. Obligingly, Gamarra signed a law on 29 November 1839 making all *libertos* subject to their mother's masters for the next fifty years and legalizing the sale of the services of all *libertos*.[38] But this was not all; following some judicious arm-twisting, the Peruvian national legislature abrogated (27 November 1840) both San Martín's decree of 24 November 1821 and the anti-slave-trade provision of 22 September 1829, thereby legalizing Peruvian participation in the nefarious traffic.[39] Still, some minimal concession to moral sensibilities was deemed necessary. After 1840, therefore, disembarked bondmen were euphemistically designated "African colonists," the inference being that they had somehow arrived in the country of their own free will.[40] It is difficult to believe that anyone was fooled by this fatuous gesture, and the reinauguration of the traffic incensed the British government, which brought diplomatic pressure to bear on Ramón Castilla, Gamarra's eventual successor. Employing both positive and negative inducements, London finally persuaded the Peruvians to sign a commercial treaty on 10 April 1850 that included a provision condemning the slave trade. Nevertheless, diplomatic condemnation and termination of the traffic remained unconnected entities as far as Peruvians were concerned.

An incident that probably accomplished more toward hastening an end to both the traffic and the institution of slavery was the slave rebellion of August 1848, which erupted on sugar plantations in the vicinity of the town of Trujillo. A large number of armed blacks marched on the town and captured it with the aid of bondmen inside the gates.⁴¹ On 15 August 1848 they presented a specious but nonetheless revealing proclamation:

> Our brothers of Chancoy, Pisco and Lima are also free ... they have risen against their unjust oppressors; their valour has saved them from servitude. The laws of nature and those of the state protect our cause; our personality is equal to theirs [i.e., the whites], and so are our rights; the slavery of some is an affront to the liberty of others. We would already be free as they, if it had not been lodged in [us] the cowardice of degradation, but it is of no importance. ... We will proclaim this very day the liberty of all slaves in the square of Trujillo.⁴²

The supposed uprisings in the other towns never took place. Finally realizing that they were alone, on the nineteenth of the month the ex-slaves began executing those whites who had not already fled the town. Although government troops recaptured Trujillo before the end of August and slaughtered an undetermined number of the Negroids implicated in the revolt, the tale of this bloody insurrection sent shock waves of fear reverberating throughout the Peruvian slavocracy.

The final abolition of slavery came as a result of civil war that broke out in November 1854. Lacking what he deemed a sufficient number of troops, President José Rufino Echenique declared that all slaves who served in his army for two years would be freed. But Ramón Castilla, the man Echenique had succeeded and his present adversary, was a master at one-upmanship. He called for slave enlistment in his forces, and on 5 December 1854 he declared involuntary servitude totally abolished – provided, of course, that he was ultimately triumphant. Achieving his goal in January 1855, Castilla made peace with the furious slaveholders by promising them financial compensation. No more than 17,000 slaves were actually owned, but the new government accepted a figure of 25,505 bondmen and undertook to pay a debt of 7,651,500 pesos. Payments by 1860 totaled 2,217,600 pesos, but no annual payments were made after 1872.⁴³

In Peru the *liberto* system had never really been put into

effect, and the raw bribe offered by Castilla to the slaveholding interests highlights the power this group exercised in the nation. As for the freedmen, abolition meant the abandonment of the sugar plantations and the mass exodus to the cities where, according to one account, "cane brandy nourished the black euphoria, day after day, week after week."[44] At length, however, the celebration of emancipation abated, and the harsh realities of hunger and poverty forced the freedmen to seek employment. Some chose to return to the coastal plantations, scenes of their past servitude, but others remained in cities like Lima, Callao, and Trujillo, eking out a scrubby existence as day laborers, domestics, and service workers. Slavery had been abolished, but the only persons who benefited financially from the emancipation had been the slaveholders themselves.

The Afro-Peruvian since emancipation

The decisive difference between the bondage system in Peru and that in Uruguay, Argentina, or Chile was that in 1854 Peruvian plantation interests still considered servitude to be economically profitable and an operational necessity. It was not enough, then, that Castilla buy off the slavocracy;[45] the plantation owners had to find another kind of slave, one whose importation would not be thwarted by Great Britain's maritime resources. Recall that during the colonial period Spain never had such an alternative; the Peruvians, however, soon found one.

Even before 1850 a few Chinese coolies had been brought to Peru, but between 1855 and 1865 this trickle became a flood; by 1875 there were 80,000 Orientals in the country. The Chinese were bondmen in all but name, and, among other things, they were forced to mine the dreadful guano deposits in the Chincha Islands. Of the 3,000 put to work on these islets between 1855 and 1865, no more than 600 survived. With white owners raking in the profits, black and mulatto overseers – many ex-slaves themselves – drove the coolies to their graves.[46] Meanwhile, on mainland plantations, Afro-Peruvian strong-arm squads were used to quell rioting Chinese. Such practices naturally poisoned relations between the Orientals and Negroids. Yet there was another even more satiric factor to the situation.

Before 1854 the slaves who worked the coastal fruit and sugar plantations had provided a necessary labor function. With abolition, the mass entry of the Chinese, and the gradual movement of many Indians and *mestizos* from the interior highlands to the coast, the Afro-Peruvian lost his importance in the labor market. He became just another job hunter faced with increasing competition from his Indian, *mestizo*, and Chinese counterparts.

The Afro-Peruvian in the national culture

A 1791 colonial census established that there were 1,232,122 inhabitants in the Viceroyalty of Peru. Negroids represented about 7 percent: 40,336 were slaves (presumably black), and an additional 41,256 persons were classified as blacks, mulattoes, or *zambos*.[47] Unfortunately, the slaves counted were those listed on tax rolls and administrative lists, and in Peru these were hopelessly inadequate.[48] Viceroy Ambrosio O'Higgins estimated the Negroid population to be at least 130,000 persons in 1799,[49] and an 1836 tabulation taken for the Department of Lima alone reported 17,431 slaves and 71,104 other blacks or mulattoes.[50] For reasons not explained, however, national censuses taken in 1836, 1850, and 1862 did not provide any racial statistics.[51] The 1876 census included a section on racial origins that listed 44,224 persons, only 1.94 percent of the population, as *negro*. The 1940 census listed 29,054 Afro-Peruvians, roughly 0.47 percent of the aggregate.

If these figures suggest anything, it is that the Afro-Peruvian is fast disappearing, or, as one author hypothesized, "the black race dissolved itself in the cities and small towns, mixing with the *cholo*, with the Indian and the white."[52] But Fernando Romero, a leading student of Peruvian racial relations, sharply disagrees. He finds that both the 1876 and 1940 censuses listed many persons as "mixtures" or "diverse crossings"; in short, no effort was made to separate *zambos* and mulattoes from *mestizos*. Also, since the "existing racial prejudice led every offspring of mixed union to seek classification as a 'white,' " many individuals claimed Caucasian ancestry no matter what their actual racial background.[53] Romero's final conclusion was that "the census [sic] of 1876 and 1940 are false through defect."[54]

What this Peruvian scholar is arguing is that there has been at least a semiconscious effort on the part of both the officials and the populace to make Peru appear as white as possible. Still, it must be acknowledged that some Peruvian census takers have demonstrated an acute awareness of the ambiguities of the situation. Officials making the population survey for the Department of Lima in 1931 emphasized that "mestizos, [and] Indians describe themselves as white [and] the blacks as ... trigueños."[55] A similar observation was recorded when government agents attempted a population survey of the city of Tacna in 1935. A kind of crisis developed because a significant number of the citizenry desired "to change their race intending to improve it." Ultimately, the declaration of the individual as to his race was usually accepted since to do otherwise would have caused a good deal of social friction.[56] Contemporary government policy makers have solved this problem and simultaneously avoided the defects of the surveys 1876 and 1940. Statistical headcounts since the 1961 census have included no racial classifications whatsoever.

Given the factors cited, it is not surprising that the postabolition attitude of national intellectuals toward Afro-Peruvians has been largely hostile. Javier Prado y Ugarteche, for example, insisted that "the Negro [is] ... a robber from the moment he is born, and forever the victim of a lascivious nature, that is bequeathed by African blood."[57] Alejandro O. Deustua portrayed the Afro-Peruvian as shiftless, lazy, and vice-ridden, an opinion shared by César Antonio Ugarte.[58] Most acerbic of all these thinkers was Francisco García Calderón, who wrote that "in South America, civilization depends upon the ... triumph of the white man over the mulatto, the Negro, and the Indian."[59] Curiously enough, Peruvian Marxist philosophers have hardly been more charitable. José Carlos Mariátegui, often touted as the founder of the Peruvian Communist party, felt that in comparison with the Chinese "the contribution of the Negro, who came as a slave, appears to be even more worthless and negative."[60] For Mariátegui and kindred spirits, the rise of the Indian was the key to socialist revolution in the nation.

Mulattoes, chiefly because they wished to be white, were misguided and useless, while Afro-Indians were believed to be genetic and cultural abominations. According to Mariátegui, "when he has mixed with the Indian, [the Negro] has corrupted him [the Indian] with his false security and exhibitionist and morbid psychology."[61]

Peruvian intellectuals treating racial conditions since World War II have been more concerned with describing real conditions rather than with discussing or analyzing theoretical psycho-biological relationships. Luis E. Valcárcel admitted candidly that "the Negro is at the bottom of Peruvian society both economically and socially." Color prejudice has kept him there, and "even when he has earned much money, he is unable to improve his status. The tradition of being a slave is heavy upon him."[62] Nevertheless, Valcárcel insists that the mulatto and *zambo* are readily accepted in Peruvian society; for them, "there are no restrictions."[63] Such frankness is not as perceptible in the work of Roberto MacLean y Esteños. This scholar insists that no formal segregation exists in Peru and that black and mulatto nationals are not ashamed of their racial origins. His own problem becomes manifest in his discussion of national matrimonial practices. In that regard, MacLean y Esteños admits that custom has established a "certain endogamic limitation,"[64] that is, white men may have Negroid mistresses, but they do not marry them. He cannot admit, however, that such traditional attitudes are symptomatic of racial bias.

The noted Peruvian novelist, Mario Vargas Llosa, has none of McLean y Esteños's inhibitions, and the social situation that he reproduces generally bears out the findings of Valcárcel. In *La ciudad y los perros* (*The City and the Dogs*, 1962), an interesting racial etiquette is manifested, but this thin curtain of social courtesy fails to mask the fact that blacks and *zambos* are looked down upon by all other racial groups. Tersely explicit is a white Peruvian, Alberto, who, in speaking about Ambrosio, a black chauffeur, remarks that "you could tell in his eyes that he is a coward, like all Negroes."[65] In Vargas Llosa's novels, *mestizos* may receive more flattering cultural designations, and mulattoes do what they can to become "white." But the black is like the leopard, he simply cannot change what he is.

Perhaps the most outspoken criticism of the prevailing attitudes toward Negroid peoples has flowed from the pen of Luis Millones, who argues that "a flagrant but a subtle racist attitude"[66] has always existed in his homeland. Consider the example that illustrates his remarks:

> Today as in the sixteenth century, it is hoped that the
> index of criminality in the poorer districts will be higher
> among the Negroes, and one is accustomed to believe that
> a visit to the Lima jails will render similar percentages to
> those which the Viceroy Toledo found in the first list of
> criminals prepared by the royal *audiencia* of Lima in
> 1570.[67]

In Peru even the Indian has had eloquent and resourceful defenders, but the Afro-Peruvian has had almost none. While solid historical and sociological works have appeared on the Afro-Uruguayan,[68] studies of a similar character have yet to flow from Peruvian pens. The truth may be that Afro-Peruvians are not as numerous as Indians or *mestizos*, and they represent the one racial or ethnic group that all the rest can agree is despicable. Recall that in 1540 Francisco Pizarro sent a black to Manco Capac bearing gifts.[69] The Indian accepted the presents but killed the black. As Luis Millones suggested above, not a great deal seems to have changed since the sixteenth century.

The future of the Afro-Peruvian

Whereas Argentina remembers Falucho and Colonel Barcala, and Chile has José Romero, Peruvian history reveals no renowned military or political figure of African or part-African origin. In the cultural realm, there is José Manuel Valdés, a person whose distinguished medical and literary careers spanned both the late colonial and independence epochs, but no Afro-Peruvian of similar stature has emerged since Valdés's death in 1844. Furthermore, with the possible exception of Valdés, perhaps the most written-about black in nineteenth century Peru was the notorious desperado León Escobar. During the civil strife that convulsed the nation in 1835, Escobar and his gang raided the capital city of Lima and demanded a heavy ransom in exchange for their peaceful departure. For four hours, while the city fathers struggled to collect the required tribute, Escobar amused himself by holding audiences and issuing commands from the presidential offices.[70] He was the first and last Afro-Peruvian to have ever occupied this seat of power.

Aside from Agustín Vallejos, a mulatto who headed the sugar workers' union and subsequently served a term in the federal congress during the 1940s,[71] the most prominent twentieth century Afro-Peruvian may well be Nicomedes Santa Cruz Gamarra, a poet, musician, and choreographer. In 1959 this artist founded the Compañia Cumanana, a repertory group dedicated to the presentation and preservation of Afro-Peruvian song and dance forms.[72] But it is for his fiery poems that Santa Cruz Gamarra is best known, and works like his *"Oiga Usté Señor Dotor"* ("Listen, Mister Doctor") spotlight his consciousness of racial heritage and the intensity of the prejudice he perceived:

> The black man who is your chauffeur
> – Who is my sister's husband –
> Has invited you for tomorrow
> To my wife's birthday [party]
> I will try to entertain you
> Giving you the best
> And since you do me the favor
> Of mingling with my race,
> Before you step into my house
> Listen, Mister Doctor
>
> If you come as a tourist,
> Sing, dance, have fun
> But never call me "boy" [Negree]
> Because I have a Christian name
> . . .
> Oh, if your wife doesn't come
> Don't you bring your mistress
> My wife has her pride and
> Gets easily offended

...
I want you to become convinced
That the well-brought up Blacks,
Even though they don't turn red,
Know shame.[73]

Unfortunately, the literary and cultural effects of Santa Cruz
Gamarra and a few others do not seem to have had much influence upon the mass of Afro-Peruvians. In this regard, the observation of George Schuyler, an Afro-American newspaperman,
would still seem to be essentially valid. Writing in 1948, Schuyler concluded that Peruvians of Negroid ancestry were "about
where the free Negroes were in our northern states in 1776, and
as a group they are not going forward."[74]

ECUADOR

The Afro-Ecuadorean "menace"

Since colonial times the Negroid population of Ecuador has
been ensconced on the Pacific coastal plain, where the mass of
them have functioned as forced laborers. This situation was
somewhat modified as a result of the successful military campaign fought from 1821 to 1823 by Simón Bolívar against the
resident Spanish forces. An undetermined number of slaves
either enlisted or were forcibly recruited into the liberating
armies, but the Ecuadorean slavocracy succeeded in retaining
control of a sizable number of their human properties. Undoubtedly, these oligarchs also supported the City Council of
Guayaquil when in 1823 that body demanded that Bolívar allow no more Negroid military officers to be stationed in or near
the city.[75] The mere presence of these emboldened blacks and
mulattoes irritated the white aristocrats, and the lack of deference paid them by these darkskinned soldiers may well have
been a factor in the 1825 and 1827 slave rebellions that later
shook northwestern Ecuador. These uprisings were soon
crushed, and even though Spanish domination ended, the social
class system was not essentially disturbed.

The architect of Ecuadorean independence in 1830 was Juan José Flores, another of Bolívar's generals and a native of Venezuela. The main prop of Flores's unabashedly authoritarian regime was the army, many of whose officers and lower ranks were black and mulatto veterans born in Colombia and Venezuela. It was this situation that Vicente Rocafuerte, a wealthy inhabitant of Guayaquil, chose to exploit in his 1835 campaign for the presidency. He argued that the presence of these foreign Negroid troops was a threat to the national security. Rocafuerte's case was strengthened by the controversial activities of Colonel José Otamendi, a black who killed and wounded several upper-class whites in the town of Riobamba because they had allegedly snubbed his wife.[76] Such a violent act of retribution would have been condemned under any circumstances, but since a black was responsible, it became doubly abominable.

Rather than face a civil war in which the racial issue could be used against him, Flores chose to step aside and allow Rocafuerte to become chief executive in 1835. By the time the latter finished his term, Negroid officers had become as rare as fleas on porcelain dogs.[77] Flores resumed the presidency in 1840, but, following the 1845 insurrection in Guayaquil, he fell from power. During the next fifteen years, eleven presidents or executive committees attempted to rule, and three new constitutions were drafted; perhaps unnoticed by the myriad of contestants for power, the nation sank into political anarchy.

The problem of abolition in Ecuador

As a part of Bolívar's federated republic of Gran Colombia, Ecuador was legally bound by the antislavery law of 19 July 1821, which stipulated that descendants of slaves born after that date were free. Nevertheless, these *manumisos*, as they were called, were to remain in the care of the masters of their mothers until they reached the age of twenty-one. In addition, *juntas de manumisión* ("committees for the manumission of slaves") were to be formed in every administrative district in order to collect taxes and purchase the freedom of older slaves.

In 1823 the first committee was established in the town of Riobamba, and another began functioning in the capital of

Quito in 1826. Records show that, over a ten-year period, 333 slaves were considered for emancipation by the Quito *junta*; as a result of outright purchase or some other form of emancipation, 91 (26.7 percent) became free citizens.[78] A cursory analysis of these figures might support the supposition that the emancipatory exertions of the Quito *junta* were woefully inadequate. But, in reflecting upon the scandalous operation of the *liberto* system in Peru or Uruguay, a sounder conclusion would be that the *junta*, although feeble, did enjoy a modicum of success. Furthermore, of the 6,804 slaves reputedly in the country in 1825, over three-fourths lived in the coastal provinces of Guayas, Esmeraldas, and Manabí,[79] where slaveholders either prevented the establishment of *juntas de manumisión* or succeeded in rendering them totally inactive. Compared with this kind of massive obstructionism, the efforts of the Quito *junta* become heroic.

Outright resistance to the law was not the only means by which the slaveholding interests made their power felt. When on 13 May 1830 Ecuador was declared an independent republic, the Gran Colombian constitution was rendered null and void, as were the *manumiso* and *junta de manumisión* laws of 21 July 1821. After some hesitation, General-President Juan José Flores decreed on 20 September that these liberation provisions were again in effect. As part of the same decree, he allowed commercial interests "with the special permission of the Congress" to import new slaves,[80] even though in 1825 the Gran Colombian Congress had positively banned the citizens of the federated republic from participating in the external slave trade.[81] The new proviso was a direct indication of the determination of the slaveholders to find new sources of blacks and maintain the viability of the existing system of servitude. Then, in 1835 Colombians began quietly selling their unwanted "pieces of ebony" to Peruvian interests, and Ecuador became a supply station and center of reembarcation for the trade.[82] British pressure coaxed Juan José Flores into signing an anti-slave-trade treaty in 1841, but the national congress did not ratify the compact for five years; any effect the restriction had on the traffic was ceremonial.

Internally, the proslavery interests remained dominant at least through 1843. A law passed in that year reasserted the slave owner's right to import new slaves with governmental permission and raised the age of freedom for *libertos* to twenty-six.[83] The tide turned when a more liberal administration took power in 1846 and decreed all children of slaves born since 1821 free when they reached the age of eighteen. Unfortunately, this government lasted less than two years, and there is some doubt whether the law in question was ever enforced. Finally, on 25 July 1851 General-President José Urbina proclaimed the total abolition of involuntary servitude. This edict was ratified on 27 September 1852, when the congress voted to recompense the slave owners for emancipating their properties. At least 5,114 slaves were counted in Ecuador in 1839, but in 1852 the government reported only 2,389 bondmen left.[84] In return for the release of the slaves, the Urbina government undertook to pay the owners 459,857 Ecuadorean pesos, an average of 192.4 pesos per slave.[85] The deadline for total emancipation was fixed at 6 March 1854. To pay the contracted debt, the government raised or introduced taxes on gunpowder, alcohol, inheritances, imports, commercial sales, and public documents.

It is possible that the José Urbina regime intended to pay the contracted debt in full, but, if this was the case, the government utterly failed to realize that Ecuadoreans would employ every means to avoid tax payments. By 1 October 1854 the ex-slave owners had received 224,123 pesos, but, inexplicably, on the twenty-sixth of that month, the special duties levied were reduced or eliminated.[86] Intermittent payments continued until 1859, when they ceased completely. Finally, on 19 September 1873 President García Moreno arbitrarily canceled the unpaid emancipation debts. At the time this action was taken, at least 145,000 pesos were still owed to former slaveholding interests.[87]

No one need shed any tears for the former owners of blacks and mulattoes in Ecuador, however, for their compliance with the spirit of the 1851 and 1852 legislation was minimal indeed. Some of those who received government payments forced their ex-slaves to sign multiyear labor contracts, while others acted as if no laws whatsoever had been passed. In 1859 and 1860 land-lords in the province of Imbabura were still whipping their Ne-groid laborers, setting their cabins afire for petty reasons, and locking them up at night to prevent their escape.[88] As late as 1867, black and mulatto workers were still attempting to pur-chase their freedom from certain coastal plantation owners, one of whom was that celebrated advocate of Negroid troops, ex-President Juan José Flores. Not until 1894 would other freed-men be released from mysteriously indissoluble work contracts held by mine owners in the Esmeraldas region.[89]

Finally, there is the problem of José Urbino himself, whose emancipation campaign was fueled primarily by a burning desire to remain in power. Having seized control in 1851, Urbino found himself desperately short of troops, a requisite if he hoped to retain control over his strife-torn country. Urbino not only began recruiting ex-slaves for his armies but also estab-lished a special force of blacks, the *Taura* battalion, which gained a nefarious reputation for executing terror attacks against the president's enemies.[90] Urbino held the presidential office until he was toppled by one of his lieutenants, General Francisco Robles, in October 1856. Much like Urbino, the new dictator had few qualms about allowing ex-slaves-turned-soldiers to avenge themselves upon whites unfriendly to his regime.[91] Robles held on until May 1859, after which there was general anarchy until García Moreno consolidated his position as chief executive toward the end of that year. In retrospect, the history of abolition in Ecuador is hardly a record in which the national citizenry can take pride.

The Afro-Ecuadorean in the national culture

Despite its unsavory emancipatory policies, Ecuador has been one of the few Latin American nations to allow the immigation of free Negroids. Between 1862 and 1869 the government con-templated the possibility of black immigration from the United States, but President García Moreno eventually rejected the idea; in his opinion, Afro-Americans were neither sufficiently docile nor politically dependable.[92] Nevertheless, one generation later, British prompting and the need for cheap labor in the railway construction and gold-mining spheres brought about a partial reversal in policy, and at least 4,000 Jamaican-born laborers eventually settled in the country.

How many persons of African origin are presently in Ecuador is uncertain. It is also a delicate question to ask, since the word *negro* is considered demeaning, and, as elsewhere, Negroid persons seek to be identified as something else. Census reports in 1825 and 1835 failed to differentiate between the various races, but in the 1858 census the aggregate of mulattoes, *zambos*, and blacks was given as 563,000, or 28 percent of the total population.[93] The semiofficial 1936 census reported that 10 percent of the Ecuadorean population was black or mulatto.[94] More recently, the 1944 reckoning of the Dirección Nacional de Estadística y Censos ("The National Bureau of Statistics and the Census") fixed this figure at 5 percent. Unfortunately, in this computation only very darkskinned people were counted as Negroid, and other estimates made by private researchers have tended to accept the 1936 figure as accurate.[95]

Regarding the Ecuadorean people, the North American demographic student John V. Saunders has written that "few characteristics of the population are as important as race. Few are as relevant in their implications."[96] But racial categorization has often been a source of friction, and, in a nation with a long history of political instability, sleeping dogs are better left alone. Neither the national census of 1950 nor that of 1962 provides any information on the races in Ecuador, and future official tabulations will probably follow suit.

Historically speaking, the most celebrated Afro-Ecuadorean was the *zambo* who adopted the name of Francisco Eugenio de Santa Cruz y Espejo (1742–1795). In eighteenth-century Ecuador, he somehow garnered degrees in medicine and law, again spotlighting the yawning gap that existed between royal law and colonial practice. Nonetheless, racial prejudice reared its head once Santa Cruz y Espejo sought to obtain a job as a minor librarian. Embittered, he went on to advocate independence from Spain and confiscation of church properties, ideas for which he suffered imprisonment, exile, and death.[97]

National scholars seemed loathe to discuss this precursor of independence until Oscar Efrem Reyes resurrected his name over a quarter of a century ago.[98] Such reticence takes on additional significance considering that Ecuadorean intellectuals have often manifested an attitude of indifference or contempt toward blacks and mulattoes. Among the more conspicuous is Alfredo Espinosa Tomayo, who in 1918 dismissed Afro-Ecuadoreans as members of a "servile race, created in slavery" and announced his unalterable opposition to racial miscegenation on the grounds that the African was known to be cursed with "inferior mental qualities."[99] When Espinosa Tomayo vented his spleen in 1918, the influence of European Positivist thought was still prevalent in Spanish American intellectual circles, so that his beliefs can be understood, though not excused. Over a generation later, however, national thinkers were still describing the Afro-Ecuadorean's behavior in similar terms. Misael Acosta Solís concluded that the Negroids of Esmeraldas province suffered from "incurable laziness,"[100] while Alfredo Fuentes Roldán argued that they demonstrated "retarded psychic reaction."[101] Finally, the historian Roberto Andrade undoubtedly expressed the beliefs of many, stating that "when we [non-Negroid Ecuadoreans] see insolence in a negro . . . the indignation is greater than that which is inspired by criminals of other races."[102] This author insisted that he was not a racist, but he also professed to be ignorant of any contribution the Afro-Ecuadorean had made toward the improvement of the nation.[103] One may be sure that this conclusion was written before Santa Cruz y Espejo suddenly became a national hero.

Esmeraldas Province and "black power"

Today, Afro-Ecuadoreans seem to be concentrated in the extreme southern province of Loja and in the far northern provinces of Imbabura, Carchi, and Esmeraldas. In some ten valley districts in Carchi and Imbabura, 40.3 percent of the population is of full or part Negroid blood.[104] Their ancestors were brought to the region as slaves to work plantations owned by the Jesuits until that order was expelled from Spanish America in 1767. Today they work as farmers, day laborers, or miners in the saltworks near the town of Salinas. Living in mud huts in an area where only a marginal existence can be scrounged out of exhausted soil, the typical Negroid is described as "happy in spite of the misery of his position."[105]

Since 1950, however, most of the interest in the Afro-Ecuadorean has focused upon the province of Esmeraldas, which has been a preeminent center of Negroid settlement since the sixteenth century. Many of the slaves freed in 1854 migrated to this region, as did an undetermined number of the Jamaicans who entered the country to participate in railroad construction work. In 1900 there were neither paved roads nor hospitals in the provincial capital of Esmeraldas. Less than a dozen schools existed, and recurring epidemics wiped out a considerable number of inhabitants. As late as 1942, the major town of San Lorenzo had neither electricity nor paved streets, but an agricultural boom during the 1950s resulted in the construction of a railroad from the capital of Quito (via Ibarra) to this town. Some changes have since occurred, but even in 1958 San Lorenzo had only two small hotels and two saloon-restaurants, and fifth grade was the maximum schooling that most students could expect to complete.[106]

The creation of the railway link between Esmeraldas Province and Quito was also the cause of a rapid rise in social friction. Violent racial battles broke out between *mestizo* elements, brought down from the highlands to help construct the rail link, and Negroid workmen. These brawls occasionally terminated in murder, and police brutality was a frequent allegation.[107] Since the completion of the railroad in 1957, white and *mestizo* business representatives and government administrators have sought to smooth relations with blacks and mulattoes in Esmeraldas, but racial discord is still occasionally evident. In most towns, the small upper class is composed of white or *mestizo* merchants and national government officials, while the middle and lower classes are overwhelmingly black or mulatto. Towns like San Lorenzo have no darkskinned policemen, and there is an increasing awareness, even among the poor, that "negroid features have a negative value."[108]

Although developments like these could be expected to generate some Negroid militancy, Esmeraldas Province has long pos-

sessed a tradition of Afro-Ecuadorean literary protest uniquely
its own. The origin of this movement is apparently rooted in the
belief of many provincial Negroids that, from 1900 until railroad construction commenced in the late 1950s, the federal
government in Quito ignored their requests for assistance because Esmeraldas was essentially a Negroid territory.[109] The reaction in literary circles to this continuing indifference was the
exhaltation of racial origins, and the poet–author who emerged
as the most talented was Pablo Adalberto Ortiz. *Juyungo*
(1942), his first major novel, earned him lasting acclaim in
Spanish America, but poems like *Casi color* most succinctly
present his racial convictions:

> Still I remember your brotherly voice
> Telling me that one did not want to be a Negro –
> That I should be white –
> It is my silent shout –
> I want to be more black than white.[110]

More recent poets have continued to preach the gospel that
blackness is beautiful, but a few like Tomás García Pérez have
also come to espouse a more Pan-African approach:

> I sing for my Negro race
> A hymn for its liberty
> Because its blood spills in Alabama
> And in South Africa –
> But soon, they will see what is
> Going to happen when the Negro
> Slave shouts [for] liberty –[111]

Unfortunately, this literary tradition of protest has done little
to awaken the Negroid masses in Esmeraldas to the problems
they now face or to acquaint them with possible alternatives to
the developing situation. Since 1965 a lumbering boom, stimu-
lated largely by the completion of the railroad, has brought new
waves of white and *mestizo* settlers into the province. The small
number of Negroid shop owners in towns like San Lorenzo have
been bought out. In addition, persons (usually mulattoes) who
had acted as intermediaries, obtaining aid from white and *mes-*

tizo officials for the resident Negroid population, found themselves either being ignored or replaced by whites and *mestizos*.[112] In short, the new wealth being generated in Esmeraldas Province has provided few benefits for the Afro-Ecuadoreans there, and unless drastic change occurs, they will simply continue to be the hewers of wood and the drawers of water.[113]

One problem – or two?

Between 1954 and 1958 twenty-five studies and aid programs were conducted in Ecuador to improve the socioeconomic condition of the Indian population. In contrast, no program was created to aid the Afro-Ecuadorean.[114] If we are to believe Professor César Astudillo, the Negroids of the country share the same rung on the social ladder as do the unpacified Indians of the eastern jungles.[115] As in Peru, the plight of the Indian population is the most glaring problem, and so the Afro-Ecuadorean minority is simply neglected. But unlike the situation in Peru, persons of African origin are a majority in at least one province and a sizable minority in three others; thus, they are too numerous to be perpetually disregarded. Even if future governments should succeed in bringing the Indian into the mainstream of Ecuadorean life, there will still exist a Negroid minority for whom the quality of life will ultimately have to be upgraded.

9

Negroid Peoples in Colombia and Venezuela

COLOMBIA

The first push toward abolition: 1819–1830

In 1778, of some 51,999 slaves reported in what is present-day Colombia, 30,000 were allegedly in the gold-mining provinces of Popayán, Antioquia, Mariquita, and Chocó.[1] About 3,060,000 pesos of gold were extracted annually in this, the premier gold-producing area of Spanish America, and it was almost entirely the work of African slaves.[2] But from the last quarter of the eighteenth century, the problem of obtaining fresh replacements for incapacitated, dying, or escaped bondmen grew in intensity, so that by 1800 much of the precious metal produced in Antioquia was being mined by free Negroids.[3]

Because gold was the primary factor in the economic life of Colombia, its procurement and the status of the slaves who performed the manual labor become critical contingencies effecting both the progress of the wars of independence and the eventual abolition of the institution of slavery. As a result of his experiences in Venezuela in 1816, Bolívar had decided that freed slaves made excellent soldiers. Thus, on 6 February 1819 he ordered the further recruitment of 5,000 Colombian slaves. Realizing that the mass of these were concentrated in the gold-mining areas of the south and southwest, he ordered the bulk of the new conscripts be taken in the provinces of Antioquia, Chocó, Cauca, and Popayán. Liberty was offered in exchange for two years' service, and when Vice-President Francisco de

Paula Santander[4] questioned the economic wisdom of this move, Bolívar wrote:

> Is it fair that only free men should die for the liberation of slaves? Is it not proper that the slaves acquire their rights on the battlefield and that their dangerous numbers should be lessened by a process both just and effective?[5]

The conscription of slaves was carried on, the ex-owners receiving bonds or promissory notes if they cooperated, but the fighting and the imposition of republican authority sparked among many slaves the belief that general liberation was at hand. From 1820 to 1822 numerous rebellions broke out in Chocó, Popayán, and Cauca, the governor of Cauca reporting that thousands of slaves had fled or refused to work. Again, Santander had opposed Bolívar's drafting of the slaves, and the shrill cries of the mining interests galvanized him into action. The governor of Cauca was ordered to "apply the pain of death to the fugitive slaves that refused to return to their masters."[6] This drastic step was taken and order was restored. So many slaves had fled or been drafted, however, that indirectly, but unequivocally, the slave regime in Colombia had been put on the skids.

In comprehending *El Libertador*'s complex and contradictory attitude toward involuntary servitude, matters might be simplified if we approach the issue in this fashion: Bolívar, the white supremacist, felt that a stable regime would be impossible if too many Negroids survived the war. But Bolívar, the nineteenth-century liberal, believed that slavery was incompatible with natural law or republican principles. It is in this last role that he had proposed the total abolition of servitude to the constituent congress meeting at Cúcuta in 1819. Not surprisingly, the delegates balked at the suggestion. On 21 July 1821 this assembly passed a free-womb law, creating the equivalent of the *liberto* (called a *manumiso*) and establishing a *junta de manumisión* in each legislative district for the purpose of enforcing this legislation and collecting tax money to emancipate slaves born before 21 July 1821.

In supporting the idea of gradual liberation, some congressional delegates made much of "the state of ignorance and moral depredation to which this unfortunate portion of humanity finds itself reduced."[7] Several may have been totally convinced by such paternalistic prattle, but delegate José Gerónimo Torres stated the issue in its starkest terms when he reminded his colleagues that 55 percent of the aggregate investment in Gran Colombia was engaged in slaves.[8] As crucial was the fact that, without forced labor, the gold mines would cease to operate and a depression would result.[9] The act of 21 July 1821 was, therefore, still another piece of legislation designed to be all things to all men. The *manumiso* scheme in Colombia was not enforced, and the *juntas* were dominated by slave owners who refused to pay the taxes needed to finance the liberation of older slaves. But the law as passed averted a major struggle and provided the abolitionists with the comforting thought that the issue could be revived later.

In 1825 the congress sanctioned a trade treaty with Great Britain that contained an article condemning the slave trade. It also passed its own law prohibiting slave interests from procuring fresh bondmen in the West Indies.[10] Such "robust" action, however, in no way satisfied Simón Bolívar, who returned to rule the Gran Colombian Federation in September 1826. Learning that the *juntas de manumisión* had collected only enough money to free 461 slaves,[11] he promulgated new decrees aimed at facilitating the collection of taxes by the *juntas*. This was followed by another sweeping order (June 1828) calling for increased congressional vigilance over the *juntas* and more expeditious purchase and release of older slaves. But in 1827, congress learned that 52% of a reported 46,829 slaves were in the goldfields, and that forced labor remained the chief means of mining the ore.[12] Bolívar might propose, but the obstinate legislators would not ratify his policies.

Bolívar, the congress, and the slaveholders may well have been on some sort of collision course, but the Republic of Gran Colombia was collapsing even more rapidly under the hammer blows of sectionalism. When in 1830 it broke apart and Bolívar resigned as president, the slaveholding interests were able to go over to the offensive. Evidence of their resurgence is manifest in the Constitution of 1832, drawn up to govern the shrunken state of Colombia. This document mysteriously excluded all reference to the *juntas de manumisión*, the *manumiso* system, and the anti-slave-trade prohibitions signed in 1825.[13] All these laws became dead letters, irrefutable evidence that the abolitionist impulse had temporarily exhausted itself.

The slaveholders' counteroffensive and final collapse

A national census taken in 1836 revealed that there were at least 38,940 slaves in the Republic of Colombia, and that at least 55 percent of them were concentrated in the gold-producing regions of the south and southwest.[14] Meanwhile, the slavery issue became increasingly interwoven with other internal disputes. A civil war had broken out in 1839, and, when the smoke cleared, General Pedro de Alcántara Herrán, a conservative, had been elected to the presidency. Slave revolts had also wracked the goldfields in the Cauca region in 1842 and 1843, and in April of 1843 Cauca slaveholders sought from President Herrán the right to sell their slaves to eager customers in Peru. The government had received the support of the slaveholders, and it agreed to this petition; at least 800 bondmen were sold before President Tomás Cipriano de Mosquera put an end to this traffic in 1847.[15]

The 1848 revolutions in Europe also had a profound influence on the idealistic young political liberals of Colombia, and in 1849 their candidate, José Hilario López, was carried into office on the crest of a reformist tide.[16] López's ascension to the presidency was a victory for the Liberal party and its adherents over the Church, the political conservatives, the landed oligarchy, and certain gold-mining interests. Freedom of religion, freedom of the press, and the expulsion of the Jesuits followed in rapid succession. When López delivered a message to the congress in 1850 condemning slavery as "a barbarous legacy, incompatible with the philosophy of the century and the dictates of 'Christian brotherhood,' "[17] abolition became only a matter of legislative detail. Some liberals bitterly opposed indemnification, arguing that African bondage had been unjust both in origin and action, but López shrewdly realized that a gesture at reconciliation might help to ease the blow.

Some bondmen had fled, assuming that López's elevation to office meant emancipation. Many owners, banking on promises of indemnification, began releasing their properties in July 1850. On 21 May 1851 all slaves were ordered manumitted, and in June the Congress completed arrangements: As of 1 January 1852, all servitude was abolished. In return, the government of Colombia agreed to pay slaveholders about 2 million pesos for the 16,000 to 20,000 slaves then held or released since July 1850.[18] As in Ecuador, there is some suspicion that full payment was never intended; chief executives up to 1883 paid only 25 percent of the debt that López had contracted.[19]

Abolition in Colombia – an analysis

In 1851, in order to determine the amount to be paid to slave-holding interests, the López government effected a census of the slaves still held in the country. In 1778 roughly 60 percent of the slaves in what became Colombia were located in the gold-mining regions previously noted. Of the 16,468 bondmen reported in 1851, 10,486 (roughly 61 percent) were located in the same general areas (with the exception of Antioquia).[20] Since the bulk of the gold producers considered forced labor indispensable, how did their industry fare after abolition?

It would be preferable to provide clear-cut answers to a question of this nature, but the facts suggest that abolition produced a bag of mixed results. With the exception of the period from 1860 to 1864, gold production rose after emancipation, but much of the activity was confined to Antioquia, where free labor was by 1851 producing over 80 percent of the gold mined in that department.[21] In contrast, the richest areas, Chocó and Barbacoas, which had produced over 1 million pesos worth of gold in 1800, were yielding only 30 percent of that amount annually by 1880.[22] In essence, overall production rose, but the richest veins could no longer be exploited.

Gold mining was not, unfortunately, the only economic activity that suffered either unsettling shocks or losses. The sugar culture experienced a serious decline, and the entire country suffered an economic slump that was aggravated by civil war from 1854 to 1855.

Historians like Vicente Restrepo have long argued that abolition was carried out too hastily,[23] and although this position has some merit, the real culprits were the national leaders who governed the country between 1821 and 1849. If gradual abolition was the national policy, then the steady promulgation and enforcement of legislation toward that end should have been carried out. Instead, the slavocracy was allowed to turn back the clock, a situation that those sympathetic to abolition were certain to oppose violently once they took power. While the Liberal party's acts of 1851 and 1852 were poorly planned and economically disastrous, López and his followers made their country bite the bullet. For this, all Colombians owe them a debt of gratitude.

Unfortunately, in keeping with the emancipation actions taken by the nations to the south, nothing whatsoever was done to help the freedmen themselves. The latter had few if any skills, and many of those abandoning the mines in Chocó or Barbacoas simply became squatters or subsistence farmers. They took virtually no part in the national life and became forgotten men. Roughly one-half century after abolition, foreign entrepreneurs attempted to revive the mining industry in parts of Southwestern Colombia, but their offers of employment were generally spurned by local blacks and mulattoes. One Englishman remarked that "the Negroes are the laziest lot in Colombia; absolutely without ambition, they are content to live from day to day with the barest necessities."[24] The Afro-Colombians about whom this observer was speaking lived in what are today the departments of Cauca, Valle, and Chocó. Their ancestors, under duress, had worked the mines and placers of the region for roughly three centuries. Their reluctance to undertake similar labors, even for payment, is therefore hardly inscrutable.

The free Afro-Colombian in
a society of classes

The legal and social position of the freed Afro-Colombian since 1821 has been ambiguous. W. H. Rainsford, British consul in

Bogotá, reported to London in 1844 that "there is no difference in the eyes of the law between the free white and [the]
coloured man."[25] Her Majesty's local representative seemed
mysteriously uninterested in discovering how the legal equality
he reported was actually enforced. In fact, public racial clashes
were not uncommon during the presidency of Francisco de
Paula Santander (1832–1838). In the town of Mompós, for
example, race war was barely averted in 1837 and 1838, and
then only through the tact displayed by the local governor.[26]
Despite these and other unresolved racial difficulties, Colombian governments, whether liberal or conservative in party orientation, "strove noticeably to preserve the official picture of
equality and harmony." A handful of Negroid individuals were
able to obtain positions of authority, but the top political and
economic posts remained closed to them.[27]

Even more consequential were the provisions in the Constitutions of 1821, 1832, and 1843 that denied suffrage to those
who were illiterate, those who worked as domestic servants or
day laborers, and those who did not possess a sufficient amount
of unencumbered property.[28] Legal provisions like these were
not specifically aimed at the Afro-Colombian, but for all practical purposes they proved successful in keeping him away from
the ballot box both prior to 1852 and for a good many years
thereafter. Then, in 1910 the government passed new laws establishing comprehensive literacy and steep property requirements for those who would exercise the franchise.[29] Not until
the return of the Liberal party to power in 1930 and the re-
moval of these legal barriers could it be said that the Afro-
Colombian became a factor in national politics. We may thus
conclude that while Mr. Rainsford's estimate of the abstract
legal situation may have been accurate, his assessment of the de
facto one was sadly deficient.

During the twentieth century the picture has changed, but
hardly dramatically. Consider, for example, the question of the
size of the national Negroid population. In 1852 persons of full
or part African origin represented 21.1 percent of the total
population, while a 1942 census put the figure at 26.4 percent.[30] The 1912 and 1918 censuses were among the most com-

prehensive ever taken, but, for some unexplained reason, the entire black and mulatto population in the heavily Negroid departments of Bolívar and Caldas went unreported. A likely explanation for this mysterious omission is that either regional or national officials wanted to minimize the number of blacks and mulattoes in the country.[31]

Possibly the most competent student of racial population distribution in Colombia is T. Lynn Smith, the North American sociologist. He estimated that as of 1950 4,600,000 persons, or 28 percent of the population, were blacks, *zambos*, or mulattoes.[32] More conservative was a 1964 Colombian governmental survey that reported the Negroid population at 21 percent of the whole.[33] This distribution is identical in its breakdown (blacks 4 percent, *zambos* 3 percent, and mulattoes 14 percent) with that reported by the Colombian scholar Ernesto Camacho-Leyva in 1962, but smaller than that presented by the *Banco de la República* in 1963. This governmental agency concluded that 30 percent of the nation's inhabitants had some African blood.[34]

These population figures reveal that there is a substantial Afro-Colombian population in the country, but even more significantly, they suggest that Colombia probably has a greater number of Negroid inhabitants than any other Spanish American republic.[35] I have yet to see a native scholar ruminate on this prospect in print.

The Afro-Colombian in the national culture

Unflattering is the kindest way to describe the general attitude adopted by many Colombian intellectuals toward Negroid citizens. The philosophical tone and literary style for describing and analyzing the psychological makeup of the Afro-Colombian seems to have been established by European Positivist thinkers, whose influence remained pervasive well into the twentieth century. Witness the case of Juvena Mejía Córdoba, who, writing in 1918, glibly condemned the blacks and mulattoes of the Caribbean coast[36] as victims of their biological ancestry. In his opinion, this blighted racial heritage conferred upon said Negroids "the fatuity and conceit which is one of the characteristics of that race."[37] Another student of Colombian culture, Ramón Franco, characterized the Afro-Colombian in the departments of Cauca, Caldas, and Chocó in this way:

> Incapable of agricultural work, he has dedicated himself to the calling that gives most leeway to his idleness; raising and stealing cattle. On the shores of the Pacific, the Negro continued his boating, hunting, and his fishing. He is happy, amoral, without esthetic notions, fetishistic, affectionate, and lying.[38]

Although both these works were written more than three decades ago, the attitudes manifested in them have not disappeared. As recently as 1961, Juan Luis de Lannoy and Gustavo Pérez declared Afro-Colombians "more sensual" and "more superstitious" than the nation's Indian inhabitants.[39]

This kind of racial categorization could be dismissed as the work of a few eccentrics if other sophisticated studies were available, but works on the post-abolition status of the Afro-Colombian by national scholars are as rare as living saber-toothed tigers. It is true that sound, dispassionate works by Aquiles Escalante, José Rafael Arboleda, and Jaime Jaramillo Uribe[40] have been published, but not one of these scholars takes his investigation past the year 1852. To date, no major study on race relations since the abolition of slavery has been written by a Colombian citizen. It would seem that the attitudes of both the government and the scholarly community seem to coincide; Colombia is to be presented as a nation where the diverse races have become one big, happy family.

As of now, some of the most extensive research concerning contemporary social conditions for Afro-Colombians has been conducted by the anthropologist Thomas J. Price. This investigator spent several years observing the activities of the blacks and mulattoes on the Caribbean coast, chiefly arount Cartagena. Among the conclusions he reached were the following: (1) the upper strata of society is entirely dominated by white aristocrats; (2) whites and *mestizos* arriving on the coast from the national capital and other cities of the interior highlands generally consider the coastal Negroids to be biologically and intellectually inferior. "There is no question," writes Price, "that the presence of Negro blood constituted a severe social and economic handicap"; (3) Afro-Colombians believe that in legal disputes involving whites and blacks, "the decision invariably favors the white"; (4) many black and mulatto women prefer to be mistresses of white men rather than marry darkskinned males because of the "prestige value involved, and the feeling that one's own children will be lighter, and enjoy greater economic and social opportunities"; and (5) the assimilation of white cultural values is such that children lacking straight hair and possessing pronounced negroid features are deemed *maluco* ("sickly") and *feo* ("ugly") by their own parents.[41] Professor Price's message is blunt and bleak: For those who cannot become lighter, life can be hellish.

Conducting sociological research in the Cartagena area during the late 1960's were Professors Mauricio Solaún and Sidney Kronus. Initially, these investigators seem to differ markedly from Price. They argue that in Cartagena there has been a "relative acceptance of the miscegenated [mulattoes] by whites, and . . . infusion with equal status throughout all levels of the class structure."[42] The Solaún–Kronus duo also concluded that in Cartagena, two-thirds of the population are Negroid, but 76 percent of the persons belonging to the socially elite group are white; the rest are mulattoes, for access to this group is barred to blacks. Racial prejudice exists, but "it is concentrated against the polar-racial type."[43] There are apparently no whites among the lower class, but a fair number among the middle class; the mass of the mulattoes is also middle class. A few blacks are economically successful, and, although they resent the discrimination exercised against them, "it is propitious for them to accept their situation."[44]

Many of the other conclusions reached do not differ from those expounded by Professor Price. Blacks and mulattoes do their best to appear whiter, and they energetically seek to conceal or deemphasize their Negroid origins; white aesthetic standards of appearance are automatically valid for all.[45] If, however, becoming whiter is viewed as the best means of escape from the curse of blackness, what chance for acceptance does the great mass of Negroids have? This difficulty is glossed over by the two sociologists, but it would appear that concubinage (*amancebamiento*) remains the most likely method a darkly pigmented female would use in order to ensure more lightly pigmented offspring. If this is indeed the case, the Solaún–Kronus study suggests that little has changed socially since colonial times.

Wisely, these professors do not claim that white acceptance of mulattoes is the norm in other areas of the country. Unfortunately, almost nothing can be said about racial conditions in the east and central sectors of Colombia because the necessary research has yet to be attempted. Several investigations have been conducted, however, in the southwestern regions, where the Negroid population is larger. William C. Sayres studied the town of Zarfal (department of Cauca) and noted that after more than two centuries the whites, Negroids, and Indians have developed a complex but sophisticated racial etiquette. A *zambo*, for example, who performed an action his compatriots considered commendable became a *mestizo* in their eyes. Several months later, he committed a grievous *faux pas*, and his compatriots began denigrating him as an Indian.[46] This relatively innocuous discriminatory pattern did not hold when the Negroid branch of a leading family attempted to obtain a position of prominence equal to that allotted to the family's white descendants. In no uncertain terms, the place of distinction was denied the Negroids, the espoused reason being that they were "of another race."[47]

The anthropologist Paul Pavy III conducted research in the back lands of the Chocó, where virtually the entire population is either Negroid or Indian. He pointed out that even with practically no white residents in the area, the Negroids recognized at least ten different color categories, and that color was "a very important aspect of social perception."[48]

It is in the urban sector, in towns like Quibdó (capital of the Chocó), however, that the most abrasive situations abound. Prior to World War II, whites and mulattoes had combined to keep the blacks from elective and appointive administrative office, but the government has undergone some alteration since then. Nevertheless, the opening of bureaucratic positions has hardly altered the situation. According to Professor Thomas Sanders,

> in Quibdó Blacks predominate in party politics and public administration, but Whites, usually from the outside, control commerce, governmental power, the Church and the police. . . . Real power is overwhelmingly in the hands of Whites, many of whom, while not discriminating openly, have a condescending view of the Blacks . . . 99 percent of business in the city is run by Whites.[49]

Relations between the races appear amicable on the surface, but young Negroids have become increasingly aware of the disdainful attitude of the whites, and they resent it. A few even argue that the national government in Bogotá does nothing to relieve the extreme poverty of the Chocó precisely because the mass of the inhabitants are Negroid. Whites in Quibdó demonstrated both fear and consternation whenever questions regarding racial discrimination were publicly aired.[50] For most inhabitants of African blood, however, the major problems have been economic. Many understand that discrimination exists, but food, clothing, shelter, and better educational opportunities are their primary concerns. In the back of their minds, they seem to believe that the acquisition of the cudgels of success will eventually win them the respect and affection of the whites.

Although these reports and studies provide illuminating insights into the position of the Afro-Colombian, they also aptly illustrate the need for more comprehensive studies by competent national scholars. From the evidence accumulated, it should be obvious that racial prejudice and color discrimination were not eradicated root and branch with the abolition of slavery in 1852. If this fact is admitted, perhaps Colombian researchers will be able to discard their reticence in regard to racial investigations and produce the kind of responsible studies that only those who know their homeland can produce.

The Afro-Colombian reaction

Not all the black and brown citizens of Colombia are poor, illiterate fishermen or farmers. Conspicuous during the 1930s and 1940s was the small number of blacks and mulattoes who emerged as important figures in the Liberal party. These include Efraím Canavera Romero, a leading figure of long standing on the Bogotá City Council; Diego Luis Córdoba, a federal senator from the Chocó; Francisco de Paula Vargas, a federal deputy; and Arigga Andrade Addan, the governor appointed to the Chocó when that territory became a department in 1947. Other Afro-Colombians, however, have been unable to join important social clubs or to obtain jobs for which they had skills. Prior to the Korean War, for example, the exclusion of blacks from the army officer corps was the unexpressed but standard policy.[51]

The most outspoken critics of the prevailing racial situation have been Negroid musicians, writers, and novelists. In their works, many have long insisted that, although the Afro-Colombian accepts his position and tells himself that the issue is class, in reality, he is tagged by whites on the basis of race and/or color. Arnoldo Palacio's novel *Las estrellas son negras* (*The Stars Are Black*, 1949) is a typical work dealing with this theme. The hero of the book, a youth named Irrá, believes that each person is born under a particular star that then guides his destiny; his is a "black star ... black as my face."[52] Irrá is desperately poor and increasingly frustrated. Although he struggles to improve his condition, his great discovery is that there is an additional factor shackling him to his unhappy fate:

> Already he [Irrá] had lost the hope that they would give
> him employment as a porter because he was Negro, and al-
> most all the establishments give these jobs to the whites,
> or to the Negroes who lick the shoes of the [white] boss.[53]

Irrá can continue to struggle against the odds, but his prospects for success are infinitesimal. Insofar as his fight can be said to emulate the general struggle of the Afro-Colombian, the point seems to be that no universal solution exists. An occasional mulatto or a lucky black may rise in the society, but poverty, disease, and prejudice doom most Negroids to a lifetime of misery even before they are born.

In contrast to the despair that pervades *Las estrellas son negras*, a hopeful Manuel Zapata Olivella proposed an amorphous form of biracial solidarity in *Corral de negros* (*Barnyard for Negroes*, 1965). The question is never whether prejudice exists because this is an accepted fact. In Zapata Olivella's eyes, the racist Colombian oligarchs are merely lackeys of that great racist oppressor, the United States of America. Seemingly, his final solution is to smash the power of the Yankee imperialists with a Marxist-oriented, Third World coalition of like-minded (and/or darkskinned) souls.[54] Zapata Olivella recognizes that an alliance of this type may take years to build, but, concerning short-range steps, he provides no more answers than Palacios.

The works of these angry young writers do not necessarily indicate that the Afro-Colombian will soon demand the immediate termination of all forms of discrimination. Nevertheless, they do imply that, as more blacks and mulattoes become educated and realize that a new shirt or a new car may not make them "white," many of them will express sentiments similar to those intoned by Lenor González Mina in her song, "Negro, negro":

> Why do you look down on me?
> Because my skin is black?
> . . . I am not ashamed.[55]

VENEZUELA

The politics of emancipation

As the third part of Simón Bolívar's Gran Colombian Republic, Venezuela was also subject to the slave legislation of 21 July 1821. In January 1830 José Antonio Páez declared the country independent of the Gran Colombian Federation and designated 30 April as the date for the meeting of the first Venezuelan National Congress. As in Ecuador, the July 1821 legislation governing *manumisos* and *juntas de manumisión* was reaffirmed, thereby establishing public evidence of the national commitment to gradual abolition. But the old law had freed *manumisos* at the age of eighteen; the 1830 legislation inexplicably moved the age of liberation to twenty-one. Furthermore, the functioning of the system in Venezuela soon indicated that the holders of *manumisos* regarded the laws as little more than platitudes by which humanitarian citizens might assuage their guilt. *Manumisos* were hunted down if they ran away, forbidden to live in domiciles separate from those of their masters, and prohibited from marrying without the master's consent.[56] While the body of the *manumiso* was theoretically not for sale, Venezuelans employed the same legal distinctions and mental reservations made by Argentines in 1813,[57] buying and selling *manumisos* much as they had always done with slaves.

The necessity of obtaining and holding cheap labor to work the coffee and cacao plantations preordained that the slavocracy would make determined efforts to keep either the slaves or the *manumisos* from ever becoming truly liberated. The law changing the age of liberation to twenty-one temporarily appeased these agrarian interests. By 1842, however, some of the *manumisos* would have automatically become free, so rather conveniently, in 1840 the national government again intervened. New legislation made the individual *manumiso* responsible to his master (now officially dubbed "patron") until the former had reached his twenty-fifth birthday. This fresh accommodation was shabbily disguised as an apprenticeship program under which the freed Negroid was to be taught a trade, thereby transforming him into a useful member of society. Enforcement of this new program became still another task for the *juntas de manumisión*, and since in Venezuela these groups were dominated by slaveholders, the lack of enforcement of the program was all but guaranteed.[58]

More than anything else, the final collapse of slavery in Venezuela was inextricably tied to the fear of the government that the opposition intended to mobilize the slaves as troops. In 1845 General José Tadeo Monagas was elected to the presidency on the Conservative party ticket. Once in office, Monagas disavowed his former political allies and cast his lot with the Liberal party. In 1848 he expelled many opposition congressmen from the legislature and became the most powerful figure in the country. It was with Monagas's approval that a 1848 law was passed declaring all *manumisos* free at the age of twenty-one.

The 1848 statute was initially resisted by the slaveholding interests, but within a year, both *manumisos* and slaves were being liberated and then forcibly conscripted into armies led by Conservative and Liberal party chieftains. When José Tadeo Monagas completed his term of office in 1851, his brother, José Gregorio, was chosen to replace him. The prospect of indefinite rule by the Monagas brothers alienated many members of the Liberal party, a substantial number of whom joined with Conservatives in the rebellion of May 1853. By December the Monagas brothers had scotched the revolt, but it was obvious that the opposition was merely licking its wounds and anticipating the next round. The wily José Gregorio therefore chose to make a preemptive strike. On 24 March 1854 he proclaimed total emancipation, a move described by the Venezuelan historian Guillermo Morón as executed "purely in order to forestall the conspirators and to gain support."[59]

Naturally, if the slaveholding interests were to be divided or even temporarily mollified, as in Colombia and Ecuador, they would have to be proffered the required carrot. Venezuelan government records indicate that in 1854 there were 12,093 slaves and 11,285 *manumisos* in the country, valued at an estimated of 4,432,991 Venezuelan pesos.[60] Paying homage to the concept of the inviolability of private property, the abolition decree promised reimbursement for the release of all persons subject to the rigors of involuntary servitude. As in so many other cases, the number of bondmen and *manumisos* actually released by the 1854 law remains an unsettled question. There were a reported 87,800 slaves in Venezuela in 1810,[61] and 40,000 as late as 1840.[62] For the total to have shrunk in fourteen years to less than 12,093 is almost incredible. If we assume, however, that the government would pay only for slaves whose existence could be proven through previous tax reports, then the 1854 figure may well represent the minimum number of bondmen legally held at the time the emancipation decree was issued.

The question of the number of slaves released becomes even

more curious when considered from another perspective. Between 1821 and 1854 the various *juntas de manumisión* in Venezuela succeeded in freeing 1,223 slaves, an average of roughly 36 per year.[63] This dismal record is evidence of the power of the slavocracy, but it does not fully explain government policy during the period. All regimes from 1830 to 1854, whether Liberal or Conservative, wanted Venezuela to be appraised as a "progressive" republic, at least by foreigners. This entailed the creation of the illusion of movement toward final abolition, even though internal exigencies necessitated preservation of the status quo. These contradictory aims could be reconciled since the slavocracy paid lip service to the idea of future liberation, and the governments insisted that full remuneration accompany abolition. Determined to stay in power by any means necessary, the Monagas brothers used abolition as a political ploy when they declared abolition, but had they not acted, this charade might have continued for decades.

The moral question aside, abolition failed to yield the results desired by either the emancipators or the slavocracy. In three years the Monagas regime had collapsed, and not a peso of compensation was paid to the ex-slaveholders. For a change, the only profiteers from the act of emancipation were the slaves themselves.

The prospect of race war in nineteenth-century Venezuela

In post-1830 Venezuela a few mulattoes did succeed in fighting their way into positions of prominence. Possibly the most significant was José Rafael Revenga, who became a member of the congress (1844–1848) and, later, secretary of Internal Affairs under José Tadeo Monagas.[64] Balancing this picture is the case of the *Sociedad de amigos del país* ("Society of Friends of the Country"). Formed by aristocratic whites in the capital city in 1834, this organization specifically declared its membership to be open only to whites. A great hue and cry was raised against this policy, particularly by prominent mulattoes who perceived (probably correctly) that the racial clause was aimed directly at them. The *sociedad* suffered scathing denunciations in the press, but there is no evidence that it soon retreated from its position.[65]

Further indication of the continuing racial friction in early Venezuelan society is found in the diary of John S. A. Williamson, an American diplomat stationed in the country between 1835 and 1840. Williamson recorded that, despite the surface camaraderie, "a great antipathy exists between white and black here."[66] As proof of this conclusion, he cited the 1835 rebellion led by Colonel José Farfán. Williamson's report of the affair, which was subsequently substantiated by another Yankee diplomat,[67] provides a compelling explanation of why Venezuelan leaders strove diligently to preserve the official picture of racial harmony:

> The recent attempt at revolution by Colonel Farfán, from a further inquiry into its origin, would appear to have arisen absolutely from the hostility on the part of the coloured population against the whites more than from any political motive whatever. . . . The government is disposed to keep this last insurrection very silent, and without publick [sic] inquiry into its origin or its principles.[68]

The suppression of this revolt did little to lessen the apprehension of the ruling classes concerning the possibility of a new outbreak of racial violence. Early in 1844 Juan Manuel Manrique, minister of Foreign Relations, confided in Allen A. Hall, United States chargé d'affaires in Caracas, that the slaughter of whites then occurring in the war between Santo Domingo and Haiti would certainly exacerbate racial tensions in Venezuela. Hoping to forestall internal racial strife, Manrique sought United States intervention in the Haitian–Dominican War.[69] Similar feelings of panic were also expressed to Hall by President Carlos Soublette, who pessimistically predicted in December 1844 that a Venezuelan "war between the races" was an imminent possibility.[70]

The reign of the Monagas brothers (1845–1857) witnessed many accusations that José Tadeo and José Gregorio were fomenting racial conflict in an effort to maintain themselves in power.[71] After the long and seemingly senseless civil wars that followed José Tadeo's fall from power in 1857, "a fusion of the population" took place under the regime of Guzmán Blanco.[72] Racial conflict does not seem to have been a major element in subsequent political upheavals. It should be remembered, however, that in 1810 the majority of the population in Venezuela probably was of Negroid blood.[73] What may well have happened is that the whites who had dominated the society began to allow the ascension of more mulattoes into the upper realms of power. In any event, the governing officialdom has become much more circumspect in discussing racial difficulties than the Manriques and Soublettes of old.

The Afro-Venezuelan in
contemporary society

Information concerning the postabolition status of Negroids in Venezuela is exceedingly sketchy. National historians and sociologists who deal with racial issues have displayed a remarkable propensity to limit the focus of their investigations to the pre-1854 years. In fact, no comprehensive study of postabolition racial conditions and policies seems to have been published.[74] The sparse commentaries on this subject elicited from the works of Venezuelan scholars further emphasize the paucity of materials available. Possibly the outstanding authority on the Afro-Venezuelan is Miguel Acosta Saignes, whose works on the colonial period have been referred to often in this work. The clarity of explanation and meticulousness in detail that enriched his colonial studies inexplicably vanish, however, when he discusses post-1854 conditions. According to Acosta Saignes, after abolition, Afro-Venezuelans "entered into the popular mainstream as farm laborers," an occupation in which the mass of them is still to be found. As for racial prejudice, the author asserts that this passion has largely disappeared except at "certain levels" and in "some strata" of society. He does not elaborate which ones these are, but he does remark that where such bias is found, it is "deeply embedded."[75]

When it comes to concreteness and candor, the commentary of Acosta Saignes does not compare with the otherwise undistinguished account of conditions provided by Henry J. Allen.

Writing in 1940 and 1941, this author found that Venezuelan society had a place for talented mulattoes, but

> Negro immigrants from the Antilles are now prohibited. . . . There is a growing color line so far as the Negro is concerned. . . . He [the] Negro is being gently retired from the Army as officer material.[76]

One critical reason that the philosophical and socioeconomic vagaries served up by Acosta Saignes are inadequate is that they fail to provide a basic framework in which the overall issue of race relations can be studied. Among the first to undertake such an effort was José Gil Fortoul, a turn-of-the-century intellectual. The influence of this author in forging the national perception on racial questions necessitates careful analysis, and the apparent contradiction found in his *El hombre y la historia: Ensayo de la sociología venezolana* (*Man and History: An Essay on Venezuelan Sociology*, 1896) requires some explanation. He glibly informs the reader, for example, that "the preoccupations of color" that had affected the nation were disappearing. But, on the same page, he declares that in 1891 the census did not include a racial tabulation "because of the fear, perhaps, of offending the susceptibilities of the Negroes and the descendants of the slaves."[77] If Gil Fortoul is correct in this assumption, it should be obvious that his first conclusion must be drastically qualified because "the preoccupations of color" had definitely not become passé among Afro-Venezuelans. Of course, it may be that the author only meant that white Venezuelans were becoming less concerned about such problems. In any event, the seeming contradiction only emphasizes the divided nature of Venezuelan society and the means employed to gloss over the racial fissures.

Gil Fortoul's essential arguments, however, are that, since Venezuelan independence, "the man of mixed blood" has come to predominate in national affairs and that "the biological fusion of the elements" would produce a new Venezuelan population.[78] A semiofficial census taken by Giovanni Batista Agostino Codazzi in 1839 would seem to bear out Gil Fortoul's assessments (see table 12).

Table 12. Codazzi estimate of the Venezuelan population

Type	Number
Unpacified Indians	52,411
Civilized or domesticated Indians	155,000
Negroid slaves	49,782
Whites	260,000
Mulattoes, mestizos, free blacks	414,151
Total	931,344

Source: José Gil Fortoul, El hombre y la historia: Ensayo de la sociología venezolana (Paris, 1896), pp. 23–24.

Codazzi's figures were fairly speculative, but the noted sociologist Ángel Rosenblat estimated that the black and mulatto population in Venezuela still represented at least 30.7 percent of the whole in 1940.[79] The problem is that since the first national census was undertaken in 1876, a statistical compilation on the basis of race has never been made. It is therefore impossible to determine with any accuracy whether the mulatto element is growing, whether the black or zambo groups are decreasing, or whether the mestizos and whites outnumber the Negroids. Without such information, the miscegenation ethic cannot be effectively challenged, a factor that provides Gil Fortoul's hypothesis with the continuing credibility it might not otherwise enjoy.

Today the miscegenated-population dogma is constantly reiterated in materials made for students and for those curious about national values. Guillermo Morón's Historia de Venezuela, officially sanctioned as a reader for public secondary schools, categorically declares that "the Negro has been assimilated into the society without impediment."[80] Furthermore, Morón argues that the nation's success at achieving racial integration is an example that other countries (unnamed, of course) would be wise to emulate. Even more chauvinistic is the Manual de venezolanidad para extranjeros (Manual of Venezuelan Identity for Foreigners, 1964), published and disseminated directly by the government. Apparently no one responsible for this book ever asked himself whether the euphoric descriptions provided would be taken seriously by discriminating readers. We are told that Venezuela is:

> an equalitarian society . . . where there are no racial differences, no prejudices of race. . . . In Venezuela social equality is not only consecrated in the law but lies in the heart of the Venezuelan as part of his manner of being and feeling.[81]

A casual stroll down the streets of Caracas reveals that the Venezuelan people are a miscegenated lot. The question to be asked, however, is whether the political elites have sought to control the elements in the mix.

Miscegenation, *sí*; blacks, *no*

The theoretical assumptions of the writer Laureano Vallenilla Lanz have seemingly had an effect upon twentieth-century Venezuelan immigration policy. The storm of European Positivism that broke over other Latin American intellectual institutions drenched Venezuelan universities as well. This influence is unmistakable in Vallenilla Lanz's *Cesarismo democrático*, a work usually cited as a sophisticated defense for the Juan Vicente Gómez regime from 1908 to 1935. A basic theme of the work is that a miscegenated and heavily Negroid population such as Venezuela has is basically incapable of governing itself; national progress under such unfavorable conditions necessitates the rule of a benevolent but ruthless strong man.[82] What is usually overlooked is that Vallenilla Lanz did not consider this situation permanent. Racial improvement and representative democracy could eventually be attained if certain conditions were met. The answer, as Vallenilla Lanz wrote a friend in November 1920, was "white immigration, European and North American immigration."[83]

Juan Alberdi of Argentina had espoused this same cure-all over seventy years before, and although the Venezuelans were a bit late in jumping on the bandwagon, the political leadership embraced the concept with a fanatical zeal. When in 1924 the rumor spread that West Indian and North American blacks might be allowed to enter the country to assist in harvesting the sugar and cacao crops, the Gómez government made its position categorically clear:

> We need and will only allow European immigration. . . .
> The United States is preoccupied with guarding its race,
> and to this effort dictates regulations concerning immigra-
> tion. The problem for us is exceedingly grave, and a fair
> policy that is well thought out ought to have for its ob-
> jective whitening the population as much as would be pos-
> sible. All Venezuelans, equal before the law and before
> society, have in this goal, the same supreme interest.[84]

Once again we see that while the Indian-European mixture was acceptable – even Juan Vicente Gómez was a *mestizo* – mixed Negroid ancestry was often quite another matter. In 1929 the immigration of persons of African origin was banned. The law issued on 22 July 1936 established a new immigration policy but again barred the entry of Negroids.[85] Alberto Andriani, architect of the new policy and minister of the Treasury in the López Contreras government (1936–1941), argued in *Labor venezolanista* that the black man was no asset to the nation's economic development. Andriani admitted that a "homogeneous white population" was an impossible development in Venezuela, but the face of the nation could be dramatically changed if Europeans were brought in and Negroids kept out.[86]

Since 1936 the directors of Venezuelan immigration policy have operated largely within the scope defined by Andriani. The flow was initially slow, but between 1946 and 1952 at least 96,000 Europeans came to Venezuela.[87] For certain groups of Italian agriculturists, the government paid all transportation costs and provided subsidies for the creation of agricultural colonies in the interior.[88] Since 1958, more avowedly democratic regimes have risen to power in Venezuela, and, on 18 July 1966, a new immigration decree dropped all racial prohibitions. But legal change does not necessarily signify philosophical conversion. Bearing in mind past attitudes, it would be interesting to speculate on the survival of the present law if even 100,000 Negroids from the overpopulated West Indies began knocking insistently on Venezuela's door.

On Venezuelan racial harmony
and discrimination

Personal experiences in Venezuela in 1962, 1965, 1970, and 1974 provide still another view of the situation. Discussing racial questions with Afro-Venezuelans was usually a painful experience. Most of them began by denying the existence of any racial prejudice in their country. Some grudgingly admitted that they had experienced embarrassing incidents, but these they preferred to view as based on nonracial causes. Others were amazed to learn that an immigration law barring Negroid people had ever been passed but doggedly insisted that it in no way indicates any discriminatory intent on the part of the government. A few asserted that, while the nation is biologically miscegenated, the political and financial strength lies in the hands of the whites. The basic impression gained was that many Afro-Venezuelans would prefer to be white, while others are thankful that the myth of national equity has not yet been debunked, thereby allowing them to ignore the question altogether.

Perhaps because I was a foreigner, some white Venezuelans in cities like Caracas, Barquisimeto, and Maracaibo chose to discuss the race relations issue with a great deal more frankness. "A subtle prejudice exists here," several of them noted, while a university professor remarked that educated North American blacks would often be socially acceptable where an Afro-Venezuelan with a similar background would not. A white, Alabama-born petroleum technician in Maracaibo remarked that "prejudice is different here, but it's real enough." The most plain-spoken individual was the son of an Austrian immigrant who had married an attractive woman of Afro-Indian origin. "Only after I had done this [married]," he observed, "did I realize what the [racial] problem in Venezuela could be like."

Most Venezuelans seem to find the discussion of racial issues uncomfortable, but in the national literature some novelists have not hesitated to present their views while allegedly describing the background of characters. Rufino Blanco-Fombona, although admittedly a man of irritable temperament, presented the main Afro-Venezuelan character in *El hombre de oro* (1906) with undue malice:

> Andrés Rata [rat] was, physically, an ill-shaped youth, of blackish skin, an agile, bony, undersized mulatto with a hanging, blubber lip and yellowish eyes. One seeks instinctively in such a person a tail, for it is hard to tell at first sight whether this is the metamorphosis of a monkey, or the degeneration of a man who has reverted to the ape. . . . Morally, he was even worse; filthy, or infectious as the saliva of a consumptive and more vile than vileness itself.[89]

More benign presentations of mulattoes can be found in the works of Romulo Gallegos and Artur Uslar Pietri,[90] but Afro-Venezuelans as a group, are still depicted in a negative fashion. Consider Levi Marrero's *Venezuela y sus recursos: Una geografía visualizada (Venezuela and Its Resources: A Visualized Geography*, 1964), which is a textbook intended for secondary school students. This work clearly presents the Venezuelan as a mixture of the African, the Spaniard, and the Indian, but while there is a short description of the past history of each group, the story of the African in Venezuela terminates with the end of the colonial period.[91] Most significantly, the student is informed that the Venezuelan "inherited from the Negro the love of work"; on the other hand he owes to the Indian and the Spaniard "the love of liberty, valor, and lofty character."[92] But could not the Afro-Venezuelan have contributed the same virtues as the whites and the Indians? Does the African have an innate propensity toward manual labor? What does the Afro-Venezuelan who reads this textbook come to believe about himself and his ancestors? In Venezuela these questions are apparently not asked, and as long as matters remain this way, it is possible to have racial harmony and racial inequality at the same time.

10
Negroid Peoples in Central America and Mexico

CENTRAL AMERICA

Instant abolition

When the Central American states declared their independence from Spain on 15 September 1821 and later severed their political connection with Mexico (29 June 1823), they did so without the bloody carnage that characterized the struggle in other parts of Spanish America. Equally nonviolent was the transition from slave to free society, an event engineered by political liberals and proclaimed by the national constituent assembly on 16 and 24 April 1824. Indemnification of the slaveholders was provided by this law, but details and actual payment were matters to be determined by the five states that composed the Central American Federation – Guatemala, El Salvador, Honduras, Nicaragua, and Costa Rica.[1]

No one has ever been able to determine the number of slaves in Central America in 1824, but there were at least 100 in Costa Rica and 800 on two plantations in Guatemala.[2] Manumission committees were created in each state, and in accordance with the law of 24 April, 65 pesos became the minimum payment for the emancipation of an individual bondman. Legislation providing for the termination of slavery in Central America seemed aimed at preventing the slavocracy from reaping a financial windfall. Full compensation on the assessed value of a slave was to be given only on a bondman less than twelve years old; on all others, various deductions were prescribed.[3] About 80 slaves allegedly were paid for in Costa Rica,[4] but, given the intermittent civil strife that wracked the Central American Federation and finally wrought its dissolution in 1839, it is unlikely that the slaveholders received more than token payments for their properties.

The Central American abolition decree, like those passed in other Spanish American republics, was never energetically enforced, and violations of its restrictions were numerous. The most significant example of noncompliance took place in 1826, when several hundred Negroids in Guatemala claimed that they were still being held in bondage and asked the Federal Congress to investigate their plight. Unfortunately, the altruism of 1824 had apparently been dissipated, for the legislature voted to disregard this request.[5] The advocates of abolition had given little consideration to the socioeconomic consequences of their actions; still, involuntary servitude was never so critical to the Central American economic system that some version of the excrescent *liberto* system had to be introduced. The ex-slave simply became one of the mass of persons living more or less at a subsistence level.

Racial policy and the Negroid presence in Central America

No analysis of the contemporary status of the Negroid population in Guatemala, Honduras, El Salvador, Nicaragua, Costa Rica, and Panama can be undertaken without considering the geographical factors that influenced the pattern of territorial settlement. Both the Caribbean and Pacific coastal lowlands are humid and swampy, but running through the center of Central America is a rugged mountain range, intersected by plateaus, or tablelands (*mesetas*). With the exception of Managua (Nicaragua) and Panama City, the capitals of all the Central American countries are located on upland plains at least 2,000 feet above sea level. The Spanish congregated in these highlands, and the mass of the populace of each nation (except for Panama) lives there today. Most of these people know or care little about their Caribbean coast, which they consider virtually a foreign country. In contrast, since colonial times, escaped slaves, *cimarrones*, and freedmen who mated with Indians[6] established themselves along the Caribbean. The mass of the Negroid population still lives there, although the majority are the present-day descendants of West Indians who were introduced by the United Fruit Company during the early twentieth century.

Effective determination of the size of the Negroid population in Central America has been made difficult by social sensitivity and governmental practice. Colonial records reveal that the African has been present in El Salvador at least since 1548.[7] There were roughly 4,000 slaves in this region by 1650; by 1930 the census reported 72 *negros* out of a total of 1,434,361 persons.[8] Rodolfo Barón Castro, probably the ablest student of Salvadorean demographic affairs, noted that the black population of the capital city of San Salvador in 1929 was 0.5 percent.[9] It is unlikely that *zambos* or mulattoes were included in either the Barón Castro survey or the 1930 census. Since that time, no statistical information on race has been published by Salvadorean governments, and there is some doubt whether a Negroid person would officially be granted anything other than a temporary residency in the country.[10]

In Guatemala the basis for census classification since 1893 has been essentially cultural.[11] Those who speak Spanish and wear shoes are considered "western" and are identified as *ladinos*. It is assumed that all others speak an indigenous tongue primarily and wear sandals rather than shoes; they are categorized as Indians. Only in 1940 did the Guatemalan government attempt to conduct a racial survey of its citizenry. At that time, 40 percent of the population were described as "white," while about 4,000 persons (less than 1 percent) were considered *negro*.[12] Again, given this minuscule percentage, it is questionable whether *zambos* and mulattoes were included as Negroid in this tabulation. Unlike the Salvadoreans, Guatemalan governments have made their racial preferences clear. A decree (no. 1781) issued on 25 January 1936 prohibited the immigration of "individuals of the Negro race," a prohibition that was later written into the Constitution of 1945.[13] This document has been superceded, but the ban against Negroid immigrants is apparently still in effect.

Honduras presents a slightly different picture. The 1945 census suggests that 90 percent of the population were racially mixed, 7 percent were Indian, 2 percent were black, and 1 percent was white.[14] Nineteenth-century assessments of the Negroid population by William Welles and Robert Dunlap make the 2 percent figure of 1945 slightly absurd.[15] A few authors have also inexplicably assumed that the racially mixed category consisted entirely of white-Indian hybrids.[16] The investigator probably closest to the truth is Franklin D. Parker, who persuasively argues that *zambos* and mulattoes were counted as part of the mixed group and that the true number of Negroids in the country was roughly 10 to 15 percent of the total.[17] Honduran governments have since included no racial assessments in their surveys, but laws passed in March 1934 and January 1935 are still in effect, and they prohibit the entry or immigration of "Negroes," "gypsies," and "coolies."[18]

The implicit rationale behind the method of racial classification employed seems to be that both the leadership in Honduras and the literate public prefer to view themselves as mixed rather than as 15 to 20 percent Negroid. It may be that the *hondureños* quietly borrowed a few ideas from the Panamanians, who took a census using the same jargon in 1940; the racial breakdown of the Panamanian population was given as 71.8 percent mixed and 14.6 percent *negro*.[19] But in the Honduran case it can only be surmised that the data were interpreted to favor the mixed categorization; two sociological scholars argue convincingly that in Panama this was exactly what was done. Moreover, they insist that only the very darkest people were classified as *negro* and that more than half of those listed as mixed were not *mestizos*, but mulattoes and persons of Afro-Indian descent.[20] Further evidence that the Panamanians did not wish to appear too Negroid can be seen in the 1940 constitutional article that specifically prohibited the granting of citizenship to certain kind of Negroid immigrants.[21]

The most unusual color-classification scheme of all was utilized by Nicaragua in its 1920 population computation. Residents were classified as *amarillo* ("yellow"), *cobrizo* ("copper-colored"), *negro* ("black"), *blanco* ("white"), or *trigueño* ("wheat-colored"). In that census, 60,654 persons were reported as *negro* (9 percent), and Euro-Africans and Afro-Indians were counted as *trigueño* or *cobrizo*.[22] More than likely, this method of racial categorization displeased and antagonized a fair number of influential persons, for it was never tried again; in fact, Nicaragua has not reported any racial data about its population since that time. But a policy still enjoying the favor of the political elites is the racial-exclusion section of the immigration law of 5 May 1930. According to its provisions, members of the Negro, Chinese, and "Gypsy" races are ineligible for Nicaraguan citizenship.[23]

Of all the Central American nations, only Costa Rica has often attempted to pass itself off as a "white" nation. Nevertheless, Spanish officialdom in 1801 reported the black, mulatto, and *zambo* population as 17 percent of the whole.[24] While the absolute number of Negroid Costa Ricans increased, by 1950 their percentage of the total declined to 2 percent.[25] Unquestionably, miscegenation has led in the direction of total amalgamation, and executive decrees 2 (22 September 1911) and 4 (1 May 1942) banning the entry of blacks, North Africans, and Orientals – virtually everyone except northern Europeans – have speeded up the process.[26]

Given the antipathies manifested in these statutes and policy practices, it is hardly surprising that Central America has produced its share of racist intellectuals. They run the gamut from Pablo Lévy, who in the nineteenth century argued that mating with mulattoes produced inferior issue,[27] to Luis Díaz Navarro, who in the 1940s condemned the mulattoes of the Caribbean coast of Honduras as "cowards by nature" and "inclined to all kinds of evil."[28] Afro-Indians have also been subject to literary abuse. At the hands of Antonio Murchio Frascara, for example, the descendants of the *sambo-mosquitos* are depicted as subhuman brutes, devoid of humanistic instincts and hopelessly deficient in intellectual capacity.[29]

To conclude, however, that somehow Central Americans are more anti-Negroid than Colombians, Venezuelans, or other South Americans is to be ignorant of certain extenuating circumstances. During the nineteenth century, for example, the

British pushed the border of their colony Belize farther and farther west, despite vehement protests from Guatemalan governments. Because the population of Belize is overwhelmingly black, the Guatemalan exclusion policy must be understood as being partially designed to keep the "enemy" out.[30]

Another situation in which mitigating circumstances must be considered is the Chiriqui project.[31] Originating in about 1862, this plan called for the resettlement of free Afro-Americans in Central America and received the personal sanction of Abraham Lincoln. But the governments of Costa Rica, Honduras, El Salvador, and Nicaragua voiced their implacable opposition, and the Great Emancipator reluctantly scrapped the plan.[32] The Central American governments were indeed united in their adamant opposition to the settlement of Afro-Americans in their region, but questions other than race had spurred this uncharacteristic display of unity. The 1850s had seen the issuance of the Ostend Manifesto[33] and, even more crucially, the continued interference in regional affairs by William Walker, the yankee adventurer who had at one time ruled Nicaragua. Perhaps the Afro-Americans would have been model citizens, but they might also have been the spearhead for a new Washington-directed drive to establish colonies in Central America. Black or white, they were Yankees, and the *latinos* can hardly be blamed for not wanting to foster a situation that conceivably might jeopardize their national futures.

The anti-Negroid entry and immigration legislation also has its basis in the fact that the North American fruit companies, in building up their operations on the Caribbean coast (in every country except El Salvador), brought in black West Indians to perform the necessary agricultural labor. These workmen spoke no Spanish, were non-Catholic, and initially had little interest in becoming citizens of the Central American republics. Under these circumstances, any increase in their numbers was regarded as a threat to the national security of the host country. If the Antilleans had had blue eyes and blond hair, the Central Americans would have exhibited manifestly different attitudes, but the cultural differences would still have caused some friction. Thus, the immigration exclusion laws must also be viewed as attempts to preserve cultural unity and to minimize the competition that the indigenous work force might have had to face.

The Negroid position in Central American society

Culturally and racially, the Central American insists on depicting himself as "Spanish," according to Salvador Mendieta.[34] Especially in the *mestizo* and Indian states of El Salvador, Guatemala, Honduras, and Nicaragua, "Spanish origin is prized."[35] Perhaps in a fit of euphoria, Salvadorean author Pedro Fonseca even asserted that the bulk of the population in his nation possessed "the predominant characteristics of the white race."[36] The point is that whiteness or Spanish ancestry is desired, and that is why racial data in censuses was sometimes presented in the curious fashion noted in the previous pages. Now racial statistics are no longer reported, and anyone may call himself white without worrying about unpleasant facts and figures.

Obviously, dark skin and kinky hair are not prized by the society at large; in addition, it is not to be expected that the descendants of slaves would possess much of whatever society deemed worthy of having. Sonfonías Salvatierra argued that in Nicaragua "all blacks and mulattoes" were at the bottom of the socioeconomic ladder,[37] while the Honduran researcher Humberto López Villanil, reported the same to be the case in his country. The latter author also added that while no racial discrimination existed in Honduras, "there was 'ethnic isolation' for which the Negroes themselves have been partially responsible."[38] Regrettably, López Villanil did not define "ethnic isolation" and chose not to discuss why other unnamed elements helped to foster it.

In most of Central America, then, Negroids accept white values in regard to appearance and culture and do what they can to either hide or minimize their non-Caucasian physical character. There are a few groups that resist this pattern. Among these are the descendants of the *sambo-mosquitos*, but they are generally regarded as relics from a stormy and not highly regarded past.[39] There is also the Negroid majority in the Bay Islands off the coast of Honduras. Their ambivalence towards Tegucigalpa governments is well known,[40] but, even though they exercise local control over certain aspects of their society, they are too few to make the national government heed their demands.

In Costa Rica and Panama, however, the Negroid population has resisted cultural assimilation and created situations that the governments could not effectively ignore. The result has been conflict and the rise of both white and black militancy.

COSTA RICA

The rise and decline
of a banana province

Costa Rica, like several other Central American states, has two different and distinct Negroid populations within its borders. The first is composed of the descendants of the slaves brought there during the colonial period. Past census materials suggest that many of these people are concentrated in the Pacific coast provinces of Guanacaste and Punta Arenas. The 1927 national census stated that there were about 2,772 black and mulatto citizens, and in 1936, 1,402 residents of African origin were reported in the central highlands region.[41] These Hispanicized Negroids have not been a source of friction since abolition. In contrast, great difficulties have arisen because of the presence of the second group, the English-speaking Antilleans and their progeny, on the country's Caribbean coast.

A few Jamaican blacks and mulattoes originally came to Costa Rica as mercenaries to fight in the civil wars between 1830 and 1850; they began arriving in large numbers only in 1872 and 1873. A North American, Henry Meiggs Keith, had contracted to construct a railroad from Puerto Limón, on the Caribbean coast, to the capital, San José. A national law of 1862 specifically had prohibited the immigration of Africans and Asiatics, but since laborers from the *meseta central* could not be induced to work the hot, humid lowlands, Keith obtained permission to introduce Jamaican laborers. The tacit understanding seems to have been that the Negroids would depart when railway construction was completed. Instead, a sizable number of them chose to stay behind; 902 were listed as residents of Puerto Limón in 1882, roughly a year after rail construction had ended.[42]

The next "black invasion" was sponsored by Minor C. Keith, who had introduced the cultivation of the Gros Michel banana in the lowlands while the railroad was still being built. As president of the United Fruit Company, Keith signed a long-term contract in 1899 governing banana cultivation and exportation in Limón Province. This time, the San José government assumed that many Jamaicans would remain in Costa Rica, and it took steps designed to supervise their movement and residential settlement. Keith was given to understand that

> none of these negroes would be permitted to live in the *meseta central* or in any region of Costa Rica except in the area around Puerto Limón. . . . This regulation was strictly enforced for many years.[43]

Between 1881 and 1921 an estimated 33,000 Antilleans entered Costa Rica in order to work the banana plantations of *Mamita Yunai*.[44] The San José government viewed this increase of English-speaking blacks in Limón Province with distaste, but few whites or *mestizos* could be made to leave the *meseta central* for the tropical lowlands. These considerations notwithstanding, the Costa Rican government continued to demonstrate its enmity toward the Antilleans. In its 1927 census, 18,003 blacks and 419 mulattoes were reported as residents of Limón Province, but only 603 of them were considered citizens; all the rest were described as "foreigners," whether born in the country or not.[45] Efforts on the part of some West Indian workmen to obtain Costa Rican citizenship were discouraged, and the town of Torrialba in Limón Province became the frontier beyond which Negroids could not normally go. To put it bluntly, Costa Rican governments saw the English-speaking blacks and mulattoes as nothing more than banana pickers in transit.

The Antillean residents of Limón Province were aware of the hostility of the government, but, initially at least, it was a problem of minor importance. Many of them made regular trips to Jamaica, Trinidad, or Barbados and considered Costa Rica only a place where they earned "banana gold." They bought their goods at the company commissary, lived in a company-owned house, were treated at the company hospital, and received time off on all United States holidays.[46] For the *costarriqueño*, or *tico*, the West Indians had little more than contempt, since the few native whites and *mestizos* who worked as dock laborers for United Fruit were paid even less than they were.[47] The Antillean also compared his former British overlords with the Costa Rican officials he occasionally saw, and the Latins came off poorly in comparison. In essence, the Antillean in Limón Province earned United States dollars, considered himself a citizen of the British Empire, and disdained the Spanish idiom as the "language of parrots."[48] This situation was to change drastically in the 1930s.

The first outbreak of the "Panama disease" (*fusarium cubense*) occurred in 1890, and by 1926 it was killing an increasing number of trees.[49] This disaster, plus the economic slump caused by the Great Depression in the early 1930s, caused United Fruit to transfer the bulk of its operations to the fertile lands on the Pacific coast. A labor force already existed in the vicinity of the new operations, so in 1934 the government of Ricardo Jiménez promulgated a law prohibiting the passage of "persons of color" across the country to the "zone of the Pacific."[50]

With a stroke of the pen, this president had reduced the mass of the Limón Province Negroids to the status of charity cases. Thousands departed for Panama or Jamaica, but the second generation, born in Puerto Limón, were neither British nor Costa Rican citizens; as stateless persons, they had no place to go. The most grievous blow of all fell in 1938, when a widespread outbreak of *sigatoka*, or banana blight, totally destroyed what was left of United Fruit's Caribbean operation. The company abandoned some lands and rented or sold others to blacks. By 1942 the days of its profitable Caribbean operations had become nothing but memories.[51] These economic reverses not only emptied the West Indian's pocketbook, but, just as crucial, with *Mamita Yunai* far away, he was completely subject to the will of the Costa Ricans for the first time. Cases of harassment by and conflict with local authorities increased sharply, and, for the Antilleans in Limón Province, "only the message of Marcus Garvey and the world championship of Joe Louis generated hope."[52]

The perils of assimilation

The plight of Negroids on Costa Rica's Caribbean coast began to improve following the 1948 Civil War and the accession to power of José "Pepe" Figueres and the PLN (*Partido de Liberación Nacional*). A decree issued on 4 November 1949 not only canceled the 1934 law and the immigration exclusion acts of 1911 and 1942 but also created a special commission to deal with the problems of the Limón Province Negroids. National citizenship was extended to them, and between 1954 and 1958 forty-seven public schools were built in the province, an increase of 950 percent over the number constructed between 1922 and 1951.[53] All travel restrictions were dropped, and the blacks and mulattoes of the Caribbean coast were offered labor and educational opportunities in San José. The Limón Province Negroids responded by joining the PLN in large numbers, and, during his second presidential term (1970–1976), Figueres named Luis Demosthenes Bermúdez, a Puerto Limón black of part-Jamaican ancestry, governor of the province. Since 1966 two other men of Jamaican parentage, Carl Neal and Reinaldo Maxwell Kennedy, have also served as PLN federal deputies.

Paradoxically, however, the improvement in the overall condition of the Limón Province Negroids has tended to mask the fact that many have left the region and those remaining are now a minority of the total population. In the 1927 census, roughly 34 percent of Limón Province's population was designated white.[54] The departure of many Jamaicans, plus the move of many whites and *mestizos* from the *meseta central* to the coastal lowland between 1934 and 1949, brought a radical shift in the provincial racial balance. According to the 1950 census, the Negroid population receded to 13,749; 62.4 percent of the provincial population was white or *mestizo*, as was 55 percent of the population in the town of Puerto Limón.[55] This development has naturally been the source of new tensions and anxieties. In the new public schools established by the Figueres regime, racial "incidents" have markedly increased. Spanish rather than English is the language of instruction, and the increasing concern of the blacks and mulattoes is that the Jamaican variant of Anglo-Saxon culture and language will be lost or simply discarded as irrelevant by the increasingly Hispanicized youth.[56] Worse yet, black and mulatto students reported that they have been insulted or intimidated by white teachers, and certain private schools in Puerto Limón have refused to accept nonwhite applicants. Social organizations with restricted membership, such as the Miramar Club, have come into existence,[57] as have residential sections where only Costa Rican whites, *mestizos*, or Chinese live.[58] Even more acute are the economic problems. After the United Fruit interests departed, the Chinese or Costa Rican whites, many of whom live on the *meseta central*, became the owners of most of the commercial enterprises and realty concerns in Puerto Limón. Alleged insults and the gouging of Negroid customers have caused tensions to rise, but at base the problem is that the others possess, while the blacks and mulattoes are generally the poor and the underemployed.[59]

From 1949, until recently, successful Negroid intellectuals and professionals, among them Colón Bermúdez and Sherman T. Jackson, left Puerto Limón and sought their fortunes generally in San José.[60] Since the mid-1960s, however, young intellectuals such as Kathleen Sawyers Royal and Terry Wolfe have chosen to remain on the Caribbean coast and fight what they see as the "dehumanization" of the black man. These militants argue that Puerto Limón blacks and mulattoes have never received a fair deal from the San José government, and only if they bring unrelenting pressures will the situation undergo perceptible change.[61]

In the past, for the purpose of protection from exploitation, the Antillean Negroid had rallied around the United Negro Improvement Association, a branch of which was formed in Puerto Limón in 1922.[62] Over the years, the UNIA sponsored dances, provided burial funds for its members, and assisted persons in trouble with the law, but it did little to either induce or encourage Negroid militancy. Easily the most important organization formed recently to organize the Limón black and mulatto youth has been AFRUTSCO (Afro-Tico Student Committee), a group that modeled itself along the lines of the now-defunct Student Non-Violent Coordinating Committee, a black organization in the United States. Its professed goal is "to support the development of the colored population in Costa Rica and the world" and to arrest the "loss of culture."[63] AFRUTSCO enjoyed steadily increasing popularity in 1971 and 1972, and it must be regarded as a Costa Rican proponent of the "black power" philosophy.

The growth of this organization and the prospective emergence of similar ones pose a problem of fateful consequences for Costa Rica. Feeding the discontent felt by the more militant blacks and mulattoes is their growing realization that they are economically marginal persons. In this type of situation, where individuals attain importance chiefly as members of a group, differences in life style, language, and attitudes become critical symbols of group identification. Can Costa Rica somehow integrate the Limón Negroids and simultaneously allow them to maintain a system of separate culture and intellectual norms? The question is more than academic because this small country is one of the few states in Spanish America with an authentic democratic tradition. If it cannot achieve the kind of integration suggested above without violence, there is virtually no hope that other states faced with similar racial problems will solve them in a more humanistic fashion.

PANAMA

Enter the outsider

A part of Colombia until 1903, Panama differs from the other Central American states in that it has always been a region where the mass of the people possessed varying degrees of African blood. Of the 35,920 persons in the Province of Panama in 1789, 22,504 (about 63 percent) were either slaves or free Negroids.[64] In the years following the wars of independence, political changes often transpired, but they were never powerful enough to root out antagonisms of color or caste.[65] Veritable race wars shook Panama City and Colón during the 1830s; ultimately the white elements prevailed, although the picture is not at all clear as to the means (other than violence) they used to do so.[66]

These grim aspects of racial relations in Panama are conveniently overlooked by those Panamanians who hypothesize that their semiisolated portion of what was then Colombia had no racial prejudice. They are quick to point out that in February 1910 Carlos A. Mendoza, a light-skinned mulatto, became chief executive following the death of President José Domingo de Obaldía.[67] Mendoza was in office exactly eight months, however, and did not run for reelection on any political ticket. As we have already noted, the latest published statistics demonstrate that African blood is common in Panama,[68] but often overlooked is Panama's white upper class (the so-called "twenty families"), which has always striven vigilantly to guard its "racial purity."[69] Given the large number of Negroids and the small number of whites, one can surmise that, had the canal not been built by the United States, the Panamanian racial situation would be similar to that in other areas,[70] where the white elite has come over a period of time to accept the social ascension of some mulattoes.

But the canal was built, and in its construction are the roots of the triangular feud that has since developed. On 6 November 1903, with the aid of Yankee machinations, Panama declared its independence from Colombia.[71] Subsequently, on 18 November 1903 the Hay-Bunau Varilla Treaty was signed, conceding to the United States both construction rights for the interocean canal and virtual political sovereignty over a zone five miles on either side of the project route. Construction began in 1904, and, since Panamanians were neither able nor willing to provide all the manual labor necessary, the United States brought in Spaniards, Italians, and finally, 44,000 workmen from Jamaica, Barbados, and Trinidad.[72] Although the United Fruit Company had begun Panamanian operations in 1899 and had moved several thousand Jamaicans to Bocas de Toro,[73] it was the canal that brought in the great flood of West Indians.

Canal Zone policy and
the *chumbo* scapegoat

The North Americans who came to the isthmus were, for the most part, skilled technicians and engineers. As an inducement, these men were well paid in gold; eventually they became known simply as "gold employees." Manual workers were generally referred to as "silver employees." The Spanish and Italian laborers received somewhat better pay than either the Panamanians or the West Indians, the latter group averaging only 10 cents per hour, plus free housing, medical care, and a return trip ticket to their point of departure. The United States not only made few distinctions between Panamanians and West Indians, which caused the former much mortification, but also recruited supervisors from Dixie "on the theory that southerners know how to deal with Negroes best."[74] As a result, the segregation system legally sanctioned in Mississippi, Georgia, and Alabama was in part transferred to the Canal Zone.

Resentful because United States employees tended to treat almost all Panamanians as "colored" and therefore inferior, Panamanians vented their rage and frustration outside the zone on the English-speaking workers from Trinidad, Jamaica, Barbados, or anywhere else in the West Indies. This situation was further aggravated by the fact that, when the canal was officially opened in 1914, some 20,000 West Indians stayed behind. They continued performing manual labor in the Canal Zone but established residential communities in Panama proper. Furthermore, they encouraged the immigration of their relatives, continued to speak English, maintained exclusive communities, and even set up their own schools.[75]

Not unexpectedly, Panamanians were greatly disturbed by the refusal of these "guests" to accept Hispanization, and they considered them both ungrateful and dangerous. In 1926 the National Congress restricted further West Indian immigration. The growing passions against the *chumbos* peaked in the 1930s. Then, at the request of the Panamanian government (1932) and the governor of the Canal Zone, the United States appropriated $100,000 to send the West Indians elsewhere.[76] Ironically, in

1939 the United States had a major change of heart; in the tradition of Bolívar and past Latin American leaders, necessity again made the Negroid a needed friend. Modern fortifications to protect the canal from Nazi or Japanese attack were deemed necessary, and so a new wave of West Indian immigration was induced to build them. Although Panama was, and is, virtually dependent upon canal activities for revenues, the national citizenry did not abjectly reconcile itself to the prospect of a second Negroid invasion. At the urgings of Arnulfo Arias Madrid, who was elected president in 1940, a new constitution was introduced that contained a provision barring citizenship to all persons of African origin whose native tongue was not Spanish. The document was never put into effect, although six years later, a new fundamental law resurrected the language requirement, this time in ambiguous terms that allowed for the possibility of *chumbo* acquisition of citizenship.[77]

This legal stipulation only minimally diminished the popular prejudice against *chumbos*. In 1948 Arias Madrid again became president, largely by exploiting the West Indian issue. His second turbulent term was terminated in 1951, but he returned to power in 1967, only to be deposed eleven days after his 1968 inauguration. The continued participation of this perennial office-seeker in national politics is evidence that, in the eyes of many of his countrymen, the Negroid West Indian is still viewed as English by acculturation, North American by economic interest, and Panamanian only by expediency.

The *chumbo* issue and the possibility of black power in Panama

Events inside Panama have not been without some effects in the Canal Zone, but changes in United States policy have had a much greater impact. Beginning in 1946, racial segregation in the Canal Zone was gradually relaxed, so that by the 1950s legal separation had officially ended. As of 1968, both Panamanians and nonnaturalized West Indians held important posts in Canal Zone administration.[78] But the general economic differential and the tradition of separation partially conspired to defeat the intent of the laws. Some legal and social changes have taken place, but the *zonites*[79] see to it that the pace of these modifications is never too rapid.

As has already been inferred, a situation similar to the one in Costa Rica has developed in Panama. The Hispanicized blacks and mulattoes, descendants of the slaves who entered the territory with the Spanish as far back as the sixteenth century, are found throughout the country. The number of mulattoes, if we are to believe the 1940 census, is probably greater than that of the blacks.

Given the presence of so many Negroid persons in the republic, it might be assumed that some feeling of kinship would have developed between Hispanicized Negroids and the *chumbos*, but this has not been the case. Hostility toward Antilleans on the part of the indigenous blacks and mulattoes has been the rule, and this situation has prompted one observer to conclude that general West Indian–Panamanian antipathy is "not based primarily on biological [i.e., racial] grounds."[80] On its face, this judgment seems valid, but its weakness lies in the fact that overall Panamanian acceptance of *chumbos* seems directly related to their proximity to Caucasian appearance, a factor that can only be described as basically biological.[81] Race and color may not be the only causes of Panamanian hostility to the West Indians, but they certainly are critical ones. This hostility does not seem to be dissipating either. A 1971 publication sponsored by the Panamanian government castigated the *chumbos*, arguing that they

> appear incrusted like a foreign body, gathered in a
> constellation of urban islands, thinly walled in against
> foreign [Panamanian] influences. This physical isolation
> aggravated by the barrier of languages and divergence of
> cultural patterns has contributed decisively in postponing
> their integration into national life.[82]

All this is curious precisely because the Hispanicized Negroids are not necessarily acceptable to white Panamanians. Among the middle class, "barriers are not erected primarily on the basis of race distinction, but barriers that successfully eliminate the majority of certain racial groups exist."[83] In other words, the very dark Panamanian needs both money and fluency in Spanish if he expects to be socially acceptable to even middle-class whites. Moreover, Negroids are still deemed unacceptable by Panamanian aristocrats, and some exclusive clubs discreetly bar "persons of dark skin" from holding membership.[84] As of 1968 there were at least five Panamanians of notable African ancestry in the National Assembly, another acting as judge on the Panamanian Supreme Court, and two in the National Court of Appeals.[85] Conversely, the diplomatic corps remains "almost completely white by Panamanian standards at least," and no Afro-Panamanian has served as chief executive since Carlos Mendoza's brief stint.[86]

There have been few public admissions of the reality of racial prejudice in Panama. The general tendency of the population is to blame any discriminatory incidents on North American influence. That this claim is really an excuse was highlighted in an article appearing in the *Panama Tribune* on 29 October 1960. At that time, Jorge Prosperi, a newspaper reporter, cited several employment situations in Panama City and charged that Panamanians who believed that only Yankees were racists were deluding themselves. "It is only necessary," he wrote, "to go to certain public or private offices to be convinced that we are mistaken and that we live in a climate of hypocrisy."[87]

The political instability of the nation, the *chumbo* issue, the North American presence in the Canal Zone, the propensity for many mulattoes to consider themselves white – all these situations have exercised a retarding influence on the development of a racial consciousness among Negroid peoples in Panama. Nevertheless, this is the only Central American state in which a potential coalition of Negroid elements could perhaps exercise decisive political authority. Unfortunately, as long as dark-skinned Panamanians wish to believe the only Negroids in the country are the *chumbos,* this potential will remain unfulfilled.

MEXICO
The process of abolition

Alexander von Humboldt stated in *Political Essay on the Kingdom of New Spain* that as of 1803 there were "less than 6,000

Negroes" in New Spain and not more than 9,000 or 10,000 slaves.[88] Since only persons of African origin were legal bondmen in Spanish America after 1609, how there could be more slaves than Negroes, or exactly what the Prussian naturalist meant by the term, is obscure. Furthermore, the best estimates indicate that over 200,000 slaves were introduced into the Viceroyalty of New Spain between 1520 and 1817.[89] Assuming the correctness of Humboldt's statistics, by 1803 this number had shrunk to less than 10,000, a totally fantastic decline.

A contradictory picture is presented by Sherburne F. Cook, who was probably the first investigator to make a careful analysis of the 1793 royal census. Cook reveals that Spanish authorities estimated *zambos*, blacks, and mulattoes at 12 to 15 percent of the viceroyalty's 5,200,000 inhabitants.[90] Reinforcing Cook's analysis and simultaneously explaining Humboldt's conclusions is the 1810 census, which reported that there were only 10,000 black inhabitants in what is today Mexico and the southwestern United States. However, the count of *zambos* and mulattoes brought the grand total of Negroid subjects to 624,461, or 10.2 percent of the total.[91] Humboldt, like numerous contemporary census takers in Latin America, seems to have counted only the darkest persons as "Negroes" and listed Negroids of mixed blood in other categories.

In 1817 the slave trade to Mexico was prohibited, and a tabulation in 1821 listed less than 3,000 still in legal bondage. A legislative statute passed on 27 September 1822 legally ended the colonial caste system and removed such terms as *mulato, pardo, zambaigo,* and so forth from the national legal and ecclesiastical nomenclature. All white, Indian, *mestizo,* and Negroid inhabitants were declared equal before the law, and in 1829 slavery was permanently abolished (except for Texas). After less than a decade of independence, the new Republic of Mexico had confronted the problem of racial inequity and had committed itself to the propagation of human equality.

As usual though, attempts to translate paper promises into socioeconomic reality foundered. After centuries of deprivation, it was most unlikely that the Afro-Mexican would immediately become an able competitor in the struggle for power that characterized the history of Mexico before 1910. While the national leadership was exercised by whites or *mestizos*, the black man gradually disappeared; *zambos* and mulattoes either became further involved in the process of miscegenation or strove to hide their Negroid origins.[92] Evidence of the existence of some sort of prejudice can be seen in the policies of Porfirio Díaz during the years he ruled Mexico (1876–1910). This dictator saw the Indian merely as a laborer. He courted European immigrants feverishly and positively banned the immigration of persons of African descent.[93]

"Little Africa" in Mexico

How many Afro-Mexicans are there now? The answer could only be a conjecture based on a shred of evidence. No census seeking racial information was permitted until 1921, and there have been none since, although between 1930 and 1940 matrimonial license forms did stipulate that the applicant indicate his or her race.[94] Credible estimates range from 120,000 to 300,000 identifiable Afro-Mexicans.[95] In any event, their total appears to represent approximately 1 percent of the national population.

Although it would seem that Negroid Mexicans were almost totally assimilated into the greater population, a few communities exist where they maintain a separate and distinct cultural identity. In the southwestern corner of the state of Guerrero lies the municipality of Cuajiniculapa, informally and somewhat sardonically called "Little Africa"; About 9,600 persons live in this 276-square-mile area, and 90 percent of them are Negroid.[96] Most are either descendants of *cimarrones* or escapees from a slave ship that was wrecked off the coast during the seventeenth century. This wild and rugged area proved easily defendable, so the Spaniards eventually decided to leave the fugitives alone.

The people of Cuajiniculapa build their homes in a circular pattern with wattle (reed) walls and conical, thatched roofs, quite reminiscent of Africa. Women seen in Cuijla, the municipality's chief settlement, go about their tasks with jugs on their heads and offspring on their hips, again in dim memory of their ancestral past.[97] The people speak of themselves as *prietos*, stating that "Negroes are donkies."[98] Many of them are farmers, and, as a result of the agrarian reforms effected since 1910, they work chiefly on *ejidos*, or communally owned enterprises. Their important money crop is sesame seeds, although some beans, corn, and peppers are also raised.

Whatever business exists in the municipality is owned by whites,[99] who are considered to be the region's upper social class. Persons of mixed African and white heritage are called *blanquitos* ("little whites") rather than mulattoes, and they generally occupy middle-stratum positions such as clerks.[100] No school was established in the Cuajiniculapa region until 1940, and an all-weather highway into the region was completed only in 1965. Most of the Negroids still cannot read or write, and they speak a Spanish heavily laced with words better understood in Ghana or Nigeria than anywhere west of the Atlantic. Nonetheless, the illiteracy and poverty of these people has not dulled their political and psychological alertness. All local political positions are in the hands of the *prietos*, the whites being informally barred from this sphere of activity. Moreover, among these Afro-Mexicans there exists "a complex of aggressive hostility against the whites and the Indians," and manifestations of these feelings emerge whenever the *prietos* feel their basic interests threatened.[101]

The Afro-Mexican in disguise

The inhabitants of Cuajiniculapa are not the only Negroid peoples in Mexico who cling to their ancestral customs, accepting assimilation on their own terms, if at all. New research indicates the presence of a large Negroid colony near Melchor Múzquiz in the northern deserts of Coahuila.[102] There are others reported in Oaxaca and Quintana Roo and especially in the state of Veracruz, where the descendants of Yanga still survive.[103] Today many of the latter (now mostly *zambos*) labor on the coffee plantations near the towns of Orizaba and Córdoba. They display an awareness of their heritage, but not of one of its most ironic aspects:

> On Córdoba's outskirts and athwart Mexico #150
> highway, Veracruz city-bound motorists may descry the

'Ῡanga General Hospital' and nine miles later dip through 'county-seat Ῡanga' . . . This was the very locale of the pre-doomed plantation colony founded by stubborn General Jo Shelby, C.S.A. . . . after the War Between the States.[104]

At present, the Afro-Mexican presents no major social problem. In the future, improved education and the rising level of expectations could cause the inhabitants of Little Africa, for example, to seek economic as well as political control of their community. There can be little doubt that such a move would heighten racial tension, but success might do little more than increase the speed of assimilation.

Beginning in the 1920s, Mexican intellectuals, led by José Vasconcelos and Moisés Sáeñz, sponsored the *indigenismo* movement, paying tribute to the Mexican Indian and his contribution to the national culture, and recognizing the necessity of his regeneration for the benefit of the nation.[105] In 1936 a Department of Indian Affairs was established in the state of Chiapas. Appreciation of the fact that Mexico is indeed an Indian nation was a long time in developing, but recognition of the nation's African background is somehow totally ignored.

If Aguirre Beltrán is correct, there probably are many persons of Afro-Indian blood in Mexico,[106] but because it is better to be Indian than Negroid, the latter is ignored. As in Peru, Bolivia, Ecuador, and much of Central America, the Indian remains the officially recognized sufferer from oppression, and there is no desire either to add another group to this category, or to delve into the issue of African cultural contributions.

11
Negroid Peoples in
Santo Domingo and Cuba

SANTO DOMINGO

Abolition through foreign intervention

Until 1697 Spain had exercised or claimed sovereignty over the entire island of Hispaniola. It had introduced the first African slaves there in 1502, but, as its continental settlements expanded, its Caribbean insular possessions declined in importance. Santo Domingo gradually became an economically insignificant settlement, populated chiefly by mulattoes and blacks, with a thin upper stratum of white oligarchs. During the last half of the seventeenth century, however, France consolidated its hold on the western third of the isle and rapidly increased the number of slaves in order to facilitate sugar-cane production in the colony they called Saint Domingue.

The mushrooming wealth of the French sugar colony was a phenomenon watched by Spain with envious eyes; it tried earnestly to emulate French success in the Spanish two-thirds of Hispaniola. Importation of slaves was allowed at reduced tariff rates, and in 1785 a new slave code, the *Código negro carolino*, was adopted. But a radical turn of events would make Cuba, not Santo Domingo, the future source of Madrid's sugar supply. In 1791 the slaves rebelled in Saint Domingue, and, after thirteen years of bitter fighting, achieved their independence. This long and bloody struggle had ominous consequences for the Spanish-speaking territory. After a disastrous war in Europe in 1795 Madrid was forced to cede Santo Domingo to France. In 1802 and 1805 black armies from Haiti invaded the territory and attempted to foment slave uprisings, but the inhabitants eventually drove them off. Early in 1808 Spain regained nominal suzerainty over the colony, but Ferdinand VII could do nothing when Dominican rebels declared independence in 1821. The calculating president of Haiti, Jean Boyer, had not forgotten the failures of 1802 and 1805, and he possessed the military means that the Spanish king lacked. In 1822 he sent his army into Santo Domingo and established a dominion that lasted for twenty-two years.

Sumner Welles described Santo Domingo during the Haitian period as

> under the domination of a tyranny which had for its chief object not only the eradication of the Caucasian race but also the obliteration of the foundation of European culture.[1]

This view has been consistently propagated by Dominican writers like José G. García, who also charged that Boyer encouraged black immigration in an effort to "Africanize the Spanish-speaking portion of the island."[2] It is true that the Haitian leader sanctioned the entry of 6,000 to 13,000 blacks from the United States in 1824. Nonetheless, Boyer's critics usually ignore his abolition of slavery in Santo Domingo (1822) and rarely mention that the "atrocious" colonization scheme enjoyed only initial success.[3] The basic fear that the white oligarchy of Santo Domingo had was that the Haitians would attempt to terminate the socioeconomic hegemony they and their ancestors had exercised for over three centuries. In fact, Boyer did decree the prohibition of land ownership by whites, but he and succeeding rulers became too involved in Haitian internal affairs to enforce this decree comprehensively. Furthermore, the mass of Negroids could not read or write, had no knowledge of finance, and lacked the political and economic skills to take advantage of the options offered.[4] Even though the Haitians were never able to effect the changes they would like to have initiated, José García and writers like him seem interested only in focusing their attention on the racial aspects of the conflict. Their preoccupation with this issue is, perhaps, a clear manifestation of the degree to which race and color questions have permeated the national intellectual consciousness.

Negroid leaders and color questions

In February 1844 a group of conspirators moved to destroy Haitian rule in the Spanish-speaking two-thirds of the island. Called the *trinitaría* ("trinity"), this cabal was composed entirely of whites, most of whom were from the Iberian peninsula, the Canaries, and the Balearic Islands.[5] Independence was proclaimed in the city of Santo Domingo on 27 February 1844, but on the following day a group of ex-slaves led by an African-born black, Santiago Basora, announced its opposition to the rebels. These blacks suspected that the white rebels intended to reintroduce slavery; if this was true, the blacks were ready to fight alongside the Haitians. *Trinitaría* leaders realized the explosive nature of this situation and moved rapidly to defuse it. On 28 February provisional President Tomás Bobadilla and Vice-President Manuel Jiménez conferred with Basora and his supporters, and on the following day slavery was again declared abolished.[6] Thereafter, the struggle against Haiti moved toward a successful conclusion, free of racial acrimony.

Since that time, except when Spain or the United States ran the country,[7] several of the presidents of Santo Domingo have been mulattoes. In fact, during the nineteenth century the door of the chief executive's office opened still further to allow the entry of two black occupants: the illiterate Pedro Guillermo, in office very briefly, and the crafty Ulíses Heureaux. The presence of these rulers seemed to create a great deal of anxiety both inside and outside the country. For example, Pedro Francisco Bono, a white intellectual urged General Gregorio Luperón, a mulatto, to challenge Heureaux in the 1888 election for the "glorification of the Negroes and mulattoes in America":

> Who better than you [Luperón] could know how
> necessary the white race is for the achievement of the goal,
> but at the same time recognize the superiority of the
> combinations of the great race. And who better than you
> could melt, amalgamate and shape a homogeneous whole.[8]

Fear may well have generated the bulk of white support for a mulatto chief executive; certainly the black man's electoral triumph gained him few admirers among whites abroad. The French newspaper, *La Revue Diplomatique*, reported in 1888 that the new president "hates the foreigners because they are white, the blacks because he is one of them."[9] There is no way to prove the accuracy of this tabloid's accusation, but, after a decade in power, Heureaux came to be despised by Dominicans of all complexions. In 1899 he was assassinated on a public street.

Since that time, the possibilities of political ascent for decidedly darkskinned persons seems to have been limited,[10] and one highly sardonic situation deserves notice here. Rafael Trujillo, the bloody dictator who ruled the nation between 1931 and 1961, would have been considered a mulatto in some other Spanish-American states. Still, he was much lighter than his brother, Héctor, who served as puppet president between 1952 and 1959. The latter was often referred to derisively as "the Negro Trujillo" and was kept out of the public spotlight because of his dark skin. The critical nature of the question of color can be seen in that, after putting Héctor in office, Rafael deemed it wise to "touch up" his brother's public photographs to make him appear less Negroid.[11]

Race and color questions in Santo Domingo

Consideration of other aspects of contemporary Dominican culture reveals that race and/or color bias is not restricted to candidates for high political office. Although the immigration of Europeans, Chinese, and Middle Eastern peoples was encouraged from the 1880s, the informal entry of numerous Haitians was not an uncommon event. The Haitian influx has been discouraged since 1937, when Rafael Trujillo massacred an unknown number of his French-speaking neighbors. For Dominicans, Haitians are the favorite whipping boys, and some citizens espouse the belief that there is no racial prejudice in Santo Domingo, only a national prejudice against Haitians. Unexplained and ignored by these proponents is a 1939 immigration law that imposed a payment of $500 on all immigrants who are neither Caucasian nor American Indians.[12]

The conduct of the national census and the use of census statistics demonstrate still another national prejudice. The 1940 data revealed that 13 percent of the citizenry were white; 19 percent, black; 0.02 percent Oriental; and the rest, mulatto. The 1950 census raised the number of whites to 28.1 percent, dropped the number of blacks to 11.5 percent, and fixed the mulatto percentage at 60.4; mysteriously the figure for Orientals remained at 0.02 percent.[13] No racial study has been attempted in subsequent censuses, and analyses conducted by foreign scholars imply that the official figures are, at best, inaccurate.[14] The key to the situation is apparently that the nation's mulattoes, especially if they are economically successful, prefer to consider themselves white. More than one observer has written that a popular expression in Santo Domingo is that "a rich Negro is a mulatto. A rich mulatto is white."[15] The census, then, is not so much an index of racial distribution as it is a sign of both social rank and aspiration.

The actual situation would seem to be that a predominately Caucasian elite still dominates the society, although this group includes a few persons who elsewhere would be adjudged mulattoes. The growing middle sector is largely of mixed blood, but even these "usually consider themselves white," and they are "more likely to check closely the family history of the person their children associated with."[16] The lower class is mulatto and black, but, even within it, social barriers based on skin color exist and Caucasian features are highly prized.[17]

Commenting on the social situation with respect to color, M. A. Mejía Ricart, a Dominican social scientist, has argued that acceptability to the highest social class in Santo Domingo is based on a variety of factors, but persons exhibiting a distinct Negroid appearance are excluded.[18] Many years ago, Sumner Welles wrote that "among all classes and among all shades, there is a universal desire that the black may be obliterated by the white."[19] Finally, the Dutch sociologist Harry Hoetink expressed a similar idea in somewhat different terminology, stating that "in Dominican society . . . the white somatic norm is dominant in regard to social prestige."[20]

In *La comunidad mulata* (*The Mulatto Community*, 1967), Pedro Andrés Cabral presents the thesis that Santo Domingo's ills stem from the fact that it is essentially a mulatto country. The crossing of African and Caucasian has produced an unstable hybrid, he believes, and plans for solving national problems that do not consider this biological contingency are foredoomed to failure.[21] Such a thesis smacks exceedingly of outmoded Positivist notions and is ample evidence of the fascination that such ideas continue to hold for some Latin thinkers. Still, there would seem to be at least one element of truth in Cabral's approach: A mulatto nation situated in the Negroid Caribbean is undoubtedly ailing if it cannot accept its racial image. Dominicans may feel constrained to call each other white, but it is hard to say who is deceived. In view of these considerations, the glorification of Caucasian features by the mulatto majority is disturbing and, for the black minority, psychologically disjunctive.

CUBA

The rise of sugar

In the wake of the first Spaniards, the African slave reached Cuba in 1511. Initially, the colony was of some importance, for *conquistadores* such as Cortés used it as a base in their search for gold and glory on the mainland. Nevertheless, Cuba declined in importance because of the establishment of the vice-royalties of Peru and New Spain and the 1615 *cédula* that established Cartagena and Veracruz as the ports of entry for slaves. As of 1760, a combination of cattlemen and tobacco farmers dominated the island's economic life, but their contribution to the overall wealth of Spanish America was small indeed.

After the English capture of Havana in 1762,[22] Cuba's mixed economic system was gradually transformed into a monoculture based almost entirely on sugar-cane production. Following the Saint Domingue slave rebellion in 1791, many French planters fled to Cuba, where they sought to duplicate the plantation economy they had previously known. Spanish officials shrewdly took advantage of the elimination of Saint Domingue as a supplier by removing taxes from refined sugar and by allowing the shipment of Cuban cane brandy to European ports. By 1826 Cuba had become the richest jewel in the Bourbon crown, producing almost 55,000 long tons of sugar per year. This economic consideration, plus the loss of all its other American territories except Puerto Rico, made Madrid fanatically determined to retain its control over the island.

The great paradox was that, during the first half of the nineteenth century, the Industrial Revolution in Europe had already begun the displacement of men with labor-saving machines, but during the same period in Cuba, the demand for cheap manual laborers increased sharply. Cuban sugar barons knew of only one place where their needs could be speedily and easily met: Africa.

The trade in forced labor to Cuba: 1789–1875

As of 1774, the number of freed Negroids in Cuba was virtually the same as the number of slaves.[23] All told, between 1511 and 1788 no more than 100,000 slaves are estimated to have been imported into the island.[24] Then, on 28 February 1789 Charles IV permitted both foreigners and Spanish subjects to sell unlimited numbers of slaves in several Indies ports, including Havana. Subsequently, in 1792 Cuban merchants were allowed to import slaves directly from Africa. Once this happened, the situation changed drastically, and masses of black captives poured into the Pearl of the Antilles. The figures listed in table 13, at best only estimates, provide some indication of the magnitude of the traffic.

Most of this traffic was completely illegal, for in 1817, Great Britain had paid Spain £400,000 to terminate it. In return, Ferdinand VII agreed to reimburse injured slave traders and to prohibit all Spaniards from traffic participation after 1820. A special Mixed Commission was later established in Havana to deal with intercepted slave ships and to arrange for the future livelihood of their black cargoes. Ferdinand, however, needed the revenues that Cuban sugar generated, and he deeply resented dictation from an England that had formerly been the world's largest dealer in captive Africans. In any case, Cuban

Table 13. *Slave traffic to Cuba*

Years	Estimated totals of slaves landed
1789–1865	436,953
1820–1865	500,000
1791–1820 } 1830–1850 }	572,449
1801–1865	616,200

Sources: Franklin Knight, *A History of Slavery in Cuba during the Nine-teenth Century* (Madison, 1970), p. 22; Hugh Thomas, *Cuba: The Pursuit of Freedom* (New York, 1971), p. 169; Arthur Corwin, *Spain and the Abolition of Slavery in Cuba: 1817–1886* (Austin, 1967), pp. 16, 54; Philip Curtin, *The Atlantic Slave Trade: A Census* (Madison, 1969), p. 40.

sugar barons had no problem raising sufficient funds to bribe local officials or to outfit slaving vessels. Sugar culture demand-ed cheap labor, and the prospect of profit apparently obliter-ated any moral considerations that slave traders may have had. As one Afro-Cuban succinctly wrote: "Life is cheap, and sugar, Sir . . . is gold."[25]

Between 1820 and 1839 British anti-slave-trade squadrons operated north of the equator along the Atlantic coast of Africa and off the Cuban coast. To evade them, slave ships proceeding from Cuba often employed foreign flags and false sets of papers. They traded south of the equator in an effort to avoid intercep-tion, and they often landed their cargoes in one of the innumer-able small bays or inlets that dot the Cuban coastline. In 1835 more British pressure forced Spain to allow the mutual search of all ships even suspected of slave-trade activities. Madrid also agreed to enact legislation punishing those citizens involved in "blackbird" activities, but Spain's *amour propre* had once again been grievously offended, and a decade would pass before such decrees were promulgated. After 1839 British antislavery squad-rons began operating south of the equator as well. Cuban slavers then began to trade in Portuguese Angola and Brazil, and they often flew the standard of the United States of America in order to escape detection.[26]

With the annual loss of plantation slaves averaging 8 to 10 percent, Cuba resembled a wealthy drug addict who could pay for his habit but could not withstand restrictions on his supply. So, despite the steadily increasing scope of British interception efforts, the annual landing of thousands of new slaves continued. By 1841 there were 436,495 slaves on the island, and even this number was deemed insufficient.

Not until 1850 did royal officials in Havana finally shake off their lethargy and attempt to enforce statutes that had been on the books for many years.[27] Ultimately, however, the decisive events leading to the extinction of the African slave trade took place neither in Havana, nor in Madrid, nor off the African coast. Abraham Lincoln, keenly aware that cotton-hungry interests in Great Britain wished to force diplomatic recognition of the Confederacy, moved judiciously to thwart this dreaded contingency. Late in 1862, he outflanked the pro-Confederacy forces and satisfied anti-slave-trade sentiment in England by sanctioning a treaty allowing British warships to stop and search suspected slaving vessels flying the United States emblem. Ships carrying captive blacks now had no flag to hide behind except the Jolly Roger. In addition, the collapse of the South in April 1865 psychologically settled the issue. Madrid simply could no longer countenance Cuban participation in "a trade which had been deplored by all the leading powers of the western world."[28]

In 1859 the value of the human properties held by Cuban slave interests stood at $76.5 million. With the old channels of resupply gradually being shut down, a devastating labor crisis might have ensued, but other developments had already begun to modify the situation. The advent of more sophisticated mechanical equipment eased the strain for wealthy sugar barons, but the temporary saviors of the status quo were Chinese coolie laborers. Between 1853 and 1873 over 132,000 Asians were landed in Cuba[29] and were immediately signed to eight-year contracts under which they were paid $4 a month. The expense for the upkeep of coolies was less than that for slaves, and they were often treated worse than the Africans; few ever returned to their homeland alive.

Still another human resource used and abused by the planters in their desperate search for more cheap laborers was a group of some 25,000 *emancipados* landed in Cuba between 1824 and 1866. Removed from Cuba-bound slavers by British interceptor patrols, these Africans were allegedly free when disembarked on the island. Unfortunately, what generally occurred was that they were signed to seven-year contracts and then reenslaved in all but name.[30] The English investigator Robert Madden attempted to determine the fate of the *emancipados* once their labor contracts had expired, but his initiatives failed to pierce the smoke screen generated by Spanish colonial administrators in order to conceal the tragedy.[31]

Indeed, life was cheap, sugar was gold, and those willing to debase others in order to line their pockets proved once again that man's most dangerous enemy is man.

Cuban slave practice and Spanish slave law

In obtaining "black ivory" to replenish the resident slave-labor force, the attitude of the Cuban slavocrats appeared to differ little from that of their South American counterparts: It was cheaper and less troublesome to obtain new slaves than it was to raise them.[32] The island's sugar kings may have regretted this policy after 1855 when prices began rising sharply, but until that time, field slaves were constantly induced to achieve their maximum output, and were considered worn out in 7 to 10 years. Commenting on the ferocity of nineteenth-century Cuban slavery, David Turnbull has written that

> the experience of the years had taught me to believe that the Spaniards are a kind and warmhearted race, and as I had frequently been told that the slave owners of . . . Habana were the most indulgent masters in the world, I was not a little surprised to find . . . that in the last particular, I had been most miserably deceived. . . . When we get into the country and visit the coffee, and especially the sugar plantations . . . we see how differently the unhappy negro is treated.[33]

Turnbull's militant abolitionism unquestionably biased his views, but evidence suggests that no testimonials need be written about the nature of Cuban slavery. In 1841 about 79 percent of all slaves lived in rural areas, and fourteen years later this figure stood at 82 percent.[34] A majority of the rural bondmen worked on sugar plantations, so that a valid depiction of Cuban slave society, as Turnbull suggests, requires an examination of rural conditions.

On sugar plantations, hard work was the order of the day, especially during the *zafra*, or cane-harvesting season. During these five to six months (December to June), cane cutters, mill hands, and other assorted field slaves labored sixteen to twenty hours a day. Some slaves expired from overwork, many collapsed exhausted, and serious accidents were frequent. They were given two hours to eat two meals, and the remainder of their released time was usually spent resting. A half-pound of jerked beef (fresh beef was available in a few areas), a half-pound of rice, and twelve ounces of corn meal constituted the standard daily diet, with fruit and yams added by more magnanimous owners.[35] Milk and leafy vegetables were rarely provided, and hygienic conditions in the slave quarters were generally poor.[36] It is this sanitation problem that contributed to the magnitude of the epidemics that killed thousands of bondmen from 1833 to 1834, 1852 to 1853, and 1858 to 1859. Even during the *tiempo muerte*, or "dead time" (July to December), slaves were kept busy clearing ground, packaging the product, and preparing the fields for the next harvest. An ex-slave who fled a sugar plantation provided the most terse summary: "Everything was based on watchfulness and the whip."[37]

It is true that the Spanish government felt some moral obligation and attempted to provide the slave with certain rights, but Cuba was thousands of miles across the ocean from Madrid. The *Código negro* of 1789 met a sad fate,[38] and half a century passed before Spain issued new regulations governing conditions in its Caribbean sugar colonies. In 1842 a new code was promulgated, although it too fell victim to slaveholder resistance. Among the rights conceded to slaves under the new regimen was that of *coartación*, which allowed the slave to purchase his free-

dom on the installment plan at a price fixed in court. Still another part of the code guaranteed to the slave a limited period
during which he could seek a new master who might purchase
him. In rural Cuba, however, the *coartación* right was often
disregarded, and the slave seeking time off to find another
owner was usually asking for punishment. The 1842 code also
prohibited masters from lashing a slave more than twenty-five
times for any single offense. Some diabolical masters chose to
contravene this stipulation by having their bondmen flogged less
than twenty-five strokes, but repeating the punishment on several different occasions.[39]

To assume that Spain would antagonize the Cuban sugar
lords and jeopardize a critical source of revenue in the interests
of African slaves or *emancipados* is to assume the presence of a
moral conscience rarely evidenced by any nation. The laws theoretically protecting bondmen against brutal treatment succeeded in providing Europeans with the image of a semihumane
Spain that was making the best of a bad situation. As long as
most Europeans knew no more about slavery in Cuba than
David Turnbull claimed he had known when he arrived in 1836,
one could rationally assume that the protective provisions were
generally enforced. The reality of the situation was that Madrid
did not make even nominal efforts to determine how many
slaves were residents on Cuban plantations until 1854.[40]

Slave revolts and Spanish policy

Like other Africans involuntarily transported to the New World,
the slave in Cuba fought back against his oppressor in a variety
of ways. Since belief in African religions, witchcraft, and sorcery[41] was widespread, many slaves sought vengeance through
the use of charms and spells.[42] For other captives suicide was
the best solution, while some found liberation through flight.
The jungle-covered slopes of Oriente Province and the marshes
of Zapata (in Santa Clara Province) hid many a *mambí*, where
fugitive slaves lived an independent existence. Apparently, the
problem of escaped slaves was deemed a serious one by nineteenth-century Spanish authorities, for hundreds of slave hun-

ters (*rancheadores*) were commissioned, and the use of semiwild dogs in this endeavor was widely accepted.

Because of the growth of the sugar monoculture on the island, the slave population increased and, with it, the intensity of slave rebellions and conspiracies. Many local disturbances were essentially spontaneous affairs involving one or two plantations. In these situations, the slaves' major objective was probably the modification of intolerable conditions. There were also a number of planned insurrections and large-scale uprisings, however, in which free Negroids sometimes participated and in which the destruction of white rule was a major goal. These include nine major revolts on the provincial level between 1795 and 1843.

Spanish reaction to these challenges was quite violent, especially when far-flung conspiratorial designs were discovered or suspected. After the Camagüey explosions in 1805 and 1812, such severe repression was undertaken that no notable rebellion took place for at least a decade.[43] An 1825 uprising in Matanzas Province was crushed only after twenty-four plantations had been destroyed; fifteen whites and forty-three slaves were killed.[44] Bloodiest of all were several Matanzas uprisings which transpired during 1843 and were suppressed only after heavy fighting. At least 275 slaves were killed during these revolts, and specially trained bloodhounds were used to hunt down and terrorize countless fugitives.[45]

The rebellions in Cuba were not unique, and Spanish efforts at repression were usually predictable. Each revolt, however, resulted in the death or flight of large numbers of bondmen. These had to be replaced of necessity, but during the nineteenth century the prices for new *bozales* from Africa continued to spiral upward. Resistance to these increasing costs, or the inability to pay them, forced the importation of coolies, the transfer of urban slaves to plantations, an increase in work load when replacements were not forthcoming, and, of course, more revolts. Profits and paranoia went together in this tropical paradise, with the sugar barons possessors of both, and the slaves victims only of the latter.

The abolition of slavery in Cuba

The end of the slave trade to Africa was the fatal blow for the Cuban system of involuntary servitude, but it was the Ten Years' War (1868–1878) that provided the *coup de grâce*. The origins of this long conflict between loyalists and patriots are numerous and complex, but slavery does not initially seem to have been a major issue. A familiar pattern can be discerned, however. In October 1868 Carlos Manuel de Céspedes, the first chief of the rebels, freed his slaves and "enlisted" them into his army.

Well aware that slaves were joining the rebel forces and that Yankee intervention might tip the balance, Madrid took rapid action. Spanish Minister Segismundo Moret y Prendergast unveiled a law (28 May 1870) that provided for (1) freedom for all slave children born from that date on; (2) purchase by Spain of all persons born into bondage since April 1868 for $125 each; (3) freedom for all slaves who served in the Spanish army, with compensation for their masters; and (4) freedom for bondmen over sixty.[46] The plan represented an ingenuous effort to satisfy both the planters and pacify the slaves, but opposition by the masters prevented implementation of this law until 1873. Thereafter, although its enforcement was spotty, the most prominent effect of the ruling was the emancipation of the young children of bondmen.

The rebels, in contrast, failed to make maximum use of what could have been a psychologically powerful issue. In April 1869 Céspedes declared all slaves freed but bound them to their masters for an indefinite period. Then, in October of that year, the rebels began encouraging slaves to rise, but only on those plantations belonging to loyalist planters. Céspedes came close to advocating unconditional abolition in 1872, but this proposal raised the ire of many of his supporters and proved to be a factor in his swift downfall. It is known that a large number of slaves served with the rebels, however, because one of the provisions of the Pact of Zanjón (1877), which terminated hostilities, was amnesty and freedom for all coolies and slaves who had fought with the insurgent forces.

With the end of the conflict, the diminution of the slave-labor force was accomplished. In 1872 there were 379,523 slaves; in 1877 the number was reduced to 199,094.[47] Death, flight, hostilities, and the Moret y Prendergast law all had a hand in bringing about this reduction of nearly 40 percent in the number of bondmen. In addition to the destruction caused by war, the rise of sugar-beet production cut down the post-1868 cane market. This development meant that by 1878 Germany had replaced Cuba as the world's largest sugar producer. The combination of these factors was a sign that total emancipation could not be long delayed. An 1880 law abolished slavery but gave owners patronage rights over the slaves they possessed for another eight years. In this fashion, Spain recognized the principles of compensation, thus mollifying die-hard interests and escaping the necessity of making further financial commitments. Six years later (7 October 1886) this system of indemnification through labor was terminated, and the remaining 30,000 slaves were released.[48]

The abolition of slavery proved no real hardship for the Cuban slaveowner since he actually made more money by paying workers than providing for slaves. In fact, the standard of living of slaves emancipated during the 1870s actually declined, for the freedman had to pay for services (such as housing) that formerly had been provided.[49] Not the least of the problems was that those freed in the 1870s and 1880s had no occupational skills, and they could earn a living only as farm workers. Freedom provided psychological gains but not necessarily material ones.

The intriguing question is why Cuban sugar lords, even though slavery was becoming increasingly uneconomical, resisted abolition so fiercely. The answer would seem to lie in the essence of the slave culture that had developed on the island. The possession of slaves provided social status, and, as long as it did so, the possessors would struggle to retain their success symbols even though it might cost them heavily to do so. Also, abolition would have swelled the ranks of freed Negroids, a group that the white ruling elements had come to regard with increasing suspicion.

The freed Afro-Cuban to 1860

The census of 1774 revealed the presence of some 36,301 free Negroids in Cuba. This figure was probably a minimum estimate since in Cuba, as elsewhere, there were a small number of fair-skinned mulattoes who passed for white or sought certificates declaring that they possessed "clean" (white) blood. There existed, as in the rest of colonial Spanish America, enmity between blacks and mulattoes and legal restrictions on the social mobility of those identified as Afro-Cubans. Even so, as cigar makers, cobblers, launderers, tailors, petty craftsmen, and domestic servants, they came to occupy a middle stratum between the slaves and the wealthier whites.[50] In general, the nonenslaved Negroids performed necessary service functions that secured for them a position of importance in the society before sugar became king.

The emergence of a plantation economy tied to the production of sugar cane had a disastrous impact upon free Afro-Cubans. Between 1820 and 1850 white Cuban authors such as Joaquín Suárez and Pedro J. Guiteras produced polemical works justifying both slavery and the slave trade on the basis of the biological inferiority of the African.[51] Some Spanish writers, among them Jacinto de Salas y Quiroga, lauded the society created by the Cuban oligarchy, arguing that "the Negro is as the ox and the horse: a means for increasing the wealth of the landowner."[52] More sophisticated racists such as the noted historian José Saco opposed the slave trade primarily because it promoted the Africanization of Cuba, an eventuality that he deemed catastrophic.[53] Narrowly construed, these arguments dealt only with slavery and the slave trade, but their larger import could not be easily dismissed by the free Negroid population. It was but one short step from the justification of slavery on the basis of racial inferiority to the legal establishment of the emancipated descendants of slaves as second-class citizens.

While these theoretical arguments are evidence of white bigotry in nineteenth and twentieth-century Cuba, the persecution of free blacks and mulattoes had actually begun during the last decade of the eighteenth century. In 1793 there were thirty-nine schools on the island in which the majority of the teachers were mulattoes; the following year, laws were promulgated providing for the phasing out of all Negroid instructors.[54] These regulations were superceded in 1809 by another decree that banned free blacks and mulattoes from either teaching in or attending a Cuban school.[55] The next step was an 1816 regulation banning them from owning land.[56] In the light of these indignities, it should come as no surprise that when in 1827 a mulatto named Ana del Toro sought permission to open an educational institution for Negroid children, the government brusquely rejected her petition.[57]

By the 1820s legal prohibitions against *castas* were disappearing from the statute books of most Spanish American republics, but in Cuba the reverse was occurring. The island's status as the major sugar producer and the fact that slaves were believed to be the *sine qua non* for successful plantation operation were the primary causes of this development. More sugar production meant more *bozales*, and the presence of an educated Negroid populace that did not work the cane fields and could challenge white authority would make the intimidation of the *bozales* exceedingly difficult. In addition, since the cultivation and shipment of sugar had become the *raison d'être* for Cuba's existence, the refusal of free Negroids to work the plantations stamped them as subversive persons.[58] Those who by their actions failed to support the reign of "King Sugar" soon felt his wrath.

The period of greatest crisis for Afro-Cubans began during the 1830s. In 1832 Ferdinand VII sought information as to whether "the existence of the free colored population is convenient."[59] Captain General Mariano Rocafort replied in the negative to the monarch's query, citing their refusal to work the plantations, but he cautioned that any action taken to remove them from Cuban soil might cause greater problems.[60] Madrid then definitely decided that a free black and mulatto population was of little use in Cuba and that their presence was not to be encouraged. On 12 March 1837 a royal *cédula* was issued prohibiting Negroids from landing in the country. This law was rather strictly enforced, for disembarking black and mulatto seamen from other countries found themselves imprisoned until the vessels upon which they had arrived were ready to depart.[61] Then, in the new national census of 1841, the traditional practice of classifying Afro-Cubans separately as blacks or mulattoes was terminated; from then on, all persons of full or part African blood would be considered the same, a portent of the future and a psychological blow that left fair-skinned Negroids incredulous.

It was the 1844 "Conspiracy of the Ladder" that clearly demonstrated how Spanish officialdom viewed the free Negroid. Matanzas Province had been shaken by several slave revolts in 1843, and the governor of the island, Leopoldo I. O'Donnell, took unprecedented security measures when in January 1844 a female slave reported that a new rebellion was being plotted. Over 4,000 slaves, free Negroids and whites were taken into custody. Seventy-eight free blacks and mulattoes, including the distinguished mulatto poet Gabriel de la Concepción Valdés were eventually executed. Hundreds of slaves were flogged to death, and a total of 1,292 persons received penal sentences.[62]

Historians disagree as to whether a conspiracy had actually been planned in Matanzas,[63] but O'Donnell chose to believe that the free blacks and mulattoes had been ringleaders in the alleged rebellion. He ordered that "all free colored persons who by their conduct give reason to believe that they are prejudicial to the repose of the country" were to be deported, and he promptly shipped 200 of them to Mexico.[64] Another of his decrees, dated 31 August 1844, stipulated that no Negroids except slaves would be allowed to return to Cuba if they happened to leave the island. A third instruction ordered local Cuban authorities to collect and detain all black and mulatto vagrants in camps or prisons for an indefinite period. Particularly despicable were the minor government officials in Matanzas Province who, sent to carry out O'Donnell's orders, extorted sexual favors from Negroid women with promises of leniency for their imprisoned sons, brothers, and husbands.[65]

But the subsequent repercussions of the 1844 affair would be just as deleterious for Afro-Cubans outside Matanzas Province. Believing that virtually no person of African origin was trustworthy, O'Donnell ordered the disbandment of the *pardo* and *moreno* militia units that had been in existence for roughly two centuries.[66] In addition, he closed down *El Faro*, the first newspaper to be published by Negroids in the island.[67] The harassment did not cease with O'Donnell's departure in 1848. Under Lieutenant General José Gutiérrez de la Concha, a pass system for black and mulatto Cubans was inaugurated (1855), and two years later all Negroid men, women, and children were ordered to register and pay a fixed annual sum for the purchase of an identity card.[68]

Considering the strained atmosphere that pervaded Matanzas Province in 1843 and 1844, it is quite likely that O'Donnell initially believed a plot had been formulated to abolish slavery and/or to create a black-dominated state. But as the investigation proceeded, the political goal became the persecution and intimidation of free Negroids in Matanzas and elsewhere. Especially after 1844, Spanish policy toward free Afro-Cubans was designed to project the following message: You are of little use since you will not perform the work we want you to do. Unless you remain submissive, you will suffer execution, exile, and/or incarceration.

The Afro-Cuban to 1959

Partially because of the oppressive policies implemented by Spanish officials after the 1844 conspiracy, a large number of the infantry fighting in the rebel armies during the Ten Years' War (1868–1878) were free Afro-Cubans. Despite the presence of many Negroid troops, however, occasional manifestations of racial prejudice indicated that powerful revolutionary leaders had not rejected the tenet of white supremacy. In 1876 they successfully engineered the retirement of Antonio Maceo, a mulatto who had risen to the rank of brigadier general. The latter was by no means ignorant of the reason for his fall from grace. In a letter to provisional president, Estrada Palma, Maceo noted that "I have known for sometime, Mr. President, that ... a small circle exists which has indicated that it did not wish to serve under my orders because I belong to the colored race."[69] It cannot be argued that racial dissension was the primary cause for the rebel defeat in the Ten Years' War, but, quite obviously, such discord did nothing to enhance their prospects.

During the war of independence from 1895 to 1898, Afro-Cubans fought on both sides, but they unquestionably composed the bulk of the rebel infantry forces. Apparently a lesson had been learned, for this time the specter of racial disharmony did not significantly manifest itself during the struggle. Afro-Cubans played prominent roles in both the military and political aspects of the conflict. In addition to the return of Antonio Maceo, there were black military leaders such as Flor Crombet, "Perico" Pérez, and Isidro Acea, while the civil representation of the insurgents included two mulattoes, Martín Morúa Delgado and Juan Gualberto Gómez.

As a result of the war, Cubans finally wrenched themselves free from Madrid's domination, but they hardly improved their situation. North American assistance had been necessary to defeat the Spaniards, and Washington was wealthier, stronger, and geographically more able to make its wishes felt. The Platt Amendment[70] was forced on a reluctant Cuba in 1902; politically, the nation became little more than a satellite of the United States.

There were critical changes of another kind as well. By decree, Madrid had ended segregation in public accommodations in 1889 and opened public schools to all persons in 1893. Other discriminatory policies persisted, but after 1898, public strife would break out between darkskinned Cubans and United States Army personnel.[71] General Leonard Wood, appointed military governor of the island, demonstrated his feelings on the racial issue by prohibiting the immigration of any persons of African descent into Cuba. In effect, independence meant the continuation of the old patterns of racial discrimination and the introduction of the Yankee variety as well.

Economically, the final victory over Spain and the establishment of a semiindependent republic did almost nothing for most Afro-Cubans. As of 1899, no recognized black or mulatto owned a farm of 100 acres or more or rented one of over 165 acres. Afro-Cubans represented 32.1 percent of the population, but they owned only 5 percent of the nation's farms.[72] The

1907 census further demonstrated how little progress was being made in reference to the increased acquisition of jobs and financial resources. Whereas 44.8 percent of all Afro-Cubans were farm laborers, an infinitesimal 1.6 percent were salesmen, clerks, or office employees. A reported 153 Negroids held academic degrees. As for professional workers, there were 14 engineers, 4 lawyers, 9 physicians, 40 dentists, and 5 engravers. Even these paltry numbers must be taken with a grain of salt, for among those listed as nonwhite professionals were an undetermined number of Chinese.[73]

Only the political route seemed relatively open for opportunistic Negroids. The two mulatto figures prominent in the independence struggle, Juan Gualberto Gómez and Martín Morúa Delgado, eventually became powerful in the Cuban National Congress. Morúa Delgado was the first – and last – Afro-Cuban elected president of the Senate (1909). Even so, President Estrada Palma (1902–1906) would never invite Morúa Delgado's darkskinned wife to social functions at the presidential palace, an insult that the senator felt deeply.[74] The success of these two Negroids was no doubt gratifying to the few qualified persons who might follow in their footsteps, but, for the rest of the black and mulatto population, the new Cuba was hardly an improvement over the old. Indeed, in 1906 the government showed its contempt for this segment of its population by passing a law appropriating approximately $1 million solely for the promotion of European immigration.[75]

Discontent bred action, and the Independent Negro Party (*Partido independiente de color*) was founded in 1907 under ex-General Evaristo Esteñoz and Pedro Ivonet. As a political aggregation intended to wring from the existing government specific benefits for the island's black and mulatto population, the party called for free university tuition, special education for Afro-Cubans, and a land-distribution plan to aid poor farmers. Curiously, the most vociferous public opposition to the new party came from the Negroid elected representatives, Morúa Delgado and Gualberto Gómez. These leaders argued that an Afro-Cuban political party would generate its antithesis, an all-white party, and racial war would result. Although Morúa Delgado died early in 1910, his law prohibiting the formation of parties on a racial basis was passed on 2 May of that year. Both Esteñoz and Ivonet continued organization activities despite this statute and their temporary incarceration until 20 May 1912, when a general revolt of Afro-Cubans, spearheaded by the party faithful, shook the island.

The full story behind this "black power" revolt has never been completely unraveled, but a hypothesis accepted by several authors is that President José Miguel Gómez knew of the conspiracy and planned to exploit it as a means of furthering his own plans for reelection. If this was his intention, his strategy went sour almost from the beginning. By September the rebellion had been drowned in blood; at least 3,000 blacks and mulattoes, including Esteñoz and Ivonet, lost their lives.[76] For the second time since 1844, a presumed Afro-Cuban threat to the status quo had been mercilessly liquidated.

From September 1912 to the collapse of the Gerardo Machado dictatorship in August 1933, an unwritten but fairly consistent policy was implemented in regard to the societal position of Afro-Cubans. A few mulattoes were assigned to preferential posts in government: Ramón Vasconcelos became commercial attaché in Paris, General Manuel de Jesús Delgado served temporarily as secretary of Agriculture, and President Ramón Grau San Martín appointed a Negroid judge during his first term of office (September 1933–January 1934). But after Gualberto Gómez retired from active politics in 1922, no Afro-Cuban would become as influential a political leader or wield the patronage powers that he had.

From January 1934 until January 1959, the history of Cuba was dominated by Fulgencio Batista, a man of uncertain racial background.[77] As far as rural Afro-Cubans were concerned, Batista did nothing directly to improve their condition of life, but those living in urban areas were able to share in the general prosperity that the island enjoyed. By 1943, 74 percent of all acknowledged Afro-Cubans were reported to be literate. There was also a total of 560 black and mulatto lawyers, 124 doctors, and 3,500 teachers.[78] During the second presidency of Grau San Martín (1944–1948), four or five Afro-Cubans became senators, and perhaps a dozen served as national congressmen. There was a perceptible increase in the number of darkskinned army officers, the highest ranking being General Gregory Querejata.

On the other hand, Negroid Cubans were prevented by indirect means from joining the navy or air force officers corps and were excluded from such trades as baking and pastry making.[79] Preference in certain occupations was often made on a color basis, a practice that strengthened the aloofness of the mulatto elite and that naturally fueled black resentment.[80] Some public beaches and parks, especially in the interior of the country, remained segregated, and minority efforts to end such discrimination often touched off bloody racial confrontations such as the one that engulfed the city of Trinidad on 7 and 8 January 1934.[81] Cuban aristocratic circles still "closed the door to persons of black complexion," and in exclusive yacht clubs, restaurants, and cabarets, blacks and mulattoes "found themselves barred from entry."[82] George Schuyler, who visited Havana in 1947, reported that, while Negroid physicians and dentists could be found, there was "only one Negro doctor on the staff of a public hospital." He also reported an imbalance in bureaucratic positions; the lower echelons were heavily filled by Negroids, while the higher positions remained lily white.[83] Schuyler did not visit the countryside, but another investigator, Lowry Nelson, reported that in rural Cuba a perceptible color line existed and that even blacks and mulattoes displayed a pronounced preference for Caucasian features.[84]

Other than ignoring the situation or merely hiring a few more Afro-Cubans to occupy petty government sinecures, national political officials from 1912 through 1959 did little to remedy these evils. Article 20 of the Constitution of 1940, for example, declared all discrimination on the basis of sex, race, or class illegal, and Article 74 called upon the minister of Labor to take action against "discriminatory practices."[85] Unfortunately, no permanent governmental commission was ever established to provide free and rapid investigation of alleged cases of racial bias. Furthermore, political instability and long years of racial antagonism made the elimination of racism by statute a dubious business even under the best conditions.

That Cuban governments did little to combat notions of white superiority can be seen in their practice of aiding and abetting census distortion. In 1912 the United Fruit Company persuaded President José Miguel Gómez to allow Haitian and Jamaican workers to enter the country for seasonal labor during the harvest, but not for permanent residence. Between 1913 and 1928 350,000 to 400,000 of them traveled to the island.[86] Considerable numbers remained, however, even after thousands were finally deported during the Great Depression. Amazingly, nothing in the censuses taken before or after the period from 1913 to 1928 reveals that any unusual immigration took place. The 1901 census reported that 32 percent of the population were black or mulatto. In 1919 the figure was 27.2 percent; in 1931, 27.2 percent; in 1943, 25.6 percent; and in 1953, 27.2 percent.[87] Numerous observers believe that these figures are grossly inaccurate and that, in reality, at least half the Cuban population has African blood.[88] Pre-Batista rulers had established the pattern of census alteration, but the governments from 1934 to 1959 were not averse to continuing it. As in Santo Domingo and elsewhere, if Cubans wanted to believe that their nation was getting whiter, census statistics would be provided to help them preserve their beliefs.

Although in some nations Negroid protest has been curiously muted, at least since the time of Gerardo Machado's second term in office (1928–1933), Afro-Cuban intellectuals have been conspicuous in exclaiming their displeasure with the prevailing pattern of racial relations. In the vanguard of the ranks of the disgruntled were journalists like Gustavo Urrutia, and poets like Marcelio Arozarena and Regino Pedrosa.[89] But the most indomitable source of Afro-Cuban dissent came to be the pen of Nicolás Guillén. Often credited with founding the *negrismo* school of Cuban poetry,[90] this mulatto's indignation and virtuosity are both evident in these sarcastic but stinging verses:

> The cabaret that never opened
> to the people of color
> (This is a [private] club, you understand?
> What a pity. If not . . .)
> . . .

In the bank
only white employees
(There were exceptions: sometimes
the one who swept and the doorman).[91]

In the face of massive indifference, however, words became impotent weapons, a factor that may well have influenced the decision of a number of prominent mulattoes and blacks to join the Cuban Communist Party. Among them during the 1930s and 1940s were the aforementioned Nicolás Guillén; Salvador García Agüero, writer and teacher; Lázaro Peña, first secretary-general of the Confederation of Cuban Workers; Arascelio Iglesias Díaz, Havana dock-labor chief; and Jesús Menéndez, boss of the Negroid sugar workers' federation (*Federación nacional obrera azucarera*). Unlike Sandalio Junco, who denounced Joseph Stalin as a betrayer of the working class and was later executed for his brashness,[92] most Afro-Cuban Communists remained in good standing with the party at least through January 1959.

For other black and mulatto Cubans, organization on racial lines remained the classic defense against injustice. The *Organización celular asteria*, formed during the 1930s, argued that since half of all Cubans were Negroid, the same percentage of government jobs must be held by Afro-Cubans. Employing a more legalistic approach was the *Comité por los derechos del negro* ("Committee for the Rights of the Negro"), which sought through court action the elimination of racist employment policies in Cuban industry. The same goal was also adopted by the *Federación nacional de sociedades negras de Cuba* ("National Federation of Negro Societies in Cuba"), a group that attempted to promote racial awareness through social activities. The problem with all these groups was that their membership was small and primarily urban. The uneducated Negroid tenant farmer or cane cutter was outside the scope of these consciousness-raising efforts and probably preferred not to think about this kind of problem.[93]

Unlike in Colombia and Venezuela, many intellectuals in Cuba were not averse to recognizing the existence of a racial problem. Alberto Arredondo and Ramón Cabrera Torres, to name but two, had flatly argued that further development of the country was impossible unless discrimination was ended and the Afro-Cuban was brought into the mainstream of national life.[94] Fernando Ortiz Fernández, whom C. Eric Williams has dubbed "the Caribbean whiteman at his best,"[95] preached the doctrine that the "Indian of Cuba was the Negro."[96] But as far as many white Cubans were concerned, the Indian had long ago been exterminated, and the Negroids knew better than to cause too much trouble. In short, race and color discrimination was very real in pre-Castro Cuba, but treatment of this disease could not be undertaken since the patient was loathe to admit his illness.

Racial questions in revolutionary Cuba

Afro-Cubans fought on both sides during the civil war from 1956 to 1959, but since the majority probably served with Batista's forces, it is doubtful that they considered Fidel Castro Ruz the great liberator who would solve the island's racial problems. Castro himself maintained a conspicuous silence regarding all such issues until after he had taken power in January 1959. He made a few peremptory remarks at a 23 January press conference, but not until 22 March did the guerrilla leader-turned-premier present a clear indication of future policy. He acknowledged that racial discrimination existed in the "centers of recreation" and in the "centers of work," the latter being the worst and the one that "we have to eradicate" with the utmost urgency. He followed this declaration by stating on 25 March during an interview that racial discrimination in Cuba was "possibly the most difficult of all the problems that we have to confront."[97]

Unlike previous Cuban dictators and presidents, Castro had publicly admitted the inadmissible: Racial discrimination was prevalent in Cuba, and the government had to take positive steps to root it out. In Spanish America the undertaking of such a commitment was in itself revolutionary; even if Cuban socialism had been a failure in every other way, the steps taken to implement the antiracist pledge would still have attracted widespread attention.

How successful the new Cuba has been in striking down the racist "dragon" is, however, a matter of controversy. The official position expressed in *Cuba: Country Free of Segregation* argues that racial discrimination was "basically an economic phenomenon"; with the departure of the Cuban bourgeoisie and Yankee capitalists, "racial discrimination had disappeared from Cuba."[98] For the most part, authors sympathetic to the revolutionary state have presented similar views. There is Adolfo Gilly, who unequivocally declared that "the Revolution has, of course, erased racial differences."[99] Others, such as Joseph A. Kahl, who spent one month in Cuba, displayed an even more euphoric attitude, "For the first time, Cuba's Negroes . . . share equally in the goals and services and the civil respect of their society. They have been fully integrated in the schools and on the jobs."[100]

A sympathetic but not uncritical view of the racial situation was presented by Elizabeth Sutherland in her book, *The Youngest Revolution*. A North American who spent several months in Cuba in 1967, Sutherland noted that "racism as it once existed in Cuba had been wiped out."[101] She maintains, however, that aesthetically the preference for Caucasian appearance was still inordinately pervasive. Furthermore, virtually all the major officeholders were white, and magazines and billboards did not suggest that a large minority of Cubans had African blood. Government officials did not deny the accuracy of Sutherland's observations about cultural racism, but they contended that after a generation or two of revolutionary equity, these problems would be rectified. She seemed constrained to accept this promise, although her reasons for doing so were not immediately manifest.[102]

Still sympathetic but considerably more skeptical was a West Indian observer, Barry Reckford. In his *Does Fidel Eat More Than Your Father?* he reported numerous incidents that seemed to justify tentatively that: (1) many Cuban whites still believe Afro-Cubans inferior by virtue of racial heritage alone; and (2) the old enmity between blacks and mulattoes still smolders beneath the surface. Specifically, Reckford reported that Afro-Cubans whose views on racial matters did not agree with those of the state were prevented from speaking at an international cultural conference held in Havana in 1968. He also found that some Afro-Cubans believed that a special government program would have to be undertaken if their children were to be able to compete with whites, but that the government refused to accept this argument.[103]

Indirect support for some of Reckford's findings exists in a study of lower-class Cuban refugees by Geoffrey E. Fox. This sociologist was somewhat disconcerted to find that both black and white Cubans generally argued that no racial discrimination had been evident in pre-revolutionary Cuba. Black and mulatto refugees, in particular, displayed a considerable reluctance to discuss racial problems, and very few did so with any candor. His major conclusion was that, for most Cubans, as long as there was no public protest and the blacks and mulattoes "stayed in their place," there was no racial problem. Efforts on the part of the Castro government to end discrimination and to provide blacks and mulattoes with opportunities for social mobility have fueled resentment among the whites and confusion among some Afro-Cubans; therefore, in contemporary Cuba there now exists a "race problem."[104]

Criticism directed at the revolutionary government's racial policies has come chiefly from Negroid Cuban expatriates and Afro-American nationalists. Among the first group is Juan René Bettancourt, appointed by Castro in January 1959 as supervisory delegate of the *Federación de sociedades negras de Cuba* ("Federation of Negro Societies in Cuba"). Bettancourt had several disagreements with his superiors and was subsequently fired. In his opinion, "one can truthfully say, and this is without the slightest exaggeration, the Negro Movement [in Cuba] died at the hands of Señor Fidel Castro."[105] Another bitter attack came from the pen of Carlos Moore, a Cuban black who charged in 1965 that the regime altered statistical data to make the national population appear whiter and also moved conspiratorially to keep blacks out of high government office.[106]

Some Afro-American militants leaving for Cuba to escape persecution in the United States have not found the Cuban racial scene to their liking. Robert Williams, who between 1963 and 1966 did propaganda broadcasts over "Radio Free Dixie," explained that he left Cuba because "I wasn't going to be an Uncle Tom for capitalism or for socialism either."[107] The world press paid a good deal of attention when Black Panther leader Eldridge Cleaver personally denounced Fidel Castro as a racist and moved to Algeria,[108] but John Clytus, who stayed in Cuba from 1964 to 1967, has probably written the most controversial commentary from a black nationalist viewpoint. This Afro-American worked as a translator for *Granma*, the official government newspaper, and taught English at the University of Havana. He reports that, in addition to being hypocritical, the Castro regime "did not allow black people to identify with black."[109] It would be an understatement to say that he took a dim view of any argument that racism was dead in revolutionary Cuba.

The problems of Afro-American nationalists are understandable, but to a great extent they are hardly the fault of the regime. Had Robert Williams, Eldridge Cleaver, and John Clytus read the past history of the island, they would have understood that racism in Cuba is centuries old. It was naïve to assume that a complete racial change could be achieved in only a decade or two. Moreover, Castro certainly was not about to let these gentlemen go freely about the island spreading black nationalist ideas that could prove antithetical to the interests of his regime.

Afro-Cuban or Afro-American nationalists would seem to be on much better ground in their criticism of the revolutionary regime for failing to recognize that the Afro-Cuban may need special help if he is to take his rightful place in society.[110] The Castro pledges of March 1959 said nothing about additional assistance, nor did they even pay lip service to black nationalism. Castro promised, in effect, that if a Negroid Cuban was qualified, he could get the job he deserved, and, if he could afford it, he could go to any restaurant, theater, or dance hall he wished. This was all that was promised. In other words, the Afro-Cuban was a typical proletarian, only slightly more deprived. But Marxist theory aside, the Afro-Cuban, like the other Africans in the Americas, is subject to psychological and other burdens resulting from slavery that resolution of the class prob-

lem may never relieve. Nevertheless, in view of its political orientation, the Castro regime can hardly afford to acknowledge
this fact. A large-scale effort to provide compensatory assistance
could (1) set Afro-Cubans apart, thereby emphasizing racial differences; (2) anger white Cubans who would not favor special
help for blacks; (3) cost large sums of money that would normally be allocated elsewhere; and (4) erode the revolutionary
government's credibility.

In regard to the question of cultural racism that Elizabeth
Sutherland raised, the Cuban government is not likely to find it
appropriate to make any radical changes or to embark on any
crash program producing new textbooks that emphasize the
deeds of darkskinned Cubans. What should not be forgotten is
that Fidel Castro is not only a socialist but is first and foremost
a Latin. Thus, his views on the raising of Afro-Cuban racial
consciousness may differ very little from those of Simón Bolívar. In addition, Castro could not fail to be aware of the bloody
events of 1844 and 1912. True or false, therefore, the official
position continues to be that, under socialism, all Cubans have
become brothers.

Unquestionably, the regime enjoys the support of the mass of
black and mulatto Cubans; it is they who have been especially
helped by literacy programs, medical aid, and agrarian reforms.
But if improved education eventually results in the rise of a
Negroid elite, there will undoubtedly be more persons like Juan
Bettancourt asking questions in the future. What the attitude of
white Cubans will be when large numbers of Afro-Cubans begin
competing for prestigious economic and political posts is uncertain. The problem is that racial bias seems to be like weeds in a
garden: You may think that you have rooted them out, but
next spring will bring a new crop.

12

The Future of the Afro-Latino

A LEGACY OF DECEIT

On 17 March 1794 the Royal Council of the Indies sent a directive to its administrators in America pointing out, among other things, that slavery under Spanish rule was more humane than it was in the American regions governed by Britain, France, Portugal, or the Netherlands.[1] Absolutely no explanation of how these august councillors had arrived at this remarkable conclusion was provided.[2] In any event, no more than a brief recall of the history of slavery to 1810 would serve to demonstrate that the council's evaluation of the historical situation was intended only for those who were already predisposed toward accepting the conclusion offered.

Both slavery and Spain's American empire have disappeared, but this bombastic claim continues to be elevated to the status of scholarly writ. Frank Tannenbaum, Stanley Elkins, and N. A. Micklejohn in Anglo-Saxon America,[3] and Homero Martínez Montero, Javier Malagón, and Restrepo Canal in Spanish America[4] have all produced studies supporting the essentials of the 1794 declaration. In addition, the Chilean historian Gonzalo Vial Correa writes that "it is admitted without much discussion, that the Spanish treated the Negro better than the English or the French."[5] Nor can we overlook Gustavo Godoy, who imperiously announced that the Spanish conquest of America was "eminently anti-racist."[6]

This obsession with establishing the superior benevolence of the Spanish system of slavery is surpassed only by the determi-

nation of some Spanish-American writers to prove that the regimen of servitude that existed in their particular nation was the
least rigorous of all. Thus, the Argentine José M. Ezcurra Massini blandly reports that slavery in the Río de la Plata region –
all three centuries of it – was indubitably "kind and humane."[7]
His contention is significantly qualified by Josefina Plá, who
insists that slavery in Paraguay was milder than in any other
place in Spanish America.[8] The aforementioned Javier Malagón
stoutly maintains that in his native Santo Domingo slavery was
"more humane" than in Cuba or Venezuela.[9] This view must be
contrasted with that of Fernando Ortiz Fernández, who describes in detail the merciless nature of slave labor on Cuban
sugar plantations but somehow concludes that in his native land
"slavery was . . . not as cruel as in other countries."[10] Finally,
there is the Chilean Guillermo Feliú Cruz, who would have us
believe that, by and large, African captives in his homeland were
almost permanently on holiday.[11]

The history of African slavery in Spanish America differs in
many respects from the history of this institution in Anglo-
Saxon America, but this assertion in no way justifies the sweeping claims so impetuously advanced by the scholars mentioned
above. Among other things, it should be evident from the materials thus far presented that British diplomatic initiatives and
the power of the Royal Navy were much more responsible for
shutting off the African slave trade than were the often ignored
prohibitions promulgated by the Spanish American states. The
semifarcical *liberto-manumiso* schemes were nowhere successful, while in Peru, Paraguay, Venezuela, Cuba, and Ecuador,
final abolition was decreed for reasons that could hardly be
described as humane. Worst of all, aside from Argentina and
Venezuela no Spanish American republic sought to create an
organization like the Freedman's Bureau in the United States,
which, no matter how poorly it functioned, did assist the slave
in adjusting to his new status.[12]

It may be argued that Spanish America was too poor to have
initiated a similar program and that the integration of the slave
into the great mass of poor Indians, *mestizos*, and freed Negroids was all that was envisioned by the creators of the emanci-

pation laws. On the other hand, in Ecuador, Colombia, Venezuela, Cuba, Peru, Argentina, and Central America, the rights of the slave owners over their ex-properties were recognized, and, in all these states except Venezuela and Argentina, compensation of some kind was eventually forthcoming. If property rights of the owner deserved recognition, was not the slave also owed something more than the right to become a peon, domestic, or day laborer? It is revealing that none of the authors previously mentioned discusses the slavery question from the perspective of the rights of the slave as well as those of the owner. This situation further illustrates one of the theses of this study: The glorious tradition of Spanish American or Iberian benevolence toward black bondmen is essentially historical fiction.

Naturally, the rejection of a legend of this sort cannot demolish it and will probably change few attitudes because, ultimately, the real credibility of the hypothesis lies in its ability to service certain philosophical and psychological needs. The poor white farmer in Alabama, Georgia, or Mississippi, for example, had to believe in the biological inferiority of the Afro-American. Otherwise, there was absolutely no one left, and he would have been faced with the unbearable realization of his own place at the bottom of the social and economic ladder. Similarly, the Spain of Charles IV and Ferdinand VII was an impoverished, third-rate nation bereft of everything except its pride. The claim of moral superiority was the only one an impotent Spain could make. Indeed, the formulation of justifications for past improprieties is an understandable task for empires upon which the sun has obviously set.

Spanish American authors, faced with the "Gringo Goliath" to the north, have often experienced feelings of inferiority. Strip away their claims of moral rectitude vis-à-vis the United States (or even some neighboring Spanish American state), and what is there left? Historical scholars such as Óscar Gil Díaz,[13] Jaime Jaramillo Uribe,[14] and Hugo Tolentino[15] have attempted to dispel the notion that slavery in their countries was somehow humane, but these efforts are often ignored or treated as inconsequential palaver. Moreover, historical texts and learned jour-

nals aside, the spirit of March 1794 lives on, although in a
different sense, in the hearts of many Spanish Americans. Time
and again, I have been earnestly informed by educated and
otherwise likable Latins that there is no racial prejudice in their
countries. How adamantly this belief is held can best be demonstrated by several examples.

After completing a musical performance at a university in El
Salvador in March 1962,[16] I had a long chat with a number of
friendly Salvadorean students, all of whom assured me that racial problems were nonexistent in their country. When I questioned the accuracy of their judgment, it was decided that this
topic warranted further discussion at a nightclub, one that supposedly had "the best women." These Salvadoreans remained
very amicable, but a crisis of sorts developed when another
black American musician from the musical group sought the
favor of one of the prostitutes plying her trade in the establishment. The students offered to pay her fee, but the lady announced, with some heat, that she did not "service Negroes."
My Salvadorean friends apologized profusely, but they refused
to view this incident as evidence of racial prejudice in their
country.

All the Salvadoreans in question were either whites or *mestizos*, but in Spanish America many persons of African descent
do not want to discuss these problems either. In January 1970 I
was chatting about comparative race relations with a mulatto
musician in a Caracas nightclub when that gentleman happened
to state that while he "was not a Negro," he sympathized with
the civil rights crusade led by the late Dr. Martin Luther King,
Jr. Somewhat perturbed by this man's attitude, I asked him
what he was if not a Negro. He replied, "I'm a Venezuelan." My
retort was that his nationality was not in dispute. I told him
that the previous day I had visited a diplomatic adviser in the
cancillería of his government, and the only person I had seen in
the building who seemed even remotely Negroid had been push-
ing a broom. This comment engendered an angry denial of any
race or color bias in Venezuela, but no information regarding
the accuracy of my observation. Later, I was able to reflect a bit
more objectively about what had occurred, and I ultimately

concluded that in the mind of the mulatto musician, the absence of race or color prejudice in Venezuela was not a debatable proposition; it was dogma. But I still wonder whether that Afro-Venezuelan ever thinks about the point I raised.

Admittedly, my experiences may seem a bit unusual, but other Afro-Americans who have spent years in Spanish America have reported similar incidents and encounters. Audrey Miles, a Peace Corps volunteer in the department of Boyacá, Colombia, was assigned to work in schools in the town of Chiquinquirá. She was informed by another teacher that Colombian Negroids could teach children subject matter but could not "give them values for living."[17] Even more to her dismay, she discovered that the local population generally believed black Colombian women to be prostitutes. As a result, she was propositioned by numerous local males who did not immediately recognize her as a black North American. She summed up her experiences succinctly:

> Generally, I've come to realize that the more *moreno* [dark] one is, the uglier he is in the eyes of the average Colombian. Everyone in Colombia wants to be *blanco* [white] so negros are *feos* [ugly]. *Negra fea* means, if we can't be white, we must constantly remind you that you are darker than we are.[18]

Less angry but hardly complimentary was Walter F. Thomas, an associate director of the Peace Corps in Venezuela in 1974. He pointed out that skin color did not appear to be a particularly important factor in rural areas, but in towns like Caracas, dark skin and Negroid features were considered negative characteristics.[19]

To understand the position of many Latins, it is necessary to comprehend that their replies to questions regarding race or color prejudice are often predicated on a number of basic psychological and social considerations. Since no system of legal segregation as pervasive as that found in Dixie between 1890 and 1960 existed in postcolonial Spanish America, Latins can say "we have no discrimination in our country." Because separate drinking fountains and separate elevators were never cre-

ated, many Latins go right on denying the existence of discrimination in their nations. They doggedly insist that any problems
are entirely the result of either class consciousness or some
linguistic misunderstanding. But a Colombian friend, speaking
with utmost candor, stated why he felt that only North American racism is a fit topic for discussion, "You Yankees, black or
white, are rich and powerful. . . . You cut back on purchases of
our products and we suffer a depression. . . . We must struggle
to make even minor gains. . . . When we are rich, perhaps we
will be able to recognize our weaknesses."

It may well be that the recognition of racial problems in
Spanish America awaits its achievement of a "place in the sun."
But suppose all the countries do not make it?

THE PROBLEMS OF THE PRESENT

Possibly the most striking factor in the history of the black man
in Spanish America has been the absence of significant change
in his overall position. Admittedly he is no longer in bondage,
but, in his deprived state, the Hispanic black or mulatto is generally excluded from competing for society's premier awards
and positions. The Spaniards brought the African to the New
World to perform manual labor; four hundred years later, this is
still his primary function.[20]

On the surface, the problem of the Negroids would seem to
be nearly identical with that of the countless Indians and *mestizos* in Spanish America. Nonetheless, even though these peoples
are poor, uneducated, and exploited by a wealthy minority that
calls itself white, there are also significant differences. In Paraguay, the Andean states, and Mexico, a *mestizo* or even an
Indian who speaks educated Spanish and wears Western clothes
can become "white." Moreover, in Peru and Mexico and to a
lesser extent in other countries, the creed of *indigenismo* has
received official sanction, and a claim to Indian blood is, in
varying degrees, fashionable. Note that in contrast, there is no
place in Spanish America where blackness is encouraged by government fiat. While doing research in Bolivia and Paraguay in
1965, I met numerous top-level diplomatic personnel and mili-

tary officers who were distinctly of Indian ancestry. It is doubtful if there is any place in Spanish America where persons as distinctly Negroid as these gentlemen were Indian could occupy so many positions of power. To put it bluntly, the black and mulatto are "in" nowhere and are among the "have nots" everywhere.

The assorted methods by which the Spanish were able to keep the blacks, mulattoes, and *zambos* divided into contentious groups have been discussed at some length. The *gracias al sacar* program provided a mechanism whereby potential leaders could be separated from the Negroid masses, while the socioracial schemes based upon the alleged degree of Spanish blood one possessed gave the mulattoes a rationale for lording it over the blacks. Independence ended the caste system on paper, but it did not make everyone white. What has since evolved in many areas is a flexible concept called "social race," which allows anyone to be whatever he wishes under limited circumstances.[21] An example is the situation in a government-built housing project in Barranquilla, Colombia. Of the people living in the development, "no one is to be seen who would not qualify as a Negro in the United States."[22] But the machinations of the social race concept are evident in that these same residents "declare themselves 'white persons,' and castigate slum dwellers as 'Negros.' "[23] Nevertheless, the inescapable fact is that this system of social categorization remains under the control of whites. Thus, the "black white men" in the Barranquilla housing project may say that only "Negroes" live in slums, but few phenotypically white persons are going to invite either the "Negroes" or the "black white men" home to dinner! The Negroid individual may choose to believe that race and/or color is only one of many ingredients in the determination of his social position, and the upper class white would agree that this is true. But the white is also well aware that, when it comes to certain job categories and entrance into the more elevated levels of society, skin color becomes critically important.

Assuming the veracity of the argument as developed thus far, what is the prospect of some sort of racial awakening among Spanish American Negroids? According to the English author

Julian Pitt-Rivers, post-World War II industrialization and the spreading technological revolution have had a powerful, though not always understood, impact upon conditions in Spanish America. He wrote that "Clothing, speech and culture are losing force as indicators of status in the context of expanding cities, but color is becoming more crucial. . . . Under modern industrial conditions, much of Latin America is moving from the system of social race that flourished in the communities of yesterday to a system of ethnic class."[24]

The emergence of many persons of African origin in the proletarian class could indeed spark some sort of racial awakening. But even though the social-race concept may lose its attractiveness, the emergence of a racial consciousness based on patterns found in the United States or some other area is by no means a certainty. Consider that Nicolás Guillén, the celebrated Cuban poet, established himself as an implacable foe of race and color bias in Cuba, but after Fidel Castro took power, Guillén ceased to write about the problem. Appointed president of the National Union of Artists and Writers of Cuba, Guillén used his talents to praise the new regime, thereby implying that the socialist revolution had solved all racial problems.[25]

Nearly as caustic in his past comments about racism in Ecuador has been another poet, Pablo Adalberto Ortiz. A diplomatic representative for his country in both Mexico and Ecuador, Ortiz depicts himself as an advocate of "negritude," but he believes that this concept is solely a means of expression and definitely "not an end in itself, as some extremist political theoreticians . . . would argue, because such a position would lead us to a . . . variety of black nazism."[26]

There is always the possibility that the personal success of these literary figures may have tempered their views. Nevertheless, the antipathy or indifference they display toward the formulation of Negroid social and political organizations is probably shared by the great mass of Hispanicized persons of African origin. Historically, light-skinned mulattoes and Afro-Indians have been acculturated to view themselves as different from blacks; a call for united action, therefore, is not likely to gain their support. Moreover, the fate of the *Partido auctóctono* in Uruguay[27] and the 1912 War of the Negroes[28] in Cuba suggest that no matter what their goals, a militant Negroid organization simply cannot expect the support of poor whites, *mestizos*, or Indians. Add to these considerations the fact that in most Spanish American republics, blacks and mulattoes are in the minority, and it becomes evident that south of the Río Grande, there are powerful circumstances that militate against the creation of the equivalent of the Black Panthers or even the NAACP. Thus, some individuals will continue striving to gain power and position on a personal basis, while the Negroid masses can expect to achieve the social change they desire only through collective action with other impoverished racial and ethnic groups.

Ample evidence exists that the hypothesis stated above is at least provisionally valid. Professor Thomas Sanders noted that young blacks and mulattoes in the Colombian Chocó were well aware that discrimination was prevalent in the capital city of Quibdó; nevertheless, they were more concerned with improving their individual economic position and going to the university than with working collectively to eradicate racial bias.[29] The attitude of these Afro-Colombians is different from that of Afro-Cubans but is definitely in harmony with the collective action approach previously noted. A black reporter from the United States visited Castro's revolutionary state early in 1973 and reported that "there is a slowly emerging black identity in Cuba," but for Afro-Cubans the necessity of making the Revolution a success took precedence over Negroid solidarity – at least for the present.[30]

Some North American blacks look with disfavor on such attitudes and decry the lack of "negritude" among the Negroid peoples of Latin America.[31] Such critics overlook a basic consideration, one that George Schuyler emphasized over a quarter of a century ago: Poor Afro-Americans possess greater socioeconomic opportunities than middle-class whites in most of Spanish America.[32] This reality does not mean that Afro-Americans must give up their struggle and cease to demand the rights that are duly theirs. But by the same token, blacks in the United States should realize that the Afro-Peruvian and Afro-Venezuelan want items like electric lights and indoor plumbing first.

Only after these things have been obtained will they worry about black history courses in schools, the impact of white standards of beauty upon the black consciousness, or the necessity of racial solidarity. In short, both Afro-Americans and Spanish-speaking blacks and mulattoes are striving to achieve a sense of liberation; they will, however, follow different roads in reaching this goal.

SPECULATION ON THINGS TO COME

In 1919 W. E. B. DuBois organized the first Pan-African Congress. Since that time, a number of conferences have been held in which people from African states and some from the Americas have come together to express their feelings of kinship and to cement the bonds that similarity of blood and origin seem to engender. But if there are Pan-African congresses and conferences, why have there been no such meetings exclusively for those who share both African origin and a common heritage of slavery in the Americas? Admittedly there would be economic, cultural, and linguistic difficulties, but they could be surmounted. Peoples of the African diaspora – Afro-Americans, Afro-Uruguayans, Jamaicans, Afro-Ecuadoreans – might discover that they have as much, or more, in common with each other than they have with Africans in Africa. If this book, no matter what its failures may be, contributes to the eventual organization of such a meeting, it will have been a successful effort.

APPENDIX 1

Prices of Slaves

Year	Place	Cost (in pesos)	Observation/ Comment
1528–1532	All Spanish New World possessions	45	Price established in the Ehinger-Seiler *asiento* of 1528. It is rather unlikely that this price level was honored by slave dealers.
1535	Cuba	47	
1536	Hispaniola	80–100	Settlers on the island complained that, at this price, dealer profits averaged almost 100%.
1536	Lima (Peru)	360	
1548	Santiago (Chile)	300	
1555	Antilles	100	The highest prices
	Caribbean coast (Panama, Colombia, Venezuela)	110	set by Charles I at which slaves were to be sold. They were
	Mexico	120	ignored by dealers
	Northwestern South America (Ecuador, interior of Colombia)		and dropped by the crown in 1561.

Appendix 1 (cont.)

Year	Place	Cost (in pesos)	Observation/ Comment
	Peru, Río de la Plata	150	
	Chile	180	
1564–1565	Chile (via Cartagena-Porto Bello-Panama City-Callao-Valparaiso)		
1595	Chile (via Buenos Aires)	280 70–74	Legal price Price for contraband *bozales.*
1600	Chile	300–400	Prices for female slaves were generally lower.
1609	Mexico	300–500	This price was changed only for the best properties.
1620	Peru (via Porto Bello-Panama City-Callao)	640	Average price paid for good prime *bozales.*
1622	Captaincy General of Guatemala (Central America)	500	Established price for a prime *bozal.*
1630	Peru	500–600	Prices established for a *bozal* shipped on the Cartagena-Porto Bello-Callao route.
	Audiencia of Charcas (Bolivia)	800	Price charged for quality *bozales* brought to Potosí.
1637	Mexico	410	
1655	Colombia Panama Venezuela	180	
1670–1680	Chile	480	Price for *bozales* shipped from Cartagena (via Panama).

Appendix 1 (*cont.*)

Year	Place	Cost (in pesos)	Observation/ Comment
1696–1701	Colombia Venezuela Panama	375	Average price paid for a male *pieza* when the Portuguese Royal Company of Guinea was *asentista*. Females sold for 350 pesos, *muleques* for 350, and *mulecas* for 250. By 1701 the price for males had dropped to 350 pesos; for females and *muleques*, to 300; and for *mulecas*, to 200.
1702–1713	Colombia Venezuela Panama Río de la Plata	300	Maximum price for slaves as stipulated in the *asiento* granted to the Royal French Company of Guinea. The actual average price for males at Cartagena was 240 pesos; at Buenos Aires, 250; and at Porto Bello, about 290.
1713–1740	Colombia Panama Venezuela Río de la Plata	150	Price fixed by the Spanish government for the South Sea Company. In fact, males and females at Cartagena were generally sold for 220 to 250 pesos while *muleques* and *mulecas* went for 180 to 220 pesos.

Appendix 1 (*cont.*)

Year	Place	Cost (in pesos)	Observation/ Comment
1713–1740	Chile	370	Average price paid for good *bozales* brought through Buenos Aires during the years the South Sea Company controlled the trade.
1737	Mexico	300	South Sea Company price for prime male *piezas* at Veracruz.
1740–1760	Cuba	144	Legal price charged by the Royal Company of Havana, which held a monopoly on Cuban trade.
1765	Mexico Venezuela Colombia Cuba Santo Domingo Panama	290	Price established in the contract under the terms of the Uriarte *asiento*. The price for *muleques* was 260 pesos; for *mulecas*, 230 pesos.
1768	Cuba	270	Price for *muleques* was 240 pesos. The average for *mulecas* was 225 pesos.
1769	Venezuela	270	
1777	Venezuela	224	
1780	Peru	500	Price for prime *bozales*.
1784–1786	Venezuela Trinidad	150–155 150	Price at which an English Company, Dawson and Becker Ltd., agreed to deliver slaves.
1785	Mexico	150	

Appendix 1 (*cont.*)

Year	Place	Cost (in pesos)	Observation/ Comment
1786	Cuba Venezuela	185	Price established for the second Dawson and Becker contract in 1786. *Mulecones* were to be sold at 175; a price was not set for *muleques.*
1972	Cuba	200	
1793	Chile	150–200	Demand decreased, and the free-slave trade reduced the prices. General price for all slaves sold there.
1802–1803	Cuba	300–350	
1805	Colombia Ecuador Panama	250	Average price
1807	Cuba	225–265	
1821–1827	Cuba	350–600	Prices varied widely because of supply uncertainties.
1828–1845	Cuba	250–350	Supply appears to have been relatively constant.
1846–1872	Cuba	500–2,000	As early as 1855, prices for slaves of all sexes, ages, sick or well, topped 1,000 pesos. With the increasing pressure against the international slave trade, the supply dried up.

Appendix 1 (*cont.*)

*Sources:*Miguel Acosta Saignes, *Vida de los esclavos en Venezuela* (Caracas, 1967), pp. 49, 53–54, 116; H. H. S. Aimes, *A History of Slavery in Cuba: 1811 to 1868*, Octagon Books Edition (New York, 1967), pp. 267–69; Domingo Amanátegui Solar, "La trata de negros en Chile," *Revista Chilena de Historia y Geografía* 44, no. 48 (1922): 33, 38–39; Frederick Bowser, *The African Slave in Colonial Peru: 1524–1650* (Stanford, 1974), p. 80; Federico Brito Figueroa, *Estructura económica de Venezuela colonial* (Caracas, 1963), pp. 108–10, 128, 131; Aquiles Escalante, *El negro en Colombia* (Bogotá, 1964), p. 16; Francisco de Paula García Peláez, *Memorias para la historia del antiguo reino de Guatemala*, 3 vols. (Guatemala City, 1943–1944), 2: 27; Rolando Mellafe, *La esclavitud en Hispano-América* (Buenos Aires, 1964), pp. 67–68; idem, *La introducción de la esclavitud negra en Chile: Tráfico y rutas* (Santiago, 1959), pp. 25, 204, 245, 252–53; Diego Luis Molinari, *La trata de negros* (Buenos Aires, 1944), pp. 74–77, 502, 507; Jorge Palacios Preciado, *La trata de negros por Cartagena de Indias: 1650–1750* (Tunja, 1973), pp. 71, 144, 203; José Antonio Saco, *Historia de la esclavitud de la raza africana en el Nuevo Mundo y en especial en los países américo-hispanos*, 4 vols. (Havana, 1938), 2: 176–83, 260, 273; Elena F. Scheüss de Studer, *La trata de negros en el Río de la Plata durante el siglo XVIII* (Buenos Aires, 1958), pp. 272, 329 fn.; Gonzalo Vial Correa, *El africano en el reino de Chile: Ensayo histórico-jurídico* (Santiago, 1957), pp. 21, 38, 52, 96–97.

APPENDIX 2
Examples of Restrictions on Slaves

1. Order from the *cabildo* of Lima, 1537:
   Slaves may not cut down trees or pick fruit or corn. First offenders receive 100 lashes, and a 10-peso fine is levied against the master. A second offense results in loss of a genital member of the slave.

2. Order from the *cabildo* of Lima, 1537:
   Any slave found changing the course of an irrigation channel will suffer 100 lashes.

3. *Cédula* to the viceroy of New Spain (Mexico) 10 July 1538:
   A slave who marries a free person remains a slave, as do the children of such a union.

4. Order from the *cabildo* of Lima, 1538 and 1549:
   Slaves are prohibited from wearing capes or selling wine.

5. General *cédula*, 1545:
   Slaves may not ride horses. Ten lashes for the first offense, 200 for the second.

6. *Cédula* to the viceroy of Peru, 19 November 1551:
   Slaves may not have Indians in their service. Offending slaves will receive 100 lashes for the first offense; the ears will be cut off for the second.

7. *Cédula* to the viceroy of Peru, 12 October 1560:
   The slave must reside with his master. The first escape brings 100 lashes; the second, 200 lashes.

8., Order from the *cabildo* of Santiago, Chile, 1577:
   Slaves are not to play cards. First offenders will receive 50 lashes; second offenders, 100 lashes; third offenders, 200 lashes.

9. Order from the *cabildo* of Mexico City, 12 September 1605:
   Slaves may not work in printing unless the master is in direct control. Upon the death of the master, the slave may not continue in the same profession unless he is under direct control of the new master. The offending slave will receive 200 lashes; the offending master, a 20 peso fine.

APPENDIX 3

Examples of Restrictions on Free Negroids

1. *Cédula* to the viceroy of New Spain (Mexico), 7 August 1535:
   Negroids may not carry arms. Offenders will receive 50 lashes and the loss of the weapon.

2. *Cédula* to the *audiencia* of Bogotá, 27 February 1549:
   No mulatto or illegitimate person may hold public office.

3. Order from the *cabildo* of Mexico City, 10 May 1574:
   Mulattoes may not be candle makers or sellers, on pain of twenty months in the mines.

4. Order from the *cabildo* of Mexico City, 7 September 1584:
   Free blacks and mulattoes are restricted from working with silk.

5. Order from the *cabildo* in Cuzco, Peru, 25 September 1591:
   No free Negroid may have a public store or make clothes. First offenders will receive a fine of 10 pesos of gold; second offenders, 20 pesos of gold; and third offenders, 50 pesos of gold.

6. Order from the *cabildo* of Mexico City, 12 June 1598:
   No blacks or mulattoes may be gold workers, on pain of a 100-peso fine to the owner of the factory or store.

7. Order from the *cabildo* in Lima, 19 March 1604:
   Blacks and mulattoes are excluded from lace and embroidery work.

8. Order from the *cabildo* of Mexico City, 12 September 1605:
   Blacks and mulattoes may not be printers unless they are working for a Spaniard, on pain of 200 lashes.

9. *Cédula* to the viceroy of Peru, 7 February 1636:
   Mulattoes and illegitimate persons may not be ordained as priests.

NOTES

1. The Iberian Connection

1   *Reconquista* is the name given to the centuries of conflict during which the Christians drove back the Muslims and gradually regained political control of the Iberian Peninsula. This struggle did not become essentially militant in character until after the discovery of the alleged tomb of St. James the Apostle in Galicia during the ninth century. A shrine was built at Santiago de Compostela to commemorate miracles wrought through the intervention of the saint, and the Christian north of Iberia was galvanized into a more unified whole. By the eleventh century the Reconquista had become a crusade, with soldiers entering combat to the cry of "Santiago." This historical epoch ended in 1492, when the last Moorish stronghold, Granada, was captured.

2   Edmundo Correia Lopes, *A escravatura: subsídios para a sua historia* (Lisbon, 1944), p. 1: W. Montgomery Watt and Pierre Cachia, *A History of Islamic Spain* (Lisbon, 1965), pp. 47-49; Charles Verlinden, *L'esclavage dans l'Europe médiévale*, 2 vols. (Bruge, 1955), 1:616-17, 622, 630.

3   Anthony Luttrell, "Slavery and Slaving in the Portuguese Atlantic (to about 1500)," in *The Transatlantic Slave Trade from West Africa*, Centre of African Studies (Edinburgh, 1965), p. 64.

4   Until A.D. 640 Egypt and all of North Africa had been Christian, constituting part of the Byzantine Empire. Muslim Arabs then conquered Egypt (640 to 642) and by 698 tribes professing Islam had taken the entire North African coast. The Portuguese, therefore, claimed that they were only reinstating Christian rule where it had existed until the seventh century.

5   Gomes Eanes de Zurara, *Chronique de Guinée* (Ifan-Daker, 1960), pp. 66-68. See also Duarte Pacheco Pereira, *Esmeraldo de situ orbis*, series 2, vol. 79 (London, 1937), pp. 61-66.

6   For a good discussion of European monetary problems and the increase in the monetary value of coins, see A. H. de Oliveira Marques, *History of Portugal*, 2 vols. (New York, 1972), 1:139; and Vitorinho Magalhães Godinho, *L'économie de l'empire portugais aux XV et XVI siècles* (Paris, 1969), pp. 39-40, 152-56.

7   Eanes de Zurara, *Chronique*, p. 30.

8   All latitudinal calculations in this section are from Domião Peres, *História dos descobrimentos portuguesas* (Pôrto, 1943), p. 78; and Oliveira Marques, pp. 148-50. These calculations were corroborated by the geography staff of Michigan State University. The Rio de Ouro appears to have been a bay rather than a river.

9   Domião Peres, *História*, p. 82. This would make the place of capture northern Mauritania.

10 The *azenagues* are a Berber people, part of the greater *tuareg* family of tribes. The Portuguese noted their reddish-brown complexion and Islamic religious beliefs. They spoke a tongue different from the Barbary Coast Moors.

11   The best account of Antão Gonçalves's 1441 and 1442 voyages is found in
      Eanes de Zurara, *Chronique*, pp. 78-79, 90-93. Vitorinho Magalhães Godinho
      argues that Gonçalves was always under Nuno Tristão's command (*Documentos sobre a expansão portuguesa*, 3 vols. [Lisbon, 1945?-1956], 2:176-77).

12   Or "black moor." By this title, the Portuguese differentiated Arabs and Berbers from the blacks whom they also believed to be Muslims.

13   Magalhães Godinho, *Documentos*, 1:143. Since medieval times the land of the
      black people had been referred to as "Guinée" by Europeans. Nuno Tristão,
      upon reaching the mouth of the Senegal River, thought it was a branch of the
      Nile and assumed he was in lower Ethiopia — a portion of the kingdom of
      Prester John.

14   Pacheco Pereira reported that "below Cape Verde" the rate of exchange was
      ten slaves for each horse, but that the figure had dropped to six by 1500
      (*Esmeraldo*, p. 80). Luttrell argues that between 1450 and 1460 the Portuguese received fourteen to fifteen slaves for each horse ("Slavery," p. 69). This
      same figure is found in Magalhães Godinho, *Documentos*, 1:93.

15   These figures are found in Oliveira Marques, *History*, 1:158; and Luttrell,
      "Slavery," p. 68. Eanes de Zurara reduces the number to 927 (*Chronique*, p.
      93). The mass of these blacks had been obtained at Arguim.

16   This is the name by which the Senegambia region was long known.

17   The lowest figure (41,256) is found in Oliveira Marques, *History*, 1:260, while
      the highest number (100,000) is from Luttrell, "Slavery," p. 77. This last
      figure is based on a 3,500 annual total found in Pacheco Pereira, *Esmeraldo*, p.
      100. Verlinden attempted to determine the average number of slaves landed at
      both Lagos and Lisbon. He arrived at a figure of 883 captives per year, which
      would bring the total to 44,150 for the period from 1450 to 1500 (*L'esclavage*, 1:627-28).

18   Oliveira Marques, *History*, 1:159. Profits from the sale of the gold dust, spices,
      ivory, and blacks bartered at Arguim sometimes exceeded 100 percent of cost
      (Ibid., p. 160).

19   Oliveira Marques, *History*, 1:217. According to A. H. de Oliveira Martins,
      1,000 ducats were equal to 200,000 *reis* (*The Golden Age of Prince Henry the
      Navigator* [London, 1914], p. 218). Verlinden points out that the Florentine
      merchant Bartolomeo Marchione paid 6,300,000 *reis* for each year he held the
      contract, that is, from 1493 to 1495 (*L'esclavage*, 1:625). This was better than
      a 1,000 percent increase.

20   On the conspicuous participation of Genoese and Venetian seamen and commercial interests in the exploration of the western coast of Africa and the
      operation of the slave trade, see Oliveira Marques, *History*, 1:217, 258; Luttrell, "Slavery," pp. 64, 67; and Magalhães Godinho, *L'économie*, pp. 176-77,
      183.

21   Verlinden, *L'esclavage*, 1:622-23. The Cortes argued that black slaves "are a
      cause of prosperity for the state" and as such should remain in Portugal. The
      official response was that the direction and licensing of traders was a royal
      prerogative. Evidence that most of the blacks obtained were being sold in
      Spain is found in Oliveira Marques, *History*, 1:159; and Luttrell, "Slavery," p.
      74.

22   On this opposition and the nature of the changing position of the Church
      relative to Christian slavery, see David B. Davis, *The Problem of Slavery in
      Western Culture* (Ithaca, 1966), pp. 98-101.

23   For varied and conflicting interpretations of these papal bulls see Verlinden,
      L'esclavage, 1:620, 838; Davis, *Problem*, p. 100; and José Antonio Saco, *Historia de la esclavitud de la raza africana en el Nuevo Mundo y en especial en
      los países américo-hispanos*, 4 vols. (Havana, 1938), 1:52-53.

24 Eanes de Zurara, *Chronique*, pp. 111-13.
25 Aristotle, *Politics*, bk. 1, chap. 4, sec. 4-5; chap. 5, sec. 11.
26 Luttrell, "Slavery," p. 70.
27 Gen. 9:22-26.
28 Eanes de Zurara, *Chronique*, pp. 93-94.
29 Ibid., p. 112.
30 Pacheco Pereira, *Esmeraldo*, pp. 90, 98, 136.
31 Ibid., p. 82, 175. Pacheco Pereira claimed that these reptiles were "a quarter of a league long." A Spanish league is 800 Spanish yards, or almost four English miles. A quarter of a league would then be roughly one mile, or 5,280 feet. He probably concluded that any place with reptiles that long represented hell on earth.
32 Verlinden, *L'esclavage*, 1:631.
33 Ibid.
34 Louis Bertrand, *The History of Spain* (New York, 1934), p. 54.
35 E. Lévi-Provençal, *Histoire de l'Espagne musulmane*. 3 vols. (Paris, 1967), 3:74.
36 By the Sudan, the Moors meant the lands of the black people, south of the Sahara Desert.
37 Lévi-Provençal, *Histoire*, p. 177.
38 Ibid., p. 75.
39 Ibid., pp. 177-78.
40 Ibid., p. 178.
41 J. A. Conde, *History of the Dominion of the Arabs in Spain*, 3 vols. (London, 1854-1855), 2:218.
42 Lévi-Provençal, *Histoire*, 3:178.
43 On this traffic and Spanish interests, see José Franco, *Afro-América* (Havana, 1961), pp. 72-73; and Verlinden, *L'esclavage*, 1:225-26, 325, 358-62.
44 Diego Ortiz de Zúñiga, *Anales eclesiásticos y seculares de la noble y muy leal ciudad de Sevilla*, 6 vols. (Madrid, 1795), 3:78. The trade at Cádiz must have occasionally been extensive, for it was said to have provided the royal treasury in that town with "*quintos* (i.e., the royal fifth) considerably useful" (Ibid., p. 77).
45 On the shortage of gold and silver, coin debasement in Spain, and the role played by these financial difficulties in impeding trade, see Magalhães Godinho, *L'économie*, pp. 39-40, 137-40.
46 Ibid., pp. 77-78.
47 A concession of this nature was probably made in order to persuade Alfonso V of Portugal to recognize Isabella's claim to the throne of Castile.
48 Vicenta Cortés, *La esclavitud en Valencia durante el reinado de los Reyes Católicos* (Valencia, 1964), p. 60. The year of the greatest number of black entrants (800) was 1495.
49 Antonio Domínguez Ortiz, "La esclavitud en Castilla durante la edad moderna," in *Estudios de historia social de España*, 2 vols. (Madrid, 1952), 2:380. The same census reveals that there were less than 400 blacks in Granada and "in the provinces of the North, a Moor or a Negro was truly rare" (Ibid., pp. 381; see also 383).
50 Ibid., pp. 376-77; Juan de Mata Carriazo, "Negros, esclavos y extranjeros en el barrio sevillano de San Bernardo," *Archivo Hispalense* 20, nos. 64-65 (1954): 11-27.
51 Georges Scelle, *La traité négrière aux Indes de Castille, contrats et traités d'assiento*, 2 vols. (Paris, 1906), 2:707.
52 Vicenta Cortés, *La esclavitud*, pp. 57-58.
53 Ibid., pp. 103-4. Unfortunately, Vicenta Cortés speaks of prices in pounds (£)

but does not give a conversion figure. The traditional exchange rate (£ = $4.86, or 25.20 *pesetas*) is therefore employed.

54 Domínguez Ortiz suggests that the galley slaves were generally Moors or captives who were Muslim ("Esclavitud," 2:405). Verlinden argues that many galley slaves were blacks and that the determining factor was not simply religious but whether or not the captive was considered to be a "barbarian" (*L'esclavage*, 1:842).

55 Since the fourteenth century Spanish and Portuguese ships had visited the Canary Islands in order to kidnap and enslave the indigenous population found there. The present-day population of these isles is primarily Portuguese, the *guanches* having been absorbed or eliminated.

56 Juan de Mata Carriazo, ed., *Crónica de los Reyes Católicos*, 2 vols. (Seville, 1951), 1:185.

57 Joaquín Miret y Sans, "La esclavitud en Cataluña en los últimos tiempos de la edad media," *Revue Hispanique* 41 (October 1917): 1-109. Vicenta Cortés states categorically that in Valencia, "in accordance with Roman law, slaves were considered as if they were nothing" (*La esclavitud*, p. 65, fn. 1). Domínguez Ortiz argues that whatever slave rights existed in theory, the de facto rights varied from household to household ("Esclavitud," 2:399).

58 Vicenta Cortés, *La esclavitud*, p. 133; Miret y Sans, "La esclavitud en Cataluña," pp. 72-75, 92-105.

59 Miret y Sans, "La esclavitud en Cataluña," pp. 72-75, 92-105.

60 Concerning the power of *guanche* chieftains at the royal court, see Vicenta Cortés, *La esclavitud*, p. 145.

61 Domínguez Ortiz, "Esclavitud," 2:396. For a short biographical sketch of the mulattoes mentioned, see pp. 376-97.

62 *Portero de camara* or gentleman usher.

63 In fifteenth century Spain a *loro* denoted a brown-skinned person and, in this context, undoubtedly a mulatto.

64 Ortiz de Zúñiga, *Anales*, 3:78.

65 For one version of the origin of Juan Latino, see Domínguez Ortiz, "Esclavitud," 2:396. According to George Ticknor, Juan Latino called himself a "Son of Ethiopia" (*Filius Aethiopum*) (*History of Spanish Literature*, 3 vols. [New York, 1965], 2:582). V. B. Spratlin analyzes the opinions of various Spanish authors and concludes that Juan was not born in Ethiopia proper, but somewhere on the western coast of Africa (*Juan Latino: Slave and Humanist* [New York, 1938], pp. 5-8).

66 On his degree status, the aid given to him by Archbishop Pedro de Guerrero, and his student days at the university, see V. B. Spratlin, *Juan Latino*, pp. 10-11.

67 Ibid., pp. 12, 17. Juan Latino did receive an appointment to the chair of Grammar at the Cathedral School where he had begun his studies, but only after a long struggle in which racial abuse was heaped upon him. He obtained the position after Archbishop de Guerrero overruled the appointing committee (Ibid., p. 19).

68 Lope de Vega, *La dama boba*, act 2, sc. 21. Here Juan Latino is described ostensibly meeting his future wife while teaching her Latin. Naturally, Cupid shot the fatal arrow while Juan was teaching Doña Ana how to conjugate the verb *to love*.

69 No one knows exactly when Juan Latino actually died although Antonio Marín Ocete makes the most comprehensive study and concludes that the date was somewhere between 1594 and 1597 (*El negro Juan Latino* [Granada, 1925], pp. 197-199). No one can say with certitude when Diego Jiménez de

Encisco (1585-1632) originally wrote *la famosa comedia de Juan Latino*. V. B. Spratlin discusses this question with clarity and believes that the work could not have been written after 1620, and that most likely it was done during the first decade of the seventeenth century (*Juan Latino*, p. 206).

70   Verlinden, *L'esclavage*, 1:840-41. The author makes it clear, however, that the proposal did not become law.

71   Domínguez Ortiz, "Esclavitud," 2:386. Jaime Vicens Vives notes that this practice of exclusion began as early as 1466 in Majorca (ed., *Historia social y económica de España y América*, 4 vols. in 5 [Barcelona, 1957-1959], 2:220).

72   On the black brotherhoods, see Domínguez Ortiz, "Esclavitud," 2:392-93; Luttrell, "Slavery," p. 73; and Verlinden, *L'esclavage*, 1:529-30.

73   This is a movable feast, held the first Sunday after Trinity Sunday (usually in June).

74   Domínguez Ortiz, "Esclavitud," 2:394.

75   Literally, "in (a) good war." The black sold as a slave to the Portuguese was considered a warrior in an unholy cause, and enslavement therefore became his just dessert.

76   Domínguez Ortiz, "Esclavitud," 2:406.

77   Lope de Vega, *Los peligros de ausencia*, act 2, sc. 7.

78   Lope de Vega, *El major imposible*, act 1, sc. 2.

79   On the negative use of the word *negro* in Spanish plays and elsewhere, see Alonso Zamara Vicente, *Lope de Vega: Peribáñez y el comendador de Ocaña y La dama boba* (Madrid, 1963), p. 182, fn. 2.

80   Africa was not yet fully known and, thus, the term *negrería* referred to the totality of western Africa occupied by black people.

81   For further evidence on the condescending and paternalistic views held about blacks and mulattoes in Spain, see Domínguez Ortiz, "Esclavitud," 2:391-92; idem, *The Golden Age in Spain 1516-1679* (London, 1971), pp. 162-64; and William E. Wilson, "Some Notes on Slavery during the Golden Age," *Hispanic Review* 7 (April 1939): 171-74.

82   Hipólito Sancho de Sopranis, *Las cofradías de morenos en Cádiz* (Madrid, 1958), p. 43.

83   See Magnus Morner, *Race Mixture in the History of Latin America* (Boston, 1967), p. 16. Many of the Indians shipped to Europe died, and Queen Isabella admonished Columbus for his callousness. See also Arthur Helps, *The Conquerors of the New World and Their Bondsmen*, 2 vols. (Miami, 1969), 1:170.

84   The distinction in this instance is crucial. Isabella was queen of Castile, and Ferdinand was king of Aragon. These kingdoms would be joined when Charles I ascended both thrones in 1517, thereby creating the nation-state of Spain. Technically, the New World was a Castilian holding, and only Castilians were originally free to exploit its riches. Indeed, merchant groups in the Castilian towns of Cádiz and Seville were so powerful that their monopoly over most of the Indies trade was not completely broken until 1778.

85   Helps, *Conquerors*, 1:170.

86   On the early arrivals and activities of *ladino* slaves in Santo Domingo, see Carlos Larrazábal Blanco, *Los negros y la esclavitud en Santo Domingo* (Santo Domingo, 1967), pp. 14-16; and Richard Konetzke, ed., *Colección de documentos para la historia de la formación social de Hispano-América*, 3 vols. in 4 (Madrid, 1953-1962), 1:81-82.

87   José Gámez, *Historia de Nicaragua* (Managua, 1889), p. 151. Despite this optimistic assessment, many blacks did indeed become casualties. See also Helps, *Conquerors*, 1:237.

88   See Franklyn J. Franco Pichardo, *Los negros, los mulatos y la nación domini-*

cana, 2nd ed. (Santo Domingo, República Dominicana), p. 14. There were some 689 whites then in Hispaniola and perhaps 1,000 blacks. Franco Pichardo also notes the Spaniards' apprehension over the situation.

89   Consejo de la Hispanidad, *Recopilación de las leyes de los Reinos de las Indias*, 3 vols. (Madrid, 1943), 3:313.

90   Konetzke, *Colección*, 1:80. The *cédula* of 11 May 1526 took the view that the *ladinos* had "bad habits" and encouraged *bozales* to rebel. The *gelofes* were blacks usually shipped from the port of Santiago in the Cape Verde Islands. They were thought to be both Muslim in orientation and the *bozal* element that had sparked the 1522 uprising.

91   Diego Luis Molinari, *La trata de negros*, 2nd ed. (Buenos Aires, 1944), pp. 148, 169, 194, 219.

92   Morner, *Race Mixture*, pp. 45-46. Important also is idem, "Teoría y práctica de la segregación racial en la América colonial," *Boletín de la Academia Nacional de la Historia* 44 (Caracas, 1961), pp. 185-221.

93   Elizabeth Donnan, ed., *Documents Illustrative of the History of the Slave Trade to America*, 4 vols. (Washington, D.C., 1930-1935), 1:343. In the 1685 Council of the Indies report, the statement is again made that the importation of *ladinos* had to end because their "ill advice" caused the loss to the Spaniards of many *bozales*.

94   Lev. 25:45-46.

2. The Slave Trade to Spanish America

1   Peter Boyd-Bowman, "Negro Slaves in Early Colonial Mexico," *The Americas* 26 (October 1969): 139-42. This writer argues that the "Brom [Brome, Bran]" peoples were inhabitants of "Region I," or what he calls "the general area between Senegal and Sierra Leone." What he defines as "Region II" is that territory "east of Sierra Leone" (Ibid., pp. 141-42).

2   Aquiles Escalante, *El negro en Colombia* (Bogotá, 1964), pp. 90, 191 (fig. 4). He describes the *bran* as a nation who lived slightly "to the north of the Gold Coast" (Ibid., p. 90). Gonzalo Aguirre Beltrán places these same people among those whom he calls *tribus de la costa de Mina* ("tribes of the Mina Coast"). He fixes their position at slightly north of the Ashanti, making them indisputably Gold Coast inhabitants (*Población negra de México, 1519-1810: Estudio etnohistórico* [Mexico, D.F., 1946], pp. 125-26, unnumbered map at back of book). Dr. Alfred Opubor, director of the African Studies Center at Michigan State University established that the correct name for these people is not *bran* or *bron*, but *brong*. He further determined that the *brong* nation inhabits the central region of Ghana called Brong-ahafo. They speak a dialect called *brong* and are related to the Ashanti-Fanti peoples. He also pointed out that São Jorge de Mina and Cape Coast (in Lower Guinea) were the ports from which they would most likely have been shipped as slaves. (Interview, 2 August 1973)

3   Miguel Acosta Saignes, *Vida de los esclavos negros in Venezuela* (Caracas, 1967), p. 132.

4   The name of a branch of the Ewe-Fon peoples living in what is now Togo and Dahomey.

5   The name given to blacks loaded at Old Calabar, Bony, and other ports on the Niger River delta.

6   On the *yorubas* as *lucumí*, see Escalante, *El negro*, p. 92; and Aguirre Beltrán, *Población*, p. 132.

7   *Castas de rios de Guinea* were also called *cabos verdes*, since they were generally shipped from the slave port of Santiago in the Cape Verde Islands.

8   On the large number of Angola-Congo blacks shipped to Mexico after 1600, see Aguirre Beltrán, *Población*, p. 244. The list of castas and the slave entrepôts under the Portuguese correspond to those found in Rolando Mellafe, *La esclavitud en Hispano-América* (Buenos Aires, 1964), pp. 53-55.

9   Aguirre Beltrán states that all slaves brought by the Manila-Acapulco route, regardless of their ethnic or national origins, were called *chinos* (*Población*, p. 143). See also Mellafe, *Esclavitud*, p. 56.

10 The positions of the Dutch on the Gulf of Guinea during the seventeenth and eighteenth centuries are geographically depicted in J. D. Page, *An Atlas of African History* (Bungay, Suffolk, 1965), pp. 30-31.

11 Ibid.

12 G. Michael Riley, "Labor in Cortesian Enterprise: The Cuernavaca Area, 1522-1549," *The Americas* 28 (January 1972): 271-87. Unfortunately, Professor Riley accepts the same regional categorizations employed by Boyd-Bowman (see note above), although he duly acknowledges his source (Ibid., p. 285).

13 Boyd-Bowman, "Negro Slaves," p. 141. If we deduct those listed as *bron* (a total of 24), then only 88 of 164 (about 53.9 percent) were from "Region I."

14 Gonzalo Aguirre Beltrán, "Tribal Origins of Slaves in Mexico," *Journal of Negro History* 31 (July 1946): 312-15; idem, *Población*, pp. 149, 244.

15 Carlos Larrazábal Blanco, *Los negros y la esclavitud en Santo Domingo* (Santo Domingo, 1967), p. 81; see also pp. 82-88. According to this author, *gelofes* (thought to be Muslims), *mandingos* (Upper Guinea inhabitants), and *angolas* were also found in large numbers in Santo Domingo (Ibid., p. 81).

16 Carlos Meléndez, "Los orígenes de los esclavos africanos en Costa Rica," in *Actas y Memorias*, XXXXVI Congreso Internacional de Americanistas, 4 vols. in 5 (Seville, 1966), 4:389-90.

17 Fernando Ortiz Fernández, *Hampa afro-cubana: Los negros esclavos; Estudio sociológico y de derecho público* (Havana, 1916), pp. 56, 58.

18 Acosta Saignes, *Vida*, pp. 129-30, 141.

19 Escalante, *El negro*, p. 24. Still, a fair number of slaves seems to have reached Mexico (Aguirre Beltrán, *Población*, p. 244).

20 Carlos Sempat Assodourian, *El tráfico de esclavos en Córdoba de Angola a Potosí* (Córdoba, 1966), pp. 3-28; José Luis Lanuza, *Morenada* (Buenos Aires, 1946), pp. 106-7; Carlos Rama, *Los afro-uruguayos* (Montevideo, 1967), pp. 11-13, 61; and especially Elena Fanny Schüess de Studer, *La trata de negros en el Río de la Plata durante el siglo XVIII* (Buenos Aires, 1958), pp. 323-24; and Ildefonso Pereda Valdés, *Negros esclavos y negros libres: Esquema de una sociedad esclavista y aporte del negro en nuestra formación nacional* (Montevideo, 1941), pp. 21-22.

21 Escalante, *El negro*, p. 110.

22 Ibid.; and Ortiz Fernández, *Hampa afro-cubana*, p. 58.

23 Aguirre Beltrán, "Tribal Origins," p. 321. These slaves were probably *yorubas*. The *terra nova* blacks were apparently shipped from Porto Novo to San Tomé to Veracruz.

24 José Antonio Saco, *Historia de la esclavitud de la raza africana en el Nuevo Mundo y en especial en los países américo-hispanos*, 4 vols. (Havana, 1938), 3:175.

25 Ibid., 4:276.

26 Diego Luis Molinari, *La trata de negros*, 2nd ed. (Buenos Aires, 1944), p. 148.

27 Bartolomé de Las Casas, *Historia de las Indias*, 3 vols. (Mexico, D.F., 1951), 3:275.

28 A precursor of St. Peter Claver (dubbed "the Apostle of the Negros"), Sandoval performed his ministry among the slaves landed in seventeenth-century Cartagena (Colombia). Although a minor figure compared to Claver, Sandoval published his doubts and misgivings concerning the morality of the slave trade.

29   For the arguments of these Spanish dissenters, see David B. Davis, *The Problem of Slavery in Western Culture* (Ithaca, 1966), pp. 190-91; Saco, *Historia*, 2:79-85, 110-113; and Silvio Zavala, *The Political Philosophy of the Conquest of America* (Mexico, D.F., 1953), pp. 74, 88-90.

30   Established in 1532 by King João III, this tribunal was formed to aid in the resolution of juridical and administrative disputes, especially those having to do with moral and legal questions.

31   For Sandoval's letter and Padre Luis Brandão's reply, see Alonso de Sandoval, S.J., *De instauranda aethiopum salute* (Bogotá, 1956), pp. 90-100.

32   J. H. Parry, *The Spanish Seaborne Empire* (London, 1966), p. 195. For the colonial jurist's view on African slavery in the Indies see Juan de Solórzano Pereira, *Política indiana*, 5 vols. (Madrid, 1872), 1:132-34.

33   Zavala, *Political Philosophy*, p. 88.

34   See Saco, *Historia*, 2:83-84. A fuller presentation of Albornoz's views is found in *Obras escogidos de filosofos*, Biblioteca de Autores Españoles, vol. 65 (Madrid, 1873), pp. 231-32.

35   The background of these events can be followed in full in Elizabeth Donnan, ed., *Documents Illustrative of the History of the Slave Trade to America*, 4 vols. (Washington, D.C., 1930-1935), 1:335-49.

36   See Georges Scelle, *La traité négrière aux Indes de Castille, contrats et traités d'assiento*, 2 vols. (Paris, 1906) 1:713.

37   Jorge Palacios Preciado, *La trata de negros por Cartagena de Indias* (Tunja, 1973), p. 349.

38   Ibid., p. 348. A bit of light on the subject is also shed by Serafim Leite, S.J., *História de companhia de Jesus no Brasil*, 10 vols. (Rio de Janiero, 1936-1945), 6:350-52. Leite argues that in Brazil, at least, the tremendous shortage of cheap labor made African slavery the only alternative to Indian slavery. The Spanish American situation was similar, but Spanish authors were rarely so frank.

39   Between 1713 and 1750 Spain had continuous problems with both the South Sea Company and the British government, the company's protector.

40   Donnan, *Documents*, 1:41-42. See especially Scelle, who (*Traité*, 1:139-61) relates the story behind the sale and resale of this award.

41   These men were headquartered in Seville and Lisbon. Among them were Gaspar Centurión and Melchor Centurión, who was in Santo Domingo.

42   Arthur Helps, *Spanish Conquest in America and Its Relation to Slavery*, 4 vols. (London, 1861), 2:13, fn. 1. As late as 1534 *licencias* sold as part of Garrevod's award were still being circulated.

43   Saco, *Historia*, 1:135. Saco argues that the license renewal was terminated in 1523. This interpretation is questioned by Scelle, *Traité*, 2:155-6. Larrazábal Blanco accepts Saco's interpretation (*Negros*, p. 26), while Donnan accepts Scelle's conclusion (*Documents*, 1:16). This question has never been settled, but the contract renewal of 1521 appears to have been canceled. The tacit decision of Charles apparently was to allow the first agreement (1518-1526) to run its course.

44   For the slave supply problems of the House of Welsher, see Larrazábal Blanco, *Negros*, p. 30, and Federico Brito Figueroa, *Estructura económica de Venezuela colonial* (Caracas, 1963), pp. 98-100.

45   *Licencias* during this period were generally granted to the following parties:

      1. Royal officials, crown representatives, or religious persons could bring in slaves as their personal property, usually free of taxes.
      2. *Conquistadores* or soldiers in their entourage were often allowed to introduce slaves without duties or a *licencia* payment as a reward for their efforts in expanding Spain's empire.

3. City governments and trade associations purchased *licencias*.

4. Persons friendly to the crown and partisans of the court, the Council of the Indies, or the Casa de Contratación were able to buy *licencias*.

5. Businessmen and merchants who had dealings with the crown purchased *licencias* but often received them as payment for a service to the state. For details and observations, see Mellafe, *Esclavitud*, pp. 32-34.

46 Brito Figueroa, *Estructura*, p. 101. Ochoa de Ochandiana had already obtained *licencias* allowing him to ship 4,000 blacks to the Indies. In his 1553 proposal, this dealer offered to pay 100,000 ducats down and the remaining 84,000 over a period of several years. Scelle and Saco argue that protests from many elements (especially merchant groups from Seville) caused the cancellation of this arrangement (*Traité*, 1:205; *Historia*, 2:38-9). No one knows, however, if any slaves were actually shipped, or if any money was returned to Ochoa de Ochandiana.

47 Mellafe, *Esclavitud*, p. 30. At the same time, the *aduanilla*, or customs charge on each permit, was raised to 20 *reales*.

48 Brito Figueroa, *Estructura*, p. 99.

49 The Treaty of Tordesillas was a formal declaration of an agreement between Portugal and Spain dividing between them the rights to conquer and colonize whatever non-Christian lands they might discover. All territories west of the line (the Americas except for Brazil) would fall under Spanish control. All territories east of the line (Africa, except for the Canary Islands, and Asia) would belong to Portugal. Because this arrangement froze France, England, and later, the Netherlands, out of the scramble for possessions, none of these states recognized its validity.

50 Brito Figueroa, *Estructura*, p. 102. The contract stipulated that all the slaves had to be males, that fixed prices were to be charged on slaves landed on the Venezuelan coast, and that no customs tax would be charged on one-third of the blacks delivered.

51 Molinari makes it clear that this was his position, although Brito Figueroa disagrees (*Trata*, pp. 50, 58-9; *Estructura*, pp. 103-4). Mellafe and Saco hold that this was the first multiclause contract signed (*Esclavitud*, p. 35; *Historia*, 2:99-100).

52 Saco and Aguirre Beltrán maintain that the Medici, Strozzi, and Piazzi families (the first two were Florentine) were heavy investors in the slave traffic during the period of Portuguese suzerainty (*Historia*, 2:89; *Población*, p. 26).

53 See Larrazábal Blanco, who points out that on 21 June 1595 Philip II issued a decree declaring that no slave could enter the Spanish Indies without his permission or that of the *asentista*. In the period from 1601 to 1609 Philip III ordered a cessation of the importation of slaves from the Philippine Islands into Mexico, thus aiding the *asentistas* (*Negros*, p. 42). As Brito Figueroa notes, however, throughout the period *licencias* were sold or granted allowing for the annual introduction of at least 500 additional blacks (*Estructura*, p. 102).

54 Mellafe, *Esclavitud*, p. 36; C. H. Haring, *The Spanish Empire in America* (New York, 1963), pp. 303-4, 309.

55 On slave smuggling through Buenos Aires, see C. H. Haring, *The Spanish Empire in America* (New York, 1963) pp. 309-10; Saco, *Historia*, 2:137-39; and Rolando Mellafe, *La introducción de la esclavitud negra en Chile: Tráfico y rutas* (Santiago, 1959), pp. 238-55.

56 Brito Figueroa, *Estructura*, pp. 103-4.

57 Donnan, *Documents*, 1:105.

58 Palacios Preciado (*La trata de negros por Cartagena*, pp. 29, 39, fn.) indicates that, over an eleven-year period, Grillo and Lomelin legally shipped over

17,000 *piezas* to the New World. Admittedly these *asentistas* did obtain some slaves from the Dutch, but they also tried to obtain others from the British at Jamaica. Grillo and Lomelin concealed this stratagem from the Spanish crown, but the Anglo-Dutch war from 1664 to 1668 prevented the Royal African Company from delivering to Jamaica all the slaves they had requested. For details on the English arrangement, see A. P. Thornton, "Spanish Slave Ships in the English West Indies, 1660-1685," *Hispanic American Historical Review* 35 (February 1955): 374-85. As for the dependency of the other *asentistas* on the Dutch, see Donnan, *Documents*, 1:105-7, 344-45.

59 See Donnan, *Documents*, 1:106-7; Scelle, *Traité*, 1:599, 620; and Thornton, "Spanish Slave Ships," pp. 382-83. The Consulado, emulating the Grillo-Lomelin example, sought to buy slaves at Jamaica, but both the London-based Board of Trade and the Jamaican planters were convinced that supplying the Spanish Indies would result in shortages and higher slave prices in the British West Indies. The Dutch rendered the Consulado's endeavors unfruitful because the Dutch West India Company claimed that it had suffered heavy losses gathering slaves for Antonio García (the latter was jailed in 1675 for nonpayment of debts). Recompense was sought in Madrid, but the Spanish government insisted that García's arrangements with the Dutch company were not governmental business. Madrid also suggested that the Dutch claim was a gigantic hoax because the blacks ostensibly collected for García had probably already been smuggled into the Spanish colonies. The Consulado wound up bearing the brunt of Dutch anger, for the latter closed all its slave stations except those in Curaçao to Consulado ships.

60 Donnan gives the details of the efforts of John Coymans to regain either the 200,000 *escudos* given by Balthasar Coymans to the crown or control of the *asiento*, which was technically awarded to Porcio (*Documents*, 1:367-70, 373-77). See also Larrazábal Blanco, *Negros*, pp. 45-46. A rapprochement between Porcio, the Coymans heirs, and the Dutch West India Company was in the making in 1692, and this appears to have been one reason that Madrid chose to get a new *asentista*.

61 Escalante concludes that the Dutch were guilty (*El negro*, p. 39). Scelle notes that directors of the Companhia de Cacheu had lent Marin de Guzmán 27,800 pesos by 1694; he was literally under their thumb (*Traité*, 2:43).

62 Scelle, *Traité*, 2:44-45. A group of London merchants offered £60,000 for the contract, but the Spanish apparently believed that once the British were able to penetrate the Indies markets legally, it would be impossible to push them out.

63 Peace with France would not occur until after the 1697 Treaty of Ryswick.

64 For a history of this Portuguese company, see Renato Mendonça, *A influência africana no portugues do Brasil*, 2nd ed. (São Paulo, 1933), pp. 52-57.

65 On the participation of unnamed Jewish interests in London, see Scelle, *Traité*, 2:54. Originally, the Portuguese arranged to buy 3,000 slaves at 110 pesos per *pieza* in Jamaica. They eventually bought many more at prices varying from 114 to 170 pesos per *pieza* (Palacios Preciado, *La trata de negros por Cartagena*, pp. 71, 72).

66 For conflicting interpretations on the actions of Diego del Rios and Juan Díaz Pimienta at Cartagena, see Scelle, *Traité*, 2:54; Escalante, *El negro*, pp. 42-43; and Palacios Preciado, *La trata de negros por Cartagena*, pp. 55-56.

67 Palacios Preciado, *La trata de negros por Cartagena*, pp. 56-57.

68 Ibid., p. 54. Díaz Pimienta claimed that these contraband blacks had a market value of 1,200,000 pesos. How he reached this figure is unrecorded.

69 Ibid. The tax of 112.5 pesos per *tonelada* was paid, not on the gross tonnage of slaves, but on the net tonnage (i.e., discounts were given on old, sick,

disabled, and young slaves). What the Portuguese apparently did was to have able-bodied slaves classified as ill or disabled. Assuming that a slave with defects would be counted as one-half a *pieza*, six of these slaves would be equal to a ton. But if four or five were actually in good health, the Portuguese would have escaped the payment of the proper tax. If such evasions were practiced constantly, the sum not paid would become quite significant.

70   Ibid., p. 46.
71   Ibid., p. 106. At least 40,640 pesos were still owed by the Portuguese Royal Company of Guinea when the contract was annulled in 1701.
72   Georges Scelle, "The Slave Trade in the Spanish Colonies of America: The *Assiento*," *The American Journal of International Law*, 4, no. 3 (1910): 639-40. The pact was negotiated by Admiral Jean Ducasse, who had been largely responsible for the sacking of Cartagena in 1697. Subsequently, Ducasse also became a major stockholder in the French Royal Company of Guinea. See also Donnan, *Documents*, 2:2-3, fn.
73   This combination eventually included Britain, the Netherlands, Austria, Brandenburg-Prussia.
74   Palacios Preciado, *La trata de negros por Cartagena*, pp. 109-11. Article 11 of the August 1701 agreement called for the payment of 200,000 *patacas*. Since this coin was the equivalent of the peso, the sum represents Spanish repayment of the money advanced in 1696. In Article 11 Philip V obligated himself to pay a sum of 300,000 *cruzados* which was a good deal more than the 1701 Portuguese damage claim. The treaty itself was negotiated by Rouillé, the French ambassador to Portugal. The councillors of Philip V were vehemently opposed to this pact, so "Louis XIV had to interfere directly with his grandson" and make known his wish to conclude the agreement. This quotation and other information pertaining to French influence in Madrid after 1700 are found in Scelle, "The Slave Trade in the Spanish Colonies," p. 638.
75   Palacios Preciado, *La trata de negros por Cartagena*, p. 112.
76   Ibid., p. 58. Not until a new accord was reached on 6 February 1715 did Spain resume making any payments to Portugal.
77   Charles Woolsey Cole, *French Mercantilism: 1683-1700* (New York, 1943), p. 105. Although it was signed on 27 August 1701, the slave-trade agreement was not to go into effect until 1 September 1702. It provided that if war commenced while the treaty was in effect, only 38,000 *piezas* would be shipped to Spanish America. If hostilities terminated or did not break out, an additional 10,000 *piezas* were to be shipped, and the French could have two additional years (i.e., twelve all told) to complete the transaction. A duty of 33 1/3 pesos was to be paid on each *pieza*.
78   Scelle, "The Slave Trade in the Spanish Colonies," p. 641; Curtis Nettles, "England and the Spanish American Trade," *Journal of Modern History*, 3, no. 1 (March, 1931): 18.
79   Palacios Preciado, *La trata de negros por Cartagena*, p. 118.
80   Ibid., p. 119.
81   For the incident involving *La Gaillarde* see Ibid., p. 136. In the struggle with Díaz Pimienta, Philip V sided with the French.
82   On the shipment of Cabo Verde slaves into Spanish America before 1701, see Saco, *Historia*, 3:185. Mina was the general name given to slaves obtained from the main Dutch slaving station of São Jorge da Mina (as it had been known while the Portuguese held it). It should be evident that the intent of the Council of the Indies and the Casa de Contratación was harassment of the French. See also Palacios Preciado, *La trata de negros por Cartagena*, p. 123.
83   Donnan, *Documents*, 2:3, fn. The British government strongly considered launching a naval campaign to completely disrupt French slaving operations on

the coast of western Africa. See Nettles, who argues that laws passed in 1702 and 1703 prohibited English merchants from selling goods to French or Spanish sources, but that the Dutch decision to sell slaves to anyone at Curaçao eventually led to a change in British policy in 1704 ("England and the Spanish American Trade," p. 20). Refer also to Cole, who points out that in 1705 the charter of the French company (handed down by Louis XIV in 1685), allowing it to operate on the western coast of Africa south of Sierra Leone, expired. In addition, the sole trading station held by the company in Lower Guinea (at Assinie on the Ivory Coast) had to be abandoned in 1705 (*French Mercantilism*, p. 104).

84   Palacios Preciado, *La trata de negros por Cartagena*, p. 159.
85   Ibid., pp. 122, 137. An indication of the widespread nature of Anglo-Dutch contraband activity was the fact that 17 percent of all slaves sold between 1703 and 1713 at the French station in Cartagena were blacks captured from smugglers or apprehended after they had been illegally landed.
86   Ibid., p. 125. The standard method for delivering contraband by the French company was to land goods at Buenos Aires (where the officials seem to have been notoriously corrupt) and claim that the merchandise was being disembarked only in order to maintain the health and welfare of the slaves already landed. A much more detailed account of French contraband practices is found in Scelle, *Traité*, 2: chap. 7.
87   Palacios Preciado, *La trata de negros por Cartagena*, p. 165.
88   Scelle, "The Slave Trade in the Spanish Colonies," pp. 648-49. The French Royal Company of Guinea provided loans for Philip V to pay mercenaries until 1709. Scelle argues that the company collapsed in 1710, but technically it remained the nominal supplier of slaves to Spanish America until 1713.
89   Palacios Preciado, *La trata de negros por Cartagena*, pp. 127-28.
90   Solid evidence of the English intent is found in John Somers, ed., *A Collection of Scarce and Valuable Tracts*, Newberry Library Special Collection, 2nd ed., 23 vols. (London, 1819), 13: 117.
91   This was to be a cargo ship of no more than 500 to 600 tons. Technically such vessels were to arrive only when the *galeones* (name given the periodic fleet sent from Spain to Cartagena and Porto Bello) were dispatched.
92   For the details concerning this treaty, see *The Asiento or Contract for Allowing the Subjects of Great Britain the Liberty of Importing Negroes into Spanish America*, Newberry Library Special Collection (London, 1713), pp. 32-34. The king of Spain was to receive 28 percent of all company profits; Queen Anne, 22½ percent; and Manassas Gilligan, 7½ percent. The queen and Gilligan immediately ceded their directorship rights to the company. See also Saco, *Historia*, 2:181-85.
93   Scelle, "The Slave Trade in the Spanish Colonies," p. 655.
94   Jean McLachlan, *Trade and Peace with Old Spain, 1667-1750* (Cambridge, 1940), p. 61.
95   The illegal traffic was directed by specially appointed subgovernors. Those appointed between 1721 and 1739 were Sir John Eyles, Sir Richard Hopkins, and Peter Burrell. The South Sea Company's illegal practices and plans are sometimes dispassionately viewed by John G. Sperling, *The South Sea Company: An Historical Essay and Bibliographical List* (Boston, 1952), pp. 20-24, 40-48. Sperling believes that profits from the clandestine trade were limited to "certain members of the directorate," some company representatives, and sea captains operating in the Indies. Interpretations distinctly more critical of the company and arguing for a greater number of culprits are found in Saco, *Historia*, 2:198; Aguirre Beltrán, *Población*, p. 78; and especially G. H. Nelson, "Contraband Trade under the Asiento, 1730-1737," *American Historical Review* 51 (October 1945): 55-67.

96 On the secondary nature of the slave trade itself to company directors, see Scelle, "The Slave Trade in the Spanish Colonies," p. 656. Despite its secondary nature, this traffic was generally profitable (Palacios Preciado, *La trata de negros por Cartagena*, p. 203). The South Sea Company paid the Royal African Company the equivalent of 60 pesos for each slave delivered from Africa to their base at Jamaica. They charged between 220 and 290 pesos for good quality slaves delivered to Cartagena and Porto Bello.

97 Evidence for all these activities is found in Vera Lee Brown, "South Sea Company and Contraband Trade," *American Historical Review* 31 (July 1926): 668.

98 Palacios Preciado, *La trata de negros por Cartagena*, p. 185; see also p. 207. Also accused of taking bribes from the South Sea Company prior to 1726 were the viceroy of Mexico, numerous governors, and customs officials.

99 Ibid., p. 269.

100 Ibid., p. 326; see also p. 75. British permission ships arrived regularly even if the annual Spanish fleet did not. This move, originally announced by the viceroy of Peru in 1728, was sanctioned by Philip V in an effort to keep large quantities of gold and silver from falling, legally or illegally, into British hands.

101 Ibid., p. 325.

102 *Convention between the Crowns of Great Britain and Spain, Concluded at the Prado on the Fourteenth of January, 1739*, Newberry Library Special Collection (London, 1739), p. 1.

103 *The King of Spain's Declaration of War against Great Britain*, Newberry Library Special Collection (London, 1739), p. 7.

104 Palacios Preciado, *La trata de negros por Cartagena*, pp. 32-33. By 1753 about 1,847 slaves, or 1,794 *piezas*, had been delivered.

105 In an anonymous pamphlet, a payment of £95,000 was demanded for alleged damages to company ships and cargoes (*A Review of All that Passed between the Courts of Great Britain and Spain Relating to Our Trade and Navigation*, Newberry Library Special Collection [London, 1739], pp. 39-40). Sperling argues that the Spanish offer of £100,000 represented the largest payment that most of the company shareholders had received since the 1730s (*The South Sea Company*, pp. 48-50).

106 Elizabeth Donnan presents an anonymous Spanish report that lists 18,447.91 *piezas* introduced between 1715 and 1731 (*Documents*, 2:443). The total was divided as follows: Buenos Aires, October 1715 — January 1731, 8,600 *piezas*; Portobello, September 1715 — July 1723, 3,994.75 *piezas*; Cartagena, December 1714 — April 1724, 2,808.25 *piezas*; Habana, July 1715 — February 1725, 1,580.66 *piezas*; and Veracruz, April 1716 — January 1731, 1.464.25 *piezas*. The total figure is 18,447.91 *piezas*. Elena Schüess de Studer lists another 2,672.33 *piezas* who landed at Buenos Aires between 1731 and 1738 (*La trata de negros*, p. 232), while Palacios Preciado produces figures that demonstrate that between May 1724 and November 1736, 7,225 *piezas* passed through the port of Cartagena (*La trata de negros por Cartagena*, pp. 311, 342).

107 The figure of 20,000 is found in Brito Figueroa, *Estructura*, p. 110, but it includes *licencias* given to other parties as well. No total is found in the seminal work of Roland Hussey, *The Caracas Company: 1728-1784* (Cambridge, 1934), pp. 172, 208, 219, 237-38, 243. Data found on the pages noted reveal, however, that between 1754 and 1765, 11,750 blacks were obtained by the company.

108 The figure of 11,000 is from Jaime Vicens Vives, ed., *An Economic History of Spain* (Princeton, 1969), p. 573, while the smaller figure is found in Molinari, *Trata*, p. 62. See also Ortiz Fernández, who claims that 4,986 slaves were introduced into Cuba by the Company, at least 910 of which were landed illicitly. He also wrote that the local government officials knew what was

happening but usually turned a blind eye to the activities because of the severe labor shortage (*Hampa afro-cubana*, pp. 79-80).

109   Vicens Vives, *Economic History*, p. 573. The author also provides further verification for the contention that the Royal Havana Company's largest profits came from the contraband slave trade.

110   James Ferguson King, "Evolution of the Free Slave Trade Principle in Spanish Colonial Administration," *Hispanic American Historical Review* 22 (February 1942): 38. The *asentista* also was obliged to bring more slaves into the colonies if the crown demanded it.

111   On the *ad hoc* slave trading activities that developed at Cartagena between 1740 and 1763, see chap. 2, p. 80 of this work, and James Ferguson King, "Negro Slavery in New Granada," in Adele Ogden and Engel Fluiter, eds., *Greater America: Essays in Honor of Herbert Bolton* (Berkeley, 1945), pp. 305-6.

112   B. Torres Ramírez, *La Compañía Gaditana de Negros* (Seville: 1973), pp. 15-43, 79-84.

113   By the terms of this convention, no customs duties whatsoever were to be imposed and the Englishmen agreed to charge no more than 150 pesos for each black delivered.

114   Brito Figueroa, *Estructura*, pp. 128-31. This author claims that Barry was only a front man for Baker and Dawson, Ltd. A contract was signed in 1795 calling for the delivery of 4,000 blacks to the Captaincy General of Venezuela, and between 1801 and 1805 Barry continued to make sporadic deliveries, although how many slaves were actually delivered is unclear.

115   Molinari, *Trata*, pp. 62, 76.

116   Ibid., pp. 87-90.

117   For the story of the unfortunate Royal Company of the Philippines, founded in 1733 and reorganized in 1785, see Aguirre Beltrán, *Población*, pp. 87-88; Vicens Vives, who points out that Charles III was one of its largest stockholders (*Economic History*, p. 576); and Molinari, *Trata*, pp. 76-77, 83, 87, and 94. The withdrawal of the company from the slave trade did not mean that the entire company collapsed; only that division dealing with slave traffic became inoperative.

118   The document authorizing the trade was technically known as the *Real cédula por lo que su majestad concede libertad para el comercio de negros con las islas de Cuba, Santo Domingo, Puerto Rico y provincia de Caracas a los españoles y extrajeros* ("Royal decree by which His Majesty concedes liberty for the trade in blacks (slaves) with the islands of Cuba, Santo Domingo, Puerto Rico, and [the] province of Caracas to Spaniards and foreigners").

119   The 1662, 1674, 1701, and 1713 contracts speak of the incoming slaves as *piezas de Indias*.

120   Palacios Preciado, *La trata de negros por Cartagena*, p. 127.

121   Jacques S. des Beuclons, *Universal Dictionary of Trade and Commerce*, trans. Malachy Postlethwayt, 2 vols. (London, 1751-1755), 1, pt. 1:131; Donnan, *Documents*, 1:106, fn.; and Scelle, *Traité*, 1:505.

122   The contracts of Barrosó-Porcio (1682), Balthasar Coymans (1685), and the Royal Portuguese Company (1696) speak of *toneladas* of slaves.

123   The definition of *tonelada* is from Martín Alonso, *Enciclopedia del idioma*, 4 vols. (Madrid, 1958), 3:3979.

124   Mellafe, *Esclavitud*, p. 40.

125   Palacios Preciado, *La trata de negros por Cartagena*, p. 61.

126   An indefinite term sometimes used to describe a sick, useless, or youthful slave considered too young to perform heavy labor.

127   Ibid.

128   Helps, *Spanish Conquest*, 3:215.
129   Brito Figueroa, *Estructura*, p. 134; and Gonzalo Vial Correa, *El africano en el reino de Chile: Ensayo histórico-jurídico* (Santiago, 1957), p. 74.
130   Scheüss de Studer, *Trata*, p. 103.
131   Edmundo Correia Lopes, *A escravatura: Subsidios para a sua historia* (Lisbon, 1944), pp. 148-49.
132   Brito Figueroa, *Estructura*, p. 109.
133   Ibid., p. 110. This number was obtained through the addition of the author's legal importation figures from 1773 to 1799 to those for the period from 1800 to 1810 that are found in another column on the same page.
134   Alexander von Humboldt, *Ensayo político sobre la isla de Cuba*, 2 vols. (Havana, 1930), 1:150-51. Humboldt lists 33,409 arrivals for the period from 1764 to 1790. The slave entries for 1791 to 1820 are thereafter listed by year.
135   Philip Curtin, *The Atlantic Slave Trade: A Census* (Madison, 1969), pp. 22-23.
136   Ibid., p. 31; table 8, p. 35. Professor Curtin writes that "the Cuban slave trade of this period from 1774 through 1807 was investigated by Baron von Humboldt, one of the first scholars to take a serious interest in historical demography" (Ibid., p. 31). For the period from 1774 to 1807, Curtin obtains his figures from H. H. S. Aimes, *A History of Slavery in Cuba, 1511-1588* (New York, 1907), p. 269. Curtin admits that Aimes used Humboldt's figures for his computations, and the Humboldt-Aimes figures for the acknowledged slave traffic from 1774 to 1807 are virtually identical. But, Humboldt also reported that 56,000 slaves were smuggled in or landed at ports in eastern Cuba between 1791 and 1820 (*Ensayo*, 1:151). So, by using Aimes' figures Curtin effectively does not deal with the question of illicit traffic to Cuba during the years he cites.
137   Mellafe, *Esclavitud*, pp. 48, 58-59.
138   In 1542 Charles I issued decrees calling for good treatment of the Indians, prohibiting their enslavement, and abolishing compulsory personal service by the indigenous people to the Spanish settlers. Had these decrees been fully implemented, it would have meant the end of the Indian as a source of cheap labor.
139   Haring, *Spanish Empire*, pp. 51-53; Helps, *Spanish Conquest*, 4:176-78, 201, 206. The provisions, for example, suppressing the system of *encomiendas* (rights of control over a group of Indians) were ignored entirely.

3. The African Slave in Spanish America

1   Unlike the first two diseases, *mal de San Lázaro* was not contagious, although the Spanish thought it was. In general, they used the term to refer to any ulcerous skin disease.
2   Concerning the medical practices of *protomédicos* at Cartagena, see David L. Chandler, "Health and Slavery: A Study of Health Conditions Among Negro Slaves in the Viceroyalty of New Granada, 1600-1810" (Ph.D. diss., Tulane University, 1972), pp. 70-85. The major health issue for the royal port authorities was the prevention of epidemics, many of which they believed were introduced by incoming Africans. A slave with scurvy, yaws, or dysentery was healthy enough to be disembarked, but a slave with smallpox was not. At the same time, to condemn an entire crew would mean financial loss, and this problem was aggravated by the fact that some prospective slave buyers reached the ships and began selecting slaves even before the inspection process was complete. Thus, the division of *bozales* into those seen as disease carriers and those considered not infected was at best a haphazard process. On these issues,

refer also to Ángel Valtierra, *Peter Claver: Saint of the Slaves* (Westminster, 1960), pp. 121-23, 144.

3   For these steps and processes, see Chandler, pp. 64-85.

4   Valtierra, *Peter Claver*, p. 123. There were twenty-four of these barracks, also called *casas de negrería* ("houses of Negros"), in Cartagena by the mid-seventeenth century. A common practice of some sea captains was to employ the patios and rear areas of their homes as *barraconas*.

5   Valtierra provides a good description of the abominable health conditions in the *barraconas* (*Peter Claver*, pp. 132-34, 139-40). The most graphic portraits of life inside these poorly ventilated, unsanitary dormitories is found in Alonso de Sandoval, *De instauranda aethiopum salute* (Bogotá, 1956), pp. 108-9. Occasionally a buyer attempted to "fatten up" a slave he wished to buy during the two or more weeks between the time the slave was landed and the initiation of the *palmeo* process. Such schemes often failed because the large quantities of rich food that the slave consumed were too much for his ravaged system, and the dysentery he invariably contracted in the filthy *barraconas* often finished him off.

6   Elena F. Scheüss de Studer, *La trata de negros en el río de la plata* (Buenos Aires, 1958) pp. 201, fn., 327, fn.

7   Ibid., pp. 127, 128, 201, 204.

8   On the two week waiting period in Cartagena, see Chandler, "Health and Slavery," p. 93. On the apparent lack of same in Buenos Aires, see Scheüss de Studer, *La trata de negros*, p. 327.

9   The height of the slave was measured by means of an official standard called a *listón*. This was a wooden measuring stick over six feet long and divided into *palmos*, a length of roughly about 8.6 inches. A full *pieza de India* had to be at least 7 *palmos* tall. Assuming that a slave was otherwise considered as 1 *pieza*, he would be taxed accordingly if he had any of the following illnesses or maladies: scurvy, 3/4 *pieza*; benign hernia, 3/4 *pieza*; ringworm, 5/6 *pieza*; blind in one eye, 1/2 *pieza*; slowness of hands (*torpeza de manos*), 1/2 *pieza* (Jorge Palacios Preciado, *La trata de negros por Cartagena de Indias* [Tunja, 1973], p. 156).

10   After 1784 a royal *cédula* prohibited the branding of slaves.

11   A fine description of the steps following the arrival of slave ships is found in James Ferguson King, "Negro Slavery in New Granada," in Adele Ogden and Engel Fluiter, eds., *Greater America: Essays in Honor of Herbert Bolton* (Berkeley, 1945), p. 308.

12   Ibid.

13   For Duarte's full story see Rolando Mellafe, *La introducción de la esclavitud negra en Chile: Tráfico y rutas* (Santiago, 1959), pp. 170-76.

14   Philip Curtin, *The Atlantic Slave Trade: A Census* (Madison, 1969), pp. 28-30; Arthur Corwin, *Spain and the Abolition of Slavery in Cuba: 1817-1886* (Austin, 1967), pp. 111-12; King, "Negro Slavery," p. 302. The most comprehensive discussion of this question is found in a study written by Gwendolyn Midlo Hall, *Social Control in Slave Plantation Societies: A Comparison of St. Domingue and Cuba* (Baltimore, 1971), pp. 13-31. The latest research on this issue is found in Nicholas P. Cushner, S.J., "Slave Mortality and Reproduction on Jesuit Haciendas in Colonial Peru," *Hispanic American Historical Review* 55, no. 2 (May 1975): 177-200. It is shown that even on Jesuit plantations, where treatment was better than on most, slaves still did not reproduce themselves, and new supplies had to be bought to keep up with the work.

15   Diego Luis Molinari, *La trata de negros*, 2nd ed. (Buenos Aires, 1944), p. 49. Mellafe succinctly states that the preference for male slaves to females was "the general situation in all America" (*Introducción*, p. 197).

16   See appendix 1; José Antonio Saco, *Historia de la esclavitud de la raza africana en el Nuevo Mundo y en especial en los países américo-hispanos*, 4 vols. (Havana, 1938), 1:272, 326; and Gonzalo Aguirre Beltrán, *Población negra de México, 1519-1810: Estudio etnohistórico* (Mexico, D.F., 1946), p. 18.

17   Fernando Ortiz Fernández, *Glosario de afronegrismos* (Havana, 1924), pp. 26, 227-78.

18   See chap. 2, pp. 41-2.

19   Rolando Mellafe, *La esclavitud en Hispano-América* (Buenos Aires, 1964), p. 68; Frederick P. Bowser, "The Free Person of Color in Mexico City and Lima: Manumission and Opportunity, 1580-1650" (paper delivered at the Conference on the International Comparison of Systems of Slavery, Rochester, N.Y., 9-11 March 1972), graphs I, II.

20   Miguel Acosta Saignes, *Vida de los esclavos negros en Venezuela* (Caracas, 1967), pp. 53, 101, 114. A cacao-for-slaves form of barter also was employed in seventeenth-century Costa Rica (Quince Duncan and Carlos Meléndez, *El negro en Costa Rica* [San José, 1972], p. 26).

21   Domingo Amanátegui Solar, "La trata de negros en Chile," *Revista Chilena de Historia y Geografía* 44, no. 48 (1922): 28-29.

22   This was especially true after Portuguese control of the *asiento* ended in 1640 (Ibid., pp. 33-34).

23   For this cynical but fascinating tale, see Carlos Restrepo Canal, "Documentos sobre esclavos," *Boletín de Historia y Antigüedades* 24 (August 1937): 486-89.

24   Ibid., p. 489. Salvador Lara's defense is difficult to understand, and the impression is that the defendant did not really believe it necessary to formulate one.

25   Information and quotations from Amanátegui Solar, "Trata," pp. 31-32.

26   Jaime Jaramillo Uribe, "Esclavos y señores en la sociedad colombiano del siglo XVIII," *Anuario Colombiano de Historia Social y de la Cultura* 1, no. 1 (1963): 17.

27   Saco, *Historia*, 1:256.

28   Jaramillo Uribe, "Esclavos," p. 15.

29   Ibid., p. 16. Jaramillo Uribe believes that the "gift" was really a bribe intended to persuade the viceroy to give Anchederreta a special license that would allow him to bring 1,000 slaves into Cartagena, possibly without the payment of customs duties.

30   Amanátegui Solar, "Trata," p. 35. After independence, the Casa de Moneda housed the executive offices of the president of Chile.

31   Saco, *Historia*, 1:181-82. I have never discovered any source that revealed the name of this unfortunate man.

32   For an accurate account of the adventures of Esteban, or Estebanico, see the original account of Pedro de Casteñada, "Relación de la jornada de Cíbola," trans. George Parker Winship, *14th Annual Report of the Bureau of Ethnology* (Washington, D.C., 1892-1893), 14, pt. 1, pp. 418-19. Casteñada maintains that Esteban did not get along well with the monk Marcos de Nieza, who was his superior. Popular versions of the adventures of this *ladino* are found in J. A. Rogers, *Africa's Gift to America* (New York, 1961), pp. 67-68; and Albert John Lathuli, *Black Heroes in World History*, Bantam Pathfinder Edition (New York, 1969), pp. 34-43. Both are sensationalist in approach and defective in detail. See also George Winship, "The Coronado Expedition 1540-1542," *14th Annual Report of the Bureau of Ethnology*, pp. 355-62. Estebanico had apparently been ordered to obey Marcos de Nieza "in everything under pain of serious punishment" (Ibid., p. 355).

33   Peter Boyd-Bowman, "Negro Slaves in Early Colonial Mexico," *The Americas*

26 (October 1969): 151. These were Indians of the valley of Toquiqua, between the Maule and Nubile rivers. A royal decree dated 26 October 1541
specifically prevented Negroids from having Indians in their charge under any
circumstances (Richard Konetzke, ed., *Colección de documentos para la historia de la formación social de Hispano-América*, 3 vols. in 4 [Madrid, 1953-
1962], 1:206). This means that technically Valdivia's grant to Juan Valiente
was illegal. The *zambo* Juan Beltrán would also receive a similar grant in 1579.

34   Boyd-Bowman, "Negro Slaves," p. 151.

35   For a history of slave activities in the mines of Peru and Chile, see Antonio
Vázquez de Espinosa, *Compendium and Description of the West Indies*, trans.
Charles U. Clark (Washington, D.C., 1942), pp. 342-43; and Mellafe, *Introduc-
ción*, p. 61.

36   A series of plateaus averaging ten to twelve thousand feet in altitude and
situated between two ranges of the Andes Mountains. The mass of Bolivia's
population today lives on the *altiplano*.

37   See Mellafe, *Introducción*, pp. 62-63; and Amanátegui Solar, who points out
that blacks were not supposed to have been used in Chilean mines either, but
"this proscription was never to be obeyed" ("Trata," p. 27).

38   Ignacio Marques Rodiles, "The Slave Trade in America — Negroes in Mexico,"
Freedomways 2 (Winter 1962): 39.

39   See Mabel Farnum, *Street of the Half-Moon* (Milwaukee, 1940), p. 70; and
José R. Arboleda, S.J., "The Ethnohistory of the Colombian Negroes" (M.A.
thesis, Northwestern University, 1950), p. 34. In eighteenth-century Peru,
slaves worked all year crushing sugar cane in mills on Jesuit-owned plantations.
They rose at 4:30 AM in the winter and 5:15 in the summer (Cushner, "Slave
Mortality," p. 186).

40   A royal *cédula* of 7 August 1535 directed to the viceroy of New Spain prohibited the public or secret possession of weapons by slaves. Another, directed to
the viceroy of Peru on 19 November 1551, prohibited the possession of weapons by any Negroid, free or slave (Konetzke, *Colleción*, 1:167, 290). That
these laws were violated by Spaniards who armed their bodyguards can be seen
in José Franco, *Afroamérica* (Havana, 1961), pp. 120-21.

41   Robert S. Smith, "Indigo Production and Trade in Colonial Guatemala," *His-
panic American Historical Review* 39 (February 1959): 185, 187; Murdo J.
MacLeod, *Spanish Central America: A Socioeconomic History, 1520-1720*
(Berkeley, 1973), pp. 186, 190-91.

42   Carlos Federico Guillot, *Negros rebeldes y negros cimarrones: Perfil afroaméri-
cano en la historia del Nuevo Mundo durante el siglo XVI* (Buenos Aires,
1961), pp. 206-7; and Vázquez de Espinosa, *Compendium*, p. 315.

43   On slave prostitution, see Jaramillo Uribe, "Esclavos," p. 32; and Konetzke,
Colleción, 2:589, 3:113.

44   See Emilio Harth-terré, "La trata y comercio de esclavos negros por los indios
del común durante el gobierno virreinal en el Perú," *Actas y memorias*,
XXXVI Congreso Internacional de Americanistas, 4 vols. (Seville, 1966),
4:381-83.

45   Marques Rodiles, "Slave Trade," p. 49.

46   The possible manumission of a slave through marriage is considered in the
Siete partidas, law 1, title 5, pt. 4. See E. N. Van Kleffens who claims that this
code was never adopted *in toto* in Castile (*Hispanic Law until the End of the
Middle Ages* [Edinburgh, 1968], pp. 170-214). The provisions of the *Siete
partidas* were applied only in certain kinds of cases (pp. 210-11; see also pp.
264-65). Note also that while titles 24 and 25 of section 7 deal with the Jews
and Moors, there is no section that pertains to black Africans *per se*.

47   Saco, *Historia*, 1:245. Recall that the import of mulatto slaves or any slave of

mixed African blood was prohibited. See also Konetzke, *Colleción*, 1:31-33, 134, 185.

48   Edgar Love, "Legal Restrictions on Afro-Indian Relations in Colonial Mexico," *Journal of Negro History* 55 (April 1970): 137; Konetzke, *Colleción*, 1:290-91.

49   Mellafe, *Introducción*, p. 90. Evidence that castrations actually took place despite royal orders to the contrary can be seen in Gonzalo Vial Correa, *El africano en el reino de Chile: Ensayo histórico-jurídico* (Santiago, 1957), p. 131.

50   N. A. Micklejohn, "The Observance of Negro Slave Legislation in Colonial Nueva Granada" (Ph.D. diss., Columbia University, 1968), p. 58.

51   Jaramillo Uribe, "Esclavos," p. 5.

52   For these *cédulas*, see Micklejohn, "Observance," pp. 215-17.

53   Ibid.; Konetzke, *Colleción*, 3:553-72.

54   Konetzke, *Colleción*, 3:643-52.

55   See chap. 2, pp. 60-1.

56   On the Spanish interest in creating a giant sugar-cane producing colony, see Elsa Gouveia, "The West Indian Slave Laws of the Eighteenth Century," *Revista de Ciencias Sociales* 4, no. 3 (1960): 78-83.

57   See chap. 2, pp. 34-5.

58   Louisiana in this case refers essentially to the territory that roughly encompasses the present state. Under the 1763 Treaty of Paris, France yielded the Louisiana Territory to Spain.

59   For varying historical interpretations concerning the *Código negro español*, see Micklejohn, "Observance," pp. 64-67, 133; Fernando Ortiz Fernández, *Hampa afro-cubano: Los negros esclavos; Estudio sociológico y de derecho público* (Havana, 1916), pp. 363-66; Saco, *Historia*, 3:16-17; Eugenio Petit Muñoz et al., *La condición jurídica, social, económica, política de los negros durante el coloniaje en la Banda Oriental* (Montevideo, 1948), p. 80; and José Torre Revello, "Origen y aplicación del Código negrero en la América española," *Boletín del Instituto de Investigaciones Históricas* 15 (1932): 492-500.

60   Vial Correa, *El africano*, pp. 136-37.

61   Muñoz, *Condición*, pp. 85, 88-159.

62   Miguel Acosta Saignes, "Los negros cimarrones de Venezuela," in *El movimiento emancipador de Hispano-América*, 3 vols. Mesa Redonda de la Comisión de Historia del Instituto Panamericano de Geografía e Historia (Caracas, 1961), 3:389; Ortiz Fernández, *Hampa afro-cubana*, p. 363.

63   Jaramillo Uribe, "Esclavos," p. 23.

64   Ibid., p. 34.

65   Juan B. de Quiros, "El contenido laboral en los códigos negros americanos," *Revista Mexicana* 5 (1943): 495-96, and 500.

66   Acosta Saignes, "Negros cimarrones," pp. 214-18.

67   Konetzke, *Colleción*, 3:732.

68   Only Torre Revello bothers to cover the final stages of the life of this controversial slave code ("Origen," p. 50).

69   Micklejohn, "Observance," p. 65.

70   See chap. 2, p. 67.

71   See chap. 2, p. 60.

72   The most notable proponents of these ideas have been Herbert Klein, "Anglicanism, Catholicism, and the Negro Slave," *Comparative Studies in Society and History* 8, no. 3 (1966): 306-27; Micklejohn, "Observance," pp. vii, viii, 323, 338-39; Frank Tannenbaum, *Slave and Citizen: The Negro in America* (New York, 1947), pp. 52-82; and Stanley Elkins, *Slavery: A Problem in American Institutional and Intellectual Life* (Chicago, 1959), pp. 52-80.

73   Luis Millones, "Gente negra en el Perú: Esclavos y conquistadores," *América Indígena* 31 (July 1971): 595.
74   It was technically illegal for blacks to have power over Indians, but this was sometimes contradicted by fact. See appendix 2 for a listing of restrictions on slaves.
75   Konetzke, *Colleción*, 3:565-69.
76   Ibid., 1:88.
77   James Lockhart, *Spanish Peru: 1532-1560, A Colonial Society* (Madison, 1968), p. 190.
78   *Coartación* supposedly was of Cuban origin (H. H. S. Aimes, "Coartación: A Spanish Institution for the Advancement of Slaves into Freedmen," *Yale Review* 17 [February 1909], 412-31).
79   Bowser, "Free Person," pp. 10, 11, 16.
80   Acosta Saignes, "Negros cimarrones," 3:386.
81   Konetzke, *Colleción*, 3:565-68. The new code virtually prohibited the owner from freeing a slave gratuitously.
82   Roberto Rojas Gómez, "La esclavitud en Colombia," *Boletín de Historia y Antigüedades*, 4 (May 1922): 101-2.
83   Bowser, "Free Person," p. 8; Vial Correa, *El africano*, p. 111.
84   Federico Brito Figueroa, *Ensayos de historia social venezolana* (Caracas, 1960), pp. 112-13.
85   Jaramillo Uribe, "Esclavos," pp. 29-30. Similar conditional manumissions are related in Bowser, "Free Person," p. 9.
86   For the case of Julián Cayetano de Liendo and his wife, see Eduardo A. Farias et al., eds., *La obra pía de Chuao: 1568-1825* (Caracas, 1968), pp. 380-90.
87   Félix de Azara, *Descripción e historia del Paraguay y del Río de la Plata* (Buenos Aires, 1943), pp. 191-94.
88   Konetzke, *Colleción*, 3:566.
89   Vial Correa, *El africano*, pp. 165-66; Paulo de Carvalho Neto, *El negro uruguayo: Hasta la abolición* (Quito, 1965), p. 119.
90   Vial Correa, *El africano*, pp. 165-66.
91   Bowser, "Free Person," pp. 16-17.
92   These figures are based on the grand total of cases Bowser cites (Ibid.).
93   Carvalho Neto, *Negro uruguayo*, p. 89; Carlos M. Rama, *Los afro-uruguayos* (Montevideo, 1967), p. 18. Rama argues that, although a few slaves were freed as a result of bad treatment and some were allowed to buy their freedom, liberation was "only a possibility" for most of them.
94   Duncan and Meléndez, *El negro*, pp. 30-31.
95   Farias, *Obra*, p. 309.
96   Concolorcovo, *El Lazarillo: A Guide for Inexperienced Travelers Between Buenos Aires and Lima — 1773* (Bloomington, 1965), p. 79.
97   For the full story, see James J. Parsons, *Antioqueño Colonization in Western Colombia* (Berkeley, 1968), p. 52; and Eduardo Posadas, *La esclavitud en Colombia* (Bogotá, 1933), p. 26.
98   Carvalho Neto, *Negro uruguayo*, pp. 117-18.
99   Duncan and Meléndez, *El negro*, pp. 30-31.
100 Acosta Saignes, *Vida*, pp. 309-10.
101 For the opinions of the supporters of this thesis, see Elkins, *Slavery*, pp. 52-80; Klein, "Anglicanism," 306-27; idem, *Slavery in the Americas: A Comparative Study of Virginia and Cuba* (Chicago, 1967), pp. viii-ix, 2-126, 254-58; Sir Harry Johnston, *The Negro in the New World* (London, 1910), pp. iii-iv, 89-99; and Tannenbaum, *Slave and Citizen*, pp. 52-82, 97-119. For the arguments of the opponents of this thesis, see David B. Davis, *The Problem of Slavery in Western Culture* (Ithaca, 1966), pp. 223-88, and especially 262-63

and 287-88; Hall, *Social Control*, pp. 1-12, 152-54; and Marvin Harris, *Patterns of Race in the Americas* (New York, 1964), pp. 69-75.

102 Micklejohn, "Observance," pp. viii, 338-39; Jaramillo Uribe, "Esclavos," p. 54.

103 For the full history of these mines during the seventeenth century and the lives of the slaves who were made to work them, see Acosta Saignes, *Vida*, pp. 158-70.

104 In 1767 the Jesuits were expelled from Spanish America; thereafter the slaves were managed entirely by members of the Franciscan order.

105 José Walter Dorflinger and Geferino Garzón Maceda, "Esclavos y mulatos en un dominio rural del siglo XVIII en Córdoba (República Argentina)," *Revista de la Universidad Nacional de Córdoba* 2 (1961): 627-40.

106 Ibid., p. 638; Acosta Saignes, *Vida*, pp. 158-70.

107 See p. 78 of this chapter.

108 Love, "Legal Restrictions," p. 137.

109 Alexander von Humboldt, *Political Essay on the Kingdom of New Spain*, 4 vols. (New York, 1966) 1:236. He writes that "we may go through the whole city of Mexico without seeing a black countenance. The service of no house is carried on with slaves." Unfortunately, he does not tell us exactly what service the remaining bondmen still supplied.

110 MacLeod, *Spanish Central America*, pp. 190-91. Those who wanted slaves in Central America had to trade indigo to get them, and slave traders would not regularly take this product in exchange for *bozales*. Efforts to get Madrid to have *asentistas* extend special credit to the Central American interests also failed. Another stumbling block was that administrators in the region believed that African slaves too easily escaped to the Caribbean lowlands, where they constantly harassed Spanish commercial interests.

111 Jaime Jaramillo Uribe, "La controversia jurídica y filosófica librada en la Nueva Granada en torno a la liberación de los esclavos y la importancia económico-social de la esclavitud en el siglo XIX," *Anuario Colombiano de His-toria Social y de la Cultura* 4 (Bogotá, 1969): 65.

112 Paul D. Pavy, III, "The Negro in Western Colombia" (Ph.D. diss., Tulane University, 1967), p. 80.

113 Ricardo Palma, *Tradiciones peruanas completas* (Madrid, 1904), p. 138.

114 See appendix 1.

115 Vial Correa, *El africano*, p. 44.

116 José Luis Masini, *La esclavitud negra en Mendoza: Época independiente* (Mendoza, 1962), p. 10; Emiliano Endrek, *El mestizaje en Córdoba: Siglo XVIII y principios del XIX* (Córdoba, 1966), p. 12.

117 Federico Brito Figueroa, *Estructura económica de Venezuela colonial* (Caracas, 1963), p. 58. In the Venezuelan case, the exact percentage was 9.7.

118 Josefina Plá, *Hermano negro: La esclavitud en el Paraguay* (Madrid, 1972), p. 36.

4. Slave Rebellions and Negroid Resistance

1 For evidence of both forms of castigation, see Paulo de Carvalho Neto, *El negro uruguayo: Hasta la abolición* (Quito, 1965), p. 92; and José Luis Lanuza, *Morenada* (Buenos Aires, 1946), pp. 101-2. A 1784 *cédula* banned the *carimba* ceremony (branding), and the 1789 *Código negro* forbade all forms of branding.

2 N. A. Micklejohn, "The Observance of Negro Slave Legislation in Colonial Nueva Granada" (Ph.D. diss., Columbia University, 1968), p. 223.

3   Quince Duncan and Carlos Meléndez, El negro en Costa Rica (San José, 1972), p. 18.
4   Carvalho Neto, Negro uruguayo, p. 91.
5   Lanuza, Morenada, pp. 33-37. This slave was referred to in the records by several slightly different names: José Ramón Olatera, Joseph Ramón, Joseph Romualdo, and José Romero.
6   The same conclusion is suggested in the Duncan and Meléndez account (El negro, p. 18).
7   Roberto Rojas Gómez, "La esclavitud en Colombia," Boletín de Historia y Antigüedades, 4 (May 1922): 94.
8   Rolando Mellafe, La introducción de la esclavitud negra en Chile: Tráfico y rutas (Santiago, 1959), p. 91.
9   Franklyn J. Franco Pichardo, Los negros, los mulatos y la nación dominicana, 2nd ed. (Santo Domingo, 1970), pp. 20-21. A freed Negroid who allowed an escaped slave to remain in his house was also to have iron shackles placed on both ankles.
10 Micklejohn, "Observance," p. 108.
11 Eduardo A. Farias, La obra pía de Chuao: 1568-1825 (Caracas, 1968), pp. 384-410.
12 Franco Pichardo, Negros, p. 21.
13 Micklejohn reports that some masters preferred their runaway slaves to be sold rather than returned ("Observance," p. 106). See in particular, Acosta Saignes, who relates the story of Pedro Quiroga, a skilled bell maker. Pedro escaped from the Concorote mining area several times, but he was never severely punished. His owner would not allow him to go free, but a severe punishment might have resulted in an injury that would have impaired Pedro's skills. Thus, escape for this skilled bondman became a game (Vida, pp. 166-67).
14 Jaime Jaramillo Uribe, "Esclavos y señores en la sociedad colombiano del siglo XVIII," Anuario Colombiano de Historia Social y de la Cultura 1: no. 1 (1963): 22; Mellafe, Introducción, pp. 86, 91.
15 Carlos Federico Guillot, Negros rebeldes y negros cimarrones: Perfil afroamericano en la historia del Nuevo Mundo durante el siglo XVI (Buenos Aires, 1961), p. 68.
16 Ibid., p. 70.
17 Miguel Acosta Saignes, "Los negros cimarrones de Venezuela," in El movimiento emancipador de Hispano-América, 3 vols. Mesa Redonda de la Comisión de Historia del Instituto Panamericano de Geografía e Historia (Caracas, 1961), 3:393.
18 Jaramillo Uribe, "Esclavos," p. 22.
19 Guillot, Negro rebeldes, p. 81. Franco Pichardo, who gives a more comprehensive description of the affair, argues that many of the blacks captured after the battle near the hacienda of Melchor de Castro were hung on the spot (Negros, pp. 14-15). Consult also Larrazábal Blanco, Los negros y la esclavitud en Santo Domingo (Santo Domingo, 1967), pp. 143-45.
20 Guillot, Negros rebeldes, p. 113. For a comprehensive history of the event, see Ibid., pp. 111-15; or J. F. Ramírez, Proceso de residencia contra Pedro de Alvarado y notas y noticias biográficas, críticas y arqueológicas (Mexico, 1847), pp. 114-17.
21 José Saco, Historia de la esclavitud de la raza africana en el Nuevo Mundo y en especial en los países américo-hispanos, 4 vols. (Havana, 1938), 2:106-7; José Franco, Afroamérica (Havana, 1961), p. 117; José Cantú Corro, La esclavitud en el mundo y en Méjico (Mexico, 1926), pp. 217-18. The thirty-six included twenty-nine men and seven women.
22 Guillot, Negros rebeldes, p. 127.

23   David M. Davidson, "Negro Slave Control and Resistance in Colonial Mexico, 1519-1650," *Hispanic American Historical Review* 46, no. 3 (August 1966): 248-50.
24   William B. Taylor, "The Foundation of Nuestra Señora de Guadalupe de los morenos de Amapá," *The Americas* 26 (April 1970): 442-46.
25   Ibid., p. 446.
26   Ibid., p. 441. The priest also added that "the salvation of these souls is more certain."
27   The *costa chica* ("pretty little coast") refers to an area of Mexico's Pacific seaboard near Acapulco, in the state of Guerrero.
28   See chap. 10, pp. 280-1.
29   Jorge Fernando Iturribarria, *Historia de México* (Mexico, D.F., 1951), p. 324.
30   For a comprehensive explanation of the origins and emergence of the *sambomosquitos*, see Troy S. Floyd, *The Anglo-Spanish Struggle for Mosquita* (Albuquerque, 1967), pp. 22-23. A somewhat different and unsympathetic discussion of this group is found in Francisco de Paula García Peláez, *Memorias para la historia del antiguo reino de Guatemala*, 3 vols. (Guatemala City, C.A., 1943), 2:116.
31   Floyd, *Anglo-Spanish Struggle*, pp. 159-79.
32   Rodolfo Barón Castro, *La población de El Salvador....* (Madrid, 1942), p. 155. The author notes that in the present territory of El Salvador, 2,000 slaves attempted a rebellion on Easter Sunday, 1625. See also Murdo J. MacLeod, who relates that "officials [of the Captaincy General of Guatemala] were never happy about it [African slave trade to the region]; the empty, tropical areas of the Caribbean coast provided refuge for a growing number of *cimarrones....* Their harassment of communications with the Caribbean coast was a nuisance" (*Spanish Central America: A Socioeconomic History, 1520-1720* [Berkeley, 1973], p. 190).
33   Aquiles Escalante, *El negro en Colombia* (Bogotá, 1964), p. 122.
34   T. Lynn Smith, "The Racial Composition of the Population of Colombia," *Journal of Inter-American Studies* 8 (April 1966): 229.
35   Antonio Vázquez de Espinosa, *Compendium and Description of the West Indies*, trans. Charles U. Clark (Washington, D.C., 1942), p. 341.
36   Escalante, *El negro*, p. 118.
37   Jaramillo Uribe, "Esclavos," p. 44.
38   For the story of the *palenque* of San Basilio, see Escalante, *El negro*, pp. 115-17.
39   Jaramillo Uribe, "Esclavos," p. 44.
40   For a history of King Miguel, see Miguel Acosta Saignes, *Vida de los esclavos negros en Venezuela* (Caracas, 1967), pp. 154-56.
41   Ibid., p. 257.
42   Alexander von Humboldt, *Personal Narrative of Travels to the Equinoctial Regions of America during the Years 1799-1804*, trans. and ed. Thomasina Ross, 3 vols. (London, 1853), 2:66.
43   Acosta Saignes, *Vida*, p. 272.
44   Ibid., p. 283.
45   This region is part of the present Venezuelan state of Yaracuy. The conflict was also felt in what became the nearby state of Carabobo.
46   Carlos Felice Cardot, *La rebelión de Andresote (Valles del Yaracuy 1730-1733)* (Bogotá, 1957), p. 55.
47   Ibid., p. 88. In general, the account of the Andresote rebellion is more comprehensively told in this work. A shorter, less detailed but interesting analysis is provided in Federico Brito Figueroa, *Las insurrecciones de los esclavos negros en la sociedad colonial venezolana* (Caracas, 1961), pp. 46-49. The *ley*

de fuga, or "the law of flight," is a Spanish American expression referring to a situation in which a victim is shot while supposedly trying to escape.

48   This town is located in the contemporary state of Falcón.

49   For the melancholy story of this *zambo*, see Pedro M. Arcaya, *Insurrección de los negros en la serranía de Coro* (Caracas, 1949), pp. 28, 55-56; and Brito Figueroa, *Insurrecciones*, pp. 60-76.

50   Brito Figueroa, *Insurrecciones*, p. 76.

51   On the Ecuadorean *zambos*, see Guillot, *Negros rebeldes*, pp. 242-46; and Victor Wolfgang von Hagen, *Ecuador and the Galapagos Islands* (Norman, 1949), pp. 144-45. Hagen notes the names of the resident Indian tribes, the Mantas and Malabas.

52   Guillot argues that the cooperation given by the *zambos* to the English corsairs Drake and Oxenham was the primary reason for the Spanish campaigns against them in 1578 and 1588 to 1589 (*Negros rebeldes*, p. 245). See Vázquez de Espinosa for a description of the *zambo* chieftains as they appeared in 1599 (*Compendium*, p. 375).

53   For varying versions of the story of Alonso de Illescas, see Norman E. Whitten, *Class, Kinship, and Power in an Ecuadorean Town: The Negros of San Lorenzo* (Palo Alto, 1965), p. 23; Jacinto Jijón y Caamaño, *El Ecuador interandino y occidental antes de la conquista castellana*, 4 vols. (Quito, 1941-47), 2:71-73; and Hagen, *Ecuador*, p. 148.

54   Luis Millones, "Gente negra en el Perú: Esclavos y conquistadores," *América Indígena* 31 (July 1971): 598.

55   Mellafe, *Introducción*, p. 96.

56   This idea is presented persuasively in James Lockhart, *Spanish Peru: 1532-1560, A Colonial Society* (Madison, 1968), pp. 171-73.

57   For a history of *La recontonería* and its operation in sixteenth-century Mexico City, see Guillot, *Negros rebeldes*, p. 128; and Edgar Love, "Legal Restrictions on Afro-Indian Relations in Colonial Mexico," *Journal of Negro History* 55 (April 1970): 133.

58   Mellafe, *Introducción*, p. 97.

59   An uprising in the Viceroyalty of New Granada caused chiefly by a determined effort on the part of the royal authorities to collect sales taxes to pay for the war that had broken out with Great Britain. See Germán Arciniegas, who, although he may not present the best study of this insurrection, specifically discusses Negroid participation in the affair (*Los comuneros*, 2nd ed. [Bogotá, 1939], pp. 232-47).

60   On the participation of the Negroid in Mexico City riots, see Chester L. Guthrie, "Riots in Seventeenth Century Mexico City: A Study of Social and Economic Conditions," in *Greater America* (Berkeley, 1945), pp. 244, 247, 251, 253.

61   Millones speaks only of colonial Peru, but his terse generalization is probably accurate: "In each indigenous rebellion, the black slaves adopted the position of their masters" ("Gente negra," p. 616).

62   Micklejohn, "Observance," p. 112. One reason for the ambivalence of the Spanish concerning anti-*cimarrón* campaigns was their high cost. Between 1599 and 1619 Spanish attacks on the *palenque* established by King Benkos (San Basilio) resulted in expenditures of 36,613 pesos. None of these attacks proved successful, which is probably a major reason why the Spaniards resented the expense.

63   Saco, *Historia*, 3:48.

5. Free Negroids in Colonial Spanish America

1 Magnus Morner, *Race Mixture in the History of Latin America* (Boston, 1967) pp. 55-56. A clear understanding of these concepts can be gleaned from Francisco Cartera Burgos, "Fernando del Pulgar and the Conversos," in Roger Highfield, ed., *Spain, the Fifteenth Century: 1369-1586* (London, 1972), pp. 296-353.

2 C.H. Haring, *The Spanish Empire in America* (New York, 1963), p. 201.

3 Gonzalo Aguirre Beltrán, *Población negra de México, 1519-1810: Estudio etnohistórico* (Mexico, D.F., 1946), pp. 165-72; and Edgar F. Love, "Marriage Patterns of Persons of African Descent in a Colonial Mexico City Parish," *Hispanic American Historical Review* 51 (February 1971): 79-91.

4 On *chinos* as a variety of the Afro-Indian combination, see Rolando Mellafe, *La esclavitud en Hispano-América* (Buenos Aires, 1964), p. 89; and Alexander von Humboldt, *Political Essay on the Kingdom of New Spain*, 4 vols. (New York, 1966), 1: 245. The latter holds that persons of Afro-Indian blood were called *chinos* in Lima and Havana as well.

5 On the racial terminology prevalent in Costa Rica, see Norberto de Castro y Tosi, "La población de la ciudad de Cartago en los siglos XVII y XVIII," *Costa Rica, Revista de los Archivos Nacionales* 28 (July-December 1964), fold-out sheet, and pp. 151-61.

6 Jorge Juan and Antonio de Ulloa, *A Voyage to South America* (New York, 1964), pp. 27-28.

7 Humboldt, *Political Essay*, 1:244-46.

8 On these developments in Santo Domingo and the *Código negro carolino*, see Carlos Larrazábal Blanco, *Los negros y la esclavitud en Santo Domingo* (Santo Domingo, 1967), pp. 106-23, especially p. 106. Refer also to Franklyn J. Franco Pichardo, *Los negros, los mulatos y la nación dominicana*, 2nd ed. (Santo Domingo, 1970), pp. 73-74.

9 On Uruguayan practices, see Eugenio Petit Muñoz et al., *La condición jurídica, social, económica, política de los negros durante el coloniaje en la Banda Oriental* (Montevideo, 1948), 1:393-94.

10 Sergio Bagú, *Estructura social de la colonia: Ensayo de historia comparada de América Latina* (Buenos Aires, 1952), p. 147. See also Gonzalo Vial Correa, *El africano en el reino de Chile: Ensayo histórico-jurídico* (Santiago, 1957), p. 133. The viceroy wanted the Negroids separated from the *mestizos* and both of these from the Indians because he felt that otherwise Spain could not rule in the Viceroyalty of Peru. He further suggested that *fiestas* and diversions of a social nature would be quite useful in keeping the subject peoples from concerning themselves with political affairs.

11 Larrazábal Blanco, *Negros*, p. 122.

12 William L. Schurz, *This New World: The Civilization of Latin America* (New York, 1954), p. 180. In the 1603 and 1611 *cédulas* to the viceroy of Peru and the governor of Cartagena (Colombia), the king lamented the lack of religious education being given the *negros* (slaves) and ordered that separate parishes be set up for them. These churches and their clergy would be maintained through a ½-peso head tax to be paid by owners for each slave. It is doubtful whether either of these decrees was ever put into effect (Richard Konetzke, ed., *Colección de documentos para la historia de la formación social de Hispano-América*, 3 vols. in 4 [Madrid, 1953-1962], 2:99-100, 179-80).

13 Vial Correa, *El africano*, p. 121.

14 Refer to chap. 1, p. 20 on the brotherhoods in Europe.

15 Larrazábal Blanco, *Negros*, pp. 136-37.

16 Vial Correa, *El africano*, p. 112.

17   José Luis Lanuza, *Morenada*, (Buenos Aires, 1946) p. 26. In Cordoban *cofradías*, religious devotion of Our Lady of the Blacks and Mulattoes (*Nuestra Señora de los Negros y Mulatos*) was prevalent at least during the eighteenth century.

18   Vial Correa, *El africano*, p. 119.

19   Ibid.

20   Ibid.

21   Germán Arciniegas, *Latin America: A Cultural History* (New York, 1967), p. 140.

22   An *auto da fé* (literally, "edict of faith") was a public pageant or exposition given by the inquisitors at which prisoners were presented and sentenced.

23   Manuel Tejado Fernández, *Aspectos de la vida social en Cartagena de Indias durante el seiscientos* (Seville, 1954),pp. 107-8. For other gruesome tales of Negroid suffering at the hand of the inquisitorial bodies, see Luis Millones, "Gente negra en el Perú: Esclavos y conquistadores," *América Indígena* 31 (July 1971): 614-15.

24   Petit Muñoz, *Condición*, 1:510.

25   A discussion of the problem of a paucity of priests in many areas outside the large urban areas is found in N.A. Micklejohn, "The Observance of Negro Slave Legislation in Colonial Nueva Granada" (Ph.D. diss., Columbia University, 1968), p. 59.

26   Morner, *Race Mixture*, p. 43.

27   Konetzke, *Colección*, 3:107-108.

28   Larrazábal Blanco, *Negros*, pp. 139-40.

29   Aguirre Beltrán, *Población*, p. 274

30   For a typical presentation of such opinions, see Frank Tannenbaum, *Slave and Citizen: The Negro in America* (New York, 1947) pp. 4, 120-26.

31   Ángel Rosenblat, *La población indígena y el mestizaje en América*, 2 vols. (Buenos Aires, 1954), 2:159.

32   For the 1778 sanction and the quoted material, see Konetzke, *Colección*, 3:438-42.

33   Ibid., 3:439.

34   Aguirre Beltrán, *Población*, p. 253.

35   Emiliano Endrek, *El mestizaje en Córdoba: Siglo XVIII y principios del XIX* (Córdoba, 1966), p. 96.

36   Konetzke, *Colección*, 3:829-31.

37   Morner, *Race Mixture*, pp. 65-67; Love, "Marriage Patterns," pp. 79-91; Aguirre Beltrán, *Población*, pp. 251-53.

38   José Luis Lanuza, "El negro en la historia argentina," *Revista de América* 1 (Bogotá, September 1947): 374.

39   Endrek, *Mestizaje*, p. 96. Such a marriage was sanctioned in 1798, however, between María Mercedes Heredia, a white, and Pedro Bracamonte, a black. The marriage was said to have been allowed "since there did not exist opposition on the part of the father of the bride" (Ibid., p. 90).

40   Located about 60 kilometers southeast of Buenos Aires.

41   Romulo Cabria, *Los Orígenes de Chascomús* (La Plata, 1930), p. 14.

42   In March 1973 this writer examined the entirety of the *Documentos parroquias* [sic] ("parish documents") found in the town of Chascomús (Buenos Aires Province). The *Libros de matrimonios* and *Libros de bautismos* are complete from 1804 on, white, Negroid, and Indian weddings and baptisms are recorded together and not in separate volumes. These records are to be found in the church of *Nuestra Señora de la Merced* ("Our Lady of Mercy") in the care of Father Pedro Leonhardt.

43   J. F. Dauxion-Lavaysse, *A Statistical, Commercial and Political Description of*

Venezuela, Trinidad, Margarita and Tobago (New York, 1969), pp. 72-73.
44 Morner, *Race Mixture*, p. 39, fn. 15.
45 Konetzke, *Colección*, 3:477.
46 Endrek, *Mestizaje*, pp. 51-52.
47 Ibid., p. 48; Aquiles Escalante, *El negro en Colombia* (Bogotá, 1964), p. 141.
48 Endrek, *Mestizaje*, pp. 52-53.
49 Jaime Jaramillo Uribe, "Mestizaje y diferenciación social en el nuevo reino de Granada en la segunda mitad del siglo XVIII," *Anuario Colombiano de Historia Social y de la Cultura* 2, no. 3 (Bogotá, 1965): 40-41.
50 Alfredo Castillero Calvo, *La sociedad panameña: Historia de su formación e integración* (Panama City, 1970) p. 105; Larrazábal Blanco, *Negros*, pp. 139-40, 176-77.
51 Endrek, *Mestizaje*, p.48.
52 Escalante, *El negro*, pp. 141-42.
53 Endrek, *Mestizaje*, p. 43.
54 A manto or mantilla is a large shawl, usually black, worn by upper class women in public (usually to church). Sumptuary laws were common in sixteenth-century Europe but in the New World the discrimination was based on race rather than religion or caste.
55 Schurz, *This New World*, p. 180.
56 José Franco, *Afro América* (Havana, 1961); Endrek, *Mestizaje*, pp. 87-88.
57 See chap. 4, pp. 121-2.
58 Pedro Tobar Cruz, "La esclavitud del negro en Guatemala," *Antropología e Historia de Guatemala* 17 (January 1965): 12. The basis for the town council's decision was that numerous disorders had occurred in which blacks and mulattoes were involved. A black or mulatto could gain authorized entry into the town only by paying a fee of 10 pesos.
59 Lanuza, "Negro," pp. 106-10. Control of the *barrios* rested in the hands of the Negroid officials resident there. The *alcade del barrio* ("district or ghetto mayor") was to communicate with the police on the last day of every month, informing the latter of the name of all persons settling into or moving out of the *barrio*. No dances or festivals were to be held in the *barrio* except on Sundays and certain holy days.
60 Quince Duncan and Carlos Meléndez, *El negro en Costa Rica* (San José, 1972), pp. 33-35.
61 Franco Pichardo, *Negros*, p. 73.
62 Lanuza suggests that the prohibitions were not enforced in Buenos Aires, but it is known that the carnival celebration for 1778 was canceled because Viceroy Cevallos believed that the *castas* utilized the festivities as an excuse to insult whites and carry on disreputable activities ("Negro," p. 106). See also Alicia Nydia Lahourcade, *La comunidad negra de Chascomús y su reliquia* (Chascomús, 1973), p. 18. For prohibitions in Asunción, see Paulo de Carvalho Neto, "Antología del negro paraguayo," *Anales de la Universidad Central* 91 (Quito, 1962): 61-62. On the situation in Montevideo, see Petit Muñoz, *Condición*, 1:393-94. He comments caustically that this ordinance and several others passed on 26 September 1807 did not distinguish between free or enslaved blacks and mulattoes and were "dictated solely in the interests of the owner class" (Ibid., p. 394).
63 José Pérez de Barradas, *Los mestizos de América* (Madrid, 1948), p. 171.
64 Ibid., pp. 171-72.
65 Vial Correa, *El africano*, p. 100.
66 Ibid., pp. 100-01.
67 For an explanation of *amparo*, see chap. 3, pp. 89-90.
68 Francisco de Paula García Peláez, *Memorias para la historia del antiguo reino*

de Guatemala, 3 vols. (Guatemala City, 1943-44), 2:516.

69   Consejo de la Hispanidad, *Recopilación de leyes de los reinos de las Indias,* 3 vols. (Madrid, 1943), 1:600.

70   Castillero Calvo, *Sociedad panameña,* p. 103; Larrazábal Blanco, *Negros,* p. 177; Vial Correa, *El africano,* p. 53; Ildefonso Leal, *Historia de la Universidad de Caracas (1721-1827)* (Caracas, 1963), p. 318; Ildefonso Pereda Valdés, *Negros, esclavos y negros libres: Esquema de una sociedad esclavista y aporte del negro en nuestra formación nacional* (Montevideo, 1941), pp. 46-47.

71   Leon G. Campbell, Jr. *"The Military Reform in the Viceroyalty of Peru: 1762-1800"* (Ph.D diss., University of Florida, 1970), p. 299, also 288-89.

72   Federico Brito Figueroa, *Las insurrecciones de los esclavos negros en la sociedad colonial venezolana* (Caracas, 1961), p. 18; Millones, "Gente negra," p. 610. *Cédulas* prohibited the training of blacks, mulattoes, and, of course, zambos to be master craftsmen in many fields.

73   On Negroids as colonial businessmen, see Castillero Calvo, *Sociedad panameña,* p. 105; and Duncan and Meléndez, *El negro,* p. 35.

74   For Panama, see Castillero Calvo, *Sociedad panameña,* pp. 102-3; and Larrazábal Blanco, *Negros,* pp. 176-77. According to Castillero Calvo, the free Negroid population (mostly mulatto) represented 65 percent of the total population of the province of Panama in 1794 (p. 100). According to Franco Pichardo, the 38,000 free blacks and mulattoes (which he notes were primarily of mixed blood rather than black) was the largest class in Santo Domingo in 1794 (*Negros,* p. 72).

75   Alexander von Humboldt, *Personal Narrative of Travels to the Equinoctial Regions of America during the Years 1799-1804,* trans. and ed. Thomasina Ross, 3 vols. (London, 1853), 2:159-60. He observed: "We were struck with the singularity of finding in the vast solitude a man believing himself to be of European race, and having no other shelter than the shade of a tree, and yet having all the vain pretensions ... and errors of (a) longstanding civilization" (Ibid., pp. 159-60).

76   For the full story of this incident, see Juan Bromley, *Virreyes, cabildantes y oidores* (Lima, 1944), p. 93.

77   This was considered part of the tribute that Negroids were expected to pay as vassals of the king of Spain. But it was not regularly collected — a major reason why they did not wish to pay.

78   Leon G. Campbell, Jr., "Black Power in Colonial Peru: The 1779 Tax Rebellion in Lambayeque," in S. Ikahukwu Mezu, ed., *The Meaning of Africa to Afro-Americans* (Buffalo, 1973), p. 173.

79   Ibid., p. 142. Campbell explains in more detail in "Military Reform," that the argument over the question of "tribute" was complicated by the fact that, while blacks and mulattoes were expected to pay such taxes, royal officials in Peru had not bothered to collect them on any regular basis for two centuries (p. 124).

80   The quoted matter is from Campbell, "Black Power," p. 145. The story can be followed in Ibid., pp. 145-54, or in idem, "Military Reform," pp. 124-29.

81   Jacques Houdaille, "Negros franceses en América Central a fines del siglo XVIII," *Antropología e Historia de Guatemala* 6 (January 1954): 65-66; quotations from p. 66.

82   These blacks hoped at one time to obtain land and establish a community on the Caribbean coast, but the Spanish government vetoed the idea, deciding that "these foreigners would be able to make revolutionary propaganda among their brothers of race who are already numerous enough in that region" (Ibid., p. 66).

83   James F. King, "The Case of José Ponciano de Ayarza: A Document on gracias

al sacar," *Hispanic American Historical Review* 31 (November 1951): 643-44. For the financial details and the move of the government toward the sale of these dispensations, see Ibid., p. 642, fn. 5. The lower price for *pardos* is understandable in that, even if they bought the exemption, what the holder could do with it might be exceedingly limited.

84 Ibid., pp. 645-47.
85 Ibid., p. 647.
86 Fernando Romero, "José Manuel Valdés, Great Peruvian Mulatto," *Phylon* 3, no. 3 (1942): 295-302.
87 José Gil Fortoul, *Historia constitutional de Venezuela*, 3 vols. (Caracas, 1942), 1:80-82. The council also wanted the crown to oblige *pardos* to work the land.
88 Information and quotations from Leal, *Historia*, p. 326.
89 Konetzke, *Colección*, 3:814-16.
90 Ibid., p. 814.
91 Quotations from Leal, *Historia*, pp. 329, 331.
92 Konetzke, *Colección*, 3:821. The trouble with this *cédula* is that it reverses that of 7 April 1805, which specifically dispenses "from the quality of *pardo* . . . Diego Mexías de Bejerano and his sons" (Ibid., p. 815).
93 Ibid., p. 831.
94 Leal, *Historia*, p. 332.
95 Petit Muñoz, *Condición*, 1:68.
96 Jean Descola, *Daily Life in Colonial Peru: 1710-1820* (New York, 1968), p. 33.
97 Francisco Depons, *Viaje a la parte oriental de Tierra Firme en la América Meridional*, 2 vols. (Buenos Aires, 1960), 1:120-21. One reason the whites may not have worried too much about this usurpation of what had been an exclusive privilege was the fact in Caracas they often attended one church, mulattoes another, and blacks still a third (Morner, *Race Mixture*, p. 64).
98 Konetzke gives the background to this proposal and its more specific details (*Colección*, 3:823-29).

6. Negroid Soldiers in the Wars of Independence

1 This political change, instituted from 1782 to 1786, provided for the reorganization and centralization of colonial administration. Judicial, political, and military power was concentrated in the hands of an intendant and his subordinate, a *subdelegado*. The most important task of the intendants was the collection of royal revenues, and strenuous efforts on their part to accomplish this provoked colonial resistance and generated the suspicion that Madrid desired to increase its de facto control of the Indies.
2 John Lynch, *The Spanish-American Revolutions, 1808-1826* (New York, 1973), p. 13.
3 Ibid., p. 18.
4 Sir A. P. Newton, ed., *Thomas Gage: The English-American: A New Survey of the West Indies 1648* (London, 1946), pp. 74-76. This renegade priest provides an excellent description of the rivalry and mutual hatred between Spanish and *criollo* friars.
5 Lucas Alamán, *Historia de México desde los primeros movimientos que prepararon su independencia en al año de 1808 hasta la época presente*, 5 vols. (Mexico, 1883-1885), 1:57 (fn.), 58 (fn.).
6 Jaime Eyzaguirre, *Ideario y ruta de la emancipación Chilena* (Santiago, 1957), p. 58.

7   Alexander von Humboldt, *Political Essay on the Kingdom of New Spain*, 4 vols. (New York, 1966), 1:204.
8   There is no question that the 1810 revolutions were initiated by a minority of the population, and leaders like Bolívar candidly admitted it. See R. A. Humphreys and John Lynch, eds., *The Origins of the Latin American Revolutions 1808-1826* (New York, 1966), pp. 5-6, 244, 264.
9   Jaime J. Vicens Vives, ed., *Historia social y económica de España y América*, 4 vols. (Barcelona, 1957), 4:342.
10   Diego Luis Molinari, *La Trata de negros*, 2nd ed. (Buenos Aires, 1944), p. 99.
11   Ibid.
12   Alicia Nydia Lahourcade, *La comunidad negra de Chascomús y su reliquia* (Chascomús, 1973), p. 19.
13   Ibid., pp. 19-20.
14   José Luis Lanuza, *Morenada* (Buenos Aires, 1946), p. 143.
15   Emiliano Endrek, *El mestizaje en Córdoba: Siglo XVIII y principios del XIX* (Córdoba, 1966), p. 83.
16   Evelyn P. Meiners, "The Negro in the Río de la Plata" (Ph.D. diss., Northwestern University, 1948), chap. vi, p. 25.
17   Ibid., chap. vi, pp. 25-28; Ricardo Rodriguez Molas, "Negros libres rioplatenses," *Revista de Humanidades* 1, no. 1 (1961): 104. The conscripted *pardos* and *morenos* were paid less than their white counterparts as well.
18   Guillermo Feliú Cruz, *La abolición de la esclavitud en Chile: Estudio histórico y social* (Santiago, 1942), p. 75.
19   Ibid., p. 77.
20   Cuyo comprised the present-day provinces of Mendoza, San Juan, and San Luis. Until 1814 the Intendancy of Córdoba included Cuyo and Córdoba. In that year Cuyo was made a separate province.
21   José Luis Masini, *La esclavitud negra en Mendoza: Época independiente* (Mendoza, 1962), p. 20.
22   Ibid., p. 32.
23   Ibid., p. 18.
24   Ibid., p. 34.
25   J. C. J. Metford, *San Martín the Liberator* (New York, 1950), p. 67. Returning to Argentina sometime after the battle of Maipú, San Martín stopped on the battlefield and called the attention of his companions to the heroism displayed by the Negroid troops on that occasion.
26   Ildefonso Pereda Valdés, *Negros esclavos y negros libres: Esquema de una sociedad esclavista y aporte del negro en nuestra formación nacional* (Montevideo, 1941), p. 123.
27   Lanuza, *Morenada*, pp. 140-141.
28   Meiners, "The Negro," chap. vi, p. 33.
29   On the exploits of Lorenzo Barcala, see Vicente P. Sierra, *Historia de la Argentina: de la anarquía y la época de Rivadavia a la revolución de 1828*, 2nd ed., 2 vols. (Buenos Aires, 1970), 1:541. Most likely, neither Sosa nor Morales, who also commanded segregated units, reached these ranks until the 1850s (Domingo Sarmiento, *Obras completas*, 52 vols. [Buenos Aires, 1953-1956], 37:66).
30   Read José Vásquez Machicado, "La última palabra sobre la nacionalidad de Bernardo Monteagudo," *Boletín del Instituto de Investigaciones Históricas* 20 (1936): 35-71.
31   The Afro-Argentine scholar Sergio Monteiro spent several occasions in March 1974 discussing the history of Falucho with me. Monteiro argues persuasively that Falucho never really existed and that the Argentine statesman and historian Bartolomé Mitre concocted much of the story. Falucho thus becomes

merely the symbol of all the heroic nonwhites who played a role in the independence struggle.

32 Bartolomé Mitre, *Episodios de la revolución* (Buenos Aires, 1960), pp. 29-32. According to this author, Falucho's real name was Antonio Ruiz (Ibid., p. 31).
33 On Juan Manuel Rosas, see chap. 7, pp. 190-1.
34 See Lanuza for the fabulous career of this soldier of fortune (*Morenada*, pp. 83-84). His experience in battle and his abilities are attested to in Rudolfo de Ferrari Rueda, *Historia de Córdoba*, 2 vols. (Córdoba, 1968), 1:189-92.
35 Samuel W. Medrano and Faustino J. Legón, *Las constituciones de la República Argentina* (Madrid, 1953), p. 258.
36 Ibid., p. 279.
37 Lanuza, *Morenada*, pp. 83-84. Ferrari Rueda points out that Barcala's sole command in 1829 was a "Negro Battalion" (*Historia*, 1:189). Laws in Buenos Aires Province specifically kept militia units separated (Provincia de Buenos Aires, *Registro Oficial de la Provincia de Buenos Aires* [Año 1825], pp. 121-22; [1830], p. 14). This information was brought to my attention by Professor David Bushnell, Department of History, University of Florida, and forwarded to me on 2 July 1974.
38 Humphreys and Lynch, *Origins*, p. 24.
39 The *llaneros* were the horsemen who tended the herds on the grasslands (*llanos*) of central Venezuela. Many of them were of Negroid origin.
40 Laureano Vallenilla Lanz, *Cesarismo democrático: Estudios sobre las bases sociológicas de la constitución efectiva de Venezuela*, 4th ed. (Caracas, 1961), p. 96.
41 James F. King, "A Royalist View of the Colored Castas in the Venezuelan War of Independence," *Hispanic American Historical Review* 33 (November 1953): 528-30.
42 Norberto de Castro y Tosi, "La población de la ciudad de Cartago en los siglos XVII y XVIII," *Costa Rica, Revista de los Archivos Nacionales* 28 (July-December 1964), p. 164. This issue is discussed in greater detail in Chester J. Zelava Goodman, "Nicaragua en sus primeros años de vida independiente, 1821-1825," *Revista Conservadora del Pensamiento Centroamericano* 54 (March 1965): 64-67.
43 Vicente Lecuna, ed., *Cartas del libertador*, 11 vols. (Caracas, 1929-1941), 1:213.
44 William P. Marsland and Amy L. Marsland, *Venezuela through Its History* (New York, 1954), p. 171.
45 King, "Royalist View," pp. 527, 534-35. Montalvo also pointed out that the *castas* much preferred to shoot at whites.
46 Gerhard Masur, *Simón Bolívar* (Albuquerque, 1948), p. 309; the same story is related in David Florencia O'Leary, *Bolívar and the War of Independence*, ed. and trans. Robert F. McNerney (Austin, 1970), p. 114.
47 Masur, *Simón Bolívar*, p. 311.
48 Alfred Hasbrouck, *Foreign Legionnaires in the Liberation of Spanish America* (New York, 1928), p. 97.
49 Vicente Lecuna and Harold A. Bierck, eds., *Selected Writings of Bolívar*, 2 vols. (New York, 1951), 1:223. Cudinamarca refers to what is today the entire country of Colombia.
50 Robert L. Gilmore, *Caudillism and Militarism in Venezuela: 1810-1910* (Athens, 1964), p. 187. I am indebted to Professor Malcolm Deas of St. Antony's College, Oxford University, who informed me of Páez's exact title. Concerning the negative Ecuadorean response to the appearance of numerous black and mulatto officers, see chap. 8, p. 226 of this text.
51 Salvador de Madariaga, *Bolívar* (New York, 1969), pp. 268-69.

52 A federation founded in 1819, composed of what are today Ecuador, Colombia, and Venezuela.

53 Madariaga, *Bolívar*, pp. 268-69.

54 Harold A. Bierck, Jr.., "The Struggle for Abolition in Gran Colombia," *Hispanic American Historical Review* 33 (August 1953): 378-85.

55 Lecuna and Bierck, Selected Writings, 2:490. Bolívar's attitude is clear, but according to José Pérez de Barradas, Bolívar had a great grandmother, María Josefa Marín de Narváez, who was a mulatto. This meant that he had "6.25% of Negro blood!" (*Los mestizos de América* [Madrid, 1948], p. 182).

56 Lecuna, *Cartas*, 5:12, 262.

57 Lecuna and Bierck, *Selected Writings*, 2:628-29.

58 Ibid., 2:625. The full statement reads: "I do not say this lightly, for anyone with a white skin who escapes will be fortunate. The sad part of it all is that the ideologists, who are the vilest and most cowardly of men, will be the last to perish."

59 Charles C. Griffin, "Economic and Social Aspects of the Era of Spanish American Independence," *Hispanic American Historical Review* 29 (May 1949): 177-79; Magnus Morner, *Race Mixture in the History of Latin America* (Boston, 1967), pp. 81, 88; Randall Hudson, "The Negro in Northern South America, 1820-1860," *Journal of Negro History* 41 (October 1964): 229. See also Madariaga, who gives an excellent description of Infante, apparently a black man (*Bolívar*, p. 524). Madariaga calls Padilla a *zambo* rather than a mulatto (Ibid., p. 556).

60 Juan Pedro Paz-Solán, *Cartas históricas del Perú*, 2 vols. (Lima, 1921), 1:39-40.

61 Madariaga, *Bolívar*, p. 524. Then a town, Petaré is today a district of the city of Caracas.

62 Ibid., pp. 524, 620.

63 David Bushnell, *The Santander Regime in Gran Colombia* (Newark, Del., 1954), p. 172.

64 On Hidalgo, see Lynch, *Spanish-American Revolutions*, pp. 305-10.

65 See chap. 5, p. 139.

66 Wilbert H. Timmons, *Morelos: Priest, Soldier, Statesman of Mexico* (El Paso, 1963), pp. 49-50. The same incident is related in Alfonso Teja Zabre, *Morelos* (Buenos Aires, 1946), p. 61; and Enrique Cárdenas de la Peña, *Imagen del Morelos* (Mexico, D.F., 1964), p. 174.

67 Ezequiel A. Chávez, *Morelos* (Mexico, D.F., 1957), pp. 48-49.

68 Morner, *Race Mixture*, p. 89. Morner leans a bit on the earlier findings of Griffin, "Economic and Social Aspects," pp. 171-78.

69 That Santa Cruz was a *mestizo* is verified by Griffin, "Economic and Social Aspects," p. 177; and Alfonso Crespo, *Santa Cruz: El condor indio* (Mexico, D.F., 1944), p. 21. J. A. Cova argues that Páez's father was white, although his mother had some Indian blood (*Páez y la independencia de Cuba* [Havana, 1949], p. 16). Pedro M. Arcaya relates that Páez's father was denied the right to carry pistols because the *alcalde* asserted that he did not have pure blood. This decision was appealed to the governor, who reversed the *alcalde*'s decision, thereby establishing Páez's father as white. Given his mother's mixed origins Páez might be adjudged a *mestizo* (*Estudio sobre personajes y hechos de la historia venezolana* [Caracas, 1911], p. 53). Manuel de Mendiburu discusses Gamarra's origins and establishes him as white in *Biografías de generales republicanos* (Lima, 1963), pp. 88-89. This is the most complete investigation of the topic, and one cannot deduce from it that Gamarra was a *mestizo*. Certainly, the antimulatto campaign Gamarra led in Bolivia in 1827 seems to indicate that he had no obvious Negroid ancestry (Ibid., chap. 8). Vicente

Guerrero represents a greater problem. Arthur H. Noll argues that the Mexican president and ex-guerrilla leader had African and Indian origins (*From Empire to Republic* [Chicago, 1903], p. 78), while Henry Bamford Parks concludes that Guerrero was of "mixed Spanish, Indian and Negro descent" (*A History of Mexico*, 3rd ed. [Boston, 1960], p. 165). William F. Sprague ducks the question, simply arguing that Guerrero was of "low mestizo" descent (*Vicente Guerrero, Mexican Liberator: A Study in Patriotism* [Chicago, 1939], p. 1). Alfonso Teja Zabre presents the approved view of the Ministry of Foreign Affairs, i.e., Guerrero had "Indian parents" (*Guide to the History of Mexico: A Modern Interpretation* [Mexico, D.F., 1935], p. 259). Hudson Strode and Charles C. Cumberland argue that Guerrero was of Indo-Spanish origins (*Timeless Mexico* [New York, 1944], p. 105; *Mexico: The Struggle for Modernity* [New York, 1968], p. 126). Perhaps these opinions are little more than educated guesses, but it is interesting that Gonzalo Aguirre Beltrán, who notes Morelos's Negroid origins, says nothing about Guerrero. *Mestizo* origins ceased to be a handicap for ambitious young men, but detectable Negroid ancestry continued to be an obstacle.

70   Morner, *Race Mixture*, p. 83. In Argentina, however, parish record books continued to describe persons as *mulato, de color bajo,* or *de color* until 1855 (Lahourcade, *Comunidad negra*, p. 46).

7. Negroid Peoples in the Río de la Plata Countries

1   The story of the revolution of 25 May 1810 and evidence that it was hardly a "popular" uprising is found in Ricardo Levene, ed., *Una historia de la Nación Argentina*, 10 vols. in 15 (Buenos Aires, 1939-1947), 5(1): 297-98, 303-10; and Carlos Roberts, *Las invasiones inglesas del Río de la Plata (1806-1807)* (Buenos Aires, 1938) pp. 389-91. A somewhat more readable account of these events is found in Ricardo Levene, *A History of Argentina* (Chapel Hill, 1937), pp. 220-30.

2   Levene, *Una historia*, 5(2): 694-95, 726-29. San Martín, Alvear, and Zapiola were chiefs of the *logia lautaro* ("Lautaro Lodge"). On 8 October 1812 they overthrew the triumvirate of Manuel Sarratea, Juan José Paso, and Martín Pueyrredón. San Martín and the others did not take power themselves. Instead, they set up a second triumvirate of Rodríguez Peña, Juan José Paso, and Antonio Alvarez Jonte, men approved by the *logia lautaro* chieftains.

3   Orlando Carracedo, "El régimen de castas, el trabajo y la Revolución de Mayo," *Anuario Instituto de Investigaciones Históricas*, Universidad Nacional del Litoral, 4 (Rosario, 1960): 171-72. On 9 April and 14 May 1812 the First Triumvirate issued decrees prohibiting the slave trade, but the legitimacy of this body and its right to issue orders for other provinces could certainly be questioned.

4   Ibid., p. 172.

5   Ibid. This rule did not hold for female *libertas*, who were supposedly emancipated at age sixteen.

6   Ricardo Rodríguez Molas, "Negros libres rioplatenses," *Revista de Humanidades* 1, no. 1 (1961): 104.

7   Carracedo, "Régimen," p. 175.

8   Article 14 of this treaty reads: "His Britannic Majesty being extremely desirous of totally abolishing the slave trade, the United Provinces of the Río de la Plata engages to cooperate with his Britannic Majesty for the completion of so beneficent a work, and to prohibit all persons inhabiting said United Prov-

inces, or subject to their jurisdiction, in the most effectual manner . . . from taking any share in such trade" (Ibid.).

9   Rodriguez Molas, "Negros libres," p. 104.

10 Carracedo, "Régimen," p. 177.

11 Evelyn P. Meiners, "The Negro in the Río de la Plata," (Ph.D. diss., Northwestern University, 1948), chap. iv, p. 27. According to the incomplete 1778 survey conducted by Viceroy Vertiz in what are today the provinces of Tucumán, Córdoba, and Mendoza, there were 126,000 persons, 55,711 of whom were Negroid.

12 José Luis Masini, *La esclavitud negra en Mendoza: Época independiente* (Mendoza, 1962), pp. 65-67.

13 Emiliano Endrek, *El mestizaje en Córdoba: Siglo XVIII y principios del XIX* (Córdoba, 1966), pp. 63-65.

14 Masini, *Esclavitud*, p. 68.

15 Irene Diggs, "The Negro in the Río de la Plata," *Journal of Negro History* 36 (July 1951): 301.

16 Carracedo, "Régimen," pp. 179-80.

17 John Lynch, *The Spanish-American Revolutions, 1808-1826* (New York, 1973), p. 86.

18 Samuel W. Medrano and Faustino J. Legón, *Las constituciones de la República Argentina* (Madrid, 1953), p. 279.

19 Meiners, "The Negro," chap. iv, p. 24. Slightly different figures are provided by Lynch, who records that six out of ten blacks and three out of ten mulattoes were slaves (*Spanish-American Revolutions*, p. 85).

20 Endrek, *Mestizaje*, p. 53.

21 Ibid., pp. 65-67.

22 Ibid., pp. 67-68.

23 See chap. 5 of this text, p. 148, concerning segregated residential arrangements in the city of Buenos Aires; and José Luis Lanuza, *Morenada* (Buenos Aires, 1946), pp. 110-16. Police sanction for these residential arrangements appears to date from 1821.

24 See Rodriguez Molas and Meiners, who explain that these clubs charged about 4 pesos as an initiation fee. Annual dues were 4 pesos for bachelors and 2 pesos for married men with children ("Negros libres," pp. 105-06; "The Negro," chap. v, p. 37).

25 Meiners, "The Negro," chap. 5, p. 38. The seven most powerful societies were *la sociedad cubunda* (*cabinda?*), *la sociedad bangala* (*benguela*), *la sociedad de moros, la sociedad mina, la sociedad de rubulo, la sociedad angola,* and *la sociedad conga.* The names of these groups is a further indication of the Congo-Angola origins of most of the slaves in the Río de la Plata region.

26 On this question, see Lynch, *Spanish-American Revolutions*, p. 86, and Comisión Nacional del Centenario, *Documentos del archivo de San Martín*, 8 vols. (Buenos Aires, 1910), 2:28. In a letter (2 July 1974), Professor David Bushnell of Gainesville, Florida, referred me to such discriminatory acts as the continuance of the segregated militia units, passed in Buenos Aires Province (1825) by a government in which Bernardino Rivadavia was the driving force (La Provincia de Buenos Aires, *Registro Oficial de la Provincia de Buenos Aires* (Año 1825), pp. 121-22.

27 The situation is somewhat confused because between 1820 and 1853 no national government legally existed in Argentina. The governor of Buenos Aires province generally acted in the name of the others in foreign affairs, but often interior leaders did not always abide by the arrangements agreed to. In this regard, Rosas proved much more successful than those officials who had ruled before him.

28   Meiners, "The Negro," chap. 7, pp. 14-15. See also Jean A. V. Martín de
      Moussy, *Description géographique et statistique de la confédération Argentina*,
      3 vols. (Paris, 1860-1869), 2: 242-43.
29   Ysabel F. Rennie, *The Argentine Republic* (New York, 1945), p. 43.
30   Meiners, "The Negro," chap. ix, forward; chap. vi, pp. 25-33. See also Rodrí-
      guez Molas, "Negros libres," p. 110.
31   Lucio V. Mansilla, *Una excursión a los Indios rangueles*, 2 vols. (Buenos Aires,
      1939), 1:178.
32   Except for the period from 1949 to 1955, the Constitution of 1853 has
      continued to serve as the instrument of governmental organization.
33   Juan Alberdi, *Bases y los puntos de partida para la organización política argen-
      tina*, 4th ed. (Buenos Aires, 1928), pp. 14, 16.
34   This is from chap. 1, art. 25.
35   Alberdi, *Bases*, p. 18.
36   In *Civilización y barbarie* (Civilization and Barbarism), 1846.
37   Domingo Faustino Sarmiento, *Obras completas de Sarmiento*, 52 vols. (Bue-
      nos Aires, 1948-1956), 37:65.
38   Carlos Octavio Bunge, *Nuestra América: Ensayo de psicología social*, 7th ed.
      (Madrid, 1926), p. 217.
39   Ibid., pp. 127, 145-46. The italics are Bunge's.
40   This claim was made in Arthur P. Whitaker, *Argentina*, 2nd ed. (Englewood
      Cliffs, 1965), p. 62.
41   Ingenieros even argued that attempting to assist a people deemed inferior was
      antiscientific. José Ingenieros, *Al margen de la ciencia* (Buenos Aires, 1908),
      pp. 267-84.
42   José Ingenieros, *Evolución de las ideas argentinas*, 2 vols. (Buenos Aires,
      1951), 2:560-70.
43   Germán Arciniegas, *Latin America: A Cultural History* (New York, 1967), p.
      395.
44   José Ingenieros provides perhaps the only figures available. He estimates that
      around 800,000 persons lived within the territorial boundaries of Argentina in
      1852. Approximately 553,000 of these were *mestizos*, and while they consid-
      ered themselves white, Ingenieros certainly did not. He argued that there were
      only about 22,000 real whites in Argentina at that time (*Sociología argentina*
      [Buenos Aires, 1918], p. 451).
45   This figure is an estimate since the varied sources disagree. Preston E. James
      reports that between 1857 and 1900, 1,200,000 persons migrated to Argen-
      tina and remained (*Latin America*, rev. ed., [New York, 1950], p. 315).
      Whitaker finds that about 2,160,000 entered Argentina between 1871 and
      1910 (*Argentina*, p. 54). Alejandro Bunge writes that 2,500,000 immigrants
      had settled in Argentina by 1914 ("Present Economic Situation in the Argen-
      tine," *Revista de economía Argentina* 34 [1935]: 206). The most complete
      study is Carl E. Solberg's *Immigration and Nationalism: Argentina and Chile,
      1890-1914* (Austin, 1970). He computes that between 1889 and 1914,
      2,351,715 persons migrated to Argentina. All were Europeans, Latin Ameri-
      cans, or from the Middle East, except for 2.11 percent listed as "others" (pp.
      35-38, 42).
46   I examined the following multivolumed works for information regarding the
      Afro-Argentine after 1852 but did not find any commentary. Levene, *Historia*;
      Roberto Leviller, ed., *Historia argentina*, 5 vols. (Buenos Aires, 1969); Vin-
      cente F. López, *Historia de la República Argentina*, 5th ed., 8 vols. (Buenos
      Aires, 1957); Ernesto Palacios, *Historia de la Argentina: 1515-1957*, 2 vols.
      (Buenos Aires, 1957); José María Rosa, *Historia Argentina*, 2nd ed., 8 vols.
      (Buenos Aires, 1967).

47   Rodríguez Molas, "Negros libres," p. 125; Sarmiento, *Obras completas*, 37:66-68; James R. Scobie, *Argentina: A City and a Nation* (New York, 1964), pp. 31-33.
48   Technically, Buenos Aires Province was not subject to the Constitution of 1853 until 1862, when it joined the national federation.
49   Rodríguez Molas, "Negros libres," pp. 120-22.
50   Ibid., pp. 118-19.
51   Ibid., p. 124.
52   Ibid., p. 125, and fn. 52.
53   República Argentina, *Tercer censo nacional levantado el 1° de junio de 1914*, 10 vols. (Buenos Aires, 1916-1917), 2:395. The total was 334 men and 189 women. Of these, 51 were in the city of Buenos Aires (p. 148), 100 in the Province of Córdoba (p. 277), and 39 in the territory of Chubut (p. 358).
54   Solberg, *Immigration*, p. 42. In 1910 there were 10 Japanese; the number increased to 2,000 by 1920.
55   Luis Grassino, "Buenos Aires de ébano," *Revista Clarín*, no. 9289 (Buenos Aires, 5 December 1971), p. 36. The only other sources for information on the Afro-Argentine between 1910 and 1940 are José Antonio Welde, *Buenos Aires desde setenta años atrás* (Buenos Aires, 1917); and Vicente Gregorio Quesada, *Memorias de un viejo: Escenas de costumbres de la República Argentina*, 2nd ed. (Buenos Aires, 1942).
56   Ibid., p. 37.
57   Ibid., p. 38.
58   Among the mulattoes I encountered was Carlos Boot, an official in the Protocol Department of the Ministry of Foreign Affairs. Ramón Carillo, another mulatto, was Minister of Public Health during Juan Perón's regime from 1946 to 1955.
59   Interview with Señora Guillermina Eloísa González de Luis, Chascomús, Buenos Aires Province, 3 March 1974. For whatever it is worth, the 1914 census lists no *africanos* in Chascomús, and Señora de Luis is over eighty years old (*Tercer censo nacional*, 2:166).
60   For pictures of the *capilla* and the statue, see Era Bell Thompson, "Argentina: Land of the Vanishing Blacks," *Ebony* 28 (October 1973): 39-40; and Alicia Nydia Lahourcade, *La comunidad negra de Chascomús y su reliquia* (Chascomús, 1973), pp. 59-60, 64.
61   Interview with Señora Guillermina Eloísa González de Luis, Chascomús, Buenos Aires Province, 3 March 1974. Some of the same frustrations regarding contemporary disinterest among the young Negroids is found in Lahourcade, *Comunidad negra*, pp. 63-65.
62   "Chascomús, una negra historia," *Siete Días Illustrados* 8 (17 March 1974): 26.
63   On the origins of the tango and its development in dance halls operated for Afro-Argentines, see Rodríguez Molas, "Negros libres," pp. 115-17; and especially Vicente Rossi, *Cosas de negros* (Córdoba, 1926), pp. 97-99, 169-226.
64   Diggs, "The Negro," p. 299.
65   William W. Kaufman, *British Policy and the Independence of Latin America: 1804-1821* (New Haven, 1951), pp. 50-51.
66   Carlos M. Rama, "The Passing of the Afro-Uruguayans from Caste Society into Class Society," in Magnus Morner, ed., *Race and Class in Latin America* (New York, 1970), p. 41.
67   Juan Carlos Pedemonte, *Hombres con dueño: Crónica de la esclavitud en el Uruguay* (Montevideo, 1943), pp. 63-65. Santa Colombo was indeed an incorrigible fellow. From his jail cell in September 1833, he helped organize another slave uprising (Ibid., p. 69).

68 Diggs, "The Negro," pp. 295-96.
69 Carlos M. Rama, *Los afro-uruguayos* (Montevideo, 1967), p. 61.
70 Ildefonso Pereda Valdés, *Negros esclavos y negros libres: Esquema de una sociedad esclavista y aporte del negro en nuestra formación nacional* (Montevideo, 1941), p. 130.
71 Rama, "Afro-Uruguayans," p. 42.
72 Pedemonte, *Hombres*, p. 137; Diggs, "The Negro," p. 301.
73 Pedemonte, *Hombres*, p. 137.
74 Ibid., p. 140.
75 Rama, "Afro-Uruguayans," p. 34, fn.
76 Pereda Valdés, *Negros*, p. 141.
77 Rama, "Afro-Uruguayans," p. 47, fn.
78 The public prejudice exhibited against blacks and mulattoes after 1853 is discussed in Rama, *Afro-uruguayos*, p. 79. The education struggle of 1878 is explained in his "Afro-Uruguayans," p. 50, fn. 2.
79 Rama discusses the question, inferring that the change was to a great degree artificial ("Afro-Uruguayans," p. 50).
80 *Marcha*, no. 812 (Montevideo, 11 May 1956): 24-26.
81 Ildefonso Pereda Valdés, *El negro en el Uruguay* (Montevideo, 1965), pp. 190-201.
82 Ibid., p. 196.
83 Ibid., p. 206.
84 Ibid., p. 207.
85 Ibid., p. 289; see also p. 207.
86 Ibid., p. 195.
87 Paulo de Carvalho Neto, *Estudios afros* (Caracas, 1971) pp. 197-200. This organization had 244 members, 103 of which were males, and the rest females. Two white males, married to mulatto women, were also members. Most of the membership did not live in the predominately Negroid district of Montevideo, but they carried on their social activities there.
88 Rama, "Afro-Uruguayans," pp. 31, 45.
89 República Oriental del Uruguay, *Compilación de leyes y decretos, 1825-1930*, 25 vols. (Montevideo, 1930) 18:354. Chap. 4, art. 27, prohibited Asian and African immigration.
90 Thomas E. Weil, et al., *United States Army Area Handbook for Uruguay* (Washington, D.C., 1971), p. 59.
91 Carvalho Neto, *Estudios afros*, pp. 37, 38, 45.
92 Pilar E. Barrios, "Tema racial," in *Piel negra, mis cantos, campo afuera* (Nendeln, Lichtenstein, 1970), pp. 48-49.
93 Carlos Pastore, *La lucha por la tierra en el Paraguay: Proceso histórico y legislativo* (Montevideo, 1949), pp. 37, 38, 45.
94 Jerry W. Cooney, "Abolition in the Republic of Paraguay," paper delivered at the *Mid-American Latin-American Studies Conference* (Muncie, Indiana, 23 October 1973), pp. 2-3.
95 A tea is made by pouring hot water over the leaves from the *ilex paraguayensis*, a kind of holly tree. It is drunk extensively in Paraguay, Argentina, and southern Brazil.
96 Cooney, "Abolition," pp. 3-5.
97 Ibid., pp. 4-6. The estimated figures on the black and mulatto population of Paraguay are on pp. 4 and 5. A discussion of slave life in Paraguay is found on pp. 6 and 7.
98 Josefina Plá, *Hermano negro: La esclavitud en el Paraguay* (Madrid, 1972), p. 70.
99 Cooney, "Abolition," p. 5.

100 Plá, *Hermano negro*, p. 36.
101 Héctor Decoud, *El campamento de Laurelty* (Montevideo, 1930), pp. 16-18. Curiously enough, this unit's greatest victories were attained against Afro-Brazilian troops.
102 Edison Carneiro, ed. *Antología do negro brasilero* (Pôrto Alegre, 1950), p. 47. This decree was incorporated as Article 25 of the Constitution of 1870.
103 Mary W. Williams, Ruth J. Bartlett, and Russell E. Miller, *The People and Politics of Latin America*, 4th ed. (New York, 1958), p. 675.
104 Mario A. Moriago, "Noticias sobre la población paraguaya en la actualidad," in Ángel Rosenblat, *La población indígena y el mestizaje en América*, 2 vols. (Buenos Aires, 1954) 1:165; Plá, *Hermano negro*, pp. 51-52.
105 International Labor Office, *Memorandum on Immigration Policy*, PMC/I/G/ rev. 1 (Geneva, 1947) n.p. Article 14 of the 1903 Immigration Law prohibited the issuance of visas to persons of African or Asian origin. This law was dropped in 1924, but immigrants continue to list their race, and an unofficial policy of exclusion was still in effect as of 1947.
106 Ibid., p. 164; Carvalho Neto, "Antología del negro paraguayo," *Anales de la Universidad Central* 91 (Quito, 1962): 59.
107 Emilio García, "Apuntes de economía política," *La Voz de Comercio* (Asunción, 23 June 1951). On the basis of an estimated 901,768 inhabitants, 3.5 percent would be about 31,500 blacks, mulattoes, and *zambos*.
108 See chap. 6, p. 170.
109 Carvalho Neto, *Estudios afros*, pp. 111-130. The earliest study of this settlement was that of Decoud, *Campamento*, p. 19.

8. Negroid Peoples in the Andean States

1 In Chile these landless farm workers and tenant farmers are called *inquilinos*. They worked the *fundos*, or large agricultural estates. On the agricultural and mining activities of African slaves in Chile prior to 1700, see Rolando Mellafe, *La introducción de la esclavitud negra en Chile: Tráfico y rutas* (Santiago, 1959), pp. 121-23, 149-54. On the replacement of African slaves, see Gonzalo Vial Correa, *El africano en el reino de Chile: Ensayo histórico-jurídico* (Santiago, 1957), pp. 46-48; Guillermo Feliú Cruz, *La abolición de la esclavitud en Chile: Estudio histórico y social* (Santiago, 1942), p. 38-40; and John Lynch, *The Spanish-American Revolutions, 1808-1826* (New York, 1973), p. 156.
2 See chap. 6, pp. 168-9
3 Feliú Cruz, *Abolición*, pp. 79-80; Francisco A. Encina, *Historia de Chile: Desde la prehistoria hasta 1891*, 2nd ed., 20 vols. (Santiago, 1952), 5:162.
4 On this problem, see Domingo Amanátegui Solar, "La trata de negros en Chile," *Revista Chilena de Historia y Geografía* 44, no. 48, 1922: 40.
5 Feliú Cruz, *Abolición*, p. 132.
6 *Sargento mayor* is the equivalent of the U.S. Army rank of major.
7 Feliú Cruz, *Abolición*, p. 132. This is also the title of the chapter beginning on page 242.
8 Encina, *Historia*, 5:165.
9 No mention is made of the Negroid Chilean after abolition in Encina, *Historia*; Francisco Frías Valenzuela, *Historia de Chile: La República*, 5 vols. (Santiago, 1949); Luis Galdames, *History of Chile*, trans. Isaac J. Cox (Chapel Hill, 1941); or Fernando Campos Harriet, *Historia constitucional de Chile*, 3rd ed. (Santiago, 1963).
10 Alfonso M. Escudero, a priest, conducted some investigations concerning the 1940 census in the Chilean Census Bureau (Dirección General de Estadística)

and reported that about 1,000 blacks and 3,000 mulattoes were residents in Chile (Ángel Rosenblat, *La población indígena y el mestizaje en América*, 2 vols. [Buenos Aires, 1954], 1:166). According to reports delivered to me from a confidential source and dated 14 June 1971, the Afro-Chilean population is about .017 percent of the whole. In 1970 the total population was estimated at 9,786,000.

11 Carl Solberg, *Immigration and Nationalism: Argentina and Chile, 1890-1914* (Austin, 1970), pp. 18-19. On the opposition to Orientals, Jews, and persons from the Middle East, see Ibid., pp. 11, 70-72. On the Chilean preference for German and Anglo-Saxon immigrants, see Ibid., p. 19; and L. E. Elliot, *Chile: Today and Tomorrow* (New York, 1922), pp. 291-97. See also Nicolás Palacios, *Raza chilena* (Valparaiso, 1904), pp. 4, 32, 48-52. He argues that the union of white European Basques and Araucanian Indians had produced a powerful and unique *mestizo*.

12 Germán Ursua Valenzuela, *Evolución de la administración pública chilena: 1818-1968* (Santiago, 1969), p. 181.

13 An article produced by the Copley News Service and appearing in the *Times of the Americas*, 11 April 1973, claimed that the Constitution of 1925 made it illegal for persons of African origin to immigrate to Chile. I wrote to Clarance W. Moore, publisher of the newspaper, seeking verification of this claim. In a letter dated 30 May 1973, Mr. Moore responded that he had received a reply from Mr. William Horsey, who had written the article for *Times of the Americas*. Mr. Horsey claimed that while he could quote no source to support his assertion, he believed that " '2 years of residence in Chile seemed to justify it.' " Several Chileans have also remarked to me that Negroid immigrants are barred from becoming citizens. This is possible, but the policy seems to be an informal rather than a stated one.

14 A confidential letter received on 14 June 1971 states that Chilean immigration laws retain provisions prohibiting the entry of any African person for purposes of permanent residence. It further reported that "the Chilean Constitution is silent on the question of exclusion but appears to give the ministries of *Gobernación* (Department of the Interior) and of *Relaciones Exteriores y Culto* (Foreign Affairs) authority over the issuance of resident permits. Each immigration case is decided on criteria not published anywhere."

15 República de Chile, Contraloría General de la República, Secretaría General, *Recopilación de reglamentos con índices por Ministerios, temático y onomástico se incluyen, además, todos los decretos supremos que, sin ser reglamentarios, tienen interés general permanente*. Decreto 5. 021, de 16 de septiembre de 1959 (Santiago, 1961), 14:11-37.

16 In late April 1962 I met two Afro-Americans living in Chile who were playing as members of a national basketball team. It appears that some Negroids are welcome in Chile, but that the prospect of their gaining citizenship may be dependent on whether or not they continue to be of use as sports performers or instructors.

17 *Washington Post*, 30 November 1973, sect. A, pp. 1, 27. According to the newspaper story, the Chilean government refused to accept a black colonel, T. M. Gafford, as military attaché in Santiago. The rejection was allegedly made on the basis of race.

18 On this social myth, passionately adhered to by middle and upper-class Chileans, see Fredrick B. Pike, "Aspects of Class Relations in Chile, 1850-1960," *Hispanic American Historical Review* 43 (February 1963): 28-33.

19 Mellafe, *Introducción*, p. 63. Hernando Pizarro had originally decided not to put black slaves in the Potosí mines because he believed the climate to be too cold for them. The crown acted on the 1554 report of the *visitador* Don Rodrigo de Medrano (Ibid.).

20 José Luis Saco, *Historia de la esclavitud de la raza africana en el Nuevo Mundo y en especial en los países américo-hispanos*, 4 vols. (Havana, 1938), 2:97-98. It seems that many of the Africans brought to Potosí were shipped illegally from Brazil. On the phenomenal price of 800 pesos in Potosí, see Mellafe, *Introducción*, p. 252.

21 Paulo de Carvalho Neto, *Estudios afros* (Caracas, 1971), pp. 259-60. The peak figure of slaves in colonial Bolivia was perhaps 4,000.

22 On the sufferings and harsh treatment of Indians forced to work the silver mines of Potosí, see Bernard Moses, *The Spanish Dependencies in South America: An Introduction to the History of Their Civilization*, 2 vols. (New York, 1914), 1:7.

23 Salvador de Madariaga, *Bolívar* (New York, 1969), p. 579.

24 Ibid., p. 580.

25 Ciro Félix Trigo, *Las constituciones de Bolivia* (Madrid, 1958), p. 223.

26 República de la Bolivia, Oficina Nacional de Inmigración, Estadística y Propoganda Geográfica, *Censo de la Población de Bolivia: Septiembre de 1900*, 2 vols. (La Paz, 1904), 2:31.

27 Trigo, *Constituciones*, p. 309.

28 República de la Bolivia, *Censo*, 2:31.

29 Ibid.

30 Ibid.

31 Gilberto Loyo, *La política demográfica de México* (Mexico, D.F., 1935), p. 485, charts following pp. 482 and 484. According to Loyo, this total is for the year 1930. No complete census was taken between 1900 and 1950. The source of the 1930 figure is not stated.

32 This, however, was not always the case. See James Lockhart, *Spanish Peru: 1532-1560, A Colonial Society* (Madison, 1968), p. 185.

33 See chap. 3, table 3, p. 95.

34 These figures are from Robert Marett, *Peru* (London, 1969), p. 83; and Santiago Tavara, *Abolición de la esclavitud en el Perú* (Lima, 1855), p. 29. Ricardo Palma gives the figure of 41,228 slaves, 33,000 of whom were on coastal plantations (*Tradiciones peruanas completas* [Madrid, 1904], p. 139).

35 Juan Carlos Zuretti, *El General San Martín y la cultura* (Buenos Aires, 1950), p. 72.

36 Quotations from Jorge Basadre, *Historia de la República del Perú*, 5th ed., 10 vols. (Lima, 1963), 2:554.

37 Ibid., p. 555; and James Ferguson King, "The Latin American Republics and the Suppression of the Slave Trade," *Hispanic American Historical Review* 24 (August 1944): 407. Palma reports that 800 slaves were brought to Peru from western Colombia after 1835 (*Tradiciones peruanas*, p. 140).

38 Basadre, *Historia*, 2:556. According to Palma, *libertos* whose services had been sold were to be paid 1 peso a week, which was roughly 50 percent of what Indian peons were getting (*Tradiciones peruanas*, p. 140).

39 King, "Latin American Republics," p. 407.

40 Rolando Mellafe, *La esclavitud en Hispano-América* (Buenos Aires, 1964), p. 102.

41 For the history of this rebellion, see Santiago Vallejo, "La raza negra en la campaña de la emancipación," *Sobretiro de la Revista Panorama* 1, no. 2 (1954): 17-20.

42 Ibid., p. 19. Vallejo argues that the horrible working conditions on the sugar plantations were the major reasons for the slave upheaval. He states that whites were killed by the Negroid rebels, but he provides no totals. No other account of this rebellion appears ever to have been published.

43 Palma, *Tradiciones peruanas*, pp. 141-42.

44 Vallejo, "Raza negra," p. 19.

45 Marett, *Peru*, p. 97. Since the slaveholding aristocrats were supporting Echenique, Castilla called for abolition as a means of striking back. Once he had won the war, however, these same forces had to be pacified. As a result, Castilla rewarded the slaveocracy handsomely for giving up their slaves and deciding to support Echenique.

46 For this sordid story, see Octavius Howe and Frederick Mathews, *American Clipper Ships, 1833-1858*, 2 vols. (Salem, Mass., 1926), 1:326-27; and Basil Lubbock, *The Colonial Clippers* (Glasgow, 1921), p. 35.

47 Fernando Romero, "The Slave Trade and the Negro in South America," *Hispanic American Historical Review* 24 (August 1944): 378.

48 Ibid., p. 379.

49 Ricardo Doñoso, *El marqués de Osorno, don Ambrosio Higgins, 1720-1801* (Santiago, 1941), p. 465.

50 Fernando Romero, "La corriente de la trata negrera en Chile," *Sphinx* 3 (May-June 1939): 93.

51 Romero, "Slave Trade," pp. 378-79. The author states categorically that many persons were listed as white who could not be called such normally.

52 Vallejo, "Raza negra," p. 20. *Cholo* is a somewhat nebulous term used in Peru and Bolivia to describe a *mestizo* or an Indian who speaks Spanish and has adopted Western customs.

53 Romero, "Slave Trade," p. 375.

54 Ibid., p. 386.

55 República del Perú, *Censo de los provincias de Lima y Callao levantado el 13 de noviembre de 1931* (Lima, 1932), p. 92. *Trigueño* essentially means "wheat-colored" or "swarthy."

56 República del Perú, *Censo de población de la ciudad de Tacna y distritos Colona y Pachia levantado el 22 de julio de 1935* (Tacna, 1936), p. v.

57 Javier Prado y Ugarteche, *Estado social del Perú durante la dominación española* (Lima, 1894), p. 165.

58 Alejandro O. Deustua, *Ante el conflicto: Problemas económico-sociales y morales del Perú* (Lima, 1931), p. 20; César Antonio Ugarte, *Bosquejo de la historia económica del Perú* (Lima, 1926), p. 50.

59 Francisco García Calderón, *Les démocrates latines de L'Amérique* (Paris, 1912), p. 338. For a study of these thinkers and an assessment of their Positivist leanings, see Jesús Chavarría, "The Intellectuals and the Crisis of Modern Peruvian Nationalism," *Hispanic American Historical Review* 50 (May 1970): 257-78.

60 José Carlos Mariátegui, *Seven Interpretive Essays on Peruvian Reality* (Austin, 1971), p. 280.

61 Ibid., p. 273.

62 Luis E. Valcárcel, *Ruta cultural del Perú* (Mexico, D.F., 1945), p. 94.

63 Ibid., p. 95.

64 Roberto MacLean y Esteños, *Negros en el Nuevo Mundo* (Lima, 1948), p. 156.

65 Mario Vargas Llosa, *La ciudad y los perros* (Barcelona, 1962), p. 24. I am indebted also to Professor James W. Brown, whose unpublished paper, "Mario Vargas Llosa on Peruvian Racism," read at the *Mid-American Latin-American Studies Conference* in Muncie, Indiana on 23 October 1972 proved quite useful.

66 Luis Millones, "Gente negra en el Perú: Esclavos y conquistadores," *América Indígena* 31 (July 1971): 595.

67 Ibid., p. 594.

68 See chapter 7 and especially the works of Ildefonso Pereda Valdés and Carlos Rama cited in notes 66, 70, and 81 of that chapter.

69 See chap. 4, pp. 117, 121.

70 Palma, *Tradiciones peruanas*, pp. 1075-76.

71 George Schuyler, *The Pittsburgh Courier*, 7 August 1948, p. 9.
72 The best examples of the work of Compañía Cumanana are found on an unnumbered LP by Nicomedes de Santa Cruz Gamarra, *Cumanana: Poemas y canciones*. The disc can be ordered through Philips Records, "El Virrey" Industrias Musicales, S.A., Avenida Mexico #238, Lima, Peru. Among the Afro-Peruvian musical artists who are members of the Compañía are Tereza Mendoza Hernández (actress, singer), Carlos H. Ramírez (bassist, composer, and arranger), and Abelardo Vásquez Díaz (singer, actor, and drummer).
73 Nicomedes Santa Cruz Gamarra, *Antología, décimas y poemas* (Lima, 1971), pp. 51-52.
74 Schuyler, *The Pittsburgh Courier*, p. 9.
75 Robert L. Gilmore, *Caudillism and Militarism in Venezuela: 1810-1910* (Athens, 1964), p. 187.
76 Roberto Andrade, *Historia del Ecuador*, 7 vols. (Guayaquil, 1932-1937), 7: 2493-94. Donald Dozer, *Latin America: An Interpretive History* (New York, 1962), p. 320.
77 Dozer, *Latin America*, p. 320.
78 Piedad Peñaherrera de Costales and Alfredo Costales Samaniego, *Historia social del Ecuador*, 3 vols. (Quito, 1964), 1:316-17.
79 Ibid., p. 324.
80 Julio Tobar Donoso, "La abolición de la esclavitud en el Ecuador," *Boletín de la Academia Nacional de la Historia* 39 (January-June 1959): 17.
81 See chap. 9, p. 238.
82 King, "Latin American Republics," p. 407.
83 Ibid., p. 408; and Tobar Donoso, "Abolición," p. 19.
84 The 1839 figure is from Tobar Donoso, "Abolición," p. 25, while the 1852 figure is from Peñaherrera de Costales and Costales Samaniego, *Historia*, 1:341. Tobar Donoso finds that 2,484 slaves were released in 1852 (p. 25), but since the latter account provides a regional breakdown of emancipation statistics, the figures used are theirs.
85 Peñaherrera de Costales and Costales Samaniego, *Historia*, 1:341. Tobar Donoso argues that 374,448 pesos (154 pesos per released slave) was the actual debt ("Abolición," p. 25).
86 Peñaherrera de Costales and Costales Samaniego, *Historia*, 1:341-42.
87 Tobar Donoso, "Abolición," p. 28.
88 Peñaherrera de Costales and Costales Samaniego, *Historia*, 1:343.
89 Julio Estupiñán Tello, *El negro en Esmeraldas: Apuntes para su estudio* (Quito, 1967), pp. 55-56, 58-59, 63
90 Carvalho Neto, *Estudios afros*, p. 301. Urbina called this group "my cannons" and treated them as a kind of proletarian guard. Attacks on dissident white citizens earned for the troops of the *Taura* battalion the epithet of "the black villains."
91 Peñaherrera de Costales and Costales Samaniego, *Historia*, 1:348-49.
92 Robert Gold, "Negro Colonization Schemes in Ecuador, 1861-1864," *Phylon* 19 (Fall 1969): 306-16.
93 José María Samper Aguelo, *Ensayo sobre las revoluciones políticas y la condición social de las repúblicas colombianas* (Paris, 1861), p. 305.
94 Luis T. Pax y Mino, *La población del Ecuador* (Quito, 1942), p. 37.
95 Lilo Linke, *Ecuador: A Country of Contrasts* (London, 1954), pp. 10-11.
96 John V. D. Saunders, *La población del Ecuador: Un análisis del censo de 1950* (Quito, 1950), p. 37. The population was categorized as to whether they wore shoes or sandals, or whether they slept in beds.
97 On the racial bias encountered by Francisco Eugenio de Santa Cruz y Espejo, see Linke, *Ecuador*, p. 19; and Mariano Picón-Sales, *A Cultural History of*

Spanish America: From the Conquest to Independence (Berkeley, 1963), p. 153.

98   Oscar Efrem Reyes, *Breve historia general del Ecuador*, 2 vols. (Quito, 1942), 2:39-48. Curiously, Reyes never mentioned that Santa Cruz y Espejo had any African blood!

99   Alfredo Espinosa Tamayo, *Psicología y sociología del pueblo ecuatoriano* (Guayaquil, 1918), p. 39. This author confidently predicted the disappearance of the blacks but was evasive concerning mulattoes.

100   Misael Acosta Solís, *Nuevas contribuciones al conocimiento de la provincia de Esmeraldas*, 2 vols. (Quito, 1944), 1:534.

101   Alfredo Fuentes Roldán, "San Lorenzo: Puerto marítimo de población negra," *Boletín de Informaciones Científicas Nacionales* 10 (November-December 1958): 372. That poor medical care or diet may have had a major effect on the perceived behavior of the Afro-Ecuadoreans in San Lorenzo would seem to have escaped this author's consideration.

102   Andrade, *Historia*, 3:2493.

103   Ibid., 3:2492-93.

104   Piedad Peñaherrera de Costales and Alfredo Costales Samaniego, *Cuanque, historia cultural y social de los negros del Chota y Salinas* (Quito, 1959), p. 56. Of the 21,358 persons in the districts noted, 9,228 were counted by the researchers as blacks, mulattoes, and *zambos*. This work should probably be considered the first scientific study of Negroid peoples in Ecuadorean history.

105   Ibid., p. 185. These authors also concluded that the Afro-Ecuadoreans studied seemed resigned to their problems, the major one being that the sterility of the land made great economic advancement impossible.

106   Fuentes Roldán, "San Lorenzo," p. 382.

107   Norman E. Whitten, Jr., *Class, Kinship and Power in an Ecuadorean Town: The Negroes of San Lorenzo* (Stanford, 1965), p. 31.

108   Ibid., pp. 56, 58, 87, 90.

109   Pablo Adalberto Ortiz, "La negritude en la cultura latinoamericana," *Expresiones culturales del Ecuador* 1 (noviembre-deciembre 1972): 16. Ortiz holds that the province was ruined in the civil wars that ended when Eloy Alfaro seized the presidency in 1895. Poor relations between the province and the capital seem to date from that event.

110   Estupiñán Tello, *Negro*, p. 102.

111   "Vergüenza," Ibid., p. 161.

112   On the changes which have come to Esmeraldas Province and the sufferings of the Negroid population especially in San Lorenzo (Esmeraldas), see Norman E. Whitten, Jr., *Black Frontiersman: A South American Case* (Cambridge, 1974), pp. 187-94.

113   Ibid., pp. 191-92. Whitten sums it up in this way: "Although the vast majority of black people will be (and are now) on the bottom of the hierarchy, there will be enough black and mulatto people in the middle (but not on top) to allow the casual observer to state that the problem is one of class relations, not race relations. But upward mobility for the few in no way negates the point of general black disenfranchisement."

114   Fuentes Roldán, "San Lorenzo," p. 372. He deals with the establishment of the *Centro de Investigaciones Indigenistas* ("Indian Research Center") in particular in "Programas indigenistas ecuatorianos: 1954-58," *América Indígena* 19 (October 1959): 289.

115   César Astudillo, "Clases y castas en el Ecuador," in República del Ecuador, Junta Nacional de Planificación y Coordinación Económica, *Memorias del Primero Congreso de Sociología Ecuatoriana*, 2 vols. (Cuenca, 1959-1960), 2:295.

9. Negroid Peoples in Colombia and Venezuela

1 Jaime Jaramillo Uribe, "La controversia jurídica y filosófica librada en la Nueva Granada en torno a la liberación de los esclavos y la importancia económica-social de la esclavitud en el siglo XIX," *Anuario Colombiano de Historia Social y de la Cultura* 4 (Bogotá, 1969), p. 65. The breakdown was Popayán, 12,441; Antioquia, 8,791; Mariquita, 4,003; and Chocó, 5,916. Slaves represented 38.7 percent of the total population of Chocó Province.

2 Vicente Restrepo, *Estudio sobre las minas de oro y plata de Colombia* (Bogotá, 1952), pp. 210-11.

3 On the shift to free labor in Antioquia because of slave shortages, see James J. Parsons, *Antioqueño Colonization in Western Colombia* (Berkeley, 1968), p. 52; and William F. Sharp, "El negro en Colombia: Manumisión y posición social," *Razón y Fábula* 8 (July-August 1968): 92. Why the system collapsed in Antioquia but not in Cauca or Chocó has never been explained. Sharp suggests that feeding the slaves had been the work of the Indians, and the decline of the indigenous population meant that the slave gangs could no longer be maintained (Ibid.).

4 When in 1819 Bolívar became president of Gran Colombia, Santander became vice-president of the same region and governor of the center state in the federation, New Granada (later Colombia).

5 Vicente Lecuna and Harold A. Bierck, eds. *Selected Writings of Bolívar*, 2 vols. (New York, 1951), 1:222-23.

6 Sharp, "El negro," pp. 95, 97.

7 Ibid., p. 94.

8 Jaramillo Uribe, "Controversia," p. 67.

9 Ibid.

10 Sharp, "El negro," p. 98.

11 Antonio José Galvis Noyes, "La esclavitud en Colombia durante el período republicano (1825-1851)," *Universitas Humanísticas*, nos. 5, 6 (December 1973): 228. On the resistance of the slaveholders to these *juntas*, see Sharp, "El negro," p. 97.

12 Galvis Noyes, "Esclavitud," p. 228. These figures were from the census taken in 1825, but they were not presented to the congress until 1827. Dr. José Manuel Restrepo reported that there were more slaves in Colombia than those revealed in the official tabulation, but many owners refused to report the full number of slaves they owned because they feared possible conscription of the males and higher taxes. Moreover, the census total cited does not include Venezuelan or Ecuadorean bondmen.

13 As far as I know, Williams, Bartlett, and Miller are the only authors who state specifically that the July 1821 laws were not reenacted (Mary W. Williams, Ruth J. Bartlett, and Russell E. Miller, *The People and Politics of Latin America*, 4th ed. [New York, 1958], p. 527, fn.). William Gibson presents a copy of the 1832 document, and nowhere in it is there any statement referring to slavery (*The Constituions of Colombia* [Durham, 1948], pp. 118-51).

14 Great Britain, Foreign Office, *British and Foreign State Papers: 1844-45* (London, 1859), 23, p. 638.

15 James Ferguson King, "The Latin American Republics and the Suppression of the Slave Trade," *Hispanic American Review* 24 (August 1944): 407-8; Ricardo Palma, *Tradiciones peruanas completas* (Madrid, 1904), p. 141. Not until 1843 was permission sought to sell slaves, although they had been dispatched to Peru as early as 1835. According to Sharp, the petition calling for the resumption of the traffic was signed by both the bishop and the governor of Popayán ("El negro," p. 98).

16   The influence of the 1848 French and German revolutions on young Colombian liberals is best explained in Milton Puentes, *Historia del partido liberal colombiano*, 2nd ed. (Bogotá, 1962), pp. 153-54; and J. M. Henao and G. Arrubla, *History of Colombia*, trans. J. Fred Rippy (Chapel Hill, 1938), p. 457.

17   Jaramillo Uribe, "Controversia," p. 81.

18   Julio César García, "El movimiento antiesclavista en Colombia," *Boletín de Historia y Antigüedades* 41 (March-April 1954): 139. A lower estimate (1,646,000 pesos) is made by José Manuel Restrepo, *Historia de la Nueva Granada*, 3 vols. (Bogotá, 1963), 2:188-89.

19   Restrepo, *Historia de la Nueva Granada*, 2:489.

20   Jaramillo Uribe, "Controversia," p. 67-68. The six departments were Barbacoas, 2,520; Buenaventura, 1,132; Cauca, 2,949; Chocó, 1,725; and Popayán, 2,160.

21   Ibid., pp. 69-70.

22   Restrepo insists that the Chocó and Barbacoas were literally "abandoned to the free Negroes" (*Estudio*, p. 167). Sharp accepts Restrepo's interpretation ("El negro," p. 100). Jaramillo Uribe disagrees ("Controversia," p. 69), as does José Galvis Noyes ("Controversia"), concerning the damage done to the national economy as a result of the abolition of slavery. Their arguments are neither as comprehensive nor as convincing as those advanced by Restrepo.

23   Restrepo blamed "our impatient Latin race" for the rapid abolition (*Estudio*, p. 211).

24   Phanor J. Eder, *Colombia* (London, 1913), pp. 197-98.

25   *British Foreign and State Papers*, 33: 637.

26   For the story of this struggle, see John Steuart, *Bogotá in 1836-37* (New York, 1838), pp. 48-50. Mompós is situated in the present-day department of Bolívar.

27   Both the quote and the conclusion are found in Randall Hudson, "The Negro in Northern South America, 1820-1860," *Journal of Negro History* 41 (October 1964): 236, 238-39.

28   Gibson, *Constitutions*, pp. 43, 83, 162.

29   Donald E. Worchester and Wendell G. Schaeffer, *The Growth and Culture of Latin America*, 2nd ed., 2 vols. (New York, 1971), 2:235.

30   W. D. Galbraith, *Colombia: A General Survey* (Oxford, 1953), p. 22.

31   T. Lynn Smith, "The Racial Composition of the Population of Colombia," *Journal of Inter-American Studies* 8 (April 1966): 216-17.

32   Ibid., p. 218.

33   A confidential letter of 14 June 1971 listed these figures as the 1964 census projection provided by the *Departamento Administrativo National de Estadística*.

34   Smith, "Racial Composition," p. 215.

35   Thomas G. Sanders, "The Blacks of Colombia's Chocó," *American Universities Field Staff, West Coast South American Countries* 17 (January 1970): 1. *The Europa Yearbook: 1971* gives the estimated Colombian population as 20 to 21 million in 1970 ([London, 1971], p. 376). Keeping in mind the percentages discussed on pages 242 and 243 of the present study, the estimated number of blacks, mulattoes, and *zambos* must be 5 to 6 million. This would easily give Colombia the largest Spanish-speaking Negroid population.

36   The Afro-Colombian population on the Caribbean is concentrated in the departments of Atlántico, Bolívar, and Guajira.

37   Galbraith, *Colombia*, p. 23.

38   Ramón Franco R., *Antropogeografía colombiana* (Manizales, 1941), p. 194.

39   Juan Luis Lannoy and Gustavo Pérez, *Estructuras demográficas y sociales de Colombia* (Madrid, 1961), p. 50.
40   Aquiles Escalante, *El negro en Colombia* (Bogotá, 1964); José Rafael Arboleda, "La historia y la antropología del negro en Colombia," *América Latina* 5 (July-September 1962): 3-17; idem, "Nuevas investigaciones afro-colombianas," *Revista Javeriana* 34 (May 1952): 197-206; Jaime Jaramillo Uribe, "Esclavos y señores en la sociedad colombiana del siglo XVIII," *Anuario Colombiano de Historia Social y de la Cultura* 1, no. 1 (1963); idem, "Controversia," pp. 63-86.
41   Thomas J. Price, "Saints and Spirits: A Study of Differential Acculturation in Colombian Negro Communities," (Ph.D. diss., Northwestern University, 1955), pp. 23-24; idem, "How Three Negro Cultures View Their African Heritage," *Trans-Action* 5 (July-August 1968): 73-75.
42   Sidney Kronus and Mauricio Solaún, *Discrimination without Violence: Miscegenation and Racial Conflict in Latin America* (New York, 1973), p. ix. This is the definition of what Professors Kronus and Solaún call the "infused racial system."
43   Ibid., p. 6. See pages 4 to 11 for a general discussion of the signs of racial prejudice.
44   Ibid., p. 128. The authors state that the lower class is "virtually devoid of whites," and the figures presented show none at all (Ibid., p. 119). There is no discussion of what would happen if the more successful blacks chose to oppose the social situation described.
45   Ibid., pp. viii, 4, 6, 24, 34-35, 143-44, 184, 220. In a letter dated 15 May 1974, I asked Professor Solaún whether there existed tension between blacks and mulattoes of the same economic classes since the latter were more likely to be "bleached" than the former. In his letter of 29 May 1974, Professor Solaún replied in the negative.
46   William C. Sayres, "Racial Mixture and Cultural Evaluation in a Rural Colombian Community," *América Indígena* 16 (June 1956): 228-29.
47   Ibid., p. 222.
48   Paul D. Pavy, III, "The Negro in Western Colombia" (Ph.D. diss., Tulane University, 1967), p. 186.
49   Sanders, "Blacks," p. 4. Of some 200,000 persons in the department of Chocó, 80 percent were considered black; 10 percent mulatto; 6 percent Indian; and 4 percent white or *mestizo* (Ibid., p. 1).
50   Ibid., pp. 6-7. Professor Sanders was actually "detained without adequate explanation" by the Quibdó police chief. They later told him that some local whites believed that he "might represent Black Power groups in the United States." The incident described in the chapter was confirmed in an interview that took place 10 October 1973, East Lansing, Michigan.
51   George Schuyler, *Pittsburgh Courier*, 14 August 1948, p. 14.
52   Arnoldo Palacios, *Las estrellas son negras* (Bogotá, 1949), p. 97.
53   Ibid., p. 42.
54   Manuel Zapata Olivella, *Corral de negros* (Cuba, 1965), pp. 189-91.
55   See Colombian recording by Lenor González Mina, "Cantos de mi tierra y de mi raza," Industria Electro Sonora Ltda., *Sonolux/LP* R-420, IES 13-38.
56   John V. Lombardi, "Manumission, *Manumisos* and *Aprendizaje* in Republican Venezuela," *Hispanic American Historical Review* 59 (November 1969): 670.
57   See chap. 7, p.   .
58   For a discussion of the mismanagement of the manumission program see John V. Lombardi, *The Decline and Abolition of Negro Slavery in Venezuela* (Westport, Conn., 1971), pp. 50-64.

59 Guillermo Morón, *A History of Venezuela*, ed. and trans. John Street (New York, 1963), p. 163. A similar conclusion is stated in Lombardi, *Decline*, pp. 136-37.
60 Lombardi, *Decline*, p. 161.
61 See chap. 3, table 3, p. 95.
62 Laureano Vallenilla Lanz, *Cesarismo democrático: Estudios sobre las bases sociológicas de la constitución efectiva de Venezuela*, 4th ed. (Caracas, 1961), pp. 10-11; Federico Brito Figueroa, *La estructura social y demografía de Venezuela colonial* (Caracas, 1961), p. 58.
63 Lombardi, *Decline*, pp. 154-55. This total includes slaves freed through purchase and through cancellation of tax debts.
64 Jane Lucas de Grummond, ed., *Caracas Diary: 1835-1840* (Baton Rouge, 1954), p. 57
65 Vallenilla Lanz, *Cesarismo*, p. 100.
66 Lucas de Grummond, *Caracas Diary*, p. 57.
67 William R. Manning, ed., *Diplomatic Correspondence of the United States — Inter-American Affairs, 1830-1860*, 12 vols. (Washington, 1939), 12:546. The diplomat in question was Allen A. Hall.
68 Lucas de Grummond, *Caracas Diary*, p. 218.
69 Manning, *Diplomatic Correspondence*, 12:545-46.
70 Ibid., p. 550; see also p. 548.
71 Robert L. Gilmore, *Caudillism and Militarism in Venezuela: 1810-1910* (Athens, 1964), p. 40.
72 Ibid. Guzmán Blanco took over in 1870 and ruled until 1888.
73 Brito Figueroa, *Estructura social*, p. 58.
74 A letter from John V. Lombardi confirmed this conclusion (8 June 1972, Indiana University, Bloomington, Indiana).
75 Miguel Acosta Saignes, "Los descendientes de africanos y la formación de la nacionalidad en Venezuela," *Anuario, Instituto de Antropología e Historia, Universidad Central de Venezuela*, 3 (1966): 39-40.
76 Henry J. Allen, *Venezuela: A Democracy* (New York, 1941), p. 65.
77 José Gil Fortoul, *El hombre y la historia: Ensayo de la sociología venezolana* (Paris, 1896), p. 24.
78 Ibid., p. 27.
79 Ángel Rosenblat, *La población indígena de América desde 1492 hasta la actualidad* (Buenos Aires, 1945), 20-21.
80 Guillermo Morón, *Una historia de Venezuela*, 3rd ed. (Caracas, 1961), p. 136. The introductory page of this work lists it as an official textbook for use in secondary schools.
81 Miguel Ángel Mudarra and Ana Adelina Ruiz de Nazoa, *Manual de venezolanidad para extranjeros* (Caracas, 1964), p. 58.
82 Vallenilla Lanz, *Cesarismo*, pp. 149-84, 207-209. The work was originally written in 1917, but a later edition was used primarily because it included important letters.
83 Ibid., pp. 213-14.
84 *Boletín de la Cámara de Comercio de Caracas* 13 (1 October 1924): 2578.
85 Edwin Lieuwen, *Venezuela*, 3rd ed. (London, 1969), p. 12. The 1929 decree banned African immigration. The 1936 law banned both African and Asian immigration. Nevertheless, some 2,500 Negroids from the East Indies apparently entered the country through the West Indies between 1929 and 1936 (Víctor Audera, *La población y la inmigración en Hispano-America* [Madrid, 1955], p. 98).
86 Alberto Andriani, *Labor venezolanista*, 2nd ed. (Merida, 1962), pp. 56-58.

87 Levi Marrero, *Venezuela y sus recursos: Una geografía visualizada* (Caracas, 1964), p. 232.
88 George Schuyler, *Pittsburgh Courier*, 24 July 1948, p. 16.
89 Rufino Blanco-Fombona, *El hombre de oro* (Madrid: Compañía Ibero-Americana, 1930), p. 66. The chapter is appropriately entitled, "The Crustacean."
90 See Romulo Gallegos, *La Trepadora* (1925) and *Pobre negro* (1937). Also notable in this regard is Artur Uslar Pietri, *Las lanzas coloradas* (1949.
91 Marrero, *Venezuela*, pp. 231-32.
92 Ibid., p. 222. See also p. 233, where the restrictive immigration policy is referred to as "selective immigration."

10. Negroid Peoples in Central America and Mexico

1 For the full details concerning the emancipation of slaves in Central America, see José Antonio Cevallos, *Recuerdos salvadoreños*, 2nd ed., 2 vols. (San Salvador, 1964), 2:96. A more enthusiastic but less informative version of the abolition of slavery is seen in Daniel Contreras and Carlos Martínez Durán, "La abolición de la esclavitud en Centroamérica," *Journal of Inter-American Studies* 4 (April 1962): 223-36.
2 L. Cardoza y Aragón, *Guatemala* (Mexico, D.F., 1965), pp. 391-92; Quince Duncan and Carlos Meléndez, *El negro en Costa Rica* (San José, 1972), p. 40.
3 For details on indemnification, see Ramón López Jiménez, *José Simeón Cañas* (San Salvador, 1967), pp. 425-29, 522; and Duncan and Meléndez, *El negro*, p. 40.
4 Duncan and Meléndez, *El negro*, p. 41; Cardoza y Aragón, *Guatemala*, p. 392.
5 Cardoza y Aragón, *Guatemala*, p. 392.
6 Recall the sambo-mosquitos, as the Spaniards called them (chap. 4, pp. 108-109).
7 Rodolfo Barón Castro, *La población de El Salvador...* (Madrid, 1942), p. 154. He argues that by 1613 there were so many blacks in El Salvador that there was fear of a general racial uprising. There were at least 4,000 to 5,000 by 1650.
8 El Salvador, Dirección General de Estadística, *El censo de 1930* (San Salvador, 1932), p. 18. There were 46 males and 26 females listed, and there is no explanation as to whether mulattoes and Afro-Indians were counted as *mestizos* or *negros*.
9 Barón Castro, *Población*, pp. 273, 526; and Ángel Rosenblat, *La población indígena de América desde 1492 hasta la actualidad* (Buenos Aires, 1945), 20-21. Rosenblat suggests that there were less than 200 blacks and mulattoes in El Salvador. Donald D. Brand reported the African population at less than 170. He does not indicate whether *zambos* or mulattoes are included in the category of Negro (ed., "The Present Indian Population of Latin America," in *Some Educational and Anthropological Aspects of Latin America* [Austin, 1951], p. 51). In any case, all these authors saw more Negroid persons than the census takers of 1930.
10 In a confidential letter I received on 14 June 1971, the following information was included: "Black persons are now allowed to travel from the airport [into the capital of San Salvador] but... permanent residence is frowned upon." See also República de El Salvador, Proveedora del Contador Centroamericano, *Recopilación de leyes administrativas*, Decreto #2772 (San Salvador, 1970), pp. 313-33. The most recent immigration-control law was written in December 1958 and, as republished in 1970, it contains no articles specifically prohibiting Negroid immigration or settlement. Section III, article 36, however, seeks racial information from prospective entrants.

11 On the presence of the blacks and mulattoes in the old Captaincy General of Guatemala, see Chester L. Jones, *Guatemala, Past and Present* (Minneapolis, 1940), pp. 131, 268-71; and J. Kunst, "Notes on Negroes in Guatemala during the Seventeenth Century," *Journal of Negro History* 4 (October 1916): 390-97.

12 Dirección General de Estadística de Guatemala, *Quinto censo general de población* (Ciudad Guatemala, C.A., 1942), n.p.

13 On this exclusion policy, see Great Britain, Foreign Office, *British and Foreign State Papers* (London, 1948), 140: 535; and (London, 1955), 149, p. 702. Discussion of the 1945 constitutional statute (originally written as a law in December 1944) is found in Laudelino Moreno, *Derecho consular guatemalteco* (Guatemala, C.A., 1946), pp. 186-87. Article 10 of the *Amended Law of Foreigners* bans "individuals of the black race" and Chinese, although the law is so written as to allow certain exceptions.

14 Franklin D. Parker, *The Central American Republics* (London, 1964), pp. 181-82.

15 William Welles estimated the black and mulatto population to be 35 percent of the whole (*Explorations and Adventures in Honduras* [New York, 1887], p. 554). Robert G. Dunlap put the figure at 10 percent (*Travels in Central America* [London, 1847], p. 334).

16 The 1945 census represents the last time the Republic of Honduras made a racial tabulation of its population. See William S. Stokes, who interprets *mestizo* to mean white-Indian hybrid (*Honduras: An Area Study in Government* [Madison, 1950], p. 14).

17 Parker, *Central American Republics*, p. 182.

18 Pan American Union, General Secretariat of the Organization of American States, General Legal Division, Department of International Law, *A Statement of the Laws of Honduras in Matters Affecting Business*, 3rd ed. (Washington, D.C., 1965), p. 4. The law of March 1934 also prohibits the settlement of Palestinians, Syrians, Lebanese, and Czechs unless they provide "satisfactory guarantees" that they will be engaged exclusively in agriculture or in the introduction of new industries.

19 Carolina de Campbell and Ofelia Hooper, "The Middle Class of Panama," in Unión Panamérica, *Materiales para el estudio de la clase media en América latina*, 6 vols. (Washington, D.C., 1950), 4:34; and Brand, "Indian Population," p. 51.

20 Campbell and Hooper, "Middle Class," p. 34.

21 Great Britain, Foreign Office *British Foreign and State Papers: 1844-45* (London, 1859), 154, p. 458. The Constitution of November 1940 prohibited the immigration of persons of "the negro race whose original language is not Spanish, the yellow race, and races originating in India, Asia Minor and North Africa" (chap. 2, art. 23). The presidency of Arnulfo Arias Madrid came to an end in 1941, and this constitution, therefore, never went into effect. The Constitution of 1946 has similar articles regarding the necessity for potential immigrants to demonstrate a familiarity with the Spanish language and culture, but no racial barriers are specifically stated (chap. 2, art. 11-14). The charge that these constitutional articles are designed to effect the same result without specifically mentioning West Indians is supported by Jean Gilbreath Niemeier, *The Panama Story* (Portland, 1968), p. 197.

22 República de Nicaragua, Oficina Central del Censo, *Censo general de 1920* (Managua, 1920), p. 8. See pages 7 to 10 for totals and a discussion of the materials.

23 Pan American Union, General Secretariat of the Organization of American States, General Legal Division, Department of International Law, *A Statement of the Laws of Nicaragua in Matters Affecting Business*, 3rd ed. (Washington,

D.C., 1965), p. 10. Armenians and inhabitants of the Middle East were also included in the ban.

24 República de Costa Rica, Ministerio de Economía y Hacienda, Dirección General de Estadística y Censos, *Monografía de la población de la República de Costa Rica en el siglo XIX* (San José, 1951), pp. 3-4.

25 República de Costa Rica, Ministerio de Economía y Hacienda, Dirección General de Estadística y Censos, *1950 censo de población* (San José, 1953), p. 87.

26 República de Costa Rica, *Colección de leyes y decretos — Año 1911, segundo semestre* (San José, 1912), pp. 172-79; idem, *Colección de leyes, decretos, acuerdos y resoluciones — Año 1942, primer semestre* (San José, 1942), p. 176. See especially article 41, which also bars "Chinese, Arabs, Turks, Syrians, gypsies, and coolies."

27 Pablo Lévy, *Nicaragua* (Paris, 1872), pp. 223, 231.

28 Rafael Helidoro Valle, *Semblanza de Honduras* (Tegucigalpa, 1947?), p. 153.

29 Ibid., pp. 170-71.

30 A good study on the Guatemala-Belize question is found in L. H. Bloomfield, *The British Honduras-Guatemala Dispute* (Toronto, 1953).

31 The Chiriqui territory was an area on the present Costa Rica-Panama border, extending from the Caribbean to the Gulf of Dulce on the Pacific. Rights to the settlement of the region had originally been purchased by the Chiriqui Company, an organization masterminded by Ambrose W. Thompson.

32 Paul J. Scheips, "Lincoln and the Chiriqui Colonization Project," *Journal of Negro History* 37 (October, 1952): 452; see also pp. 441-44.

33 This secret report was drawn up by three American ministers meeting in Ostend, Belgium, and was sent to the secretary of State. It proclaimed that if Spain would not sell Cuba to the United States, then the United States had a right to take the island. To the chagrin of the manifesto's authors, word of its existence was leaked to the press, and the secretary of State had to disavow its proposals.

34 Salvador Mendieta, *La enfermedad de Centro América*, 2 vols. (Barcelona, 1934), 1:65.

35 William L. Stokes, *Latin American Politics* (New York, 1959), p. 16.

36 Pedro S. Fonseca, *Demografía salvadoreña* (San Salvador, 1921), p. 48. Fonseca was one of the persons in charge of conducting the 1930 census, which reported that 2.1 percent of the population was white and 92.3 percent was *mestizo*. It seems evident that the opinions he expressed in 1921 were primarily intended to make the population believe that it was becoming whiter.

37 Sonfonías Salvatierra, "Ensayo sobre la clase media en Nicaragua," in Unión Panamericana, *Materiales para el estudio de la clase media en América latina*, 6 vols. (Washington, D.C., 1950) 4:95.

38 Humberto López Villanil, "Estudio de la clase media de Honduras," in Unión Panamericana, *Materiales para el estudio de la clase media en América latina*, 6 vols. (Washington, D.C., 1950) 4:80.

39 H. Blutstein, et al., *Area Handbook of Honduras* (Washington, D.C., 1971), pp. 54, 66, 132; Parker, *Central American Republics*, p. 90. There were at least 1,116 descendants of the *sambo-mosquitos* on the coast of Guatemala in 1950. There are also approximately 12,000 black Caribs on the northern coast of Honduras and in the Bay Islands, according to Blutstein (p. 66). No figures are available on the numbers in Costa Rica and Nicaragua.

40 Blutstein, et al., *Area Handbook*, p. 67. There are at least 7,800 black and mulatto inhabitants in the Bay Islands (*Islas de la Bahia*).

41 República de Costa Rica, Ministerio de Economía y Hacienda, Dirección General de Estadística y Censos, *Censo de población de Costa Rica — 11 de mayo de 1927* (San José, 1960), pp. 41, 90. Of these, 1,113 were described as blacks

and the rest as mulattoes. The same census points out that only 607 blacks were considered citizens. Since Negroids from Limón Province were not allowed to live on the *meseta central*, almost all the black citizens were probably from the Pacific coast. The 1936 figure is from Leo Waibel, "White Settlement in Costa Rica," *Geographical Review* 39 (October 1939): 549.

42 Duncan and Meléndez, *El negro*, p. 72. By 1892 the figure had decreased to 544 Jamaicans in Limón and 63 in San José who were working on the railroad.

43 Ralph Hancock, *The Rainbow Republics* (New York, 1948), p. 14. Duncan and Meléndez insist that no law specifically prohibiting Jamaicans from living in the highlands existed, although a policy of exclusion was informally enforced (*El negro*, p. 77). Hancock is supported, however, by Michael D. Olien, "The Negro in Costa Rica" (Ph.D. diss., University of Oregon, Eugene, 1967), pp. 40, 105.

44 Duncan and Meléndez, *El negro*, p. 58. *Mamita Yunai* is West Indian slang for "Mama United," or United Fruit Company.

45 *Censo de población de Costa Rica — 11 de Mayo de 1927*, p. 91. Presumably the mulattoes were considered citizens, although the census fails to clarify their status in Limón Province. According to figures in Duncan and Meléndez, roughly 5.8 percent of the Limón Province Negroids were citizens (*El negro*, p. 77).

46 Olien, "The Negro," pp. 93-94.

47 Ibid., p. 99. Apparently a contracted form of *costarriqueño, tico* is a derogatory term, and, while Costa Ricans may use it in addressing each other, they frown on its use by others.

48 Duncan and Meléndez, *El negro*, pp. 77, 92. These authors make it clear that many Jamaicans considered themselves superior to the white and *mestizo* Costa Ricans.

49 Olien, "The Negro," pp. 112-13.

50 Duncan and Meléndez, *El negro*, p. 79. The government justified this law by claiming that Limón Negroids obviously did not care about going west because they did not protest against the transfer. It also claimed that the movement of the Antilleans across the country to the Pacific side would "upset the racial pattern of the country" (Olien, "The Negro," p. 113).

51 Olien, "The Negro," p. 113.

52 Duncan and Meléndez, *El negro*, p. 95.

53 Ibid., p. 222. Only five public schools were built in the entire province of Limón between 1922 and 1951. Some twenty-three private schools existed in which English was the language of instruction.

54 *Censo de población de Costa Rica — 11 de mayo de 1927*, pp. 41, 91.

55 Duncan and Meléndez, *El negro*, p. 74. Only 33.2 percent of the population of Limón Province were listed as Negroid. A smaller number of Asiatics had also moved into the province (1 percent), and 3 percent of the populace were listed as Amerindian. Consult also Olien, who provides the figures for Puerto Limón ("The Negro," p. 127).

56 Duncan and Meléndez, *El negro*, pp. 77-79, 91-92, 116-18.

57 Olien, "The Negro," p. 144.

58 Ibid., pp. 121-23.

59 Michael D. Olien, "Levels of Urban Relationships in a Complex Society: A Costa Rican Case," in Elizabeth M. Eddy, ed., *Urban Anthropology: Research Perspectives and Strategies* (Athens, 1968), pp. 85-88; Duncan and Meléndez, *El negro*, pp. 118-21.

60 Duncan and Meléndez, *El negro*, pp. 260-72. I had the pleasure of knowing Dr. Sherman T. Jackson from 1963 to 1964. He is now a professor of Chemistry at the University of Costa Rica, in San Jose.

61   Duncan and Meléndez, *El negro*, pp. 201, 205.
62   Ibid., p. 183. Marcus Garvey had actually spoken in Puerto Limón in 1921 and 1928. According to Olien, the UNIA in Puerto Limón has made it a point to stay out of local politics ("The Negro," pp. 147-49).
63   Ibid., pp. 273-74.
64   Alfredo Castillero Calvo, *La sociedad panameña: Historia de su formación e integración* (Panama City, 1970), pp. 99-100.
65   Ibid., p. 105.
66   Ibid., p. 106.
67   Ernesto J. Castillero, *Historia de Panamá*, 7th ed. (Panama City, 1962), p. 145.
68   See p. 264 of this chapter.
69   John Biensanz, "Cultural and Economic Factors in Panamanian Race Relations," *American Sociological Review* 14 (December 1949): 773.
70   See chap. 9, pp. 264,274.
71   For a history of United States intervention in Panama in November 1903, see Howard C. Hill, *Roosevelt and the Caribbean* (Chicago, 1927), pp. 68-130.
72   Duncan and Meléndez, *El negro*, p. 58.
73   Castillero Calvo, *Sociedad panameña*, p. 106. The West Indians went to work on coconut, banana, and cacao plantations at Bocas de Toro.
74   John Biensanz, "Race Relations in the Canal Zone," *Phylon* 11, no. 1 (1950): 23.
75   Ibid., pp. 24-25.
76   Gustave Anguinzola, "Negroes in the Building of the Panama Canal," *Phylon* 29, no. 4 (1968): 358.
77   See fn. 21 of this chapter.
78   Anguinzola, "Negroes," p. 359.
79   As of 1971 there were 27,000 *zonites* in Panama.
80   Biensanz, "Panamanian Race Relations," p. 776.
81   Campbell and Hooper, "Middle Class," p. 68.
82   Castillero Calvo, *Sociedad panameña*, p. 108.
83   Ibid., p. 53.
84   An often overlooked but excellent article dealing with Panamanian society is Georgina Jiménez de López, "La clase media en Panamá," in *Unión Panamericana, Materiales para el estudio de la clase media en América latina*, 6 vols. (Washington, D.C., 1950) 4: 66-68.
85   Anguinzola, "Negroes," p. 359.
86   Biensanz, "Panamanian Race Relations," p. 778.
87   The article is found in the news section of *The Crisis*, 108, no. 1 (January 1961): p. 29.
88   Alexander von Humboldt, *Political Essay on the Kingdom of New Spain*, 4 vols. (New York, 1966), 1:236.
89   Gonzalo Aguirre Beltrán, *Población negra de México, 1519-1810: Estudio etnohistórico* (Mexico, D.F., 1946), pp. 81-90.
90   Sherburn F. Cook, "The Population of Mexico in 1793," *Human Biology* 14 (December 1942): 501-503.
91   Aguirre Beltrán, *Población*, pp. 231, 236-37. This ethnologist also argues that Humboldt increased the number of *criollos* beyond all reason.
92   Moisés González Navarro, "Mestizaje in Mexico during the National Period," in Magnus Morner, ed., *Race and Class in Latin America* (New York, 1970), pp. 148-50.
93   Ibid., p. 154.
94   Ibid., pp. 150-51.
95   Rosenblat, *Población indígena*, 20-21.
96   Gonzalo Aguirre Beltrán, *Cuijla, Esbozo etnográfico de un pueblo negro* (Mex-

ico, D.F., 1958), pp. 16-28; Loyal Compton, " 'Little Africa' on Mexico's Pacific Shore," *The News* (Mexico City, D.F.) 8 August 1971, p. 10.

97   Compton, " 'Little Africa,' " p. 11.

98   Aguirre Beltrán, *Cuijla*, p. 69.

99   Many of those considered whites are really *mestizos*.

100 Ibid., pp. 69-73.

101 Ibid., p. 132.

102 Compton, " 'Little Africa,' " p. 11. In July and August 1974 Professors David Bailey (Michigan State University) and William Beazley (North Carolina State University) performed special research in the state archives and Catholic church parish records in the city of Saltillo (Coahuila). They discovered that during the eighteenth century a large group of blacks and mulattoes were brought to Coahuila. These people disappeared, but these researchers were unable to discover why. Evidence uncovered by them in the state archives suggests that a troublesome group of "Indians" (the *mascojo* or *mascogo*), located about 200 or 220 kilometers north of Saltillo, are not Indians at all, but persons of black and Afro-Indian blood. These people may well be the descendants of some of the blacks and mulattoes brought into Coahuila during the eighteenth century. If this information is essentially correct, the claim of Gonzalo Aguirre Beltrán to the effect that after emancipation the Afro-Mexican "hid himself" can be adjudged as provisionally valid ("La etnohistoria y el estudio del negro en México," in Sol Tax, ed. *Acculturation in the Americas*, 3 vols. [Chicago, 1962], 2:166). This theory might also be qualified in the sense that the Afro-Mexican not only hid himself; intentionally or unintentionally, he has also been hidden.

103 Ángel Rosenblat, *La población y el mestizaje en América*, 2 vols. (Buenos Aires, 1954), 1:142. For the story of Yanga, see chapter 4, page 106 of the present text.

104 Compton, " 'Little Africa,' " p. 11.

105 An excellent discussion of the *indigenismo* movement in Mexico can be found in Victor Alba, *Las ideas sociales contemporáneas en México* (Mexico, D.F., 1960), pp. 345-57, 405-38.

106 Aguirre Beltrán, "Etnohistoria," p. 166.

11. Negroid Peoples in Santo Domingo and Cuba

1   Sumner Welles, *Naboth's Vineyard: The Dominican Republic, 1884-1924*, 2 vols. (New York, 1928), 2:901.

2   José G. García, *Compendio del la historia de Santo Domingo*, 3rd ed., 4 vols. (Santo Domingo, 1893), 2:121-22.

3   Harry Hoetink, "Materiales para el estudio de la República Dominicana en la segunda mitad del siglo XIX," *Caribbean Studies* 8 (October 1967): 4; idem, "Americans in Samaná," *Caribbean Studies* 2 (April 1962): 3-23.

4   These issues are discussed in depth by Franklyn J. Franco Pichardo, *Los negros, los mulatos y la nación dominicana*, 2nd ed. (Santo Domingo, 1970), pp. 142-43, 149.

5   Ibid., pp. 146, 161.

6   Ibid., p. 161. As a result of independence in 1844, Franco Pichardo concludes that "formal inequality" among the races ended. Since then there has been "informal inequality" (p. 162).

7   Spain reestablished its rule over Santo Domingo between 1861 and 1865. The United States government exercised a protectorate over Santo Domingo between 1916 and 1924.

8   Harry Hoetink, "The Dominican Republic in the Nineteenth Century: Some
    Notes on Stratification, Immigration and Race," in Magnus Mörner, ed., *Race
    and Class in Latin America* (New York, 1970), Gregorio Luperón, *Notas auto-
    biográficas y apuntes históricos*, 2nd ed., 3 vols. (Santiago, 1939), 3:250-51.
9   Luperón, *Notas*, 3:345.
10 Hoetink, "Dominican Republic," p. 119.
11 Rayford W. Logan, *Haiti and the Dominican Republic* (New York, 1968), p.
    14, fn.
12 Ibid., p. 16.
13 Ibid.
14 Confidential letter, 14 June 1971. In this source, the population was estab-
    lished at 70 percent mulatto, 15 percent white, and 15 percent black. See also
    Eugenio Chang-Rodríguez, *The Lingering Crisis: A Case Study of the Domini-
    can Republic* (New York, 1969), p. 103. The figures given here are 65 percent
    mulatto, 20 percent black, and 15 percent white.
15 Logan, *Haiti*, p. 17.
16 Howard J. Wiarda, *The Dominican Republic: Nation in Transition* (London,
    1969), p. 100.
17 Ibid., p. 75.
18 M. A. Mejía Ricart, *Las clases sociales en Santo Domingo* (Ciudad Trujillo,
    1953), pp. 27-28.
19 Welles, *Naboth's Vineyard*, 2:909.
20 Hoetink, "Dominican Republic," p. 116.
21 Pedro Andrés Pérez Cabral, *La comunidad mulata* (Caracas, 1967), pp. 27,
    51-52, 147, fn.
22 By terms of the 1763 Peace of Paris, Havana was returned to Spain.
23 Franklin W. Knight, *Slave Society in Cuba during the Nineteenth Century*
    (Madison, 1970), p. 22.
24 H. H. S. Aimes, *A History of Slavery in Cuba: 1511 to 1868*, Octagon Books
    Edition (New York, 1967), p. 269.
25 Robert Madden, *Poems by a Slave on the Island of Cuba* (London, 1849), p.
    45.
26 The United States had formally prohibited the participation of its citizens in
    any external slave trade in 1808. But in keeping with its "freedom of the seas"
    position, it refused to allow any nation to stop ships flying Old Glory. Thus
    slaves used the United States flag often, and, rather than force a confronta-
    tion, the British declined to press the issue.
27 On Spanish laxity in law enforcement, see David Turnbull, *Cuba: With Notices
    of Porto Rico and Slave Trade*, Negro Universities Press Edition (New York,
    1969), pp. 590-60; Phillip S. Foner, *A History of Cuba and its Relations with
    the United States*, 2 vols. (New York, 1962), 1:187; Hugh Thomas, *Cuba: The
    Pursuit of Freedom* (New York, 1971), p. 165; and Knight, *Slave Society*, pp.
    52-53.
28 Knight, *Slave Society*, p. 22.
29 Thomas, *Cuba*, pp. 186-87.
30 Ibid., p. 181.
31 Robert Madden, *The Island of Cuba: Its Resources, Progress and Prospects*
    (London, 1849), p. 39.
32 For a discussion of this question, see Knight, *Slave Society*, p. 57; and
    Thomas, *Cuba*, p. 170.
33 Turnbull, *Cuba*, p. 48.
34 See Ibid., p. 63; and especially Ortiz Fernández, *Hampa afro-cubana: Los
    negros esclavos; Estudio sociológico y de derecho publico* (Havana, 1916), p.
    306.
35 Ortiz Fernández, *Hampa afro-cubana*, p. 199, fn. 2.

36 Ibid., pp. 220-21.
37 Esteban Montejo, *The Autobiography of a Runaway Slave* (New York, 1968), p. 23.
38 See chap. 3, pp. 83-86
39 On the 1842 code, see Gwendolyn Midlo Hall, *Social Control in Slave Plantation Societies: A Comparison of St. Domingue and Cuba* (Baltimore, 1971), pp. 108-9; and Knight, *Slave Society*, pp. 130-31.
40 Thomas, *Cuba*, pp. 181, 223; Knight, *Slave Society*, p. 58. The 1854 registration decree was not enforced; only after 1866 were slaves annually registered on Cuban plantations.
41 African religion as manifested in Cuba was often of *yoruba* origin and was called *santeria*. Members (called *ñáñigos*) of a semireligious secret society (*Abakua*), complete with witch doctors, participated in bloody sacrifices and black magic ceremonies at least until 1959.
42 Montejo, *Autobiography*, p. 26; Thomas, *Cuba*, p. 176.
43 Elias Entregalia, "Los fenómenos raciales en la emancipación de Cuba," in *El movimiento emancipador de Hispanoamérica*, 4 vols. (Caracas, 1961), 3:329.
44 Ortiz Fernández, *Hampa afro-cubana*, p. 432.
45 Roland T. Ely, *Cuando reinaba su majestad, el azúcar* (Buenos Aires, 1963), p. 497.
46 Knight, *Slave Society*, pp. 171-72.
47 Hall, *Social Control*, p. 135. Knight found that 363,000 slaves were held in 1869, but this number dropped to "less than 228,000" by 1878 (*Slave Society*, p. 177).
48 Knight, *Slave Society*, p. 178; Corwin, *Spain*, p. 311.
49 Thomas, *Cuba*, p. 280.
50 Herbert Klein, *Slavery in the Americas: A Comparative Study of Virginia and Cuba* (Chicago, 1967), pp. 162-64; Thomas, *Cuba*, p. 172.
51 For these argumentative theories, see José Antonio Saco, *Historia de la esclavitud de la raza africana en el Nuevo Mundo y en especial en los países américohispanos*, 4 vols. (Havana, 1938), 4:249; and Foner, *History*, 1:196-97.
52 Jacinto de Salas y Quiroga, *Viajes de Don Jacinto de Salas y Quiroga* (Madrid, 1840), p. 253.
53 José Antonio Saco, *Contra la anexación*, 2 vols. (Havana, 1934), 1:82, 224.
54 Alberto Arredondo, *El negro en Cuba* (Havana, 1939), p. 48.
55 Ibid.
56 Ibid., p. 34.
57 Ibid., p. 48.
58 Knight, *Slave Society*, p. 97; Thomas, *Cuba*, p. 186. According to the latter source, free Negroids "generally would do anything, even nothing, rather than work on sugar plantations: far better to sit and starve in Havana than work in any capacity on a sugar estate."
59 Hall, *Social Control*, p. 128.
60 Ibid., pp. 128-29.
61 Ibid., p. 130.
62 Thomas, *Cuba*, p. 205; Aimes, *Slavery in Cuba*, p. 146; Foner, *History*, 1:216-17. Knight claims that only 3,000 persons were arrested, but that 300 were flogged to death (*Slave Society*, p. 81).
63 Knight denies that the threat of an alleged revolt had any basis in fact (*Slave Society*, p. 81). Hall leaves the question in abeyance (*Social Control*, pp. 57-58, 129-30). Thomas believes that a real conspiracy existed (*Cuba*, p. 205).
64 Hall, *Social Control*, pp. 126-27.
65 Ely, *Cuando reinaba su majestad*, p. 498.
66 Thomas, *Cuba*, p. 205.
67 Pedro Deschamps Chapeaux, *El negro en el periodismo cubano en el siglo*

XIX: Ensayo bibliográfico (Havana, 1963), p. 50. Another such newspaper did not appear until Martín Morúa Delgado published *El Pueblo* in 1879 (Ibid., p. 180).

68 Hall, *Social Control*, p. 132.
69 Thomas, *Cuba*, p. 265.
70 In February 1901 Secretary of State Elihu Root forwarded a letter to General Leonard Wood, military governor of Cuba, proposing that the island be made an independent nation, but that the United States maintain control over it because of its strategic geographical position and agricultural produce. Root's plan was redrafted by a Senate committee headed by Colorado Senator Orville H. Platt and was attached as a rider to the Army Appropriation Act of 1901. As adopted, it provided, among other things, that the Republic of Cuba (1) sign no treaty that would tend to impair its sovereignty, nor allow any nation (except the United States) to establish military bases on its soil; (2) consent to the right of intervention by the United States for the purpose of preserving Cuban independence or maintaining a government that would adequately protect life, individual liberty, and property; (3) make available to the United States lands necessary for coaling or naval stations; (4) include the provisions of the Platt Amendment in a permanent treaty to be signed with the United States.
71 Montejo, *Autobiography*, pp. 216-17.
72 Thomas, *Cuba*, p. 430.
73 Victor H. Olmstead, *Cuba: Population, History and Resources — 1907*, United States Bureau of the Census (Washington, D.C., 1909), pp. 225-26.
74 Leopoldo Horrego Estuch, *Martín Morúa Delgado, vida y mensaje* (Havana, 1954), pp. 202-03.
75 Duvon C. Corbitt, "Immigration in Cuba," *Hispanic American Historical Review* 29 (May 1942): 305.
76 The story of the *Guerra pequeña de mayo* ("Little War of May"), or the "Negroes' War," is concisely related in Charles E. Chapman, *A History of the Cuban Republic: A Study in Hispanic American Politics* (New York, 1927), pp. 308-13; and in Emilio Roig de Leuchsenring, *Males y vicios de Cuba republicana: Sus causas y sus remedios* (Havana, 1959), pp. 186-88. The most complete account is found in Ramón Vasconcelos, *El General Gómez y la sedición de mayo*, 2nd ed. (Havana, 1916). Fernando Ortiz Fernández took a dim view of the affair, denouncing Esteñoz as an "adventurous politicaster" (*Hampa afro-cubana*, p. 435), but a more sympathetic view is presented in Arredondo, *El negro*, pp. 66-67.
77 Batista was apparently of mixed Negroid, Oriental, and Caucasian heritage.
78 Ramón Cabrera Torres, *Hacia la rehabilitación económica del cubano negro* (Havana, 1959), p. 6; Thomas, *Cuba*, p. 1119.
79 Gustavo E. Urrutia, "Racial Prejudice in Cuba," in Nancy Cunnard, ed., *Negro Anthology: 1931-33*, 2nd ed. (Greenwood, 1969), p. 476.
80 M. A. Pérez-Medina, "The Situation of the Negro in Cuba," in Cunnard, ed., *Anthology*, p. 480.
81 Arredondo, *El negro*, p. 64. In public parks in some interior towns, certain benches were either marked or understood to be for whites only and others for Negroids only. Afro-Cuban efforts to change this situation sparked the Trinidad incident.
82 Roig de Leuchsenring, *Males y vicios*, pp. 196-97.
83 George Schuyler, *Pittsburgh Courier*, 17 July 1948, p. 16.
84 Lowery Nelson, *Rural Cuba* (Minneapolis, 1950), p. 170.
85 Cabrera Torres, *Rehabilitación económica*, pp. 3-4.
86 For the details of this illicit immigration, see Carleton Beals, *The Crime of Cuba* (Philadelphia, 1933), p. 56; and Thomas, *Cuba*, p. 524. Ramiro Guerra y

Sánchez puts the immigration for 1913 to 1928 at slightly more than 250,000 (*Sugar and Society in the Caribbean: An Economic History of Cuban Agriculture* [New Haven, 1964], p. 145).
87 Thomas, *Cuba*, p. 1117.
88 Wyatt MacGaffey and Clifford Robert Barnett, *Twentieth Century Cuba: The Background of the Castro Revolution* (New York, 1965), p. 34; Beals, *The Crime of Cuba*, p. 56.
89 Urrutia's views on both white Cuban and white American discriminatory attitudes toward Afro-Cubans is found in Urrutia, "Racial Prejudice," pp. 474-78. For poems by Marcelino Arozarena and Regino Pedroso (the latter of black and Chinese ancestry), see Ildefonso Pereda Valdéz, *Lo negro y lo mulato en la poesía cubana* (Montevideo, 1970), pp. 32-52, 107-34, 148-62.
90 On Guillén as probable founder of the *negrismo* movement in Cuban poetry, see Jean Franco, *Spanish American Literature Since Independence* (London, 1973), pp. 179-80; and MacGaffey and Barnett, *Twentieth Century Cuba*, p. 265. Structurally, *negrismo* represented a self-conscious break with traditional Castilian verse form. Poets affecting this style utilized African words and Afro-Cuban slang and occasionally tried to employ the rhythm of African drumming patterns as a basis for new literary forms. Philosophically, *negrismo* poetry both exalted the African roots of the Cubans and championed the rights of the nation's masses. Since most blacks and mulattoes in Cuba were proletarians, these two causes could be considered essentially complimentary.
91 "Cual tiempo pasado fue mejor" in Pereda Valdés, *Lo negro y lo mulato*, p. 140.
92 Sandalio Junco attempted to enter the Cuban bakers' union, but he was refused membership. He was deported from Cuba by the Machado government, and after returning from the Soviet Union, he fronted a Trotskyite party faction that eventually became part of the *Partido Auténtico*'s labor wing (MacGaffey and Barnett, *Twentieth Century Cuba*, p. 154). For the story of this amazing individual, see Cole Blasier, "The Cuban and Chilean Communist Parties, Instruments of Soviet Policy, 1935-48" (Ph.D. diss., University of Michigan, 1956), p. 59.
93 On the problems of the Negroid lower classes in Cuba, see Lowry Nelson, "The Social Structure in Cuba," in *Materiales para el estudio de la clase media en América latina*, 6 vols. (Washington, D.C., 1950), 2:64, 71-72.
94 Arredondo, *El negro*, pp. 80-82; Cabrera Torres, *Rehabilitación económica*, pp. 2, 16.
95 C. Eric Williams, "The Contemporary Pattern of Race Relations in the Caribbean," *Phylon* 16, no. 4 (1955): 379.
96 Arredondo, *El negro*, p. 45.
97 Roig de Leuchsenring, *Males y vicios*, pp. 199, 201.
98 Ministerio de Relaciones Exteriores, Dirección de Información, *Cuba: Country Free of Segregation (Pays sans discrimination raciale)* (Havana, n.d.), p. 2.
99 Adolfo Gilly, *Inside the Cuban Revolution* (New York, 1964), p. 14.
100 Joseph A. Kahl, "The Moral Economy of a Revolutionary Society," in Irving Louis Horowitz, ed., *Cuban Communism* (New York, 1970), p. 102.
101 Elizabeth Sutherland, *The Youngest Revolution: A Personal Report on Cuba* (New York, 1969), p. 138.
102 The clearest exposition of Sutherland's views is found in Ibid., pp. 138-46.
103 Barry Reckford, *Does Fidel Eat More Than Your Father?* (New York, 1971), pp. 126-28, 135.
104 Geoffrey E. Fox, "Cuban Workers in Exile," *Trans-Action* 8 (September 1971): 24-29.
105 Juan René Bettancourt, see "Castro and the Cuban Negro," *Crisis* 67 (May 1961): 273.

106   Carlos Moore, "Le peuple noir a-t-il sa place dans la révolution cubaine,"
      Presence Africaine, no. 22 (15 December 1964): 177-230. A rebuttal to
      Moore's article was written by René Depestre and published in *Presence Afri-
      caine*, no. 36 (15 December 1965): 105-42.
107   Georgie Ann Geyer, "The Odyssey of Robert Williams," *New Republic* 164
      (20 March 1971): 15.
108   See, for example, *O Estado de São Paulo* (São Paulo, S.P., Brazil), 12 February
      1969, p. 6; or *New York Times*, 26 June 1969, p. 4.
109   John Clytus, *Blackman in Red Cuba* (Miami, 1971), p. 127.
110   This issue is discussed in Clytus, *Blackman*, p. 77; Bettancourt, "Castro," p.
      273; and Geyer, "Odyssey," p. 15.

12. The Future of the Afro-Latino

1   Richard Konetzke, ed., *Colección de documentos para la historia de la forma-
     ción social de Hispano-América*, 3 vols. in 4 (Madrid, 1953-1962), 3(2):727.
2   The only real clue to the origins of this argument is reported in Ildefonso Leal,
     "La aristocracia criolla venezolana y el Código negrero de 1789," *Revista de
     Historia* 3 (February 1961): 79-80. In 1791 two Indies officials, Francisco de
     Saavedra and Juan Ignacio Urrizar, went before the Council of the Indies in
     Madrid and argued that the *Código negro español* of 1789 was not necessary
     since Spanish treatment of slaves had always been more humane than the
     British or French. How these two officials knew their judgment was valid was
     not explained.
3   Frank Tannenbaum, *Slave and Citizen: The Negro in America* (New York,
     1947), pp. 52-54, 65, fn.; Stanley Elkins, *Slavery: A Problem in American
     Institutional and Intellectual Life* (Chicago, 1959), pp. 63, 72, 77-80; N. A.
     Micklejohn, "The Observance of Negro Slave Legislation in Colonial Nueva
     Granada" (Ph.D. diss., Columbia University, 1968), p. 323.
4   Homero Martínez Montero, "La esclavitud en el Uruguay: Contribución a su
     estudio histórico-social," *Revista Nacional* 3 (August 1940): 273; Javier Mala-
     gón, "Un documento del siglo XVIII para la historia de la esclavitud en las
     Antillas," *Miscelánea de estudios dedicados a Fernando Ortiz*, 2 vols. (Havana,
     1956), 2:968; Restrepo Canal, "Documentos," p. 492.
5   Gonzalo Vial Correa, *El africano en el reino de Chile: Ensayo histórico-jurí-
     dico* (Santiago, 1957), p. 135.
6   Gustavo Godoy, "Fernando Ortiz: Las razas y los negros," *Journal of Ameri-
     can Studies* 8 (April 1966): 243.
7   José Ezcurra Massini, "Redhibitoria y esclavos en el Río de la Plata," *Archivo
     Iberoamericano de Historia de la Medicina y Antropología Médica* 18 (1961):
     214.
8   Josefina Plá, *Hermano negro: La esclavitud en el Paraguay* (Madrid, 1972), p.
     77. Plá states without qualification that "we are able to attest for certain that
     slavery was milder in Paraguay than in any other region of Spanish America."
     She fails to buttress this assertion with any comparative statistics or relevant
     information.
9   Malagón, "Documento," p. 968.
10   Fernando Ortiz Fernández, *Hampa afro-cubana: Los negros esclavos; Estudio
     sociológico y de derecho público* (Havana, 1916), p. 179. Ortiz Fernández
     believes that slavery in the "lesser Antilles" (presumably the French, Dutch,
     and English islands) was much worse than in Cuba. He discusses slavery in
     Haiti (p. 263) but otherwise provides no evidence to justify his claim.
11   Guillermo Feliú Cruz, *La abolición de la esclavitud en Chile: Estudio histórico
     y social* (Santiago, 1942), pp. 40-41.

12 In Argentina, there was the *Tesoraría Filantrópica* (see chap. 7, p. 186), while in Venezuela, there was the apprenticeship program of 1840 (see chap. 9, p. 250). Neither of these programs was ever put into effect, but they represent Latin recognition that the ex-slave needed something more than a decree of liberation in order to fulfill his potential as a citizen of a republic.

13 Óscar Gil Díaz, *Apuntes para la historia* (Santo Domingo, 1969), p. 77. He insists that it is "an absurdity" to argue that slavery was somehow benevolent in Santo Domingo, a claim made by Javier Malagón.

14 Jaime Jaramillo Uribe, "Esclavos y señores en la sociedad colombiano del siglo XVIII," *Anuario Colombiano de Historia social y de la cultura* 1, no. 1 (1963): 29-31.

15 Hugo Tolentino, *Raza e historia en Santo Domingo*, 2 vols. (Santo Domingo, 1974), 1: 124-26, 191-93.

16 I was then a member of the Paul Winter sextet, a group that had won the intercollegiate jazz group trophy in 1961 and was picked to conduct a tour of Latin American colleges and universities in 1962.

17 Audrey Miles, "The Minority Volunteer," *Peace Corps Volunteer* 3, no. 10 (September 1968): 17. Miss Miles does not specifically refer to Colombian blacks but to *costeños*, or people from the coast, which is where most Colombian blacks and mulattoes are found. The point is that in Boyacá all blacks are commonly referred to as *costeños*. As Miss Miles herself elaborated, "because it is not possible to distinguish between a *negra colombiana* and a *negra estadouinense* [from the U.S.] in appearance, I have learned what Colombian men think of *negras costeñas*" (Ibid.).

18 Ibid.

19 Interview, Caracas, Venezuela, 21 January 1974.

20 Precisely to the point is Frederick K. Branom, ed., *Commercial and Library Atlas of the World: A Pictorial Compendium of World Maps and Facts* (Chicago, 1942), p. 146. This work features a photo of three blacks carrying sacks of fruit. Under the photo is the following caption: "Most of the heavy labor of Central America and in some sections of South America is done by the black race."

21 The best discussion of this concept is found in Charles Wagley, "Social Race in the Americas," in Richard Adams and Dwight Heath, eds., *Contemporary Cultures and Societies in Latin America* (New York, 1955), pp. 531-45.

22 Julian Pitt, "Race, Color, and Class in Central America and the Andes," in John Hope Franklin, ed., *Color and Race* (Boston, 1968), p. 270.

23 Ibid.

24 Ibid., pp. 278-79.

25 On the change in Guillén's literary perspectives, see Jean Franco, *Spanish American Literature Since Independence* (London, 1973), pp. 179-80, and George Kent, "Literature of the Black Peoples of the Americas," in Keith Irvine, ed., *World Encyclopedia of Black Peoples* (St. Clair Shores, Mich., 1975), 1:62-63.

26 Pablo Adalberto Ortiz, "La negritud en la cultura latinoamericana," *Expresiones culturales del Ecuador*, 1 (noviembre-diciembre 1972): 14. Ortiz further argues that "negritude" is an "effective and logical antithesis to the humiliating universal insult that the white man has inflicted upon the black." Nevertheless, "there can be no return to Africa" and the eventual solution to the problem remains "cultural and ethnic miscegenation" (Ibid., p. 15).

27 See chap. 7, p. 203.

28 See chap. 11, p. 304.

29 See chap. 9, p. 247.

30 Ed Boyer, "An American Reporter in Cuba," *Detroit Free Press*, 28 June 1973, pp. 12a-13a.

31   A case in point is the critique found in Wilfred Cartey, *Black Images* (New York, 1970), p. 45. He was, however, referring essentially to poets and literary figures.
32   George Schuyler, *The Pittsburgh Courier*, 8 August 1948.

BIBLIOGRAPHY

Listed below are indispensable works about the African in Spanish America.

Acosta Saignes, Miguel. *Vida de los esclavos en Venezuela.* Caracas: Ediciones Hespérides, 1967.

Aguirre Beltrán, Gonzalo. *Población negra de México, 1519–1810: Estudio etnohistórico.* Mexico, D.F.: Ediciones Fuente Cultural, 1946.

Bowser, Frederick. *The African Slave in Colonial Peru: 1524–1650.* Stanford, Calif.: Stanford University Press, 1974.

Carvalho Neto, Paulo de. *Estudios afros: Brasil-Paraguay-Uruguay-Ecuador.* Caracas: Instituto de Antropología e Historia, Universidad Central de Venezuela, 1971.

Castillero Calvo, Alfredo. *La sociedad panameña: Historia de su formación e integración.* Panama: Comisión de Estudios Interdisciplinarios para el Desarrollo de la Nacionalidad, Editora Lemania, S.A., 1970.

Duncan, Quince, and Meléndez, Carlos. *El negro en Costa Rica.* San José: Editorial Costa Rica, 1972.

Endrek, Emiliano. *El mestizaje en Córdoba: Siglo XVIII y principios del XIX.* Córdoba: Universidad Nacional de Córdoba, 1966.

Estupiñán Tello, Julio. *El negro en Esmeraldas: Apuntes para su estudio.* Quito: Talleres Gráficas Nacionales, 1967.

Franco Pichardo, Franklyn J. *Los negros, los mulatos y la nación dominicana.* 2nd ed., Santo Domingo: Editora Nacional, 1970.

Guillot, Carlos Federico. *Negros rebeldes y negros cimarrones: Perfil afroamericano en la historia del Nuevo Mundo durante el siglo XVI.* Buenos Aires: Editores Fariña, 1961.

Hoetink, Harry. *The Two Variants in Caribbean Race Relations: A Contribution to the Sociology of Segmented Societies.* Translated by Eva M. Hooykaas. New York: Oxford University Press, 1967.

Knight, Franklin W. *Slave Society in Cuba during the Nineteenth Century.* Madison: University of Wisconsin Press, 1970.

Larrazábal Blanco, Carlos. *Los negros y la esclavitud en Santo Domingo.* Santo Domingo: Julio P. Postigo e Hijos, 1967.

Lombardi, John V. *The Decline and Abolition of Negro Slavery in Vene-zuela.* Westport, Conn.: Negro Universities Press, 1971.

Magnus Mörner, ed., *Race and Class in Latin America.* New York: Columbia University Press, 1970.

Masini, José Luis. *La esclavitud negra en Mendoza.* Mendoza, Arg.: Talleres Gráficos D'Accurzio, 1962.

Mellafe, Rolando. *La introducción de la esclavitud negra en Chile: Tráfico y rutas.* Santiago: Universidad de Chile, 1959.

Molinari, Diego Luis. *La trata de negros.* 2nd ed., Buenos Aires: Facul-tad de Ciencias Económicas, Universidad de Buenos Aires, 1944.

Ortiz Fernández, Fernando. *Hampa afro-cubana, los negros esclavos; Es-tudio sociológico y de derecho público.* Havana: Revista Bimestre Cubana, 1916.

Palacios Preciado, Jorge. *La trata de negros por Cartagena de Indias: 1650–1750.* Tunja, Col.: Ediciones La Rana y El Aquita, 1973.

Peñaherrera de Costales, Piedad, and Costales Samaniego, Alfredo. *Coan-gue, o Historia cultural y social de los negros del Chota y Salinas.* Quito: Editorial Llacta, 1959.

Pereda Valdés, Ildefonso. "El negro en el Uruguay." Montevideo, *Re-vista del Instituto Histórico y Geográfico del Uruguay* 25 (1965).

Plá, Josefina. *Hermano negro: La esclavitud en el Paraguay.* Madrid: Ediciones Paraninfo, 1972.

Saco, José Antonio. *Historia de la esclavitud de la raza africana en el Nuevo Mundo y en especial en los países américo-hispanos.* 4 vols. Havana: Cultural, S.A., 1938.

Scelle, Georges. *La traité négrière aux Indes de Castille: Contrats et traités d'Assiento.* 2 vols. Paris: L. Larose et L. Tanin, 1906.

Scheüss de Studer, Elena F. *La trata de negros en el Río de la Plata durante el siglo XVIII.* Buenos Aires: Departamento Editorial, Universidad de Buenos Aires, 1958.

Vial Correa, Gonzalo. *El africano en el reino de Chile: Ensayo his-tórico-jurídico.* Santiago: Instituto de Investigaciones Históricas, Facultad de Ciencias Jurídicas y Sociales, Universidad Católica de Chile, 1957.

INDEX

Abd-al-Rahman III, 14
Acea, Isidro, 302
Acosta Saignes, Miguel, 27, 112, 254-5, 328, 336, 337, 347, 349, 350, 352, 353, 377, 391
Acosta Solis, Misael, 232, 373
Adra, 28
Affonso V, 10
Afro-Argentines since abolition, 194-7
Afro-Chileans since independence, 210-14
Afro-Colombians since abolition, 236-49, 321
Afro-Cubans, since independence, 298-312; since Castro, 309-12, 321
Afro-Ecuadorians since independence, 226-35
Afro-Mexicans since independence, 280-2
Afro-Panamanians since abolition, 276-8
Afro-Paraguayans since abolition, 205-9
Afro-Peruvians since independence, 220-6, 321
Afro-Uruguayans since independence, 199-205, 224
Afro-Venezuelans since abolition, 252-60, 321
Agudelo, Lorenzo, 92
Aguilar, Nicolás de, 139
Aguirre Beltrán, Gonzalo, 27, 31, 129, 131, 134n, 282, 337, 339, 342, 344, 355, 356, 362, 382, 383, 391
Aguirre, Francisco, 58-9
Aimes, H. H. S., 328, 345, 350, 384, 385
Alamán, Lucas, 359
Alba, Victor, 383
Alberdi, Juan 191-2, 193, 257, 365
Alberto, José Antonio de, 145
Alcacovas, Treaty of (1479), 15
Al-Hakam I, 13, 14
Allen, Henry J., 254-5, 377
Al-Mansur, 14

Almagro, Diego de, 75, 76, 87
Almojarifazgo, ix
Alonso, Martín, 345
Alsina, Luciano Soler, 196
Alvarado, Pedro de, 76, 76, 127
Alvear, Carlos, 185
Amanátegui Solar, Domingo, 96n, 328, 347, 348, 368
Anchederreta, José de, 74
Andrade, Gaspar de, 47
Andrade, Roberto, 232, 372, 373
Andrade Addan, Arigga, 248
Andresote, Juan, 113, 114, 124; see also López de Rosario, Andrés
Andriani, Alberto, 258, 377
Angola, 28, 31, 32, 43, 72, 290
Angola, Francisco, 106
Angolas, 32
Anguinzola, Gustave, 382
Anne, Queen of England, 54
Antilleans (black workers), 266, 269, 270
Antilles (Spanish), 72, 77, 105
Arboleda, José Rafael (S.J.), 244, 348, 376
Arcaya, Pedro M., 354, 162
Arciniegas, Germán, 356, 365
Areche, José Antonio de, 153-4
Arévalo, Domingo, 158
Argentina, 42, 78, 92, 94, 95, 98, 120, 134, 138, 145, 147, 151, 167-8, 171, 199, 216, 217, 220, 315; since abolition, 185-97
Arias de Herrera, Francisco, 116
Arias Madrid, Arnulfo, 276
Aristegui, Lorenzo de, 58-9
Aristotle, 333
Arozarena, Marcelio, 306
Arredondo, Alberto, 307-8, 385, 386, 387

393

Uruguay, 187-200; Venezuela, 249-52
Smith, Robert S., 348
Smith, T. Lynn, 243, 353, 375
Sobremonte, Nicolás, 142, 166
Solaún, Mauricio, 245, 376
Solberg, Carl E., 365, 366, 369
Solís, Andrés, 147
Solórzano Pereira, Juan de, 34, 338
Sosa, Esteban de, 76-7
Sotomayor, José, 146
Soublette, Carlos, 253
South Sea Company, 31, 35, 36, 53, 54-5, 56, 57-8
Spain, 13-26, 33-4, 35, 37, 39, 40, 43, 48, 49, 51, 52, 53, 54, 55-61, 66, 76, 77-87, 106, 108-25, 127, 153, 154, 156-7, 163-4, 197, 210, 214, 226, 261, 283-4, 285, 289-96, 297, 302, 313
Sperling, John G., 342, 343
Sprague, William F., 363
Spratlin, V. B., 334, 335
Steuart, John, 375
Stokes, William S., 379, 380
Strode, Hudson, 363
Suárez, Joaquín, 199, 200, 298
Sucre, Antonio José de, 215
Sutherland, Elizabeth, 309, 312, 387

Tabares, Mariano, 180
Tannenbaum, Frank, 93, 313, 349, 350, 356, 388
Tavara, Santiago, 370
Taylor, William B., 353
Tejado Fernández, Manuel, 356
Teja Zabre, Alfonso, 362, 363
Terra novas, 30, 32
Thomas, Hugh, 290n, 384, 385, 386, 387
Thomas, Walter F., 317
Thomspon, Era Bell, 366
Thornton, A. P., 340
Ticknor, George, 334
Timmons, Wilbert H., 362
Tobar Cruz, Pedro, 357
Tobar Donoso, Julio, 372
Toledo, María de, 40
Tolentino, Hugo, 315, 389
Tordesillas, Treaty of (1494), 40
Toro, Ana de, 299
Torre Revello, José, 349
Torres, José Geronimo, 238
Torres Ramírez, B., 344
Tovar, Margarita de, 85

Trigo, Ciro Félix, 370
Trinidad, 162, 269, 274
Tristão, Nuno, 7, 8,
Trujillo, Héctor, 286
Trujillo, Rafael, 286
Tupac Amaru II, 122
Turnbull, David, 292, 293, 294

Ugarte, César Antonio, 222, 371
Ulloa, Antonio de, 132, 355
Uñanue, Hipólito, 128, 129n, 130
United Fruit Company, 263, 269-70, 272, 274, 306
United States, 76, 104, 163, 189, 192, 230, 249, 253, 273-4, 275, 276, 284, 285, 290, 291, 302, 310
Urban VII, 34, 35
Urbina, José, 229-30
Uriarte, don Miguel de, 58
Ursua Valenzuela, Germán, 369
Urrutia, Gustavo, 306
Uruguay, 78, 90, 95, 98, 120, 132, 134, 138, 170, 197-205, 216, 220, 228; since abolition, 201-5
Uslar Pietri, Artur, 378

Vaca, Arias, 111, 112
Valcárcel, Luis E., 223, 371
Valdés, Gabriel de la Concepción, 300
Valdés, José Manuel, 157, 224
Valdivia, Juana de, 76
Valdivia, Pedro de, 76
Valiente, Alonso, 76, 77
Valiente, Juan, 76, 77, 121
Valladolid, Juan de, 18, 19
Valle, Rafael Helidoro, 380
Vallejo, Santiago, 370, 371
Vallejos, Agustín, 225
Vallenilla Lanz, Laureano, 257, 361, 377
Valtierra, Ángel, 346
Valverde, Félix de, 113-14
Van Kleffens, E. N., 348
Varela, José Pedro, 201
Vargas, Francisco de Paula, 248
Vargas Llosa, Mario, 223, 371
Varon(es), 71, 79
Vasconcelos, José, 282
Vasconcelos, Ramón, 304, 386
Vásquez de Coronado, Francisco, 75
Vásquez de Espinosa, Antonio, 348, 353, 354
Vásquez Machiado, José, 360
Vega, Lope de, 19, 21, 334, 335
Velasco, don Luis de, 106
Vélez de Guevara, don Francisco, 88